The Biblica[

86

The Lost Coin

THE
LOST COIN

Parables of Women, Work and Wisdom

edited by

Mary Ann Beavis

SHEFFIELD ACADEMIC PRESS
A Continuum imprint
LONDON • NEW YORK

Published by Sheffield Academic Press Ltd
The Tower Building, 11 York Road, London SE1 7NX
370 Lexington Avenue, New York NY 10017-6550

www.SheffieldAcademicPress.com
www.continuumbooks.com

British Library Cataloguing-in-Publication Data

A catalogue record for this book is available from the British Library

Typeset by Sheffield Academic Press
Printed on acid-free paper in Great Britain

ISBN 1-84127-322-8 (hardback)
      1-84127-313-9 (paperback)

CONTENTS

II
Parables of Women's Work

III
Johannine Metaphors of Mother and Bride

IV
Parables of Wisdom/Sophia

V
FINDING PARABLE

ABBREVIATIONS

AB	Anchor Bible
ABRL	Anchor Bible Reference Library
AnBib	Analecta biblica
AsSeign	Assemblées du Seigneur
AV	Authorized Version
BAGD	Walter Bauer, William F. Arndt, F. William Gingrich and Frederick W. Danker, *A Greek–English Lexicon of the New Testament and Other Early Christian Literature* (Chicago: University of Chicago Press, 2nd edn, 1958)
BTB	*Biblical Theology Bulletin*
BZ	*Biblische Zeitschrift*
CBQ	*Catholic Biblical Quarterly*
CIL	*Corpus inscriptionum latinarum*
CRI	Compendia rerum iudaicarum ad Novum Testamentum
CurTM	*Currents in Theology and Mission*
EBC	Eerdmans Bible Commentary
EKKNT	Evangelisch-Katholischer Kommentar zum Neuen Testament
ETL	*Ephemerides theologicae lovanienses*
EvT	*Evangelische Theologie*
ExpTim	*Expository Times*
FCB	Femininst Companion to the Bible
FFNT	Foundations and Facets: New Testament
GNB	Good News Bible
HDR	Harvard Dissertations in Religion
HR	*History of Religions*
ICC	International Critical Commentary
JBL	*Journal of Biblical Literature*
JSNTSup	*Journal for the Study of the New Testament*, Supplement Series
JSOT	*Journal for the Study of the Old Testament*
JTS	*Journal of Theological Studies*
LSJ	H.G. Liddell, Robert Scott and H. Stuart Jones, *Greek–English Lexicon* (Oxford: Clarendon Press, 9th edn, 1968)
NEB	*New English Bible*
Neot	*Neotestamentica*
NIBC	New International Bible Commentary

NICOT	New International Commentary on the Old Testament
NIV	New International Version
NovT	*Novum Testamentum*
NRSV	New Revised Standard Version
NTM	New Testament Message
NTS	*New Testament Studies*
RB	*Revue biblique*
RevistB	*Revista biblica*
RSV	Revised Standard Version
SacPag	Sacra Pagina
SBEC	Studies in the Bible and Early Christianity
SBLDS	SBL Dissertation Series
SBLMS	SBL Monograph Series
SBLSS	SBL Seminar Series
SBT	Studies in Biblical Theology
SC	Sources chrétiennes
SNTSMS	Society for New Testament Studies Monograph Series
SVTP	Studia in Veteris Testamenti pseudepigrapha
TDNT	Gerhard Kittel and Gerhard Friedrich (eds.), *Theological Dictionary of the New Testament* (trans. Geoffrey W. Bromiley; 10 vols.; Grand Rapids: Eerdmans, 1964–)
TDOT	G.J. Botterweck and H. Ringgren (eds.), *Theological Dictionary of the Old Testament*
TSAJ	Texte und Studien zum antiken Judentum (3 vols.; trans. J.T. Willis, Grand Rapids: Eerdmans, 1977-).
TToday	*Theology Today*
TSK	*Theologische Studien und Kritiken*
WMANT	*Wissenschaftliche Monographien zum Alten und Neutestamentliche Wissenschaft*
ZNW	*Zeitschrift für die neutestamentliche Wissenschaft*

LIST OF CONTRIBUTORS

Vicky Balabanski, Lecturer in New Testament, Parkin-Wesley College, Adelaide College of Divinity, Australia

Mary Ann Beavis, Department of Religious Studies, St Thomas More College, University of Saskatchewan, Canada

Kamila Blessing, 7821 Delmar Blvd, University City, MO 63130, USA
Deborah Core, 467 Case Annex, Eastern Kentucky University, Richmond, KY 40475, USA

Elisabeth Schüssler Fiorenza, Harvard Divinity School, Cambridge, MA, USA

Elaine Guillemin, 19 Wineva Avenue, Toronto, Ontario M4E 2T1, Canada

Holly Hearon, Christian Theological Seminary, Indianapolis, IN, USA

Edith Humphrey, 52 Belmont, Aylmer, QC J9H 2M7, Canada

Linda M. Maloney, Academic Editor, The Liturgical Press, Collegeville, MN, USA

Mary W. Matthews, 1000 Granville Court N., St Petersburg, FL 33701-1529, USA

Kathleen Nash, Religious Studies Department, Le Moyne College, Syracuse, NY, USA

Pheme Perkins, Department of Theology, Boston College, Chestnut Hill, MA, USA

Barbara Reid, Catholic Theological Union, 5401 S. Cornell, Chicago, IL 60615, USA

Adele Reinhartz, Department of Religious Studies, McMaster University, Canada

Kathleen Rushton, 120 Lonsdale Street, North New Brighton, Christchurch 8009, Aotearoa New Zealand

Barbara Scheele, Brooklyn College Library, Brooklyn, NY, USA

Carter Shelley, 1504 Holly Circle, Wilkesboro, NC 28697, USA

Christin Lore Weber, 9700 Sterling Creek Road, Jacksonville, OR 97530, USA

Antoinette Clark Wire, 2617 LeConte Avenue, Berkeley, CA 94709, USA

Thirty years ago nobody had ever heard or dreamt of feminist biblical studies. Today the articles and books offering ever more sophisticated feminist biblical interpretations abound. Feminist biblical studies, together with post-colonial, Afrocentric, subaltern, Latino/a, Asian, Indigenous, queer, materialist and ideology critical studies have in the past thirty years greatly contributed to the emerging emancipatory paradigm of biblical criticism. Whereas the study of wo/men in the Bible has always been a staple of biblical interpretation, it—like the numerous books about wo/men cluttering up library shelves—expressed the interest of elite educated men, as Virginia Woolf observed some time ago. (I write wo/men in such a broken fashion in order to indicate not only the great differences between wo/men and within wo/men but also to signify that the term is inclusive of men).

While wo/men always have interpreted the scriptures, feminist biblical studies are a newcomer in theology and religious studies. Only in the context of the wo/men's movements of the nineteenth and twentieth centuries have feminist scholars begun to explore the possibilities of a critical hermeneutics that takes the institutional silencing of wo/men in biblical religions and the cultural impact of biblical texts on wo/men into account. In the nineteenth century, Elizabeth Cady Stanton initiated the project of the *Woman's Bible* because she was convinced that no area of society could be reformed without reforming all areas of it. In the twentieth century, feminist biblical interpretation has emerged. That speaks in culturally different tongues.

Popular and academic biblical interpretations by women, the reading of the bible as a woman or the interpretation of Scripture in terms of gender, however, are not simply identical with a critical feminist interpretation (understood as a practice of rhetorical inquiry that is conscious of its social location and utilizes not just a gender analysis but also a multistrategic analysis of race, class, heterosexuality, and imperialism). Feminist interpretation does not just aim to make meaning and sense out of androcentric (i.e., male centered) or better, kyriocentric (i.e., slave master, Lord, father, husband or elite, propertied, educated, male-centered) biblical texts, but it intends the formation of a critical historical and religious consciousness.

Whereas a feminist hermeneutic seeks to understand the meaning of texts, a conceptualization of feminist biblical studies in terms of rhetoric attends to the effects biblical discourses produce, how they produce them, and for whom they are produced. Hence, feminist biblical studies is best understood as a critical rhetoric that moves beyond 'mere hermeneutics' to a complex process of critical analysis. It seeks to overcome the theoretical binaries between sense and meaning, explanation and understanding, distanciation and empathy, reading 'behind' and 'in front of 'the text, interpretation and application, realism and imagination.

Insofar as religion and the Bible still play a significant role in many wo/men's lives, feminists cannot afford to neglect the Bible. Instead, feminist theology both reclaims the authority of wo/men as subjects of interpretation and reconceptualizes the act of interpretation as a moment in the struggle for self-affirmation and well-being. Popular and academic biblical interpretations by wo/men from very different socio-political ethnic and national locations, the reading of the bible as women and its interpretation in terms of gender have greatly contributed to the development and flourishing of this new field of biblical studies.

However, interpretations of the Bible by wo/men are not automatically feminist simply because they are readings done by wo/men. Insofar as Bible-believing wo/men do not employ a critical analysis of wo/men's socio-political and cultural-religious subordination and second-class citizenship, they tend to read kyriocentric biblical texts as authorization for cultural and religious femininity and subordination. By insisting that not all biblical readings of wo/men or about wo/men are feminist, one does not deny agency and respect to the individual wo/men who engage in such readings, but simply points to the cultural-religious determination of our reading lenses and approaches.

Since feminist biblical studies in all areas of inquiry have been flourishing, it is very surprising that in the past decade no book-length study on the parables has appeared. The reason for this might be that at first glance the parables of Jesus are predominantly stories about men. In 1988 Susan Marie Praeder published a small booklet *The Word in Women's Worlds* in which she discussed four parables that had wo/men characters.[1] She

---

1.   S.M. Praeder, *The World in Women's Words* (Wilmington, DE: Michael Glazier, 1988).

observed that of the thirty to forty parables which the canonical and extra-canonical gospel literature attributes to Jesus, only five portray wo/men and their worlds, whereas the rest are stories about the relationships and worlds of men.

This fascinating collection of original essays which we owe to the work of Professor Mary Ann Beavis argues to the contrary that parable studies are a rich and abundant field of inquiry which is waiting to be harvested by feminist biblical critics. This volume is a significant contribution to wo/men's and gender biblical studies which will change not only how we look at the parables of the gospels but also how we approach biblical interpretation. Searching for the 'lost coin' of parables about wo/men will change not only how we understand parable texts but also how we go about reading them.

Although it represents primarily the work of Canadian and American wo/men, this volume brings together readings from quite different theoretical and methodological perspectives. It not only features contributions by multiple authors but also multiple interpretations of one and the same text. It does not just interpret canonical texts but also those that have not made it into the Christian canon. It does not just focus on the synoptic gospels but also on that of John, not just on stories but also on simile and metaphor.

In short, this book will greatly contribute to the methodological and theoretical discussions underway in many areas of biblical studies. By focusing on stories and metaphors which tell us something about the everyday world of first-century wo/men it enriches our historical imaginations. By exploring how kyriocentric ideology is at work in the construction of stories about wo/men, it sharpens our awareness of everyday, commonsense prejudices. By placing wo/men in the centre of attention it challenges us also to de-centre the kyriocentrism of those texts that do not mention wo/men. As Wisdom's teachers, the contributors to this volume extend her invitation to us: 'Come eat of my bread and drink of the wine I have mixed. Leave immaturity and live, and walk in the way of Wisdom' (Prov. 9.5-6).

Elisabeth Schüssler Fiorenza

Introduction:
Seeking the 'Lost Coin' of Parables about Women

Mary Ann Beavis

The Genesis of The Lost Coin

As a feminist and a scholar who has published several works on the parables of the Christian Testament,[1] I have tried to apply a feminist perspective to my interpretations. By 'feminist', I mean that I have sought to uncover ways in which the parables critique the patriarchal social structures of antiquity (e.g., slavery, absentee landlords) and which open up vistas of new, non-oppressive social relations. I have challenged interpretations of the parables which cast God in the role of a harsh, vindictive tyrant—as a master with the power of life and death over slaves (Lk. 12.41-48) or as a temperamental deity prone to summary executions (Lk. 12.16b-20). More generally, I consider feminist—in the sense of subversive, unconventional, hermeneutically 'suspicious'—my attempts to bring new or unorthodox questions and perspectives to parable interpretation, to query the 'accepted wisdom'. These efforts include bringing to the discussion data about ancient reading, education and literary theory; comparisons with the Graeco-Roman fable; information about slavery in antiquity; William R. Herzog II's exciting application of Paolo Freire's 'pedagogy of the oppressed'; and Alice Miller's ideas on 'poisonous pedagogy'. To what extent I have achieved these aims I leave for my readers to adjudicate.

---

1. M.A. Beavis, 'Parable and Fable', *Catholic Biblical Quarterly* 52 (1990), pp. 473-98; 'Ancient Slavery as an Interpretive Context for the New Testament Servant Parables, with Special Reference to the Unjust Steward (Lk. 6.1-8)', *Journal of Biblical Literature* 111 (1992), pp.37-54; 'The Foolish Landowner (Luke 12.16b-20)', in V.G. Shillington (ed.), *Jesus and His Parables: Interpreting the Parables of Jesus Today* (Edinburgh: T. & T. Clark, 1997), pp. 55-68; see also M.A. Beavis, *Mark's Audience: The Literary and Social Setting of Mark 4.11-12* (JSNTSup, 33; Sheffield: Sheffield Academic Press, 1989). None of the 'women' parables discussed below are covered by the Shillington volume.

Despite the feminist approach that I so value, it struck me only recently that I had never written about a parable that actually features women characters, that depicts characteristically female activities, or that uses female imagery. And, while many of the parables extant in the Gospels are about (putatively) male characters, or are parables of nature, a substantial list of 'female' parables can be compiled: the ten virgins (Mt. 25.1-13); the lost coin (Lk. 15.8-10); the persistent widow (Lk. 18.2-5); the woman kneading dough (Mt. 13.33; Lk. 13.20, 21; *Gos. Thom.* 96); the woman carrying a jar of meal (*Gos. Thom.* 97); the nursing babies (*Gos. Thom.* 22). Several parables refer to traditionally female (or at least domestic) work such as sewing a patch on a garment (Mt. 9.16; Mk 2.21; Lk. 5.36), filling a wineskin (Mk 2.22; Mt. 9.17; Lk. 5.37-39), or spinning and carding thread (Mt. 6.28-30; Lk. 12.27-28; *Gos. Thom.* 36). Behind some parables hovers the figure of Sophia, comparing herself to a mother hen (Mt. 23.37-39; Lk. 34-35), imploring the lowly to take her yoke upon them (Mt. 11.28-30), comparing 'this generation' to a crowd of petulant children (Mt. 11.16-19; Lk. 7.31-35; cf. *Gos. Thom.* 21). The Johannine *paroimia* of 'new birth' can be defined as parabolic speech (Jn 1.13; 3.1-14).[2] And, with a little reflection, the list can be augmented: what about the female slaves explicitly mentioned in the parable of the two stewards (Lk. 12.45), or the brides whose presence is implicit in wedding parables (esp. Jn 3.29-30)?

Even a parable that seems solely occupied with the relations between men may imply female characters. Richard L. Rohrbaugh observes that the prodigal son's behaviour would have been even more damaging to the mother of the household than to the father:

> The son is expected to stay at home, and it is especially in the interests of his mother that he do so. Obviously he should maintain his father in his old age, but his presence means far more than that to his mother. He is the surety of her place in the family.[3]

Unfortunately, apart from a few sentences, the role of the mother in this story is not developed any further, but Rohrbaugh's remarks on the effects of the parable on a peasant audience are tantalizing: 'A peasant hearing of the younger son's scandalous departure...would recognize that both parents had been damaged. We usually forget about the mother, but peasants

---

2. See E.S. Johnson, *She Who Is: The Mystery of God in Feminist Theological Discourse* (New York: Crossroad, 1992), p. 80.

3. R.L. Rohrbaugh, 'A Dysfunctional Family and its Neighbours (Luke 15.11b-32)', in Shillington (ed.), *Jesus and His Parables*, pp. 151-52.

would not'.[4] Reinserting 'the mother' and other female characters is another way in which the parables could be interpreted from a feminist perspective.

I have not been alone in my neglect of these parables. To my knowledge, none of the many books that have been published on the parables in recent years approach them from an explicitly feminist perspective; nor do they contain significant interpretations of parables featuring female characters—occasionally with the exception of the well-known stories of the persistent widow, the ten bridesmaids and the lost coin.[5] The parable of the bakerwoman (Mt. 13.33; Lk. 13.20, 21; *Gos. Thom.* 96)—known in 'malestream' scholarship as the 'parable of the leaven'—has received some coverage in feminist interpretation, and is well-known through Alla Renee Boarth's poem 'Bakerwoman God',[6] but is rarely included in scholarly anthologies on the parables. There are substantive treatments of some of these parables in works of feminist New Testament scholarship,[7]

---

4.   Rohrbaugh, 'Dysfunctional Family', p. 152. Cf. B.B. Scott's treatment of the same parable, where he considers the impact of the son's behaviour on the mother and daughters of the family (*Hear Then the Parable: A Commentary on the Parables of Jesus* [Minneapolis: Fortress, 1989], p. 111).

5.   Recent monographs and edited collections on the parables confirm this impression. The parable of the persistent widow (or the 'unjust judge') is quite well covered in the literature; e.g., John R. Donahue, *The Gospel in Parable: Metaphor and Theology in the Gospel Parables* (Philadelphia: Fortress, 1988), pp. 180-93; Kenneth E. Bailey, *Through Peasant Eyes: More Lucan Parables, Their Culture and Style* (Grand Rapids: Eerdmans, 1980), pp. 114-26; William R. Herzog II, *Parables as Subversive Speech: Jesus as Pedagogue of the Oppressed* (Westminster: John Knox, 1994), pp. 215-32; Scott, *Hear Then the Parable*, pp. 175-88. It is more difficult to find significant interpretations of the ten virgins (one example is Jan Lambrecht, *Once More Astonished: The Parables of Jesus* [New York: Crossroad, 1981], pp. 146-66; see also Pheme Perkins, *Hearing the Parables of Jesus* [New York/Ramsey, NJ: Paulist, 1981], pp. 104-110) or the lost coin (see, e.g., Kenneth E. Bailey, *Poet and Peasant: A Literary Cultural Approach to the Parables in Luke* [Grand Rapids: Eerdmans, 1976], pp. 142-57; Scott, *Hear Then the Parable*, pp. 308-13; Perkins, *Hearing the Parables*, pp. 32-33). Almost never is more than one of these parables featured significantly.

6.   For the text of the poem, see E. Roberts and E. Amidon (eds.), *Earth Prayers from Around the World: 365 Prayers, Poems, and Invocations for Honoring the Earth* (San Francisco: HarperCollins, 1991), pp. 162-63. For feminist interpretations of the parable, see L. Schottroff, *Lydia's Impatient Sisters: A Feminist Social History of Early Christianity* (Louisville, KY: Westminster John Knox Press, 1995), pp. 79-90 and E. Schüssler Fiorenza, *Sharing Her Word: Feminist Biblical Interpretation in Context* (Boston: Beacon Press, 1998), p. 181.

7.   E.g., Schottroff, *Lydia's Impatient Sisters*, pp. 79-120; Schüssler Fiorenza,

but not in a volume on the parables. It is even more difficult to find interpretations of less obvious 'woman parables' (much less feminist interpretations)—parables of women's work, the mother hen, the parables unique
to the *Gospel of Thomas*.[8] This book is a feminist quest for the 'lost coin'
of parables about women, women's work and parables using female
imagery, undertaken by a group of feminist women interpreters.

The Parables
Scholars differ in their enumerations of the 'major parables' of the Gospels.[9] This is partly because the biblical understanding of parable (*māšāl,
parabolē*) includes many different kinds of metaphorical speech: proverbs,
riddles, oracles, allegories, similitudes, fables. According to the Gospel of
Mark, all of Jesus' teaching was 'in parables' (Mk 4.34). For the purposes
of this volume, Adolf Jülicher's threefold classification of Jesus' parables
in terms of similitudes, parables proper and exemplary stories is somewhat
helpful, although it does not exhaust the multifariousness of the parable
tradition.[10] A similitude is a brief narration of a typical or recurrent event
from everyday life (e.g., a seed growing secretly, a tree bearing fruit, a
woman kneading dough). The 'parables proper', or narrative parables, are
similar in form to the fables of the Aesopic tradition; they are short
narratives about one-time, fictitious events, like the rich fool (Lk. 12.16-
21; *Gos. Thom.* 63), the rich man and Lazarus (Lk. 16.19-31) or the
wicked tenants (Mk 12.1-11; Mt. 21.33-41; Lk. 20.9-16). In their original

Sharing Her Word, pp. 181-182; B. Reid, *Choosing the Better Part: Women in the Gospel* (Collegeville, MN: Liturgical Press, 1966)

8.   Scott (*Hear Then the Parable*) includes a record number of 'woman parables' in his monograph, including the persistent widow, the lost coin, the woman kneading bread, and the parable of the woman with a jar from the *Gospel of Thomas*. His interpretation of the prodigal son ('I Remember Mama', *Hear Then the Parable*, pp. 99-126) also has a feminist twist.

9.   See e.g., the lists in J.D. Crossan, 'Parables', *Harper's Bible Dictionary* (P.J. Achtemeyer, gen. ed.; San Francisco: HarperSanFrancisco, 1985), p. 748 (747-49); R.H. Stein, 'Parables', *Oxford Companion to the Bible* (B.M. Metzger and M.D. Coogan, eds.; Oxford: Oxford University Press, 1993), pp. 569-70 (567-70); and Perkins, *Hearing the Parables*, pp. 218-20. An 'Index of Parables in the Four Gospels' published on the internet lists some 67 parables from the canonical Gospels alone (http://www.rc.net/wcc/parindex.htm). Stein estimates that there are more like 80 parables in the canonical Gospels.

10.   Adolf Jülicher, *Die Gleichnisreden Jesu* (2 vols.; Tübingen: J.C.B. Mohr, 1910).

form, such stories were probably open-ended, with the audience being expected to provide their own interpretations; in the Synoptic Gospels, explanations or applications (like the 'morals' appended to many of the fables of Aesop) are often inserted at the beginning or end of the parable.[11] A third kind of parable is the exemplary story, the narration of a specific case illustrating a general principle (e.g., the shocking 'neighbourliness' of the good Samaritan). The Johannine *paroimiai* ('figures') are usually left off lists of parables, but many are similar to synoptic-style parables—such as the extended metaphor of the shepherd, the thief and the doorkeeper (Jn 10.1-18), the saying about the grain of wheat (Jn 12.24), and John the Baptist's comparison of himself to 'the friend of the bridegroom' (Jn 3.29-30). Scholars are increasingly including parables from the *Gospel of Thomas* in their interpretations.[12]

Feminist Perspectives on the Parables

As mentioned above, to date there has been no sustained attempt to identify, classify and interpret parables about women, women's work and the female, feminist or not. Among feminist interpreters who mention parables as important for feminist study are L. Schottroff and E. Schüssler Fiorenza. Schottroff criticizes any 'theory of parables' that does not take seriously the social setting of women's (and men's) lives in antiquity.[13]

> The parables speak of social reality, including the so-called parables of nature. The parables describe and then turn upside down the world of owners of large estates and farms, of the female and male daily-wage earners, tenants, and slaves. It is therefore necessary to make the social-

---

11. See Beavis, 'Parable and Fable'.

12. E.g., Scott, *Hear Then the Parable*, pp. 30-35; Crossan, 'Parables', 748.

13. Schottroff, *Lydia's Impatient Sisters*, pp. 52-53. She cites R. Bultmann (whose position is basically that of A. Jülicher) and P. Ricoeur as examples of exegetes with 'parable theories' that dismiss the 'commonplace' elements in the parables as irrelevant to their interpretation. For Bultmann, the real-life images of the parables are merely interpretive aids for the reign of God; for Ricoeur, the significance of the images is 'the scandalous disturbance of the commonplace' (p. 52). The effect, says Schottroff, is that 'the world of women baking bread and of children crying' is set apart from the realm of God's action in the world (p. 52). Cf. R. Bultmann, *History of the Synoptic Tradition* (Oxford: Basil Blackwell, 1963), pp. 171-72, 198; P. Ricoeur, 'Stellung und Funktion der Metapher in der biblischen Sprache', in P. Ricoeur and E. Jungel, *Metapher: Zur Hermeneutik religiöser Sprache–Ev. Theol.*, special no., pp. 45-70.

historical exploration of this world the point of departure. What is a drachma worth, and what does it mean when a woman who possesses ten drachmas does not stop searching for the one she lost? In order to know where in a parable God's reign upends the 'commonplace', what I call social reality, I must undertake social-historical research or else I open myself to blunders.[14]

Schottroff's feminist social history of early Christianity includes substantive chapters on the parable of the woman baking bread, the lost coin and the persistent widow.[15]

The other scholar who mentions the parables as significant for feminist biblical interpretation, E. Schüssler Fiorenza, uses four parables of women—the bakerwoman, the woman seeking the lost drachma, the persistent widow, and the parable of 'the wise and foolish young wo/men' as figures of 'the practices of feminist biblical interpretation as a boundary-breaking activity of Divine Wisdom'.[16] The leaven kneaded throughout the *basileia* by the bakerwoman is the 'fomenting' and 'corrupting' activity of Divine Sophia at work in feminist theologies.[17] The parable of the woman sweeping her house in search of the lost coin images the search of Divine Wisdom for what is lost and hidden—for those who have 'fallen through the cracks'; and the joy of the woman and her female neighbours on finding the coin brings to mind 'the lost emancipatory Christian traditions of wo/men's agency and struggle—a heritage that can be experienced by reclaiming wo/men's theologies and histories as their own heritage'.[18] The assertive widow who demands justice represents 'Divine Wisdom and her followers as forcefully fighting for justice and righting wrongs'.[19] The story of the wise and foolish wo/men serves as a caution to 'those who engage in movements and struggles against injustice to plan for the long haul: burnout is no excuse for giving up the struggle'.[20] These feminist approaches to the 'parables of women' point the way for some of the interpretations in this volume, with their focus on the realities of women's work, their aim to recover and reclaim a 'lost' body of tradition, and the attention to the 'voice' of Wisdom in the parables.

---

14. Schottroff, *Lydia's Impatient Sisters*, pp. 52-53.
15. Schottroff, *Lydia's Impatient Sisters*, pp. 69-120.
16. Schüssler Fiorenza, *Sharing Her Word*, pp. 181-182.
17. Schüssler Fiorenza, *Sharing Her Word*, p. 181.
18. Schüssler Fiorenza, *Sharing Her Word*, p. 181.
19. Schüssler Fiorenza, *Sharing Her Word*, pp. 181-182.
20. Schüssler Fiorenza, *Sharing Her Word*, p. 182.

In focusing on 'woman parables' as defined above, this collection of essays runs the risk of reducing feminist interpretation to the exegesis of texts about women as read/interpreted/experienced *by women*.[21] The project recognizes that neither 'woman' nor 'feminism' are categories with unified meanings. While the recovery and interpretation of material about women by women is an important part of feminist inquiry, it by no means exhausts the scope of feminist interpretation, which can just as easily be applied to texts and contexts with no overt references to women or femaleness (see my chapter on Luke 15.11-32). Nor can it be assumed that all women, regardless of differences such as race, class or ethnicity, share some essential nature—that all women are expressions of the category of 'Woman' or 'the Feminine'. Similarly, specifying a 'feminist' approach should not be taken to mean that the term 'feminist/feminism' has a unified meaning that crosses all class, ethnic, racial and other boundaries. As Schüssler Fiorenza observes, 'feminist' reading

> must time and time again rearticulate its categories and focus its lenses of interpretation in particular historical situations and social contexts. It may not subscribe to a single method of analysis nor adopt a single hermeneutical perspective or mode of approach. It also may not restrict itself to one single reading community or audience. Rather, it must search for appropriate theoretical frameworks and practical ways of interpretation that can make visible oppressive as well as liberative traces inscribed in ancient Jewish and Christian scriptures.[22]

Like the contributors to Schüssler Fiorenza's *Searching the Scriptures*, the group of interpreters who participated in this project articulate diverse feminist perspectives, differ somewhat as to the theoretical assumptions and analytical methods with which they approach their interpretations, and often reflect on how their own social locations and political engagements shape their interpretions.[23]

Although the majority of the chapters in this volume are written by professional biblical scholars (Beavis, Maloney, Balabanski, Perkins, Hearon, Wire, Nash, Blessing, Rushton, Reinhartz, Humphrey, Reid, Guillemin),

---

21. Elisabeth Schüssler Fiorenza warns that this kind of methodological focus on women 'is in danger of identifying women's reality with women's representation and of succumbing to the totalizing power of the grammatically masculine so-called generic text' ('Transforming the Legacy of The Women's Bible', *Searching the Scriptures, Volume 1: A Feminist Introduction* [New York: Crossroad, 1993], p. 20).

22. Schüssler Fiorenza, 'Transforming the Legacy', p. 18.

23. Schüssler Fiorenza, 'Transforming the Legacy', p. 18.

there are several exceptions. Deborah Core (Lk. 12.41-45) is a professor of
English literature; Carter Shelley (Lk. 18.2-5) is a professor of religion and
literature. Mary Matthews is a freelance editor, writer and desktop pub-
lisher; Barbara Scheele is a bibliographer of Women's Studies and
Religious Studies at Brooklyn College; Christin Lore Weber is a well-
known writer in the area of women's spirituality.[24] However, it should be
noted that the authors are mostly from Canada or the US (with the exception of Balabanski, who is Australian, and Rushton, from Aotearoa/New
Zealand), as well as middle-class, white and Christian (a notable exception
is the Jewish New Testament scholar Adele Reinhartz). As such, this
volume cannot claim to capture the vast spectrum of feminist/womanist
hermeneutical potential inherent in the task of parable interpretation and
creation.

In view of the androcentric bias of the biblical texts, I have deliberately
spun a wide web in order to capture the 'lost tradition' of woman parables.
The following classification includes parables of different genres, from the
synoptics, John and the *Gospel of Thomas*, and classifies them according
to the major themes of 'Women, Work and Wisdom':

'Women': Parables Featuring Female Characters
These are the parables that are most easily identifiable as 'parables of
women' in that they are narrative parables which focus on female characters. L. Maloney's interpretation of the parable this volume is named after
(Lk. 15.8-10) sees the woman's search for the 'lost coin' as a metaphor for
feminist theological inquiry:

> Our work is contextual and concrete; it sees the ordinary and the everyday
> as the place where God is revealed: it takes place 'in the house'. It is hard
> work; it is a struggle to find what we are seeking in the darkness that has
> covered it for so many centuries. But it is also characterized by joy and
> celebration, and by hope: a hope that assures us that God is with us. God
> has her skirts tucked up and is busy sweeping and searching, too.

Maloney's reading of the parable prepares the way for the 'hard work' of
feminist theological interpretation of the parables, as well as the rewards.
My own brief chapter on Luke 15.10 points out that the Lucan interpretation of the parable as symbolizing divine joy over one repentant sinner is

24. See Christin Lore Weber, *Altar Music: A Novel* (New York: Scribner, 2000);
Circle of Mysteries: The Women's Rosary Book (St. Paul, MN: Yes International,
1997); *A Cry in the Desert: The Awakening of Byron Katie* (Manhattan Beach, CA:
Work Foundation Inc., 1996).

problematic for persons who have suffered abuse and injustice at the hands of 'sinners'.

Several of the women who answered the initial call for contributions to this volume (Matthews, Shelley, Scheele) requested the parable of the persistent widow (Lk. 18.2-5). In view of the scarcity of substantive interpretations of this parable, I encouraged all three to submit chapters; each one provides a distinctive feminist construal of a familiar narrative, and reflects the feminist suspicion of hegemonic claims to the 'right' interpretation of a text. M. Matthews sees the judge of the parable as an image of structural injustice, and the widow as 'Everychristian', badgering unjust authority until it gives in, day after day, year after year. C. Shelley uses this story of a 'widow without wiles' to deconstruct the stereotype of the cultural stereotype of the widow as an nagging shrew. B. Scheele interprets the widow as a God-figure in the guise of Holy Wisdom, who 'both prays and actively searches for people who will be faithful to the codes of justice in scripture'.

V. Balabanski provides a much-needed contribution on the 'the wise and foolish virgins' (Mt. 25.1-13), a major parable that has received little attention in parable scholarship. Balabanski imaginatively reconstructs the story from the patri/kyriarchal perspective of the *mastaba* (village bench), where the (male) elders of the town have a good laugh at the expense of the 'foolish' young women. She then imagines the (female) view from the 'actual first century' *agora* (marketplace), where the 'foolish' women are judged as socially inadequate, and worthy of censure for their want of discretion. Both readings, Balabanski argues, make the ungracious and kyriarchal bridegroom of the parable into a type of Jesus of Nazareth, leading her to conclude that 'If we search this parable for a symbol which can speak to us of Christ the liberator, it is there only in potential at present'.

A final chapter in this section ('Making Up Stories: A Feminist Reading of Luke 15.11b-32') is my attempt to read a narrative parable with no significant 'female' content in feminist terms; in this case, the parable of the prodigal son is interpreted from the standpoint of a survivor of family abuse. If the traditional reading of the parable, which sees the son as selfish and unfilial and the father as loving and forgiving, is 'reread' from the son's point of view, the interpreter must take seriously the possibility that the son left home for a good reason. Could a parable about the return 'home' of a runaway child ever be construed in a positive way by someone who had suffered at the hands of an abusive parent? How many times have well-meaning pastoral counsellors used inappropriate biblical paradigms ('forgiveness', 'submission', 'family values') to send endangered people back to unhealthy homes, families and relationships?

Parables of Women's Work
As L. Schottroff has pointed out, the work of poor women in antiquity was not limited to unpaid domestic roles—Strabo mentions a female ditch-digger giving birth on the job and returning to work so as not to lose a day's pay.[25] Schottroff's evidence that female labourers earned half as much as men in antiquity sheds new light on the commonplace observation that the drachma lost by the woman of the lost coin parable is the equivalent of a day's wage for a 'labourer'.[26] It also suggests that it should not be assumed that a parable like the labourers in the vineyard (Mt. 20.1-15) refers only to male workers.

The interpretations in this section explicate the kinds of work, paid or unpaid, that a poor woman like the finder of the lost coin might have done. Most of the *mešhalîm* in this grouping are similitudes (Mk 2.21-22 and par.; Mt. 13.33 and par.; Mt. 6.28-30 and par.), or are extra-canonical (*Gos. Thom.* 22, 97), and thus seldom have occupied separate chapters in volumes on the parables. P. Perkins undertakes a class analysis of the parables of the patch and the wineskins (Mt. 9.16-17, Mk 2.21-22, Lk. 5.36-37), pointing to the social gap between the privileged male wine-drinkers who are the implied audience of the parable and the marginal status of the persons—female or male, slave or free, child or adult—who actually did the work of patching clothes and filling wineskins. A.C. Wire and H. Hearon's collaborative chapter on the parable of the bakerwoman (Mt. 13.33; Lk. 13.20,21; *Gos. Thom.* 96) and the similitude of the lilies of the field (Mt. 6.28-30; Lk. 12.27-28; *Gos. Thom.* 36) 'describe activities that consume the lives of many peasant and slave women today in many parts of the three-fourths world', as well as of the women of antiquity. K. Nash's interpretation of the parable of the breastfeeding infants (*Gos. Thom.* 22) reveals that the women's work of childbearing and nursing is radically devalued in the *Gospel of Thomas*, where those 'born of woman' are not eligible for the 'Kingdom of the Father'. K. Blessing's chapter on the parable of the woman carrying a jar of meal (*Gos. Thom.* 97) shows how the woman's discovery that the jar has been emptied 'on the way' is actually a moment of recognition of the *positive* value of 'emptying' in the

25. Strabo, *Geography* 3.4.17, cited in Schottroff, *Lydia's Impatient Sisters*, p. 99.
26. Schottroff, *Lydia's Impatient Sisters*, p. 99.

world-view of the Thomas community. Finally, D. Core's piece on the 'troubling tale' of the faithful and unfaithful stewards (Lk. 12.41-45)[27] finds the model of punitive justice presented by the parable to be incompatible with feminist social ethics.

It should be noted that the parables covered in this section do not fully cover the range of women's work alluded to in the parables. For example, the parable of the woman and the coin represents her doing domestic work ('sweeping', Lk. 15.8). And the distinctively female labours of birthing and midwifery underlie the Johannine *paroimiai* of (women) giving birth (see below).

Johannine Figures of and Bride and Birthgiver

The Johannine 'figures' (*paroimiai*) are usually left out of parable anthologies; however, as 'brief figurative sayings' attributed to Jesus, they fall within range of utterances identifiable as *mešhālīm*. A. Reinhartz's chapter on John the Baptist's comparison of himself to the 'friend of the bridegroom', and the messiah to '[him] who has the bride' (Jn 3.29-30) notes that, in its Johannine form, 'bride' of the saying recedes into the background, existing only in relationship to the 'bridegroom'. However, Reinhartz argues, there is room for a feminist re-visioning of the parable that ascribes mutuality to the relationship between the 'bride' (disciple) and 'groom' (Jesus). K. Rushton's chapter on the 'procreative parables' (Jn 3.1-10 and 16.21-22) is an antidote to interpretations that have overlooked or obscured the female 'language and imagery of human generation' which underlies John's distinctive christology.

Parables of Sophia

As the leading biblical image of the divine as female, the figure of Divine Wisdom/Sophia has occupied many works of feminist theology/thealogy.[28] In the parables in this section, Jesus speaks explicitly as the prophet of Sophia. E. Humphrey's chapter on the parabolic saying in which Jesus, the messenger of Divine Sophia (cf. Mt. 11.19b), invites Wisdom's 'children'

---

27. Only Luke's version of the parable (cf. Mt. 24.45-51) contains a reference to women slaves (Lk. 12.45), reflecting Luke's predilection for gender pairing (see T.K. Seim, 'The Gospel of Luke', in E. Schüssler Fiorenza (ed.), *Searching the Scriptures: A Feminist Commentary* [New York: Crossroad, 1994], p. 730.

28. E.g., E. Schüssler Fiorenza, *Jesus: Miriam's Child, Sophia's Prophet: Critical Issues in Feminist Christology* (New York: Continuum, 1994); E.A. Johnson, *She Who Is: The Mystery of God in Feminist Theological Discourse* (New York: Crossroad, 1993).

to assume her 'yoke' (Mt. 11.28-30), creatively 'declines' the logion into four distinct parables developing the themes of 'my yoke', 'rest', 'learning', and 'humility'. E. Guillemin's piece on the Wisdom metaphor of the mother hen (Mt. 23.37-39; Lk. 13.34-35) interprets this image in the context of maternal imagery in the gospel of Matthew. B. Reid's commentary on the parable of 'Wisdom's children' (Mt. 11.16-19; Lk. 7.31-35; cf. *Gos. Thom.* 21) shows that this image has both drawbacks and potential for feminist christology and ecclesiology.

'Gathering': Parabling as Women's Work
The final section of this anthology is devoted to a 'mythic' parable, 'Gathering', by feminist spiritual writer C.L. Weber. This poignant and haunting tale, rooted in earth-based spirituality rather than Judeo-Christian mythology, begins:

> There was a woman who went down each morning to the sea. There she gathered stones, feathers, driftwood and colored bits of broken glass. She placed them in a basket woven of reeds that grew along a river flowing past her home...

This parable, with its images of women's faithful and sustained labour in the pursuit of wisdom, creativity and rebirth, is an appropriate evocation of the spirit of this volume, which has 'gathered' together the submerged tradition of woman-parables, and creatively 're-formed' them through the prism of feminist interpretations. Sometimes the process is painful, reminding us of the neglect, exploitation and abuse of women and men historically and today. The perspective that is attained through the 'gathering' however, is healing and life-affirming:

> The woman who came up from the sea stood at the top of the hill. She gazed to the north and a gathering of stones that fit together perfectly. She turned and gazed to the east where a nest of feathers invited eagles. She turned to the south where sun's fire passed through coloured glass like music. And then she stood beside a tangle of driftwood that resembled a gnarled old woman. She gazed over the sea toward the horizon as though she could see what lay beyond.

This book is a kind of 'basket' of stories that have, to date, been considered the flotsam and jetsam of the parables, 'miscellaneous' or 'unimportant' stuff, often 'thrown overboard' in favour of more 'valuable' cargo. Like the women of Weber's story, the contributors to this volume have reclaimed and restored these *mešhālīm*, pointing to a 'new horizon' in parable interpretation.

Including a new parable by a woman storyteller points to the fact that not just interpretation, but also parable-making and telling, have always been 'women's work'. In antiquity, women were the tellers of 'old wives' tales'—folktales, fairytales, myths and parables told to children, family members and each other.[29] The role of Eastern European Jewish women in transmitting folk tradition through the centuries has been documented by folklorist B. Kirschenblatt-Gimblett.[30] One of her informants recalls:

> I never heard a single anecdote or fairytale (*maysele*) from my grandfather. I also never heard a single Yiddish song from him, of course. He was totally immersed in Halakah (the legislative part of the Talmud or rabbinical literature, as opposed to Aggadah), Shulhan Aruk (the collection of laws and prescriptions governing the life of an Orthodox Jew), restrained piety, praying, prayers, Torah (Pentateuch). But my grandmother, she implanted the Yiddish folk tune in me; she told me a fairytale, she asked a riddle, and while speaking to people, freely uttered proverbs and witticisms.
>
> Was my grandmother an exception then? Many grandmothers and mothers were like this.[31]

The same informant mentions that the Sabbath was the day when his grandmother would often sit him down near the warm oven and tell him stories of the *tsadiqim* (saints).[32] Another remembers:

> Sometimes during hours when the children were at leisure the *rebetsin* [*rebe*'s wife] also told them stories of ghosts and goblins which she had heard from her mother, who had heard them from her grandmother, and so on...[33]

Kirshenblatt-Gimblett notes that 'it is in the home that the mother is most important as a storyteller. She is often the one who tells stories to the children when they are very young and later to the daughters in particular, since as soon as the boys are old enough they go to the synagogue with their father'.[34]

---

29. See D.R. MacDonald, *The Legend and the Apostle: The Battle for Paul in Story and Canon* (Philadelphia: Westminster, 1983), pp. 34-53.

30. B. Kirschenblatt-Gimblett, 'The Concept and Varieties of Narrative Performance in Eastern European Jewish Culture', in R. Bauman and J. Sherzer (eds.), *Explorations in the Ethnography of Speaking* (2nd edn; Cambridge: Cambridge University Press, 1989), pp. 283-308.

31. Kirschenblatt-Gimblett, 'Concept and Varieties', pp. 284-85.

32. Kirschenblatt-Gimblett, 'Concept and Varieties', p. 294.

33. Kirschenblatt-Gimblett, 'Concept and Varieties', p. 295.

34. Kirschenblatt-Gimblett, 'Concept and Varieties', p. 294.

Reclaiming the 'Lost Coin' of Women's Parables

As argued above, the 'woman parables' are an unrecognized part of the parable tradition that has received minimal coverage in the secondary literature, and which has to date received little attention even from feminist biblical scholars. As well as filling a gap in the scholarly literature on the parables, the chapters in this book highlight these vignettes from ancient Mediterranean women's lives, and provide insights into the role of women and the female in Jesus' ministry and preaching, in the ancient *ekklēsia* of wo/men, and in early Christian theology/thealogy. As well, some of the contributions bring to the surface some of the 'submerged' female figures implicit in the parables: the bride, the birthing mother, the breastfeeding mother or wetnurse, the mother hen, the abused female slaves of Lk. 12.45, all in the spirit of Divine Sophia.

The fact that much of this material has gone uninterpreted or under-interpreted by traditional scholarship indicates the need not just for a single effort to exegete these parables, but for a multiplicity of interpretations, viewpoints and methods. This book goes some way towards addressing this need in two main ways: by encouraging collaborative efforts (e.g., Hearon and Wire, Rushton and Lee[35]); and by publishing alternative interpretations of the same parable by different contributors (Matthews, Shelley, Scheele).[36] Also included are several homiletic interpretations (Maloney, Shelley, Scheele), in addition to the more academic contributions that make up the majority of the chapters, since, as Schüssler Fiorenza asserts, feminist interpretation must include a 'hermeneutics of proclamation' that addresses 'preaching, counseling, and individual Bible study' as well as academic biblical exegesis.[37] Although not all feminist interpreters would agree that a proclamatory hermeneutic is appropriate to academic biblical scholarship, this approach recognizes that the bible functions for many as sacred scripture, and as such has the potential to have both positive and negative impacts on human lives. In particular, as many feminist exegetes have observed, the bible has fre-

---

35. As Rushton acknowledges, the chapter on the parables of labour and childbirth (John 3.1-10; 16.21-22) was initially to have been written by Dorothy Lee; Professor Lee declined the project when she realized that Ms. Rushton was about to defend a dissertation on this topic, and facilitated her contribution to *The Lost Coin*.

36. Cf. my chapter on Luke 15.10, which comments on the Lucan 'interpretation' of the parable of the lost coin.

37. E. Schüssler Fiorenza, *But She Said: Feminist Practices in Biblical Interpretation* (Boston: Beacon Press, 1992), p. 69.

quently been used to define women's roles, rights and opportunities; as Elizabeth Cady Stanton wrote in 1895:

> While their [women's] clergymen told them on the one hand, that they owed all their blessings and freedom they enjoyed to the Bible, on the other, they said it clearly marked out their circumscribed sphere of action: that the demands for political and civil rights were irreligious, dangerous to the stability of the home, the state and the church.[38]

The psychological interpretations in the chapters by Beavis and Blessing also go some way towards addressing this need. The encouragement of collaborative efforts and multiple perspectives is somewhat unusual in biblical scholarship, and deliberately reflects the feminist values of collaboration and co-operation, as well as a feminist respect for difference and plurality of viewpoints. The inclusion of an original 'mythic' parable is another departure from the norm in books on the parables in that it presents parable-making as an ongoing creative theological enterprise.

It is hoped that the volume will serve as a rich and unique source of insight for scholarship, preaching and teaching, and as an invitation to discover these 'parables of women', to recover other 'lost' traditions of women and the female, and to create new ones for the future.

A Note on God-Language

Several of the contributors to this volume (Beavis, Matthews, Reid, Guillemin) have chosen to use alternative spellings of 'God' (Godde, G*d) in their chapters. The spelling 'Godde' was suggested by Edwina Gateley, who found this archaic spelling in a prayer and hymn book used by a community of Sisters of the Mission in New Zealand. Gateley explains that having struggled with the gendered terms 'God' and 'Goddess', and finding neither satisfactory, 'I was delighted to come across a word which embraces both male and female and is rooted in an English far older than our current usage'.[39] The spelling G*d follows E. Schüssler Fiorenza, who uses it to 'indicate the brokenness and inadequacy of human language to name the Divine'.[40] Both usages remind us of what E.A. Johnson identifies as fundamental aspects of language about the divine:

38. E.C. Stanton, *The Woman's Bible* (Salem, NH: Ayer Company, 1988), p. 8. Originally published in 1895.

39. E. Gateley, *A Warm, Moist Salty God: Women Journeying Towards Wisdom* (Trabuco Canyon, CA: Source Books 1993) iii n †.

40. Schüssler Fiorenza, *Sharing Her Word*, p. 187 n. 10.

- *incomprehensibility*–the divine is fundamentally unknowable: *Si comprehendis, non est Deus*.[41]
- *analogy*–all speech about the divine is analogical and meta-phorical.[42]
- *many names*–no one image or concept suffices to comprehend the divine mystery.[43]

The term thealogy (for feminist theology), based on the feminine form (*thea*) of the Greek word for 'god/dess' (*theos/thea*), is used for similar reasons.

---

41. Johnson, *She Who Is*, pp. 104-112.
42. Johnson, *She Who Is*, pp. 113-117.
43. Johnson, *She Who Is*, pp. 117-120.

I

'LOST' PARABLES OF WOMEN

'SWEPT UNDER THE RUG': FEMINIST HOMILETICAL REFLECTIONS ON THE PARABLE OF THE LOST COIN (LK. 15.8-9)

Linda Maloney

To many practicing Christians, the parables in Luke 15.4-19 are so familiar they could probably recite them in their sleep—especially the first one, the parable of the shepherd with the lost sheep. The church is very fond of the image of Jesus the Good Shepherd—so much so that several times a year many churches have a 'Good Shepherd' Sunday, with one or the other of the gospel readings that touch on that.[1] However, the second part of the gospel reading usually gets much less attention: the parable of a woman who has lost a silver coin, a drachma. The passage reads:

> Or what woman having ten silver coins, if she loses one of them, does not light a lamp, sweep the house, and search carefully until she finds it? When she has found it, she calls together her friends and neighbors, saying, 'Rejoice with me, for I have found the coin that I had lost'.[2]

Ordinarily in Christian proclamation, the woman is just the filling in the 'sandwich' between the all-too-familiar story of the lost sheep and the long, interesting parable of the lost ('prodigal') son (Luke 15.11-32). Between the man and his sheep and the man and his son, the woman and her coin are metaphorically 'swept under the rug'. At most, the preacher says: 'Isn't that nice, Luke likes to pair stories of men and women, and here is another of those pairs, and now let's talk about something interesting, like why the owner of the sheep would risk losing ninety-nine to go looking for just one'—and so on.[3] But here,

1. E.g., Mt. 9.36; Mk. 6.34; Jn 10.11.
2. The translation used throughout this chapter is the New Revised Standard Version.
3. On Luke's use of gender pairings, see T.K. Seim, 'The Gospel of Luke', in E. Schüssler Fiorenza (ed.), *Searching the Scriptures: A Feminist Commentary* (New York: Crossroad, 1994), pp. 729-31; see also in the same volume C.J. Martin, 'The

like the woman of the parable, as a feminist interpreter I am going to go sweeping and searching and looking for a paradigm of Christian feminist praxis in a brief and often-overlooked parable about a poor woman.

Even for a feminist reader, this parable seems problematic because it appears so trivial. The man has a hundred sheep; the woman only has ten little coins. In a translation published in the 1960s, someone had modernized the story so that the woman had 'ten dimes'—even forty years ago, a small amount of money—one more example of how women's lives are trivialized and demeaned in comparison to those of men. *The Living Bible* of the 1970s reversed field and made these 'ten valuable silver coins', but even this translation does not capture the value of the money for the woman in the parable: in Graeco-Roman antiquity, a drachma was about equal to a day's wages for a male labourer—two days' wages for a female worker.[4]

This parable first came into its own for feminist Christians in 1985, when women liberation theologians from the whole South American continent and the Caribbean met in Buenos Aires at the Latin American Conference on Liberation Theology from Women's Perspective, and they took this parable as the theme of their conference. They interpreted that conference as the 'coin' that was lost and found. They said: 'The coin symbolizes our coming together and the discovery of our selves in the light of our experience of God and our daily theological work, which now are transformed into a festival. [In this celebration] we will share our different ways of seeking our coin, of doing our theology'.

As these women knew, the parable reveals a number of things about the ways contemporary feminist and other liberation theologians approach their task: the work is contextual and concrete; it sees the ordinary and the everyday as the place where God is revealed: it takes place 'in the house'—long a symbol of the believing community. It is hard work; it is a struggle to find what has been lost in the darkness that has covered it for so many centuries. But it is also characterized by joy and celebration, and by hope: the hope that 'God is with us' (Mt. 1.23). Like the woman in the parable, God has her skirts tucked up and is busy sweeping and searching, too.

Let me read the parable again in this feminist theological context: The woman has ten drachmai, and apparently that is all she has, because

Acts of the Apostles', 769-71.

4.   See L. Schottroff, *Lydia's Impatient Sisters: A Feminist Social History of Early Christianity* (Louisville, KY: Westminster John Knox Press, 1995), pp. 92-95.

she is very distressed about losing even one of them. A Greek drachma, as noted before, is about the same as a Roman denarius: two days' wages for a female labourer. We know, then, that the woman is poor, whether she has earned the money herself or her husband has left it with her for safekeeping. We also know she is poor because she lives in a mean, dark house, with a low door that doesn't let in much light. In an age when houses were sometimes taxed according to the number of windows they had, one way of estimating a person's wealth was by how light and airy his/her house was. The woman has to light a lamp, which could cause her further anxiety because of the cost of lamp oil. Even with the lamp, she can only find her coin by sweeping and listening for the rattle of the metal against the hard dirt floor. She is so happy to find the coin that in her joy, she calls all her women friends and neighbours (*philai, geitonai*) to share in her happiness, just as the owner of the sheep invites his (grammatically masculine) friends and neighbours (*philoi, geitonoi*) to celebrate the recovery of that one sheep. The tale of the lost coin is so nicely constructed that the woman, her friends, her neighbours, and the drachma she seeks and finds are all feminine in the Greek of the parable.

The parables of the lost sheep and the lost coin use parallel language. The two parables share the same sequence: having, losing, searching, finding, rejoicing. But more importantly, both stories, and the final parable of the lost son, all end with celebrations (Lk. 15.6, 9, 32). The rejoicing of the one who has found the thing lost, be it sheep, coin or son, is not complete unless it is shared by a community. In particular, it appears that the man has sheep for only one reason: so that there can be banquets. And the woman knows what money is for: it exists so that you can invite your friends to a celebration. By the time the feasting is over, more than one sheep and more than one drachma's worth of food will have been consumed.[5] But, in the narrative world of the parable, these valuables exist not to be hoarded, but to be shared.

The celebratory and communal theme of these parables can be compared to what many contemporary theologians are learning about their work: that its purpose is to create community, and to re-create it again and again. 'Doing theology' does not refer just to the work of aca-

---

5.   Interestingly, the value of a drachma was roughly equivalent to the price of a sheep c. 300 BCE, although the coin may have been worth less by the time of the parable; see D.R. Beck, 'Drachma', in D.N. Freedman (ed.), *Eerdmans Dictionary of the Bible* (Grand Rapids, MI: Eerdmans, 2000), p. 356.

demicians; it also encompasses what Christian women and men do when they 'search the scriptures' together, when they gather in study groups to ask questions about God and seek for answers, and when they gather in worship to break the bread of the word and the bread of the eucharist together. When feminist theologians—academic and non-academic—go searching for the lost coin of memory, they re-discover and form new bonds with the lost fore-sisters and brothers who have preceded them. They forge new connections with lost saints, and in doing so see themselves in a new way. The theological task of wo/men, like the work of the woman of the parable, is to sweep, and listen, and sweep again, and listen again—until there is a tiny sound that provides the impetus to go on searching for 'something' until at last it is found; 'something' that may seem so minuscule, so insignificant, that it has gone unnoticed and uncelebrated for centuries. But that tiny drachma—like this brief 'woman's parable' and the others gathered together in this volume—is just what we were looking for; it is just what we need to make it possible for us to call our friends and neighbours, our *philai* and *geitonai* (Lk. 15.9), together and say: 'Rejoice with me, because I have found the drachma I had lost'.

There are some stories in the Bible that tell people of faith how to be like God: in mutual love and forgiveness; in care for God's creation. Then there are other narratives, like the parable of the lost coin and others included in this volume, that compare God to human beings, male and female. The parables of women and men in Luke 15 portray a God who cares and searches and rejoices even more when s/he has lost something—or someone. And from the standpoint of a Christian believer, I think it can justly be said that God cares—cares more than we do, if the parable is true—when the *stories* of some of us are lost, when the *memory* of the female half of the world dies through neglect. Christians are used to the idea of Jesus the Good Shepherd, and some of the earliest Christian art has that theme. But many people of faith are not as comfortable with the metaphor of God the anxious woman, the poor woman laboriously seeking in the dark for the tiny, precious thing she has lost. This parable says that God is *like* that woman, just as God is *like* that shepherd. And if God is the one searching, then human beings are like the sheep, either the lost one or the ones at home, and like the coins, either the missing one or the ones in the purse. From a Christian theological perspective, human beings exist for only one reason: so that there can be a 'we', a community gathered together, an *ekklēsia*. Alone, people of faith are lost, out of place.

In the end, this and every Christian story points to the communion of saints—the community that rejoices together, with God and all the angels, because God refuses to have any gaps at the banquet table. If anyone is missing, there can be no real celebration. If anyone is lost and cold and miserable and frightened, the rest are, too. Because God can't rejoice without God's people, together, women friends and men friends, with the saints and the angels: one people of God celebrating, because no-one can stay lost forever. 'If we live, we live to the Lord, and if we die, we die to the Lord; so then, whether we live or whether we die, we are the Lord's' (Rom. 14.8). Nobody is superfluous, nobody is left out.

'There will be joy in heaven', says the first parable (Lk. 15.7). 'There is joy in the presence of the angels', says the second parable (Lk. 15.10). The stories in Luke 15 remind people of faith that the saints who have gone before are already rejoicing—not just because they are gathered together with God and the angels—but because they are a living presence in the faith community. In theology and practice, people of faith are pledged never to forget them, as they will never leave the community of believers.

JOY IN HEAVEN, SORROW ON EARTH: LUKE 15.10

Mary Ann Beavis

> Just so, I tell you, there is joy in the presence of the angels of God
> over one repenting sinner.[1]

Although this verse is usually regarded as a gloss added by the evangelist
to the parable of the woman searching for a lost coin (Lk. 15.3-6), it begs
for further comment from a feminist perspective. In Chapter 4 of this
anthology ('Making Up Stories: A Feminist Reading of Lk. 15.11b-32'),
this saying, which is reiterated in expanded form in Lk. 15.7, is mentioned
by survivors of sexual abuse in a Dutch study of Christianity and incest.[2]
To these women, the idea that Godde rejoices more over the repentance of
a sinner—someone like their abusers—than over a righteous person who
needs no repentance is profoundly disturbing. For one respondent,
Margaret, the saying meant that '[t]he angels rejoice for that one sinner
who repents in the last minutes of his life…[more than for] the ninety-nine
who were good their entire lives. So there'll be more rejoicing for him up
in heaven than for me when I get there?'[3] Another woman, Ellen, observed
that this is a teaching of great comfort to *offenders*, but not to victims:
'The offender knows that too. After first trying to deny everything, he
says: "I have sinned, but that doesn't matter because my redeemer will
grant me forgiveness" '.[4] Even worse, the victim of abuse may be cast in
the role of 'sinner' if she refuses to forgive her abuser; she becomes
someone who must 'repent' so that Godde can forgive *her* for *being
abused*. The survivor is doubly victimized: first by her abuser; then by the
church that teaches her that she is sinning by withholding forgiveness.
This saying, which comprises the 'moral' (*epimythium*) of the three

1. The quotation is from the New Revised Standard Version.
2. A. Imbens and I. Jonker, *Christianity and Incest* (Minneapolis: Fortress, 1992),
p. 277.
3. Imbens and Jonker, *Christianity and Incest*, p. 163.
4. Imbens and Jonker, *Christianity and Incest*, p. 163.

parables in Lk. 15 (lost sheep, lost coin, prodigal son),[5] conditions the reader's interpretation of the parables: Godde is as anxious for the welfare of the sinner as the shepherd is to find the missing sheep; to Godde, the sinner is infinitely more valuable that the lost drachma that the woman so anxiously searches out; the errant son is beloved by his father, no matter how far he strays. An abuse survivor might bitterly remark that this is good news for abusers and bad news for their victims. Sure, the sinless elder brother is reassured by his father that he is also a beloved member of the family, but the celebration and rejoicing are over the 'lost' brother.

I was recently reminded of the difference between the incest survivors' negative reaction to Lk. 15. 7, 10 and the 'standard' interpretation of this saying as a message of consolation to sinful humanity. At a public lecture given by feminist theologian Bernice Santor, five women in the biblical tradition were featured: Eve (Gen. 1-3), Huldah (2 Kgs 22; 2 Chron. 34), Mary Magdalene (Mt. 27.56, 61; 28.1; Mk. 15.40, 47; 16.1; Lk. 8.2; 24.10; Jn 19.25; 20.1, 18), the Samaritan woman (Jn 4.7-30) and Martha (Lk. 10.38-42; Jn 11.1-44).[6] Santor, an artist and quilter as well as a theologian, had crafted five beautiful quilts illustrating the stories of each of these women. Of the five, she observed, three have been misidentified in traditional, patriarchal scholarship as sexual 'sinners' (Eve, Mary Magdalene, the Samaritan woman), one has been overlooked (Huldah), and one has been typecast as a harried housewife (Martha). Santor's presentation consisted of a commentary on how each of these women had been misrepresented by 'malestream' interpretation, and each quilt symbolized the powerful and positive roles embodied in each figure. The audience reaction to Santor's feminist interpretation of the three 'sinners' is directly relevant to my commentary on Lk. 15.10, so I shall focus on her remarks on Eve, Mary Magdalene and the Samaritan woman.

Santor's first quilt depicted Eve as the pregnant *Hawa*, 'Mother of All Living' (Gen. 3.20). In Christian tradition, Eve has been seen as a seductress who tempted the man into eating fruit from the tree of knowledge (1 Tim. 2.11-14), the 'devil's gateway... the unsealer of that tree... the first deserter of the divine law', she 'who persuaded him whom the devil was not valiant enough to attack', the destroyer of 'God's image, man'

---

5. For the Graeco-Roman terminology pertaining to the 'morals' added to parables, see M.A. Beavis, 'Parable and Fable', *Catholic Biblical Quarterly* 25 (1990), pp. 482-82.

6. Bernice Santor, 'Some Women Amazed Us', Public Lecture, St. Thomas More College, January 17, 2000.

(Tertullian, 'On the Apparel of Women').[7] Santor emphasized Eve's dignity as the primal woman, who, according to Gen. 2.16-17, was not yet created when YHWH commanded Adam not to eat from the tree. Rather than being disobedient (like her husband), she is an innocent seeker after wisdom, whose worst 'sin' is to desire something good (Gen. 2. 6).

The quilt devoted to Mary Magdalene depicted her with a halo, in magnificent priestly garb, as a great leader and teacher of the early church, in accordance with her ancient title of Apostle to the Apostles.[8] Santor noted that the canonical gospels suggest that Mary was the leader of Jesus' women disciples (especially Lk. 8.2-3), and consistently identify her as the first witness to the empty tomb and to the resurrection (Mk 16.1-8; Mt. 28.1-10; Lk. 23.49; 24.1-11; Jn 20.1-18). It is Mary who proclaims the 'good news' of the resurrection to the male apostles (Jn 20.18). However, in the Western church, Mary Magdalene has been misidentified as a prostitute, due to Gregory the Great's (sixth century CE) *incorrect* conflation of Mary Magdalene with an anonymous 'woman of the city… a sinner' portrayed in Lk. 7.36-50. Traditional artistic representations of Mary have frequently depicted her as the 'repentant Magdalene', often shown holding a jar of ointment, alluding to the 'sinner' who anoints Jesus' feet (cf. Lk. 7.37), or in the *Noli me tangere* scene, where the resurrected Jesus reveals himself to the prostrate, weeping Mary (Jn 20.11-17). Although feminist interpreters are well aware that Mary Magdalene is never depicted as sinful, much less a prostitute, in the Gospels or elsewhere in Christian tradition prior to the sixth century (or in Eastern Christianity), this is the image of Mary that has endured through the centuries, especially in popular culture.[9]

Santor's quilt of the Samaritan woman ('the woman at the well') shows her running towards Sychar (Jn 4.5) to proclaim the good news that Jesus is the messiah (Jn 4.28-29). In Christian tradition, this woman is usually depicted as a horrible sinner, since, as Jesus prophesies, she has been

7. In A. Roberts and J. Donaldson (eds.), *The Ante-Nicene Fathers*, Volume 4, *Fathers of the Third Century: Tertullian, Part Fourth; Minucius Felix; Commodian; Origen, Parts First and Second* (repr.; Grand Rapids, MI: Eerdmans, 1997), p. 8.

8. E.g., in the late first or early second century *Gospel of Mary Magdalene*; see R.J. Miller, (ed.), 'The Gospel of Mary', *The Complete Gospels* (San Francisco: HarperSanFrancisco, 1994), pp. 357-66; K.L. King, 'The Gospel of Mary Magdalene', in E. Schüssler Fiorenza, *Searching the Scriptures: Volume 2: A Feminist Commentary* (New York: Crossroad, 1994), pp. 601-34.

9. See J. Schaberg, 'Fast Forward to the Magdalene', *Semeia* 14 (1996), pp. 33-45.

married five times, and the man she is currently living with is not her husband (v. 18). However, Santor observed, the idea that the woman was promiscuous, a prostitute, or an adulteress is pure speculation; it is just as likely that she had been widowed five times, or divorced through no fault of her own—a victim of misfortune, not a sexual sinner. Perhaps she had been passed down from brother to brother, according to the custom of levirate marriage (cf. Mk 12.18-23). The man whose household she occupied might have been a father, brother, or other male relative, rather than an illicit sexual partner. However, rather than emphasizing the woman's perceptiveness in recognizing Jesus as the messiah and her role in spreading the gospel, patriarchal interpretation has focused on her supposed sinfulness, and Jesus' condescension in speaking to her (a point that the disciples in the narrative do not dare to make; cf. v. 27).

The perspective on the figures of Eve, Mary Magdalene and the Samaritan woman presented by Bernice Santor was familiar to those of us in the audience—that is, most of us—who were aware of feminist theology and biblical interpretation. Several female students expressed their surprise and appreciation at hearing such a positive portrayal of these biblical women. However, two of the male audience members, one a student, and one a faculty member, had reservations. The younger man pointed out how many of the male heroes of the bible are flawed, sinful characters—Abraham, Jacob, David, Solomon—and yet Godde still used them to good purpose. The professor suggested that something was 'lost' when the 'sinfulness' of these women was taken away; surely, all human beings are sinful, and stories of Godde's love and forgiveness to sinners are a welcome message of hope.

Santor's reply was that of course all human beings are sinful; what her quilts, and her commentary on them, meant to emphasize is that patriarchal interpretation has often projected sin onto women characters unnecessarily. What I should have added to the discussion at that time (and which I shall add now, according to the principle of *l'esprit d'escalier*) was that the difference between the 'sinful' male characters cited by the student and the female 'sinners' portrayed in the quilts is that, in the biblical tradition, *patently guilty men are heroized, while relatively innocent women are transformed into sexy sinners*. Abraham is a weak character who lies about his wife's identity twice in order to save his own skin (and consequently places her in sexual peril) (Gen. 12.10-20; 20.1-18; cf. 26.7-11), has a son by a foreign slave girl and twice sends her (first pregnant, then with a baby) out into the desert to fend for herself (Gen.

16.1-16; 21.8-21), and is only prevented from offering a human sacrifice by divine intervention (Gen. 22.1-14)! Jacob is a schemer who dupes his disabled father and steals his brother's rightful inheritance (Gen. 25.27-34). David is a self-serving politician who kills (or arranges the assassination of) anyone who might be a threat to his claim on royal power (2 Sam. 1.15-16; 4.5-12; cf. 3.26-34)), a voyeur and adulterer who murders his partner's husband (and who quite possibly 'seduces' Bathsheba by means of rape) (2 Sam. 11.2-27) and cruelly mistreats his first wife, Michal (2 Sam. 3.12-16, 6.20-23), a father who turns a blind eye to his son's rape of his daughter (2 Sam. 13.1-29) and brings disaster on his people (2 Sam. 24.25). Solomon, the famous sage of Israel, imposed forced labour on his people in order to complete his grandiose building programme (1 Kgs 5.13-18, 9.15-22), a policy that eventually caused the breakup of the kingdom (1 Kgs 12.1-33). In contrast, Eve is the wise and fecund Mother of All Living; Mary Magdalene is the faithful Apostle to the Apostles; the Samaritan woman is the first person in John's Gospel to identify Jesus as the messiah. The male and female characters are hardly comparable.

It is perhaps not too much of a hermeneutical 'stretch' to suggest that these three, quite disparate, biblical stories about women have all traditionally been interpreted through the lens of the sentiment expressed in Lk. 15.10: 'there shall be joy above among the angels of God over one repenting sinner', and that this 'moral' has been erroneously applied in all three instances. These women are righteous, not sinful, and in no special need of repentance. The men, however, are overwhelmingly sinful, and yet have been elevated through centuries of patriarchal interpretation into towering heroes of the faith, their many shortcomings overlooked by recourse the same interpretive principle: Godde's love and forgiveness to sinners. To a male audience (at least insofar as the men identify with 'heroic' figures like Abraham, Jacob, David and Solomon), perhaps this message of easy grace is good news. But women listeners get a different message. They are led to identify with biblical women whose virtues have been distorted into vices—curiosity into hubris, freedom into licentiousness, coping with misfortune into punishment—and rapturously to accept 'forgiveness' for the betrayal of innocence. How much 'joy in heaven' the repentance of the innocent engenders I shall leave the reader to decide.

It is tempting to 'rescue' Lk. 15.10 by attributing it to the evangelist Luke and not to Jesus.[10] However, this saying has some claim on

10. Cf. R.W. Funk, R.W. Hoover and The Jesus Seminar, *The Five Gospels: The*

authenticity, insofar as it meets the criterion of 'distinctive discourse' laid down by the Jesus Seminar.[11] By making sinners and not the righteous the special focus of Godde's care, the saying goes 'against the social and religious grain'.[12] Surely the saying would have 'surprised and shocked' as well as 'frustrated the ordinary, everyday expectations' of Jesus' peasant, Jewish audiences.[13] Moreover, research on parable performance in Jewish folklore studies indicates that 'an epigrammatic formulation of the general principle or moral of... [a] tale in the form of a proverb or aphorism' (*muser-haskl*) is often a feature of live parable performances;[14] this casts some doubt on the supposition that Lk. 15.10 is necessarily 'an interpretive overlay or comment' added by the evangelist.[15] Another insight from the study of Jewish folklore is that it is the *aptness* of a story to the situation being discussed that is prized by listeners, even more than the story itself.[16] To apply Lk. 15.10 (or Lk. 15.7) to the situation of either the sinners or the innocents discussed above would be, to quote some traditional retorts to ineptly told parables, 'as appropriate as a smack [in reply to] "Good Sabbath"' or 'appropriate to yesterday's stuffed dumplings'.[17] In the spirit of the evangelists[18] who, according to the Jesus Seminar, frequently attributed their own statements to Jesus,[19] and in the interest of what E. Schüssler Fiorenza calls 'a critical feminist rereading of the Bible for liberation',[20] I shall suggest a *muser-haskl/epimythium* that is more appropriate to the situation of the 'lost' who are the innocent victims

Search for the Authentic Words of Jesus (New York: Polebridge, 1993), pp. 355-56.

   11. Funk *et al.*, *The Five Gospels*, pp. 30-32.

   12. Funk *et al.*, *The Five Gospels*, p. 31.

   13. Funk *et al.*, *The Five Gospels*, p. 31.

   14. B. Kirshenblatt-Gimblett 'The Concept and Varieties of Narrative Performance in East European Jewish Culture', in R. Bauman and J. Sherzer (eds.), *Explorations in the Ethnography of Speaking* (2nd edn; Cambridge: Cambridge University Press, 1989), p. 303; see also B. Kirshenblatt-Gimblett, 'A Parable in Context: A Social Interactional Analysis of Storytelling Performance', *Folklore: Performance and Communication* (Dan Ben-Amos and Kenneth S. Goldstein, eds.; The Hague/Paris: Mouton, 1975) 105-30.

   15. Funk *et al.*, *The Five Gospels*, p. 21.

   16. Kirshenblatt-Gimblett, 'Concept and Varieties', p. 288.

   17. Kirshenblatt-Gimblett, 'Concept and Varieties', p. 288.

   18. Including women proclaimers of the word (e.g., Jn 4.25; 11.17; Lk. 24.10; Acts 18.26; Phil. 4.2-3; Rom. 16.7).

   19. Kirshenblatt-Gimblett, 'Concept and Varieties', p. 23.

   20. E. Schüssler Fiorenza, *But She Said: Feminist Practices of Biblical Interpretation* (Boston: Beacon Press, 1992), p. 75.

of sin and injustice, as well as to those who sin against them:

> Likewise, I tell you, the angels of Godde rejoice more over one innocent
> person who is vindicated
> than over the repentance of the sinners who have abused them![21]

21. With a little paraphrasing, an appropriate *muser-haskl* from the synoptic tradition might be Mk 9.42: 'Whoever causes one of these little ones who believe in me to sin, it would be better for him if a great millstone were hung round his neck and he were thrown into the sea' (RSV).

Proclaiming the Parable of the Persistent Widow (Lk. 18.2-5)

Mary W. Matthews, Carter Shelley and Barbara Scheele

There was a judge in a certain city who had no fear of Godde and no shame in his dealings with humanity. A widow in that city kept coming to him and saying, 'Grant me justice against my opponent'. And for a while, he didn't feel like it. But finally he said to himself, 'Although I have no fear of Godde and no shame in my dealings with humanity, because this widow keeps pestering me, I might as well grant her justice, so that in the end she doesn't come and give me a black eye' (Lk. 18.2-5; translation by Mary W. Matthews).

Editorial Introduction

In the early stages of assembling this book, the parable of the persistent widow was the one most often requested by prospective contributors. In the end, I decided to honour the manifest appeal of the parable for feminist Christian women by including three distinctive interpretations rather than insisting on one 'definitive' reading. Like Linda Maloney's piece on the lost coin (Chapter 1), the three authors of this chapter provide more 'homiletical' or 'popular' readings of the parable than is usual in 'serious' New Testament scholarship (although it is not uncommon for feminist exegetes to bring contemporary, personal and experiential elements into their work). The editorial choice to incorporate chapters that reflect what Schüssler Fiorenza calls a 'hermeneutics of proclamation' in addition to strictly academic exegesis was deliberate, recognizing that for many people, as Scheele observes below, 'reading the bible is important' in a way that reading most other ancient texts is not, no matter how interesting or relevant they may be to scholars. Although Matthews, Shelley and Scheele read the parable in different ways, all three interpretations attest to the *social* implications of the story, especially in the context of real women's lives, ancient and contemporary.

1. *'Go Thou and Do Likewise': A Homiletical Commentary*

Mary W. Matthews

v. 2: Κριτής τις ἦν ἕν τινι πόλει τὸν θεὸν μὴ φοβούμενος καὶ ἄνθρωπον μὴ ἐντρεπόμενος. *There was a judge in a certain city who had no fear of Godde and no shame in his dealings with humanity.*

The legal system in the first century was not, of course, like our own, so the first word to examine is κριτής, judge. Obviously, in antiquity a judge was not a black-robed veteran of years and years of legal training, apprenticeship and practice. In Jesus' time, priests presided over court cases involving Jewish religious matters. The Sanhedrin, with the high priest presiding and ninety councillors (with a quorum of 23), was the supreme Jewish court. As B. Malina observes:

> Criminal proceedings were nothing but inquisitions but the judges were enjoined to unearth every conceivable argument in favor of the accused. There was no way to lodge an appeal. The sentence was pronounced in the name of God.[1]

This court decided such matters as blasphemy, violations of the Sabbath law or the Torah's purity regulations.

Although Roman proconsuls acted as magistrates in matters that concerned the overlords of the Jewish nation, for most people justice came from elders who dealt with local matters as they sat at the town gate (Amos 5.10). The judges were instructed by the scriptures to 'Consider what you are doing, for you judge not on behalf of human beings, but on YHWH's behalf; Godde is with you in giving judgment. Now, let the fear of YHWH be upon you; take care what you do, for there is no perversion of justice with YHWH our Godde, or partiality, or taking of bribes' (2 Chron. 19.6-7).[2] Since this judge had no fear of YHWH, Jesus' audience would have understood that his judgments included corruption, partiality and venality.

The last word in the verse, modifying κριτής, is the present passive participle of ἐντρέπω, which means: to have been made ashamed; to

---

1.   W. Fricke, *The Court-Martial of Jesus: A Christian Defends the Jews Against the Charge of Deicide* (New York: Grove Weidenfeld 1990, translated from the German by Salvator Attanasio), p. 151.

2.   Translation is from the New Revised Standard Version, revised to reflect more inclusive language.

respect or regard; to be ashamed; to feel fear (*entrepō*, to be 'in trepida-
tion'). Thus, another perfectly accurate translation would be, 'who
respected neither Godde nor humanity'. However, to understand the full
import of the term, the parable needs to be interpreted in terms of the
ancient ideology of honour and shame. First-century Mediterranean culture focused on male honour. Men spent a lot of their time trying to
achieve or maintain honour—that is, 'a claim to worth and the social
acknowledgment of that worth'—and to avoid shame, 'sensitivity for
one's own reputation and sensitivity to the opinion of others'.[3] Whereas
men could achieve honour, women were allowed only to try to avoid
shame. Karen Jo Torjesen explains:

> A man gained honor through challenging another man's honor successfully
> or by avenging any loss of honor of his own. A woman, however, demon-
> strated her honorability by comporting herself with shame, signifying that
> she understood her sexual vulnerability, and avoiding all appearances of
> indiscretion. Femaleness functioned as a cultural symbol for shame... In
> this sexual division of moral labor, honor was considered an aspect of male
> nature expressed in a natural desire for precedence and an aggressive
> sexuality. Shame, the defining quality of womanhood, was indicated by
> passivity, subordination, and seclusion in the household.[4]

For Jesus' audience, this judge was the opposite of what a judge should
be: he was *not* righteous and God-fearing (i.e., he was corrupt), and he did
not care about his own reputation or what others thought about him—he
was without honour. If B.E. Reid is correct in her suggestion that the widow
was the judge's own mother or sister,[5] this judge was colossally shameless.

> v. 3: χήρα δὲ ἦν ἐν τῇ πόλει ἐκείνῃ καὶ ἤρχετο πρός αὐτὸν λέγουσα,
> Ἐκδίκησόν με ἀπὸ τοῦ ἀντιδίκου μου. A widow in that city kept coming
> to him and saying, 'Grant me justice against my opponent'.

P. Hiebert comments, 'The term "widow"...has a more specific meaning in
the biblical texts than the English word conveys. The woman designated

---

3.   B. Malina, *The New Testament World* (Atlanta: John Knox Press, 1981), pp. 28,
44.
4.   K.J. Torjesen, *When Women Were Priests* (HarperSanFrancisco, 1993), p. 137.
5.   B.E. Reid, *Choosing the Better Part? Women in the Gospel of Luke* (Collegeville, MN: Liturgical Press, 1996), p. 191: 'To Jesus' first audience, the notion of a
woman arguing her own case before the judge would have been startling. Adjudication
was the domain of men. At the death of her husband, the widow's nearest male relative
would have taken responsibility for her. We suspect that her complaint is against the
very man who should have been her protector!'

by these terms was not merely someone whose husband had died; she lived outside of the normal social structure in which every female lived under the authority of some male; she was responsible to and for herself'.[6] The widows (Hebrew: *almanôt*) were the only class of women who could act on their own, with the same autonomy granted to men; unlike other women, widows had no male relative who could invalidate their vows, override their judgment, or controvert their decisions.

This independence carried a heavy price. Along with orphans and resident aliens, widows were particularly vulnerable to oppression, injustice and exploitation. A widow could not inherit from her husband; all property went to the nearest male heir. The widow could remain in her husband's family only if his next of kin would take her in levirate marriage.[7] Part of the bride-price (*mohar*) settled upon each woman at marriage was an amount equal to one year's worth of the groom's income, to be kept in trust by the bride's family in case she were ever widowed or divorced.[8] That was all that most widows had. If her husband's family did not accept her, her position was precarious indeed.

The widow would have been expected by Jesus' first-century audiences to be a victim—passive, subordinate to whatever surviving male relatives she had, silent, meek, discreet, rarely stirring out of her home. But notice the Greek ἤρχετω—the imperfect of ἔρχομαι, which principally means, 'to come'. In Greek, the imperfect expresses action in the past that was ongoing, whether just beginning ('on December 26, Christmas was coming'), prolonged ('Noah thought, "The rain just keeps coming"'), or repetitive ('the widow kept coming'). In this context, we see that the widow 'was coming (before him)' not just once, but over and over.

The words ἐκδικέω and ἀντίδικος have no easy translation into English. Ἐπιδικάζω means to avenge or punish a crime, to exact vengeance, or to avenge a person. Someone who is ἔκδικος is without law, lawless, unjust. (Later, in 18.6, Luke calls the judge ἀντίδικος, 'a person who does wrong, is unrighteous, unjust'). Δίκη, the word usually translated 'justice', meant custom, law, right, punishment, atonement, vengeance, satisfaction. An ἀντίδικος is an opponent in a lawsuit,

6. P. Hiebert, 'Widows', *Oxford Companion to the Bible* (ed. B.M. Metzger and M.D. Coogan; Oxford: Oxford University Press, 1993), p. 795.

7. R. Gower, *The New Manners and Customs of Bible Times* (Chicago: Moody Press, 1987), p. 74.

8. Gower, *Manners and Customs*, p. 64. In other words, Mary of Nazareth, upon being widowed, would have had a sum of roughly $20,000 on which to support herself, Jesus, his four brothers, and 'all his sisters' until her sons reached economic maturity.

whether defendant or plaintiff. In other words, the widow was not complaining about some trivial matter or doing the first-century equivalent of buttonholing the judge at a cocktail party. She was insisting that the judge 'get off his lazy duff' and punish the crime of which she was victim, to provide a satisfactory outcome in the lawsuit in which she was apparently plaintiff. Without money for the bribe, her only hope was to keep coming until the judge finally got sick of refusing her.

What makes this interesting is that 'Jewish women could not testify in court, since they were socially considered liars and legally considered minors'.[9] In other words, this parable must have boggled the minds of its first audiences: a mere woman, a widow—by definition, in their minds, weak, foolish, silly, impotent, chattering, useless—was not only taking part in a court case, she was browbeating the judge! She dared to invade the court, a male domain—not once, but over and over. She was assertive, autonomous, out of seclusion, and insubordinate. In the eyes of first-century Galilee, the widow was as shameless as the judge.

Jesus' parables are drawn from everyday life, but they do not necessarily portray normal, everyday life. Jesus often exaggerates or comes up with unexpected behaviour—a debt of a thousand talents is forgiven (that is, somewhere between $23 million and 1.1 billion US dollars in today's money, depending on whether the talents were silver or gold); *all* of the guests invited to an important banquet decline; *all ten* bridesmaids fall asleep. In the world of the parable, it is not even surprising that 'Jessica Fletcher' is arguing a case before the Supreme Court. The point is the contrast between lawless power and powerlessness, between utter shamelessness and what therefore must be its opposite.

> v. 4 Καὶ οὐκ ἤθελεν ἐπὶ χρόνον. μετὰ δὲ ταῦτα εἶπεν ἐν ἑαυτῷ, Εἰ καὶ τὸν θεὸν οὐ φοβοῦμαι οὐδὲ ἄνθρωπον ἐντρέπομαι…' *And for a while, he didn't feel like it. But finally he said to himself, 'Although I have no fear of Godde and no shame in my dealings with humanity…'*
>
> v. 5 διά γε τὸ παρέχειν μοι κόπον τὴν χήραν ταύτην ἐκδικήσω αὐτήν, ἵνα μὴ εἰς τέλος ἐρχομένη ὑπωπιάζῃ με: *…because this widow keeps pestering me, I might as well grant her justice, so that in the end she doesn't come and give me a black eye'.*

These verses present some interesting translation issues. The Greek θέλω (v. 4) meant to wish, want, desire, or 'like'; with a negative (such as οὐκ)

9. P.R. Smith, *Is It Okay to Call God 'Mother'? Considering the Feminine Face of God* (Peabody, MA: Hendrickson Publishers, 1993), p. 93.

it meant 'didn't care to' or 'didn't feel like it'. Μετὰ δὲ ταῦτα—literally 'with that'—meant 'afterwards', or in this context, 'after the discernible while'; here, 'finally' is an appropriate translation. The Greek κόπον (v. 5) meant 'trouble, labour, or hardship'; with the verb παρέχω, the usual translation is 'to bother or trouble someone'. In the translation process, I debated a long time between 'pestering' and 'giving me grief'. The verb ὑπωπιάζω is a boxing term that means, 'to strike under the eye' or 'to give a black eye to'; it derives from the phrase ὑπώπιον 'under the eye'.[10]

Very few translators seem to be able to accept the idea of a widow, presumably an older woman, actually striking a man who has power over her as though she were a boxer; of the many translations I consulted, only three came close: the New American ('lest she finally come and strike me'), the New Jerusalem ('or she will come and slap me in the face'), and the Amplified Bible ('lest she give me intolerable annoyance and wear me out by her continual coming *or* at the last she come and rail on me *or* assault me *or* strangle me'). Most translations bowdlerize the word, translating the boxing term by some variation on 'wear me out'. But what are they afraid of? Jesus was never afraid of exaggerating for effect, to make what he was saying memorable. Isn't there something charmingly 'sticks and stones'-ish about a judge who isn't afraid of public opinion, but who *is* afraid of being beaten up by a little old lady?

Most commentators take for granted that one of the characters in this parable must be a stand-in for Godde, and most seem bewildered by the idea of Godde portrayed as an unjust judge—a few even class this parable with the tale of the dishonest steward in Lk. 16.1-8a. Luke is particularly troubled by the idea of portraying God as corrupt, and does his best to present the parable as a typical *qal vahomer,* an analogy from lesser to greater–if arithmetic is tough, how much tougher is calculus? Or, as Luke portrays Jesus as saying,[11] 'If an unjust judge can be badgered into justice, how much more will Godde do when Godde's chosen ones bellow [βοάω, the sound an angry bull makes]?' (18.8).

J. Schaberg is not the only source to notice that Luke had a vested interest in 'appeasing the detractors of Christianity and controlling women

---

10. Rarely, someone will propound the definition 'to slander or besmirch', as in giving the judge's reputation a black eye—but Jesus has already said, twice, that this judge didn't give a fig about his reputation.

11. Most scholars agree that 18.1 and 18.6-8 are Luke's explanation of Jesus' parable.

who practice or aspire to practice a prophetic ministry in the church'.[12] For Luke, the ideal woman is silent, submissive, passive, and obedient to the men in her life. Any other sort of woman, such as the unnamed woman of 7.35-50, is almost by definition a 'sinner'. Notice that in the 'application' in 18.8, the widow is nowhere to be found. Think of how much more effective it would have been if Luke could have brought himself to say, 'If a defenceless widow can tromp a corrupt judge, when the Messiah comes, mama will spank!'

The problem with identifying Godde with the unjust judge is that it implies that Godde needs to be pestered–in 18.8, Luke as much as says so. But does Godde really need to be pestered? Not according to Jesus ben Sirach (Sir 35.14-22):

> Do not offer Godde a bribe, for Godde will not accept it; and do not rely on a dishonest sacrifice; for Adonai is the judge, and with Godde there is no partiality... Godde will not ignore...the widow when she pours out her complaint... Indeed, Adonai will not delay'.[13]

B.E. Reid, on the other hand, offers the appealing idea that, as in the parables of the lost coin and the woman baking bread, Godde in this parable is to be imaged by the woman. She says,

> If, however, like the two previous parables, the woman represents Godde, then an entirely different message emerges. Here is an unexpected twist in the parable. That Godde would be relentlessly pursuing justice is not a new image of the divine (e.g., Sir. 35.14-19). But that Godde is more akin to a victimized widow than a powerful judge is startling. She embodies godly power in the midst of apparent powerlessness... Luke faithfully preserves a story told by Jesus which shatters stereotypes and highlights the power of the seeming powerless. With his introduction, however, Luke sidetracks the reader from this message. Since this kind of role is not what he would encourage for women, he softens the parable's impact by posing the widow as an example of persistent prayer, a docile and acceptable role.[14]

If the widow is meant to represent Godde, then the unjust judge must represent humanity. Jesus was saying, in other words, that Godde keeps nagging at us until we reluctantly get around to doing the right thing. If this is so, this parable becomes a variation on the old proverb, 'Life keeps

---

12. J. Schaberg, 'Luke', in C.A. Newsom and S.H. Ringe (eds.), *The Women's Bible Commentary* (Louisville, KY: Westminster/John Knox Press, 1992), p. 275.

13. NRSV; inclusive language added.

14. Reid, *Choosing the Better Part?*, pp. 192, 194.

t

teaching the same lesson until we learn it'. Is Godde powerless, like the widow? Consciously we deny any such idea—but those of us who are 'practising' Christians still sleep late on Sunday mornings, make excuses not to give a full tithe, and ignore the lesson of the sheep and the goats (Mt. 25.31-46). The moral of the story would be, it's best to do the right thing for the right reasons, but second best is doing the right thing for the wrong reasons.

I rather like this view of the parable, but in my view, neither character images Godde. I believe that the unjust judge represents what L. Schottroff calls 'structural injustice';[15] the widow represents Everychristian. Like the widow, Everychristian is to be persistent, to keep badgering unjust authority until it finally gives in. I believe Jesus is saying to each of us: keep demonstrating outside the School of the Americas, that evil place where the CIA teaches South American bullies like Noriega (an alumnus) how to terrorize, massacre, torture, and rape. Keep pointing out to the Magisterium that Genesis 1.27 is right, and Godde created women in Godde's image; if Godde did not, then women are not merely not eligible to represent Godde at the altar, we are also not eligible for baptism, communion, or redemption. Like the persistent widow, fight injustice to the best of your ability, no matter how overmatched you are—don't envision your fight as one grand apocalyptic battle, but rather as the same sort of 'fight' as water eroding stone. As Jesus might say today: a wacky little old lady with 24 cats, sitting in a sea of chintz and writing letter after letter, *can* fight City Hall and win. So go thou and do likewise.

2. *'A Widow Without Wiles'*

Carter Shelley

Come, come my conservative friend, wipe the dew off your spectacles, and see that the world is moving. Whatever your views may be as to the...proposed work, your political and social degradation are but an outgrowth of your status in the Bible... How can woman's position be changed from that of a subordinate to an equal, without opposition, without the broadest discussion of all the questions involved in her present degradation? (Elizabeth Cady Stanton in *The Women's Bible*, 1895.)

---

15. L. Schottroff, *Lydia's Impatient Sisters: A Feminist Social History of Early Christianity* (Louisville, KY: Westminster/John Knox Press, 1995), p. 101.

Introduction

Because I have served as a Presbyterian pastor for the past 21 years, as well as having been a church conflict resolution consultant and a teacher of homiletics and literature, my contribution introduces American literature feminist scholar Judith Fetterley's resisting reader method (explained in the following) and applies it by means of a homily. Preaching as Christian feminist is a challenge I face on a regular basis. How does one read the text with integrity, yet preach it audibly to congregants who need opportunities to reflect upon their own social-political biases rather than simply walk out the door mad and rejecting every word uttered from the pulpit? It's a dilemma Jesus himself faced every day of his ministry.

In *The Resisting Reader: A Feminist Approach to American Fiction*, Fetterley deconstructs texts read as part of the American literary canon: 'Rip Van Winkle', *A Farewell to Arms*, *The Great Gatsby*, *The Bostonians* and *An American Dream*.[16] Fetterley offers this hermeneutical method to women students and teachers as a way to read androcentric texts traditionally valued for their transcendent themes and literary power. Fetterley argues that such texts must be deconstructed (resisted) by women readers if women are to maintain a sense of power and self-worth in the face of patriarchal generalizations about what it means to be female in American society:

> Our literature neither leaves women alone nor allows them to participate. It insists on its universality at the same time that it defines that universality in specifically male terms... In such fictions the female reader is co-opted into participation in an experience from which she is explicitly excluded; she is asked to identify with a selfhood that defines itself in opposition to her; she is required to identify against herself...[The] experience of being American is equated with the experience of being male.[17]

In reading such texts, Fetterley notes that the female reader often experiences a sense of powerlessness and futility, yet she often doesn't really understand why it is she feels this way. Such powerlessness pervades the woman reader's world because the best known American literature, like the best known biblical stories, define the world as male and expect the reader to identify with the male protagonists to the exclusion or detriment of female characters. Those characteristics in American literature which Fetterley names as a reality for women readers are also pervasive in the

16. J. Fetterley, *The Resisting Reader: A Feminist Approach to American Fiction* (Boston: Beacon, 1978).
17. Fetterley, *Resisting Reader*, p. xii.

Bible. With its relegation of women to second-class status and presentation of women as betrayers (Delilah), prostitutes (Rahab), objects of lust (Bathsheba and Tamar), evil influences (Queen Jezebel), unfaithful harlots (Hosea's wife), schemers (Rebekah and Rachel), mothers (Sarah, Hannah, Mary, the mother of Jesus) and virgins (Jephthah's daughter), the Bible also endorses misogyny.

Fetterley warns the reader against too easily assuming that a text's authority comes from its intrinsic worth: 'The question of who profits, and how, are crucial because the attempt to answer it leads directly to an understanding of the function of literary sexual politics'.[18] Modern deconstructionist Jacques Derrida has written that the problem posed by literary texts which too quickly achieve status as authoritative and transcendent texts is that their meaning becomes prematurely limited, restricting the text's vitality and power to suggest more and mean far more than one definitive reading, book review or commentary can provide. When the female reader too easily accedes to a text's false authority and universality, she allows that text to define her and to deprive her of a voice that is her own. Consequently, women must re-vision the lives of the women we read about, write about, and are, for ourselves. Fetterley quotes poet Adrienne Rich:

> Re-vision—the act of looking back, of seeing with fresh eyes, of entering an old text from a new critical direction—is for us more than a chapter in cultural history: it is an act of survival. Until we can understand the assumptions in which we are drenched we cannot know ourselves. And this drive to self-knowledge, for woman, is more than a search for identity: it is part of her refusal of the self-destructiveness of male-dominated society. A radical critique of literature, feminist in its impulse, would take the work first of all as a clue to how we live, how we have been living, how we have been led to imagine ourselves, how our language has trapped as well as liberated us; and how we can begin to see—and therefore live—afresh.[19]

Published in 1978, *The Resisting Reader* was one of the first crystallizations of deconstruction used in the service of feminist hermeneutics. Deconstruction offers a popular hermeneutic for feminist scholars and students because deconstruction refuses to allow androcentric texts' words about women and women's reality and purpose to go unchallenged. Because it begins with the reader's subjective response to a particular text, resisting readings can be applied by the amateur as well as the academic.

---

18. Fetterley, *Resisting Reader*, p. xx.
19. Quoted in Fetterley, *Resisting Reader*, p. xix.

Using Fetterley's four categories (listed below), in the following we compare a patriarchal, androcentric, absolutist reading of Lk. 18.1-8 by Jesus' contemporaries and many of our own, with an imaginative reconstruction of one by Jesus himself as 'resisting reader'. In this parable about the judge and the persistent widow, we shall see that Jesus offers no critique or sideways 'wink, wink, nudge, nudge' about the widow's conduct. What Jesus does do is empower one of the powerless and declare her behaviour not only necessary but laudable: 'Will not God grant justice to his chosen ones who cry to him day and night?'

Four Steps in a Feminist Hermeneutic of Deconstruction

1. Name the text's sexist subtext.

2. Expose the text's contradictory statements.

3. Undermine the text's pretensions to authority.

4. Recognize the text's fake claim to universality.

Deconstruction: The Resisting Reader

The resisting reader resists the stereotypes and subtle or not-so-subtle descriptions, assumptions and definitions of the self as categorized according to gender, race, sexual orientation, ethnicity, etc., as these appear in a particular text. A key question for the resisting reader to ask is: 'Who profits and how from this particular text and reading of it?' The resisting reader is one who reads a biblical or other literary text while aware of the standard reading and interpretation such a text receives in the academy, and then challenges that reading. For example, the parable of the Widow and the Judge is understood by the general audience of the first and twenty-first centuries to illustrate how a woman's nagging can finally wear down the worst of scoundrels, leading to the woman getting what she wants in the end. Such a reading is commonly accepted and enjoyed in androcentric cultures which relish jokes about poor, henpecked husbands and use such material as a way of suggesting that since women already (indirectly) run the world through whining and nagging, there's no reason to let them get the upper hand in other spheres.

In place of the patriarchal, androcentric, biblical text, I put Jesus of Nazareth in his historical context as a Jewish man born into an androcentric, patriarchal culture. Yet Jesus' reading of his world is that of the resisting reader. He looks at the status quo religious leaders, the Pharisees and Sadducees, and he recognizes that they possess the law but have lost both their heart and their God. At every stage of his ministry Jesus gives voice to the theological, spiritual, emotional, and physical needs of the powerless: the leper, the tax collector, the prostitute, the poor and disenfranchised. In Lk. 18.1-8 Jesus gives a resisting reader's slant to the notion of woman as nag. While Jesus' re-visioning of the world is no more gynocentric than it is androcentric, the Kingdom of God he proclaims and the parables he tells describe a world and a God very different from that of first-century Judaism, or much which purports to be twenty-first century Christianity.

Worksheet: Text: Luke 18.1-8		
	Patriarchal, androcentric world view	*Jesus' resisting reader*
1. Sexist subtext	poor judge harassed by harridan	one in need is the widow
2. Contradictory statements	poor judge can only capitulate: he is besieged by insistent, nagging, powerful woman	powerless one is the widow: no money, no strong allies: deserves sympathy and support
3. Pretension to authority	world was made for man, woman was made for man and should be subject to him, not ruling over him	God created woman and man to be in caring relationship with God and each other.
4. Fake claim to universality	God created men to be superior to women and by divine right rule over women in all walks of life. Women need to understand they are subservient and lesser beings.	God consistently is the champion of the poor, the widow, the orphan, the alien in our midst.

As the 'worksheet' above illustrates, in preparing a homily on Lk. 18.1-8, I first considered its context, past and present, as a text read within a patriarchal, androcentric culture in which understands the parable of the widow and the judge as a story about the importance of persisting in order to get what one wants. As with many other biblical stories in which one of the key characters is a woman, the story's primary meaning gets lost when the reader or interpreter gets sidetracked by culturally reinforced stereotypes of the poor judge being harassed by the relentless widow. I then re-read the text from the point of view of Jesus using it as a resisting reader, challenging his own historical context by giving the powerless widow (and, by implication members of his audience) a voice and a hearing, and attributing to them the ability to change their situation through exercise of that voice. Victimization, a reality and a concept much discussed and reckoned with in modern society, is not something we hear about in the parables of Jesus. In the parable of the widow and the unjust judge, Jesus shows that the widow does have power in that she uses what she possesses, her voice and her time, ultimately to achieve her goal. She does it alone, on her own. Jesus empowers the reader/audience to do the same and then multiplies that power with the avowal that our petitions for justice will be heard and met by God.

Homily: 'A Widow Without Wiles'

Here, we shall consider two ways in which the parable of the widow and the unjust judge is interpreted. Setting aside Luke's obvious primary focus upon the importance of prayer as a means for establishing a healthy and beneficial relationship with God, and the challenge to all listeners to have a faith worth finding when the Son of Man comes, let us look at the parable on its own. What is the basic plot? A widow needs her case heard by a judge. We don't know if she's rich or poor, young or old, pretty or pathetic. Jesus doesn't tell us.

In Western culture, there is more than one kind of widow. In the biblical story of Ruth, the Moabite widow is able to use both her mother-in-law's cunning and her own womanly wiles to seduce Boaz into taking seriously his kinship obligation to them both. The pretty and rich Widow Bolt in Anthony Trollope's first Palliser novel, *Can You Forgive Her?*, is able to play off suitor against suitor until she selects for herself the one she will have as a husband. A depressed and newly widowed Jacqueline Kennedy asserted, 'My life is over', but her own resilience, charisma, and wiles kept her from being either friendless or escortless for the next 30 years.

None of these women were without wiles or resources. But not all widows are so fortunate as to be young, pretty or rich. While Jesus provides no details about the widow in this parable, it's enough for him and his audience to know that she is a widow. The very word 'widow' conjures up images of economic insecurity, vulnerability, loneliness, and desperate need on behalf of herself and her children, if no male family member can be found to help. This widow without wiles must speak and act for herself. She doesn't seduce; she doesn't bribe; she persists—she keeps coming back. And what happens? As a judge who fears neither God nor man, suggesting his verdicts are open to the highest bidder, the judge refuses to hear her case. So she keeps returning, day after day after day, until he gives in. Does his heart soften towards her? Does he decide he wants to be a better, more honest man than he has been? No. The unjust judge just can't take it any more. He hears her case and grants her justice to get her out of his courtroom and 'off his back': 'Though I have no fear of God and no respect for anyone, yet because this widow keeps bothering me, I will grant her justice, so that she may not wear me out by continually coming' (vv. 4-5). As with everything else related to this judge, his decision stems from self-interest. It's easier to grant justice than to keep dealing with the widow.

'Hooray for the widow! Let's hear it for the underdog who's finally had her day in court!', we feminists cry. But, in traditional ways of interpreting the parable, while some readers celebrate the widow's vindication, others appreciate the unjust judge's liberation from a stereotypical nagging female. The poor judge has been harassed and brought low by that most terrifying of all beings, the 'nag'. Our culture is so saturated with nagging wife jokes that many sympathize with the judge, especially because many modern listeners recognize his discomfort and agree: 'Hell, who cares about justice? Just get this woman off the poor fellow's back!' The gender stereotypes of this text are as familiar to us as are the infinitely irritating antics of Hyacinth Bucket ('Bouquet'), wife and bully of husband Richard in the popular British television sitcom 'Keeping up Appearances'. The gender stereotypes are as old as early American literature, e.g. 'Rip Van Winkle'. Thus, the unjust judge becomes a poor, hapless man, cruelly besieged by a powerful, insistent, not-to-be-denied woman.

That is not the story Jesus told, but it's often the story we hear when this parable is read, because we too have bought into the stereotype. A classic case in point is Washington Irving's short story 'Rip Van Winkle'. We all know the plot. Gentle, sweet, easygoing Rip Van Winkle is cursed with a wife who nags him mercilessly about his laziness, his irresponsibility, his unwillingness to work. Madame Van Winkle is such an unpleasant shrew that Rip's neighbours and friends feel sorry for him and regularly conspire to protect him from the whiplash of her tongue whenever she discovers him drinking at the tavern, frolicking with other people's children or sleeping the day away. Even the reader shares in the laughter, and the dislike of this woman whom Rip Van Winkle finally escapes by sleeping for twenty years. Furthermore, the reader shares Van Winkle's relief upon waking when he discovers his wife has died and can no longer terrorize him.

When I taught this story in a college American literature survey course, I invited the women students to read this story through the eyes of Madame Van Winkle, and to write me a one-page essay on what they discovered. To their own surprise, since many already knew the story from middle- or high-school readings, they found themselves in sympathy with and ready to defend a woman they'd previously remembered as being a horrible harridan. What the students discovered was a desperate woman, powerless to make her trifling husband work or care that his house was literally falling down, that his children were underfed and clothed in rags, and that their overall situation was both pathetic and poverty-stricken. Suddenly, Madame Van Winkle became a figure of identification for the women students, and her nagging made sense. What other recourse had she in the face of Rip's indifference and irresponsibility? Was her lot all that different from an unwed teenage mother trying to survive on welfare but without child support from the baby's father? Was it not the same situation faced by countless women today, and so poignantly described in Frank McCourt's memoir *Angela's Ashes*? It's the story of many a wife whose pleading and nagging do not prevent her husband from drinking away his weekly paycheck. Nagging, the students discovered, is what someone does when he or she feels powerless to act, because the reality is that one doesn't have to nag if one has sufficient power, influence, or wealth to get what one wants in another way.

The widow of Lk. 18.2-5 is one of many people Jesus identifies as powerless in his contemporary world in which Roman rulers and soldiers, Pharisees and Sadducees, the healthy and the wealthy are the ones who have power. But what weapons or resources can the powerless proffer? Only themselves. 'Nagging' is what a woman lacking womanly wiles must do. 'Whining' is what a needy young child lacking in strength and guile must do. For many a powerless person, nagging is a necessity, but, unfortunately, it is also very risky. First, there is the risk of humiliation, disdain, resentment and scorn. Remember the joke? 'Take my wife, please!' Second, nagging is viewed as ugly and unappealing behaviour which leads to rejection by other people. Nagging annoys people, and causes them to excise the nagger from their dinner party list and to work overtime to avoid her company. Third, nagging often leads to abuse. In the fictional story 'Rip Van Winkle', the reader dislikes and rejects Madame

Van Winkle, and celebrates her husband's escape from her, but in real life, many a nagging woman can be found in the emergency rooms of hospitals having bones set and bruises salved, the victims of physical abuse inflicted by boyfriends or husbands. In today's world, many say, 'You've come a long way, baby!' But it's still true that a woman who wants to be considered attractive and nice must not be a nag. Society's other point is that powerless people who nag deserve what they get: 'Don't make me spank you', says the 140-pound mother to the 35-pound toddler. 'He got his skull smashed in during the demonstration, because he deserved it', the policeman told the reporter.

Nagging is what one does when one is powerless, *but not voiceless*. Jesus' point beyond the parable is that nagging—or as he, and we, might prefer to say, persistence in voicing one's cares or cause—works not only with unjust earthly judges; it works with God. How much better off are you and I, Jesus asks in vv. 7-8 when we have not an unjust, uncaring, unscrupulous judge, but a generous, loving, compassionate and interested God to hear our cries? That is exactly what God requires and desires–the prayers, the heartfelt cries, the aching needs, the expressions of pain and need and injustice. These prayers will be heard by God, a God who cares and shares in the suffering and hardship of the powerless faithful ones who remember God and are embraced by God. God cares and God empowers. If God cares, then so should we.

There are many powerless people in the world today, and there are also many powerful and unjust people. The parable exhorts the believing community to *pray* and *act*. *Pray* for help, for wisdom, for guidance, for persistence. *Act* through nagging, persisting, speaking on behalf of those allowed no voice, on behalf of those whose voice is discredited, on behalf of those too young to speak for themselves. God doesn't hold all the power. We human beings are given some, in the form of words, language, need, ambition, emotions, creativity, inspiration, perspiration, to act on our own behalf and on behalf of others.

The existing relationship between God and God's people is vitally important to God and to humanity: 'And will not God grant justice to his chosen ones who cry to him day and night? Will he delay long in helping them? I tell you, he will quickly grant justice to them'. God will not force those who pray to him to humiliate themselves with incessant nagging in order to get what they want. We are the chosen ones. God will hear us, and God will grant justice.

3. *'Will She Find Faith on Earth?'*

Barbara Scheele

When I was a girl, Catholics did not read the Bible. We didn't even have one at home. Instead, there were well-thumbed novenas, saints' lives, Latin–English missals, and the diocesan weekly newspaper. Other Catholic families had decorative Bibles, dusted regularly, which were opened primarily to record births, deaths, and marriages. Another biblical memory from my 1950s childhood in white working-class New York City is being teased by the Lutheran children down the street. They could quote the Bible chapter and verse and thoroughly enjoyed pointing out our deficits in that area. Those Lutheran kids knew something then that I did not: reading the Bible is important.

Elizabeth Cady Stanton knew that reading the Bible is important to women. Scripture and its institutionally directed interpretation are some powerful tools to keep women in their secondary, 'complementary' place. *The Woman's Bible* was Stanton's 1895 response.[20] Fundamentalist religion was then and remains today a formidable political opponent of increasing power for women. Stanton saw that the prevailing interpretation of scripture needed to be challenged and broadened, and proceeded to do so. *The Woman's Bible* does not read well today, but it is a milestone on the highway of feminist scripture and theology, of found women's stories and reinterpreted negative commentary on women in all cultures. Stanton's example of agency, her refusal to be 'complementary', and her persistent faith in women's rights remain for us a valuable legacy.

The widow in Lk. 18.1-8 is reminiscent of Elizabeth Cady Stanton, Susan B. Anthony, and the other women and men who fought so tirelessly for women's suffrage. Most of them were ordinary people with profound faith who endured repeated rejection and public scorn, whose friends and relations betrayed or deserted them. And they never stopped fighting for what was right. Their memories are important. Their stories have imprinted themselves in my personal 'woman's Bible'.[21] The texts we call sacred

20. E.C. Stanton, *The Woman's Bible* (Boston, MA: Northeastern University Press, 1993).

21. K. Pui-Lan and E. Schüssler Fiorenza (eds.), *Women's Sacred Scriptures* (Concilium 1998/3; London: SCM Press; Maryknoll, NY: Orbis Books, 1998). The editors expand the framework of scripture to include non-canonical works such as diaries, memories, and traditions.

must not be treated like ornaments on a shelf but grappled with in a strenuous way. It has been said that good theology is done by placing the Bible beside the newspaper. If we claim pride in our biblical values, we need to search for the outward signs of their practice, in biblical times and in our own.

The Jewish tradition values the study not only of Torah, but of the rabbinic literature which interprets and expands the text. Communities gather for vigorous argument, and the arguments themselves may be recorded. Here is a story from the Talmud which illustrates the relationship of scriptural argument and action:

> Rabbi Tarfon and the elders were reclining in the upper story of Nithza's house in Lod. The question was asked before them: 'Which is greater: study or action?' Rabbi Tarfon answered and said: 'Action is greater'. Rabbi Akiva answered and said: 'Study is greater'. Everyone answered and said: 'Study is greater because study leads to action' (*bKiddushin* 40b).[22]

The scholar who re-tells this story also tells very concretely how study leads to action. She was a member of the Women of the Wall, who acted against the prohibition on women to hold a prayer service at the Western Wall of Jerusalem. For years they went to the women's section of the wall, enduring the protests of ultra-orthodox men who invaded their section, and, with like-minded women, physically assaulted the women who refused to stay silent, refused to remove the ritual prayer shawl or the Torah scroll. The Women of the Wall refused to be exiles. When they were asked to silence themselves for the sake of peace, they took the written request and subjected it to argument and scripture study. Through their life-action, inspired by the contemporary meanings they found in Hannah's song (1 Sam. 2.1-10), they persistently claimed their homeland by their public actions.

The history of warfare over who is entitled to be the final arbiter of biblical authority is not over. Feminist critics are feared and loathed because they dare to ask the questions that traditionalists claim have been answered once and for all at some definitive point in church history. I am convinced beyond a shadow of a doubt that Jesus authorized all people of faith to probe the questions, and commissioned us to work on the answers until we see justice in action.

---

22. B.D. Haberman, 'Praxis-Exegesis: A Jewish Feminist Hermeneutic', in Pui-Lan and Schüssler Fiorenza, *Women's Sacred Scriptures*, p. 92.

This brings us to the parable of the persistent widow:

> Then Jesus told them a parable about their need to pray always and not to lose heart. He said, 'In a certain city there was a judge who neither feared God nor had respect for people. In that city there was a widow who kept coming to him and saying, 'Grant me justice against my opponent'. For a while he refused; but later he said to himself, 'Though I have no fear of God and no respect for anyone, yet because this widow keeps bothering me, I will grant her justice, so that she may not wear me out by continually coming'. And the Lord said, 'Listen to what the unjust judge says. And will not God grant justice to his chosen ones who cry to him day and night? Will he delay long in helping them? I tell you, he will quickly grant justice to them. And yet, when the Son of Man comes, will he find faith on earth?' (Lk. 18.1-8).[23]

In the core of this scripture (vv. 2-5), we learn that the widow has a legal claim against an opponent; she goes directly to a judge; the judge denies her claim; the widow returns again and again to repeat her demand; the judge gives in. The widow is an archetype of the woman who puts her understanding of biblical justice into action. She then proceeds to demand right action from the one responsible until it is done.

At the time Luke's gospel was written, the audience of disciples still identified themselves as Jews, though they were becoming increasingly isolated from mainstream Judaism. Luke appears to be writing to the disciples of the late first/early second century CE, when the fledgling Christian community, despairing over the delay of the second coming which they assumed was imminent, desperately needed protection. The entire community, men and women, could easily identify with the widow. Metaphorically they were all 'widows'. Widows and orphans in their time as in ours, were leftovers. (We still use the word-processing terms 'widows and orphans' to represent dangling lines, left over from the photographs and text they once 'lived with'.) Widowed women had the legal status of property, and when their owners died, they had to be transferred to other proprietors. Despite biblical and legal guidelines of the day which established the transfer procedures, the widows were rarely wanted in the new masters' houses. Perhaps the Lukan community was losing heart and losing faith; the persecutions seemed endless. When would they receive their due? According to J. Jeremias, Luke's purpose in this parable is to give assurance to Christian disciples that God is indeed

---

23. All scriptural references in this section are to the New Revised Standard Version.

coming as promised. God has not abandoned them.[24] They should 'pray always', and God will surely reward them.

Still, under the circumstances, it's striking that Luke used a woman to deliver this message, a woman who does *not* sit around passively praying, but takes herself bodily to confront the judge who holds the key to unlock justice on her behalf. She not only walks the walk, but talks the talk, and loudly, too. She is 'willing to be offensive, to be not liked... One must admire the spirit of a woman who did not play games to make herself attractive to the judge. She did not play up to him'. [25] Our widow had a strong sense of entitlement and the courage of her convictions, grounded in the text of the Jewish law, the Torah. The legal tradition she based her claim on was not only the written law which enshrined her rights. There was a subtext of hypocritical action, of bribery and influence peddling, which oiled the machinery of justice. The Torah taught her the community's decisions on justice for widows, what should be. To find the subtext, she had to read the actions of the elites and the judges. She had to read between the lines, for much was unsaid in public. I can see her as she listened intently to the rumors, and perhaps visited and questioned people who had waited at that same gate for justice. The widow did her homework.

As much as in Luke's time, today this parable invites a conversation on the ways of power for the oppressed and ignored. *Now* is the time to apply her knowledge of corruption, and transform it into justice. There are empowering lessons here for the *anawim* ('the poor'), those people, so beloved by Jesus, on the fringes of society. The widow breaks the code of silence. She does not voice the noise of hysteria or impotent screaming, but uses some of the power moves of her adversaries.[26] Like them, she goes directly to the judge for justice rather than sending a family member or hired representative to direct him toward a favourable ruling. She seeks the Torah justice lost in the debased and lazy bureaucracy. She finds that justice by elbowing her way through the corrupt political machine. Her adversaries have time on their side, so the widow ups the ante on the judge. She cannot compete with cash or political favours, but she *can* raise

24. J. Jeremias, *The Parables of Jesus* (2nd rev. edn; New York: Charles Scribner's Sons, 1972), pp. 153-57.

25. R.C. Wahlberg, 'The Assertive Widow', in *Jesus and the Freed Woman* (New York and Mahwah, NJ: Paulist Press, 1978), pp. 108-109.

26. W.R. Herzog, *Parables as Subversive Speech; Jesus as Pedagogue of the Oppressed* (Louisville, KY: Westminster/John Knox Press, 1994), p. 229.

the volume. This strategy threatens 'to blow the cover off the operation'.[27]
By going public and going often, she raises for the judge the spectre of
becoming a pariah, alienated from his powerful allies, who don't want
their shady practices widely known. 'The widow is forcing the judge to
reevaluate the cost-benefit ratio of her case'.[28]

For practitioners of feminist liberation theology, the widow is a role
model. She fights the lie with truth. She not only uses her voice effectively, but models the wisdom of silence.[29] For example, the widow
doesn't attack the judge, for she knows that might backfire. By focusing
on the truth and calling him to accountability, she reverses the roles. Now
he is the petitioner, wearied by her assault on him. She is the judge. Like
feminist scripture students, she sits with Torah and compares the justice it
promises with the justice administered in her time, and publishes her
findings.

The first time I read this parable, it was a scripture assigned to members
of a women's home retreat in 1986. We were to read and reflect on one
passage fifteen minutes a day for a week, then come back to the group to
discuss our reactions. Like the judge, I was bothered by this widow. She's
unattractive, I thought, so desperate, and unwanted by her community.
This is many a woman's nightmare. She's loud and demanding. I couldn't
shake her out of my mind: she was becoming my hound of heaven.

The widow challenged my fear of challenging authority. Would I ever
need to raise my voice to demand something? Like many a white woman
of my time, I was raised to be soft-spoken and passive, and would wait
around, as Schüssler Fiorenza puts it, in 'typically "feminine" fashion...
for the "all-powerful man" to come to one's rescue'.[30] Like many others
poised uneasily on the border between middle class and poverty, I sought
shelter in the illusion of security: tenure, health insurance, pension. A
husband would materialize and shelter me from the storms of life.

This widow/hound caught up to me several years ago, when I was
defeated—beaten in attempts to obtain proper medical and educational
care for my disabled brother—who had excellent health insurance, by the
way. Letters and telephone calls went unanswered. His social caseworkers

27. Herzog, *Parables as Subversive Speech*, p. 229.
28. Herzog, *Parables as Subversive Speech*, p. 230.
29. A. Goodwin, 'The Right to Remain Silent', *Pastoral Psychology* 41 (1993),
pp. 359-76.
30. E. Schüssler Fiorenza, *Sharing Her Word; Feminist Biblical Interpretation in
Context* (Boston: Beacon Press, 1998), p. 154.

couldn't be bothered and said so openly and sarcastically. 'WE are his primary care givers', said the case manager. There would be no interference with his authority. Lawyers in a state department for the protection of the disabled would not take his case, and dismissed me. Would you be surprised to know that these lawyers and the state caseworkers had offices in the same building? This cozy arrangement clarified the issue: the lawyers were there to protect the case managers. Assistance to the disabled, which they loftily claimed to be their sworn duty, is purely coincidental if my experience is typical of their work.

Naturally, I shared my tale of woe with the women in the scripture retreat group, which is still meeting today. Remembering my first reaction to this parable, one of the women said to me, 'Well, Barbara, it's time to re-read the widow in Luke 18'. And I did. Whenever despair or passivity beckons, I think of her. By now, I think of the widow as my matron saint. She taught me to bank the anger for the right moments, to find back alleys and side doors, and not to work harder but smarter. Together with the widow and the members of that retreat group, I emerged from the anger, the bullying of the bureaucracy, and depression. I bypassed the social workers and took my brother directly to specialists. The doctors' assistants befriended me, and like Shiphra and Puah, the midwives in Exodus (1.15-20), they conspired with me, and provided the information I needed to outwit the system and get a more desirable solution. Begrudgingly, and with much whimpering about their woundedness, like the judge,[31] the caseworkers developed a treatment plan and moved with exquisite slowness to implement it. Raising my voice repeatedly was the only way to speed the process along.

Best of all, I learned to get help from others. (In my solitary dialogues with the widow, I've asked her to tell me why she didn't organize, but that is another parable.) My sister worked the phones to put more pressure on the caseworkers. A friend who supervises homes for the disabled came with me to case review meetings; her guidance was the decisive factor in the group's decision to provide a more suitable educational setting for him. Discreet calls to his new teachers got me copies of documents in

---

31. Schüssler Fiorenza comments: ' "I will grant her justice so that she may not give me a black eye (bruise, batter down, or wear me out) by her nonstop coming" [v. 5]. The soliloquy of the judge expresses a typical sentiment of those who act violently; the judge blames the wo/man victim for "battering" although she only seeks her rights and vindication whereas he acts violently by denying justice to her' (*Sharing Her Word*, p. 155).

record time. I used the papers to apply to another agency. When case manager resistance escalated again, I found a good advocate, who for no fee called the reluctant agency to a meeting and intimidated them into action. By adapting the strategies of the widow, I learned that focused action and faith in one's cause replace fear. Sleeping Beauty woke up from her docile dreams.

This parable is like a large onion. To find the woman at its heart, we need to peel away many layers of Lukan interpretation within the text, and years of commentary and preaching. I have given you my lived experience with the widow at the gate, and I pray that others continue to read her and walk with her and tell us their sacred story. Otherwise the woman's bible stays on the shelf, gathering dust.

I thought this homily on the parable of the persistent widow would end here, but there is one more discovery to share. There is a riddle which I've never seen in print but heard many times:

> A father and his son were riding in an automobile. There was an accident so severe that the father died. The son was seriously injured, but found by an emergency crew and rushed to a hospital. They brought him into the operating room, where a surgeon was waiting. The surgeon said, 'I can't operate on this boy! He is my own child'. How can this be?

I didn't know the answer when I first heard it. I still am irritated, being a feminist in good standing, that I failed to see the answer that was there all the time. The surgeon is his mother. The power of stereotypes is formidable. No one is immune to the seduction of simple answers.

This parable contains a similar problem. The author tells us that Jesus was talking about prayer, about praying always. The widow is not shown praying, although she is making a petition, and we do have a tradition of petitionary prayer. The problem is really with the judge, as most commentators agree. How could such a callous and corrupt man be a God figure? The answer Luke gives (vv. 7-8a) holds that if the woman could get justice from this bottom-feeder of a judge, all the sooner will God deliver the chosen ones when they cry out. Well, maybe.

The God figure in this story, the one who seeks justice and 'faith on earth' like the 'son of humanity' Jesus invokes in the parable (v. 8b), is none other than the widow. It really works to explain to whom the disciples must turn. God, imaged as the female figure of Holy Wisdom, both prays and actively searches for people who will be faithful to the scriptural codes of justice. She models the diligent search for honesty and love within ourselves and in others. God has no hands to create the kindom of heaven but ours. People of faith can see Jesus in the joys and the hardships of our daily experience. God is here, now, suffering with us in our poverty and our doubt, like the widow. It is this God who shows us by grappling with everyday assaults on our dignity how to keep moving on prayer- and scripture-powered feet. This is an incarnate, embodied God. She, Holy Wisdom, and Jesus of Galilee are both left-overs, rejected throughout time. Wisdom spoils our fun. Jesus blows the lid off the undercover operation. Ignore them.

I nearly fell off my chair when I first encountered this interpretation of the widow.[32] First I missed a female surgeon, and then I failed to see a female figure of God. The book of Wisdom, canonical in the Catholic, Greek and Slavonic bibles, portrays Wisdom/Sophia as an ethereal, disembodied female figure: 'For Wisdom is more mobile than any motion; because of her pureness she pervades and penetrates all things. For she is a breath of the power of God, and a pure emanation of the glory of the Almighty; therefore nothing defiled gains entrance into her' (Wisd. 7.24-25).

Proverbs gives us a more incarnate, enfleshed female image. In Proverbs 8, we meet Wisdom actively crying out, much as the widow in Luke 18 calls to all who would hear:

> Does not Wisdom call, and does not understanding raise her voice? On the heights, beside the way, at the crossroads she takes her stand; beside the gates in front of the town she cries out: 'To you, O people, I call, and my cry is to all that live' (Prov. 8.1-4)

and later,

> 'I walk in the way of righteousness, along the paths of justice...' (Prov. 8.20).

Luke, who in many places demonstrates knowledge of the Jewish scriptures, might have been inspired to base the figure of the widow upon the solitary figure of Wisdom pleading at the gate in Proverbs. The gate of the town or small city was also a place where ancient Jews seeking redress of grievances would find a judge to hear them.[33]

---

32. M. McKenna, 'The Widow and the Unjust Judge', in *Parables: The Arrows of God* (Maryknoll, NY: Orbis Books, 1994), p. 105. This chapter contains an excellent example of the efficacy of this parable to stimulate discussion of the uses of power.

33. Herzog notes: 'Ideally, every town with 120 or more men was to establish a tribunal of seven judges, probably drawn from the elders of the town, to adjudicate Torah at the gate' (*Parables as Subversive Speech*, p. 224).

B. Reid observes that the grouping of God, the judge and the widow is found in the deutero-canonical Wisdom of Jesus Sirach:

> That God would be relentlessly pursuing justice is not a new image of the divine (e.g., Sir. 35.14-19). But that God is more akin to a victimized widow than a powerful judge is startling. She embodies godly power in the midst of powerlessness.[34]

Lest we think that the Lukan author was a feminist theologian, Reid reminds us that while Luke's Jesus speaks of the widow with a stereotype-shattering image of the divine, the evangelist in no way encourages that interpretation. Reid writes that 'he softens the parable's impact by posing the widow as an example of persistent prayer, a docile and acceptable role'.[35] Despite Luke's conscious intentions, however, the divine female image of Wisdom comes shining through.

As Christian feminist seekers of the whole truth in scripture, it is up to us not to *replace* the stories of the patriarchs, but rather to connect the narratives of women's courage and persistence to the canonical sacred stories. Women's prayers and poems and dreams, their tales of terror and heroic public deeds, must be known. The world is hungry for more of the story. With renewed imagination and communal sharing comes joy. Stereotypes fade. Joy—in the here and now—expands our deepest desires to heal the injuries and to do justice together for all. What brighter joy can there be than the blazing illumination of a God worthy of receiving our prayer?[36]

We need not wait at the gate for 'She Who Is'. Wisdom/Sophia is here, now. She is the godhood calling inside each of us to join in the transcendent wholeness of God. And like the widow in the parable, she is loudly and desperately seeking our attention.

34. Reid, *Choosing the Better Part,* p. 192.
35. Reid, *Choosing the Better Part*, p. 194.
36. L.T. Johnson, 'Something Fundamental is Afoot', *Commonweal* 120 (29 January 1993), p. 22. In this review essay of E.A. Johnson's *She Who Is*, L.T. Johnson says of its author: 'she has performed the most fundamental function of a true theologian, which is to provide a vision of God worthy of prayer'. The full reference for the book is E.A. Johnson, *She Who Is: The Mystery of God in Feminist Theological Discourse* (New York: Crossroad, 1992; repr. 1997).

OPENING THE CLOSED DOOR: A FEMINIST REREADING OF THE 'WISE AND FOOLISH VIRGINS' (Mt. 25.1-13)

Vicky Balabanski

Introduction

More than thirty years ago, Josephine Massingbaerde Ford noted in relation to Mt. 25.1-13 that in addition to the striking number of peculiarities which this parable carries, it also stands out for its criticism of women.[1] While I cannot agree with her that 'it is the only place in the Gospels where Jesus utters any criticism either direct or in metaphorical language against women'[2]—given the story of the Syrophoenician woman (Mk 7.24-30 *et par.)* to name the most prominent objection—nevertheless, she did identify a key aspect of this parable.

There is a remarkable dearth of published feminist comment on this parable, and, to my knowledge, no extended feminist analysis of it to date.[3] This is all the more remarkable, given the fact that the key protagonists are two groups of young women, each of which has a voice in the parable. The voices/perspectives that are expressed by these women articulate both relationship and difference, and the patriarchal context is dramatically enacted at the end by the coming of the 'kyriarch'. All of these factors invite an 'engendered'[4] reading of the parable.

---

1. J. Massingberd (*sic*) Ford, 'The Parable of the Foolish Scholars (Matt. xxv 1-13)', *NovT* 9 (1967), pp. 107-123.

2. Ford, 'Foolish Scholars', p. 107.

3. A.-J. Levine gives a brief reading of this parable in C.A. Newsom and S.H Ringe (eds.), *The Women's Bible Commentary* (2nd edn; Louisville: Westminster John Knox Press, 1998), p. 348. I will refer below to a more extended reading by P. Perkins, in *Hearing the Parables of Jesus* (New York/Ramsay, NJ: Paulist Press, 1981), pp. 104-10, which does not set out to give a feminist interpretation of the passage.

4. E. Wainwright adopts this term in her most recent book, *Shall We Look For Another? A Feminist Rereading of the Matthean Jesus* (Maryknoll, NY: Orbis, 1998), esp. pp. 20-21:

The text of Mt. 25.1-13 is as follows:

1. Then the kingdom of heaven will be like this. Ten young women[5] took their lamps and went to meet the bridegroom.

2. Five of them were foolish, and five were wise.

3. When the foolish took their lamps, they took no oil with them;

4. but the wise took flasks of oil with their lamps.

5. As the bridegroom was delayed, all of them became drowsy and slept.

6. But at midnight there was a shout, 'Look! Here is the bridegroom! Come out to meet him'.

7. Then all those young women got up and trimmed their lamps.

8. The foolish said to the wise, 'Give us some of your oil, for our lamps are going out'.

9. But the wise replied, 'No! there will not be enough for you and for us; you had better go to the dealers and buy some for yourselves'.

10. And while they went to buy it, the bridegroom came, and those who were ready went with him into the wedding banquet; and the door was shut.

11. Later the other young women came also, saying, 'Lord, lord, open to us'.

12. But he replied, 'Truly I tell you, I do not know you'.

13. Keep awake therefore, for you know neither the day nor the hour. (NRSV, modified)

> I use the term *engendered* because it is evocative of the twofold aspect of the reading being undertaken. It incorporates the word *gender,* that aspect of text, reader, and context that a feminist reading seeks to decenter and to deconstruct. Gender in this respect can function symbolically for multidimensional patri/kyriarchy. The immersion of the word itself into the term *engender* can evoke this deconstruction. The term engender, which carries the sense of 'bringing into being' or 'creating', points toward readings as productive of new meaning. Such new meaning engenders the feminist subject in the multidimensionality of sex, race, class, religious affiliation, and those other dimensions that constitute subjectivity. This subjectivity is social, constituted by society, but at the same time struggles against those socio-cultural representations that are recognized as oppressive.

Thus the scope of an engendered reading addresses the various forms of patri/kyriarchy, and enables a creative imagining of new structures and symbols.

5. Literally, 'virgins'. I depart from the NRSV translation at this point, as 'bridesmaids' has very specific cultural associations for the contemporary reader which do not correspond to those of ancient Palestine. On wedding customs in ancient Palestine, see Section 3 below.

The 'peculiarities' of the parable from a narrative point of view are listed by various writers to include the following:

- lack of clarity as to where the ten young women are as they wait for the bridegroom; do they fall asleep on the street?
- lateness of the beginning of the wedding feast;
- the idea that the oil sellers are open after midnight;
- the harshness of the 'wise' young women towards the others in sending them off when they knew that the bridegroom was about to arrive;
- the relevance of the motif of sleep, which has no apparent links with the conclusion in v. 13;
- the lack of mention of a bride.[6]

While most studies recognise the harshness of the words and actions of the 'wise' young women, it is either simply accepted by the interpreters or they seek to justify the behaviour by reference to a presumed custom, such as a proposed torch dance,[7] which accounts for the unwillingness of the 'wise' young women to share their oil. No study focuses on this unwillingness as the central problem of the story. For a feminist reading of this parable, this must be a central issue, along with the complicity of the 'wise' young women in the patri/kyriarchal *dénouement* of the story. An engendered reading must grapple with the actions and allegiances of the 'wise' group, rather than setting them aside as beyond the scope of legitimate questioning, as does U. Luz in his otherwise stimulating interpretation of this passage:

> Now we are not to ask whether their oil really would not have been enough to share (sharing their oil would have been a beautiful feature in this story!). We are also not to ask whether there really would not have been any olive oil to be found in the bride's house. Neither should we interpret the refusal of the wise women allegorically, for instance as the impossibility of substitutionary works. Rather, the narrator chooses from several possibilities the way the story is to proceed, and chooses this one, because he wants it to

6. This list is drawn from my study of this parable entitled 'Matthew 25.1-13 as a Window on Eschatological Change', in *Eschatology in the Making: Mark, Matthew and the Didache* (Cambridge: Cambridge University Press, 1997), ch. 2. This study does not give an engendered reading of the parable, but explores it as a window on the development of early Christian (pre-Matthean) eschatology.

7. The reference to a postulated 'torch dance' refers to a presumed wedding custom which J. Jeremias proposed in his article 'ΛΑΜΠΑΔΕΣ Mt 25,1.3f.7f', *ZNW* 56 (1965), pp. 196-201.

move towards a 'tragic' ending. The clever women therefore do not refuse because their torch dance takes so long and they consequently need all their oil for it, nor do they refuse because they are malicious, cruel or greedy, but because the story will have it so.[8]

While Luz may be right that the narrator controls the shape of the story we have, the narrator does not control our reading of it. An engendered reading chooses not to pass over the power dynamics and ethics of a story 'because the story will have it so', but by means of a hermeneutics of suspicion, seeks to expose them. E. Schüssler Fiorenza has shown how crucial such a critique of the text is, so that 'the kyriarchal text's rhetorical silences, contradictions, arguments, prescriptions and projections, its discourses on gender, race, class or religion can be exposed as the ideological inscriptions that they are'.[9] Only via an analysis of the rhetoric of oppression can the search for new and liberating ways of reading proceed.

The approach which I will take in this reading is as follows. Recognising what S. Schneiders has argued as to the significance of *genre* as a code which profoundly shapes the reading,[10] I will begin by addressing the genre of Mt. 25.1-13. I will then explore 'wisdom' (*phronimos*) and 'foolishness' (*mōria*), as they are constructed in this parable. At this point I will set out what can be known about marriage customs in first-century Palestine. Then, by means of an application of rhetorical, socio-historical and ideological criticisms, I will give a series of feminist reconstructions of ancient ways of hearing/reading this parable. The first is a reconstruction of a patriarchal reception of the story, which I call 'View from the *mastaba*/village bench'.[11] The second is a reconstruction of how some women may have heard this story; this I call 'View from the *agora*/

---

8. U. Luz, *Das Evangelium nach Matthäus (Mt 18-25)* (EKKNT 1–3; Zurich: Benzinger Verlag, 1985), p. 476 (translation mine).

9. L. Bormann et al. (eds.), 'The Rhetoricity of Historical Knowledge: Pauline Discourses and its Contextualizations', *Religious Propaganda and Missionary Competition in the New Testament World* (New York: Brill, 1994), pp. 460-61.

10. S. Schneiders, *The Revelatory Text: Interpreting the New Testament as Sacred Scripture* (San Francisco: Harper, 1991), p. 137.

11. I have borrowed this term from K.E. Bailey, *Poet and Peasant and Through Peasant Eyes: A Literary-Cultural Approach to the Parables in Luke* (comb. edn; Michigan: Eerdmans, 1983), p. 34. In doing so, I acknowledge the contribution Bailey has made to socio-cultural studies via this method. At the same time I wish to draw attention to the inherently patri/kyriarchal perspective of the view from the *mastaba*, where the *men* sit and talk to their *male* friends by the hour.

marketplace'.[12] This second reconstruction differentiates between two first-century women's perspectives. All of these ways of hearing will differ from the rhetoric of Matthew, for whom this parable functions as part of a wider narrative. The Matthean perspective will then be explored. Finally, having sought to discern these diverse voices, I will offer a contemporary feminist interpretation of this parable.

As I invite the reader to join me in this exploration, I should include a word about myself. As the daughter of central European parents who emigrated to Australia after the Second World War, I share in the privileges of education and the legacy of the first two waves of feminism. But as one who continues her spiritual journey within the Christian tradition, I am aware that, like the 'wise' young women, I am at times complicit in being slow to expose those contemporary ecclesiastical 'doorkeepers' who both set up the rules and then use them to invalidate those outside. This reading ultimately seeks to stand with the 'foolish' young women as those who find themselves marginalized and excluded from the feast.

The Significance of Genre

The story of the two groups of young women, one 'wise' and one 'foolish', is clearly a parabolic construct. But whose? And for what purpose? The point of departure for discourse around this parable has been determined primarily by source-critical questions as they relate to the issue of genre: what is the source of this story? Is this an allegorical construct of the early church, or a parable of Jesus? And if a parable of Jesus, to what extent has it been reworked? Our answers to these questions will shape what elements of the story we give prominence to, and ultimately our interpretation of it as a whole.

Over the past century, there have been two main approaches to the

---

12. Wainwright, in setting out her own methodology, writes of the importance of the feminist principle of difference. She sets out 'to take account of significant differences within the audience in relation to gender, ethnicity, class, and religious affiliation. Such an approach seems particularly appropriate to a study of the Matthean context since it has long been recognized by scholars that there are tensions within the text in relation to a number of key issues—ethnicity, gender and leadership, to name but a few' *(Shall We Look for Another?*, p. 36). In seeking to reconstruct a view from the *agora,* then, I am not claiming to reconstruct a perspective held by all women. This parable gives a rare glimpse of the way in which women's perspectives differ; this will be explored in the final section of this paper.

interpretation of this pericope. The first takes the story as dealing with a plausible wedding scenario, and interprets it as a parable which goes back to Jesus himself. A. Jülicher, who argued against the allegorical interpretation of parables which had been dominant until then, championed this view,[13] as did J. Jeremias, who gave two quite different interpretations of this parable.[14] The second and contrary position, represented by R. Bultmann[15] and G. Bornkamm,[16] among others, saw the story as an allegorical construct of the early church, determined by the experience of the delay, or non-occurrence, of Christ's return.

Neither position is completely convincing. The primary weakness of the first position is that the story does not seem to present a 'normal' cultural scenario, given the peculiarities listed above. Not only is there no bride mentioned; not only do all the young women seem to fall asleep on the street; not only do the ones without oil go to the vendors after midnight and seemingly successfully buy some oil, but the bridegroom himself steps out of his cultural script as host, and seemingly prioritizes punctuality over the duties of the host, in a most un-circum-Mediterranean-like way. One would expect a certain twist to the story,[17] but a twist that is integral to the metaphor of the plot, rather than a series of implausible elements.

Given these peculiarities, one would have expected that the proposal by Bornkamm and others that this is an allegorical construct of the early church would have swayed most interpreters. This, however, is not the case. If the story were constructed to address the delay of Christ's return, it is difficult to explain why certain elements are to be taken allegorically, according to Bornkamm (such as the bridegroom, and the delay), and certain elements (such as the number ten, the oil, the vessels, etc.) are not.

13. *Die Gleichnisreden Jesu* (vol. 2; Tübingen: J.C.B. Mohr, 1910), pp. 448-59.

14. *The Parables of Jesus,* first published in English translation in 1963, went through three revised editions; his article entitled 'ΛΑΜΠΑΔΕΣ' is mentioned above in n. 7.

15. *Geschichte der synoptischen Tradition* (2nd rev. edn; Göttingen: Vandenhoeck & Ruprecht, 1931), p. 191.

16. 'Die Verzögerung der Parusie. Exegetische Bemerkungen zu zwei synoptischen Texten', in W. Schmauch (ed.), *In Memoriam E. Lohmeyer* (Stuttgart: Verlag Katholisches Bibelwerk, 1951), pp. 116-26.

17. P. Ricoeur writes of 'extravagance' and 'surprise' in relation to the parables, and identifies it in this parable with the slamming of the door on the 'frivolous maidens'. 'Biblical Hermeneutics', *Semeia* 4 (1975), pp. 29-148. Luz also identifies the narrative extravagance with the bridegroom's rejection of the latecomers (*Evangelium nach Matthäus [Mt 18-25]*, pp. 467-68).

Other scholars have proposed a more continuous allegorical reading, without the overriding eschatological emphasis, but the hermeneutical keys have appeared overly esoteric or arbitrary.[18]

A third and mediating position has been developing, which takes the pericope as a parable of Jesus which has undergone a process of allegorization.[19] P. Perkins[20] argues for this, as does A. Puig i Tarrech in his monograph on Mt. 25.1-13.[21] More recently, I have argued that the clustering of allegorical motifs in vv. 5-7a is a pre-Matthean allegorizing interpolation, which shows certain early Christian communities coming to grips with the delay of Christ's return and the death of community members.[22]

18. Ford, 'Foolish Scholars', seeks to read the parable as a 'covert midrash' on the Rabbinic discussion of the Canticle of Canticles. She proposes that the parable is told against a background of conflict with certain Jewish teachers, with a view to exposing the way in which these scholars were monopolizing the nuptial imagery of the covenant on Sinai and excluding the less learned from an intimate relationship with God. While her case is carefully researched and argued, it has found few adherents, given not only the lateness of the Rabbinic witnesses upon which the case is founded, but the esoteric nature of the hermeneutical key which she proposes. A different allegorical reading of the parable was offered by F.A. Strobel, 'Zum Verständnis von Mt XXV 1-13', *NovT* 2 (1958), pp. 199-227, in which he argued for a liturgical interpretation based on a Syrian expectation of Christ's return on the evening of Passover. Once again, the hermeneutical key appears too esoteric to be convincing.

19. For a study of allegory and allegorism in the synoptic parables, see H.-J. Klauck, *Allegorie and Allegorese in Synoptischen Gleichnistexten* (2nd edn; Münster: Aschendorffsche Verlagsbuchhandlung, 1978). He distinguishes between allegory proper, allegorism (which he understands as an exegetical method which interprets a text anachronistically according to a particular philosophical or theological preconception, such as the *pesher* method of Qumran), and allegorisation (which develops and reinterprets the metaphors of an earlier text or tradition, such as is seen in the Targums). It is this third type that we find in Mt. 25.1-13, according to the position outlined above.

20. *Hearing the Parables of Jesus* (New York: Crossroad, 1981), especially Chapter 7, entitled 'Allegory: When is a Parable not a Parable?', pp. 101-11.

21. *La Parabole des dix vierges (Mt 25,1-13)* (AnnBib 102; Rome: Biblical Institute Press, 1983).

22. Balabanski, *Eschatology in the Making*, ch. 2. C. Riniker accepts a similar hypothesis, but argues for vv. 5b-6a as the pre-redactional interpolation, in 'Die Gerichtsverkündigung Jesu', Doctoral dissertation, Berne, 1991, p. 297. In my opinion, without the central vv. 5-7a, and the clearly redactional addition of v. 13 (which calls on the reader/hearer to keep awake, despite the fact that both groups of young women fell asleep), the parable may well go back to Jesus. In this context, though, my concern is not to discuss the pre-Matthean form of the parable, but to deal with the form in which it has been received.

What difference do these alternatives make to our reading of the passage? If we take it as a parable of Jesus from start to finish, we are confronted by the problem that this Jesus tells a story in which the male kyriarch, the bridegroom, acts ungraciously and against both the tenets of God's mercy and the culturally-defined imperative of the generous host. While this Jesus does not *require* the listener to identify his own person with that bridegroom, this identification is readily made, given the self-designation of Mk 2.19/Mt. 9.15 (which many scholars take to be genuine Jesus material). This ungenerous and unmerciful bridegroom of Mt. 25.11 bears little resemblance to Jesus the liberator of feminist christological discourse.[23] Feminist readers would be justified in replying to this Jesus, 'I do not know you'.

If, on the other hand, we are dealing with a purely allegorical construct of the early church, we are dealing with a story in which the bridegroom is unequivocally identified with Jesus *Pantocrator*, who is constructed in purely patriarchal terms. While this hypothesis has the attraction of attributing the ungenerous behaviour of the bridegroom not to the historical Jesus himself, but to the early church, we are left with an allegory which we may, at best, counter-read, or at worst, find altogether irrelevant to the task of feminist Christian re-visioning.

The third position, which takes this story as a parable of Jesus which has undergone a process of allegorisation, makes it necessary to distinguish between various layers and perspectives. The parable as it stands will no longer reflect the cultural practices of Jesus' day consistently, but it will have as its basis a plausible cultural scenario, and will therefore be subject to socio-cultural analysis in a way that pure allegory could not be.

If, as I have argued in *Eschatology in the Making*, this is a parable of Jesus that has undergone considerable resymbolisation in the light of the experiences of certain early Christian communities, namely the experience of the delay of Christ's return and the death of community members, we too may explore ways in which a resymbolization of the story can allow it to speak to our contemporary concerns at the opening of the third millennium. How such a resymbolization may look will be explored in the final section of this paper.

23. Cf. R.R. Ruether *Sexism and God Talk: Toward a Feminist Theology* (Boston: Beacon Press, 1983), pp. 137-38; N. Ritchie, 'Women and Christology' in E. Tamez (ed.), *Through Her Eyes: Women's Theology from Latin America* (Maryknoll, NY: Orbis, 1989), pp. 81-95.

Wisdom and Foolishness as Constructed by Mt. 25.1-13.

No sooner do we hear of the ten young women in v. 1 than they are divided into two opposing groups in v. 2: the 'foolish' (*mōrai*) and the 'wise', or 'clever' (*phronimoi*). The 'foolish' are the first to be presented, and the reader/hearer[24] is left in no doubt as to the shape of the story to follow: it will present the extent and nature of their 'foolishness' and the fate which is to befall such ones. The 'clever' are the foils against which the 'foolish' will stand out in sharp relief. As Luz has pointed out, the rhetoric of the parable hinders the reader identifying with the foolish;[25] they are defined as those whose doom is sealed.

By dividing the young women into two opposing groups, we have a perspective which was well-known in the second temple period as an aspect of wisdom teaching, namely the concept of the *two ways*. This is a rhetorical construction of binary distinctions, whereby good and evil, clever and foolish, life and death are divided by a deep chasm, and the reader is exhorted to choose the way of life. The opening of the Didache, which itself has close links with the Matthean tradition, illustrates this well:

> There are two ways: one of life, and one of death. The difference between the two ways is great. (*Did.* 1.1)[26]

There is no doubt that this way of seeing the world underlies some of the traditions we find in Matthew's Gospel. The most prominent is 7.13-14:

> Enter through the narrow gate for the gate is wide and the road is easy that leads to destruction, and there are many who take it. For the gate is narrow and the road is hard that leads to life, and there are few who find it.

This conceptualization depends not only on the metaphor of two roads that may be taken, but also on the separation of groups of people, often down the middle. This division into opposing groups or pairs lends itself particularly to eschatological paraenesis, as we find in Mt. 24.40-41:

24. From this point I will simply refer to those who receive and make meaning from this text as 'reader'.

25. *Das Evangelium nach Matthäus (Mt 18-25)*, p. 467.

26. Although the *Didache* as it stands is a Christian text, many scholars believe that the didachist is drawing on pre-Christian traditions for the doctrine of the Two Ways. Certain texts in the Hebrew Scriptures such as Deut. 30.15-20 and Prov. 12.28 provide a background for this construction. For a discussion of the Two Ways in the Dead Sea Scrolls and in Wisdom writings, see W. Rordorf and A. Tuilier, *La Doctrine des douze apôtres (Didachè)* (SC 248; Paris, 1978), pp. 23-27.

> Then two will be in the field; one will be taken and one will be left. Two women will be grinding meal together; one will be taken and one will be left.

It is the same sort of eschatological division that we find in Mt. 25.1-13. By dividing the ten young women from the beginning into those who are 'foolish' and those who are 'wise', the parable evokes the *two ways* paradigm, and conveys to the reader that these groups are already on their respective paths, the one group to life, and the other to destruction.

Feminist critical theorists have drawn attention to the way in which such binary oppositions are socially constructed and serve to maintain patriarchal and kyriarchal power.[27] The division between wise and foolish, like the construction of male/female, divine/human, sets up a system of allegiance and rejection, whereby the former is defined as good and the latter as evil. Simply to reverse the allegiance would be to maintain the binary opposition and re-inscribe it into the text. It is therefore not useful to seek to counter the rhetoric of the *two ways* by reversing what is 'wise' and what is 'foolish'. Rather, we need to expose the way in which this rhetoric divides these young women and seeks to do so with the reader from the beginning.

The nature of wisdom and foolishness in this parable deserves some further attention. The term used for wisdom is not *sophia,* but rather *phronimos.* While *sophia* wisdom, like the Hebrew *hokmah,* has a broad scope, which spans not only the quest for truth and grappling with finitude, but also everyday instruction on human interaction, the scope of the term *phronimos* is more limited. It refers to the sort of cleverness or prudence required for self-preservation, or for fulfilling one's appointed role. In the synoptic Gospels, it is used only in parables or parabolic sayings. The term occurs at the end of the Sermon on the Mount, Mt. 7.24, with reference to the prudent builder who builds on the rock. In Mt. 24.45 it describes the trustworthy slave who is put in charge of the master's household. It is also the term used to exhort the disciples to be as wise/prudent/clever as serpents and as innocent as doves (Mt. 10.16). This sort of practical 'wisdom' does not seek to plumb the depths of the human condition, but to grasp what the required preparations entail, and to complete them reliably. This is certainly part of the concept which undergirds the parable of Mt. 25.1-13: the 'wise' or 'prudent' young women are depicted as those who

27. See Wainwright, *Shall We Look for Another?*, p. 11, and the literature cited there.

are not only *willing* to fulfil their role, but *prepared* to do so as well.[28]

The most interesting parallel usage to Mt. 25.1-13 is the description of the unjust steward in Lk. 16.8 as *phronimos*. Here the term is no longer translated in contemporary versions as acting 'wisely' (as it was in the AV), but rather 'shrewdly' (NRSV, NIV, GNB) or 'astutely'(NEB, New Jerusalem). The steward's actions were of practical self-preservation. If we accept the insights from socio-cultural criticism, the steward gambled on the rich man's reluctance to lose honour before the villagers by retracting his supposed generosity.[29] The person characterized by this sort of 'wisdom' is not necessarily ethical, but one of those who 'play their cards well'.

The same could be said for the clever/astute/shrewd young women of Mt. 25.1-13. Their actions do not model an appropriate ethic for an 'ecclesia-logy of liberation'.[30] Their 'wisdom' is not the sort of *phronimos* that is needed in the struggle to move beyond patri/kyriarchy, for it is not a *relational* wisdom. Rather, it is one which sets the goal or end above the means, and is prepared to sacrifice the different or 'foolish' young women to reach those ends. Ultimately it perpetuates the binary distinctions which we have sought to critique.

In this parable, therefore, *phronimos* wisdom is in stark contrast to *sophia* wisdom. On the macro-level of Matthew's Gospel, which heightens the identification of *sophia* with Jesus,[31] we meet a wisdom which calls the heavy-laden and oppressed to herself (Mt. 11.28-30) and teaches that those who would save their life will lose it (Mt. 16.25). *Sophia* wisdom is

28. B. Witherington III, with regard to Matthew's usage, draws a christological distinction between the use of *sophos* and *phronimos*. He states that 'Matthew carefully avoids the use of *sophos* here lest it be thought that the disciples too could be sages like Jesus. Rather they can become *andris phronimo,* as opposed to what in Proverbs is seen as the stereotypical example to avoid–the fool (*andri moro*)' *(Jesus the Sage: the Pilgrimage of Wisdom* [Minneapolis: Augsburg Fortress, 1994], pp. 356-57). The choice of this term to describe practical prudence is in keeping with Matthew's interest in *doing* and *bearing fruit.*

29. See Bailey, *Poet and Peasant,* 86-118; B. Malina and R. Rohrbaugh, *Social-Science Commentary on the Synoptic Gospels* (Minneapolis: Fortress, 1992), p. 375.

30. This is a term coined by E. Schüssler Fiorenza to describe a liberating *ekklēsia* of women characterized by a feminist ethics of solidarity, which fosters respect and befriending between women. See *Discipleship of Equals: A Critical Feminist Ekklesia-logy of Liberation* (London: SCM, 1993).

31. See E. Schüssler Fiorenza, *Jesus: Miriam's Child, Sophia's Prophet* (London: SCM 1994), p. 151.

fundamentally relational and, in the case of this parable, critiques *phronimos* wisdom.

To reject the *phronimos* ethic of Mt. 25.1-13 is not to reject legitimate self-preservation. To do so would be to deny self-hood and return to the 'sin' of abdicating responsibility for oneself.[32] P. Perkins points out in relation to Mt. 25.1-13 that there are those who are always expecting others to bail them out, and 'we all find ourselves hoping that the boom gets lowered somewhere along the line on people like that even if we do help the person out of whatever jam he or she is in'.[33] While I recognize the point she is making, I find this comes close to exalting a *phronimos* ethic over a *sophia* one. It assumes that she and others like her are part of the 'wise' group, and that relationality is a burdensome necessity. In my opinion, it is necessary for a feminist re-visioning to reject the *phronimos* ethic of Mt. 25.1-13. To do so is to reject the priority of the future over the present, and the priority of the goal set before us over the current travelling companions.

To summarize our discussion of wisdom and foolishness in Mt. 25. 1-13, we have found that the rhetoric of the parable seeks to establish an identification of the reader with the 'wise' and hinders one with the 'foolish' young women. This evokes a concept of the *two ways*, which, due to its kyriarchal binary distinctions, needs to be deconstructed. We have also found that the 'wisdom' of the young women who were prepared cannot simply be adopted; the astute young women, though prepared, do not model the sort of relational ethic which is imperative in a feminist re-visioning.

Marriage Customs in First-Century Palestine

Before we move to the feminist reconstruction of the first-century reception of this parable, it will be worthwhile to set out what scholars do and do not know about the first-century marriage customs in Palestine. As marriage customs were localized, and the ancient sources inconclusive,[34] we are working with hypotheses. It is highly probable that the marriage arrangements, which took place in various stages, were brought to a

32. Cf. V. Saiving's ground-breaking article 'The Human Situation: A Feminine View', *Journal for Religion* (April 1960).

33. *Hearing the Parables of Jesus*, p. 108.

34. For a list of ancient sources, with some commentary, see Luz, *Das Evangelium nach Matthäus (Mt 18-25)*, p. 469 n. 18.

conclusion with the coming of the bridegroom to the house of the bride and the escorting of the bride to the bridegroom's house where she was to live (patrilocal marriage). Malina and Rohrbaugh, in agreement with A. Musil,[35] take the ten young women to be waiting at the groom's house to greet him, the bride and her relatives on their arrival, to await the consummation of the marriage and the blood-speckled bedsheet (cf. Deut. 22.13-21), and to participate in the feasting that followed.[36] Luz, by contrast, understands v. 1 as a title, and not as the commencement of the story, and takes the young women to be waiting with the bride at her house.[37] Given the prominence of lamps in the story, which would light the bridal party's way from one house to the other, as well as the likelihood that the young women would attend their friend rather than perform a function which could be done by the groom's family or servants, I find Luz's hypothesis the more convincing.

Perkins draws attention to the parallels between this parable and those of the shut door (Lk. 13.24-30) and the faithful servants (Lk. 12.35f), and suggests that the ten virgins of this story 'should be seen as servants, not as guests'.[38] If this were the case, it would mean that the parable was an example of the 'lazy servant' story, whose master (in this case the bridegroom) was justified in his rejection of them. While this proposal gives a useful insight into the status of unmarried women, I think nevertheless that these young women depicted in the story are portrayed as wedding guests, albeit ones with a duty and function to perform. This is suggested by the fact that at least the 'wise' are said to go in with the bridegroom to the wedding banquet (v. 10), with the implication that they took part in the banquet. Given the elaborate hierarchy of banquet etiquette in the ancient world, saying they were guests is not necessarily claiming high status for them (cf. Lk. 14.8-10).[39]

With regard to the lamps, these should be thought of not as small oil lamps, which can burn for several hours, but as long sticks which hold aloft a bowl filled with oil-soaked rags.[40] As we know from the description

35. *Arabia Petraea III,* Vienna, 1907, reprinted Hildesheim 1989, pp. 194-95.

36. Malina and Rohrbaugh, *Social-Science Commentary*, p. 148.

37. *Das Evangelium nach Matthäus (Mt 18-25)*, p. 472. See also Jeremias, 'ΛΑΜΠΑΔΕΣ', pp. 196-201.

38. *Hearing the Parables of Jesus*, p. 106.

39. For evidence of Jewish women attending banquets, though reclining separately, see K.E. Corley, *Private Women, Public Meals: Social Conflict in the Synoptic Tradition* (Peabody, MA: Hendrickson, 1993), p. 69.

40. See Luz, *Das Evangelium nach Matthäus (Mt 18-25)*, p. 471.

of the massive lamps which were erected in the Temple courts during Sukkoth (the Feast of Tabernacles) and which lit up the night,[41] the lighting of torches which push back the night mark a festive and significant occasion (not unlike the contemporary use of fireworks). The extravagant burning of olive oil marked the significance of the event and invoked the presence of God. The ten young women of the story were given what would have been seen as the honour and responsibility of carrying these processional torches. It seems that they were aware that the significance of the torches was greater than simply lighting the path for the bridal party, for which five torches would probably have sufficed. It may be that the torch bearing was perceived as a quasi-religious duty, and if so it would have been one of the very few that women performed publicly. This may account for the 'foolish' group's shared impulse to act rashly and go off into the night in search of oil.

Little more can be said with confidence about the specific marriage customs of first-century Palestine, given that there would have been strong local variations. We do not know whether there was any dancing involved,[42] nor whether ten young women in a festive procession would have been perceived as a large number, denoting high status. Our best access to the customs is via the parable itself, provided it is indeed a reworked parable rather than a continuous allegory.

On the basis of this historical material, we will now move to the task of historical imagining, by setting out several feminist reconstructions of how the story may have been received by first century audiences.

View from the mastaba/*Village Bench: Reconstructing a Patriarchal Reception of the Parable*

Young women could be referred to in a number of ways in Koine Greek. They could be referred to by means of their familial relations as 'daughter' (*thygatēr*), a term which can also function as a friendly greeting (cf. Mt. 9.22). The general term *gynē* can refer to unmarried women who had reached adulthood, the age of twelve-and-a-half. The fact that these young women are referred to as 'virgins', *parthenoi,* gives prominence to their nubility, and thus their sexual availability. This is so whether or not the term was a culturally fixed one referring to bridal/wedding attendants with

---

41. See *Sukkah* 5.1-4. Four menorahs were set up in the Court of Women, and the dancing and celebrating went through the night for the seven days of the feast.

42. As Jeremias argued. See n. 7 above.

certain roles. In a patriarchal context, opening a story with reference to ten nubile girls, five of whom were foolish and five prudent, sets the scene for a comic jest. Had the young women been referred to as 'daughters', or 'daughters of Zion' (viz. Mt. 21.5), the property rights of fathers or the honour of society would have been evoked, and the resulting tone would have been set quite differently.

As it is, the opening two verses, as seen from the *mastaba*, evoke a jest, the butt of which will be the 'foolish virgins'. Philo was presumably not alone in seeing virgins as being like 'sheet[s] of wax levelled to show clearly the lessons to be inscribed' on them (*Spec. Leg.* I 106). The description of five of them as *foolish* virgins indicates that these ones are destined from the start to have a salutary lesson inscribed upon them.

If, from the perspective of the patri/kyriarchal bench, the opening of the story evoked the expectation of humour, how would the ensuing story meet that expectation? In v. 3, the nature of the foolishness is made clear. They all had their torches. The trouble was, five of them had the sticks, the bowls and the rags, but no oil (which does *not* mean further oil reserves, as has often been assumed).

It is most likely that the ten young women would have been visualized as waiting at the bride's house, as we have seen. The surprise or twist of the parable would thus not have been in their apparently falling asleep on the street. As the parable now reads, vv. 5-6 function to delay the *dénouement* and increase the suspense of the story.

From the perspective of the *mastaba*, a strong element of humour would lie in vv. 7-9. Both groups of young women are convinced that they must at all costs fulfil their function as torch bearers, and this results in the 'foolish' ones going off to buy some oil from the merchants, as though *their* light would be the concern of the bridegroom, when he was on the way to collect his new wife and consummate his marriage with her. The 'astute' ones are only astute enough to send the others off into the night, on what could be a wild goose chase. The humour is then at the expense of both the foolish and the prudent, whose shared obsession to fulfil their kyriarchally-defined roles renders them all foolish and imprudent. Those who hurry off to the oil merchants do so without light, and after midnight. As seen from the *mastaba*, the dangers of the bridegroom's displeasure are far outweighed by the dangers of the night-time quest for oil.

Despite the expectations that the story has raised by linking 'foolishness' with 'virginity' and sending a group of desperate young women off into the night unaccompanied, the five young women return to the wedding, apparently with oil and without further incident. They are, of course, too late to perform their required kyriarchal function, but as friends of the bride, could expect a welcome nevertheless.

The twist, or sting in the tail of the story, comes in v. 12.[43] The bridegroom turns them away with the words 'I do not know you'. The joke has gone sour. What started as a joke at the expense of a group of foolish young women has come unstuck, with the kyriarchal host, with whom the men on the *mastaba* had until this moment identified themselves, now alienating the male hearers by his ungenerous and inscrutable behaviour. What began with comedy ends without resolution, and the lines of identification and sympathy have been destabilized. The amusing antics of the 'foolish virgins' had not prepared the patriarchal listener for the unaccountable rejection by the host, and leaves the question hanging in the air: if the bridegroom acts in this way to these guests, who eventually made it to the wedding against great odds, might he not do so to us as well? The joke against both the foolish and the prudent virgins might ultimately be a joke against us.

What started out as a potentially titillating story of foolish virgins, who through their night-time escapade were in danger of being 'known', ends—through their not being 'known' by the bridegroom—with a disturbing sense of injustice. The male hearer can no longer be completely confident that he would be safely in the banquet, for the foolish wedding attendants can no longer simply be defined as 'the other'. The male listeners who felt the outrage of the rejection would glimpse the world anew, and in doing so find a God who is unpredictable, a God who is not playing the game according to the rules. Far from resolving the story at the end, the closed door evokes a desire for a more just and generous resolution. For the male listener who has undergone the re-visioning described above, the story remains disturbingly open-ended.

This imaginative reconstruction posits male first-time listeners whose contact with the story is aural and pre-redactional.[44] It may be the closest we can come to reconstructing the intended audience of the story. It would have been most effective among those men who identified themselves most strongly with the kyriarch of the story: the elite and powerful men among the audience. For the religious leaders, the use of the 'bridegroom'

43. So Ricoeur, 'Biblical Hermeneutics', p. 117, and Luz, *Das Evangelium nach Matthäus (Mt 18-25)*, pp. 467, 477.

44. I.e., without v. 13. It is not dependent on the presence or absence of vv. 5-7a, which I take to be an allegorizing insertion (see n. 2 above).

may have evoked YHWH God as bridegroom, on the basis of such a text as Isa. 62.5. This would have strengthened their confidence as 'insiders', whose right and prerogative it was to be among the guests. Nevertheless, the story does not depend on this identification. It does, however, depend on the 'high context'[45] shared understanding of the honour required of a host.

View from the agora/*Market Place:* Reconstructing Women's Reception of the Parable

The most striking thing about the opening of the parable, when seen from the perspective of women familiar with the marriage customs of the day, is the lack of mention of a bride. The bride is the central focus of a wedding, for perhaps the one time in her life. Although we have no direct access to the exact customs presupposed by the story, we may be confident that these young women are seeking to perform certain duties which have a dual function. The first is to enact the transferral of ownership of the bride from her father to her husband and to symbolize that all property matters have been successfully resolved to the mutual benefit of the families. The second is to inculcate the necessity and desirability of entering the married state among young women yet to be married. It was not necessarily the case that young women looked forward to marriage, when they would be transferred to the husband's family, where they would have little status until the birth of a son, and possibly little friendship and support. The dangers of motherhood would also have made marriage a daunting prospect.[46] Given that young women from the age of twelve-and-a-half had the right to refuse a marriage proposal,[47] customs which highlight the desirability and importance of becoming a bride were fostered by the kyriarchally constructed society.

Both these functions would have prompted the women who heard this story, whether married or unmarried, to identify with the bride in the story, had there been one. The married women would recall their own wedding

45. See Malina and Rohrbaugh, *Social-Science Commentary,* pp. 11-12.

46. See A.L. Wordelman's article entitled 'Everyday Life: Women in the Period of the New Testament', *Women's Bible Commentary,* pp. 482-88. She draws attention to the poetry of a young girl named Erinna, which talks of her childhood play with a dear friend Baucis, playing with dolls and pretending they were newly married wives. Her poetry reflects the 'centrality of marriage dreams' (p. 486).

47. According to *b. Kiddushin* 2b, 79a.

day, and the unmarried would go over in their minds the concept of being a bride.

However, given that the bride is not mentioned in the best manuscripts,[48] we may assume that the lack of mention of her is part of the original shape of the story. Instead of being able to identify with the bride, therefore, the rhetoric of the story gives women two possibilities: to see themselves as part of the group of prudent women, or as part of the group of foolish ones. It seems to me unlikely that many women would have heard the story as jest, given that it relies on an androcentric viewpoint fostered to exclude female listeners.[49]

As we have seen already, the shape of the story promotes the identification with the 'wise'/prudent young women, and hinders identification with the foolish. It conveys the message to a female listener that it is imperative that she be among the prudent, and not among the foolish. In order to ensure that she is, it becomes imperative rightly to discern what the oil may be, so that she may be prepared to fulfil her appointed role.

In this way, the parabolic action of the story which we traced from the viewpoint of the *mastaba* is pushed towards allegory. The all-important feature is the oil. The key teaching which is being conveyed to the female listener by the parable is that being present, being willing to perform one's role, being a friend of the wedding party can all count for nought if one is not prepared with the oil. To slip up in one's duty–to be forgetful or carefree–may prove to be the unforgivable sin.

As a result, the dynamics of the interaction between the groups of young women become secondary. Any sense of outrage that the female listener may have had that the prudent young women did not share is rendered irrelevant. Not even the sense that the bridegroom is acting unfairly is voiced. In the perspective from the *agora*, he is the kyriarch of the story and may choose to act capriciously. From this perspective, the over-riding imperative is to be prepared with the oil and to be among the 'wise'.

The resulting theology which is conveyed and perpetuated by this identification with the 'wise' is the *phronimos* wisdom outlined above. Any objections as to the ethics of the astute young women—which

48. The words 'and the bride' (*kai tēs numphēs*) are included primarily by Western witnesses. On both external and internal grounds, most scholars are confident that they are a secondary addition.

49. It was, of course, possible for women who spent time in the company of men to enter into and excel at their witticisms. See Corley, *Private Women, Public Meals,* esp. ch.2.

override any compassion or solidarity with their peers—are ruled out. Relationship is maintained only with those who show themselves to be worthy through their actions. The 'wise' thus become an exclusive club with entry rights into the eschatological banquet. Put this way, I hope it is clear that neither the actions of the shrewd young women nor those of the bridegroom bear much relationship to the commitment and ministry of Jesus of Nazareth.

It would also have been possible for some women to identify from the outset with the foolish. If their pre-understanding was of themselves as falling short or failing to meet the patri/kyriarchal expectations placed on them, they may have resisted the rhetoric of the story and identified with the 'foolish' young women. If so, they would have found no good news in the story. Much like the 'two way' paradigm, the 'foolish' girls would have been seen to be on the path to destruction from the outset, but were themselves unaware of it. The story would confirm that nothing could have been done by their peers to avert the coming destruction, and the bridegroom's words would have served to reveal to them their own worthlessness. This is a grim perspective, which bears none of the hallmarks of the sort of good news we find confidently expressed by Mary, the more favoured young woman of a comparable age to the young women of the story, in her song of praise (Lk. 1.46-55).

Both the perspective from the *mastaba* and the ones from the *agora* set out above are concerned with the actual first-century hearers of the story. Both perspectives are, of course, my own constructs. Although imagination is involved, these are not yet examples of the 'creative imagination' Schüssler Fiorenza writes about, which, through 'historical imagination, narrative amplifications, artistic recreations and liturgical celebrations' allow women to enter the biblical text.[50] Both the first-century women's perspectives imagined here are oppressive, and cannot simply be adopted by the feminist reader of the twenty-first century. These perspectives will, however, clarify the directions which a re-visioning of this parable must take.

If the different perspectives set out above give a plausible account of how this story may have been heard in the first century, this carries some important implications. It will mean, first of all, that it is ultimately the first perspective from the *agora*, which identifies with the 'wise', which becomes the dominant one. This view comes to focus on the oil as good

50. E. Schüssler Fiorenza, *But She Said: Feminist Practices of Biblical Interpretation* (Boston: Beacon Press, 1992), p. 73.

works. The first view from the *agora* displaces the view from the *mastaba*. There may be a number of reasons for this:

- the allegorizing reading lends itself to teaching and exhortation;
- this reading type can function well when being retold many times whereas the *mastaba* type depends on the surprise of the first-time telling;
- the allegorising reading can be applied to women and men alike, while the reading from the *mastaba* requires the male listener to make the shift in identification;
- the *mastaba* perspective, with its rhetoric of jest, no longer functions once the tradition has moved from an oral to a written medium. Once Matthew set it down as part of the Gospel narrative, he set down not only the story but also the lens through which it was to be read.

The second implication is that this parable originally enabled the (male) listeners to hear with new ears and be confronted with themselves. This perspective from the *mastaba* was initially amused by the actions of the young women, but ultimately confronted by the ungenerous actions of the bridegroom. Neither the actions of the shrewd young women nor those of the bridegroom were justified by this perspective.

By contrast, the perspective from the *agora* justifies both. This latter perspective ultimately sacralizes the division into 'wise' and 'foolish', and the ethic of 'look after number one'. In writing this, I do not wish to apportion blame in this process. It seems to me that given the shift of the *Sitz im Leben* of the parable from a conflict situation to that of early church exhortation, it could hardly have been otherwise. But we have been left with a parable which continually prompts us to call bad *good*. The actions of the 'wise' young women and the actions of the bridegroom are unjustified and wrong and we need to name them as such.

The Parable from the Perspective of Matthew's Gospel

If we have had reason to question whether the bridegroom of Mt. 25.1-13 can be equated with Jesus the liberator, the evangelist Matthew has no such reservations. It is clear from the narrative sequence in which this parable is placed that the focus for Matthew is on the coming judgment.[51]

---

51. For a study which gives attention to redactional critical questions and also ones

For the evangelist, the bridegroom is none other than Christ, coming as judge and dividing not simply outsiders, but his own followers into two groups 'as a shepherd separates the sheep from the goats' (Mt. 25.32).

Verse 13, which is widely accepted to be a Matthean addition to the story, gives Matthew's 'angle' on the story. 'Keep awake/watch/take heed, therefore, for you know neither the day nor the hour'. The story illustrates this lesson only moderately well, given that *none* of the young women keep awake, and they all know the day and ultimately the hour, as the call has gone out that the bridegroom is arriving, prompting five of them to hurry off. Nevertheless, the surprise and dread of exclusion are vivid illustrations of what, for Matthew, is at stake.

Matthew's is the only Gospel in which this parable of the 'foolish' and 'wise' young women is recorded. Verses 11-12, however, show affinity to the Q material of Lk. 13.25-27/Mt. 7.21-23. The surprising rejection of those who seem to be insiders is a theme which is used by Matthew at the end of the Sermon on the Mount:

> Not everyone who says to me, 'Lord, Lord', will enter the kingdom of heaven, but only the one who does the will of my Father in heaven. On that day many will say to me, 'Lord, Lord, did we not prophesy in your name, and cast out demons in your name, and do many deeds of power in your name?' Then I will declare to them, 'I never knew you; go away from me, you evil-doers/workers of lawlessness' (Mt. 7.21-23, NRSV, modified).

Like the bridegroom of Mt. 25.1-13, the eschatological judge of this passage declares that certain followers are rejected from his presence because he 'never knew' them. These followers can point to prophecy and miracles done in the name of the 'Lord'. But it appears that the good deeds do not spring from a connection with the one in whose name they are performed, so that these 'good' deeds, according to Matthew, result in evil or lawlessness. Matthew seems to be using this tradition to critique certain leaders within his community, and to point to the day of judgment as the time when true allegiances will be revealed.

Although the surprise of rejection and the words used to express it are similar to Mt. 25.12, Mt. 7.22-23 is an aphorism rather than a parable and, unlike the parable, has a quite specific group of 'workers of lawlessness' in mind. Mt. 25.1-13 does not seem to be addressed to a specific group, though the fact that the protagonists are women may have meant that women felt particularly addressed by this parable.

of narrative sequence, see J. Lambrecht, *Once More Astonished: The Parables of Jesus* (New York: Crossroad, 1981), pp. 146-66.

The theme of the surprising rejection of seeming 'insiders' is found again in the parable of the wedding garment (Mt. 22.11-14). Here, the context of the parable heightens the surprise and unreasonableness of the rejection of the man without a wedding robe. Coming as it does after the story of the wedding banquet in which the guests had simply been dragged in, good and bad alike, the fact that one person is singled out as being inappropriately dressed is made all the more striking. How could a last-minute ring-in be expected to be wearing a wedding robe? The very un-reasonableness of the expectation pushes the reader towards a symbolic or allegorizing reading of the significance of the wedding garment. It becomes something that one must be constantly 'clothed' in, and, for Matthew, this mantle is the better righteousness set out in the Sermon on the Mount.

The associative links between the parables of the wedding garment and the ten young women prompt those who read the parables within the narrative context to interpret the wedding garment and the oil as parallel symbols. For Matthew, both are symbols of doing the will of God as expressed in the commandments of Jesus. For him, this is the better righteousness referred to in Mt. 5.20, and set out in 5.21-48. The alle-gorizing process had progressed for Matthew to the extent that he was not, it seems, troubled by the fact that the 'wise' group's unshared and thus hoarded oil was intended to represent the love that goes the extra mile and extends even to one's enemies (Mt. 5.43-48). He, like many subsequent interpreters, was confident that such (symbolic) oil could not, by defi-nition, be shared.

As we have seen, the evangelist is convinced of the way in which the final judgment will be a surprise to those who believe that they are comfortably insiders. The most striking example of this theology in the Gospel is the vivid story of the final judgment in Mt. 25.31-46. Neither the ones who are judged to be 'blessed by my Father' (v. 34), nor the ones who are judged to be 'accursed' (v. 41) seem to have had an inkling of their status. Both groups address the judge as Lord, or perhaps 'sir', which implies that they may have regarded themselves as disciples. Here is Matthew's final and most vivid illustration of his theology that 'by their fruits you will know them' (cf. Mt. 7.20), or, to use the contemporary idiom, 'actions speak louder than words'.

While Matthew has a strong eschatological motivation to his theology, he is also convinced that the final separation of insiders and outsiders must not be pre-empted. He believes that the church is, and must remain until the end, a *corpus permixtum,* a mixed group of righteous and unrighteous together. This comes through in his parables of the weeds among the wheat (Mt. 13.24-30) and the dragnet (Mt. 13.47-49).

Given this theology that the separation must not be done until the end, Mt. 25.1-13 is all the more clearly a depiction of the eschatological judgment. Although the evangelist does not add a reference to outer darkness and grief, the reader can supply these from the night-time imagery of the parable and the narrative context (cf. Mt. 24.51). For Matthew, then, this parable is exclusively a depiction of the end time judgment, not a model for ethical or righteous behaviour on the part of the 'wise' young women or the bridegroom. The reservations I have expressed about the ethics of the parable are not Matthew's concern at this point in his narrative.

For Matthew, the end times were close at hand,[52] and this conviction shaped his theology throughout the Gospel. For feminist readers, by contrast, this emphasis on eschatology is suspect. Along with other theologies of liberation, feminist theology is not content to look to the righting of wrongs in the end times, but seeks to expose, critique and change current evils via a feminist political hermeneutic. Simply to reiterate first-century eschatology, as though the intervening twenty centuries had not taken place, would be to validate and hallow a system of meaning which has served patriarchy well. While an emphasis on the end times may not be synonymous with patri/kyriarchy, one of the prime functions which eschatology has performed over the centuries is to relativize the demand for justice in the here and now.

It is therefore not open to us as feminist readers of this passage simply to adopt the Matthean perspective which we receive through the narrative context and the rhetoric of the parable itself. Although we may retain an eschatological framework, the vast majority of feminists do not share the imminent eschatology of Matthew. What we look for from this parable, then, is not end time teaching, but wisdom that can be of some 'earthly use'. In search of this wisdom, we now turn to the final section of this paper.

A Contemporary Feminist Interpretation of Mt. 25.1-13

I suggested at the outset that, for feminist readers, the unwillingness of the 'wise' young women to share their oil and their complicity in the patri/kyriarchal *dénouement* of the story is the central problematic of the

---

52. See *Eschatology in the Making*, esp. pp. 173-75.

story. We may not simply pass over these things because the rhetoric of the story will have it so, or because it symbolizes the final judgment in its narrative context, not contemporary ethics.

In our search for the 'hidden wisdom', or 'deeper lode'[53] of the story, we cannot simply take the path of the earliest hearers. I have argued that the view from the *mastaba* had liberating potential for the male first-time listeners. This liberating potential was dependent upon the willingness of the male listeners to shift their framework of identification. As such, it was a man's story told to men, and what liberation was effected for first-century women was not effected directly in the impact of the story on them, but indirectly, via their fathers, brothers, sons, religious leaders, male neighbours, masters or clients. As contemporary feminist readers, who have received this story in a narrative context and with centuries of interpretation built upon it, we cannot do more than catch an echo of this early liberating potential of the parable. The door to this reading is closed to us.

The view/s from the *agora* are not so distant. The view which identifies with the 'wise' young women and seeks to discern the symbolism of the oil in contemporary and relevant ways is a path chosen by some women.[54] One may even seek to interpret the oil as the insight and courage to pursue the journey out of patriarchy towards a liberating future. However, joining with the kyriarch, the bridegroom, who excludes the women who have not lived up to his expectation, simply in order to secure one's goals, negates whatever liberating symbolic potential there might be in the oil.

This door may not be shut to us, but *sophia* wisdom invites us to reject it in our search for an entrance to a liberating, compassionate and relational future. In order to find a door through to a liberating reading of this parable, a door which we both *can* open and *choose* to open, we will return to three aspects of the parable: the interaction between the two groups of women; the person and words of the bridegroom; and finally, the door itself. In doing so, we will use the potential of constructive historical imagining mentioned above.

Although the rhetoric of the story has indicated from v. 2 onwards that there is a division in this group of ten young women who are waiting to perform a ceremonial function, it is not until v. 8 that we see the division enacted. One group, the group without oil, asks those with oil to share. The other group, those with oil, refuse to share on the basis that there will

---

53. These terms are used by Wainwright, *Shall We Look for Another*, p. 21.
54. Such as Perkins, in *Hearing the Parables of Jesus*.

not be enough, and offer some advice to those without oil. Here we have a rare instance in a biblical text of the voicing of differences in women's perspectives. The rhetoric of the story pushes the reader to see the request of the young women without oil as unreasonable, self-centred, and an attempt to hinder the prospects of those with oil.

However, if we deconstruct this rhetorical move, what remains is a request based on the legitimate grounds of friendship. This is not a friendship grounded in utility, such as those of patrons and clients, but one based on fellow-feeling, or *oikeiosis*.[55] On the basis of their common humanity and their common task, their request for an act of friendship— the sharing of the oil—is legitimate. The legitimacy of the request is illustrated by the Jesus of Matthew's Gospel, in both the 'Great Commandment' and the 'Golden Rule':

> Teacher, which commandment in the law is the greatest?' He said to him, ' "You shall love the Lord your God with all you heart, and with all your soul, and with all your mind". This is the greatest and first commandment. And a second is like it: "You shall love your neighbour as yourself". On these two commandments hang all the law and the prophets (Mt. 22.36-40).

> In everything do to others as you would have them do to you; for this is the law and the prophets (Mt. 7.12).

The request of the young women without oil is nothing other than that they be treated as neighbours, and that those with oil act in a way which is congruent with the way that they would wish to be treated. The key to their viewpoint is friendship. If their point of view is translated into theological terms, they are looking for compassion and mercy, not only from their peers, but ultimately from God.

The reply of the young women with oil shows a differing priority. They are focused on the task at hand, and they point out that *none* of them may be able to achieve that task adequately if they meet the others' request. They are not completely unaware of the demands of compassion and mercy, for they are not comfortable simply to refuse the request, but feel the need to add a suggestion as to how the situation may be ameliorated for all. In the context of the story, the suggestion is an ineffectual one, as the arrival of the bridegroom has already been announced. We might characterize their viewpoint as one of fairness; it would not be fair that

---

55. For a discussion of friendship in the ancient world, see J. Massingbaerde Ford, *Redeemer, Friend and Mother: Salvation in Antiquity and in the Gospel of John* (Minneapolis: Fortress, 1997), ch. 5.

they be expected to give up their oil and forego the benefits to which their preparation entitled them. To translate this viewpoint into theological terms, they are looking for a kind of forensic justice, not only from their peers, but ultimately from God.

In this brief dialogue between the two groups, we find encapsulated the perennial dialogue between the justice and mercy of God. Can these opposing demands be reconciled? Which of the two should have priority?

Within the parameters of the story, these questions are resolved in favour of fairness or forensic justice. The young women with oil are the 'winners', and those who looked for friendship, compassion and mercy are the 'losers'. The kyriarch of the story resolves the tension between justice and mercy in favour of justice, and rejects any demand of relationship from those who are now the outsiders with the words 'Truly I tell you, I do not know you'.

If this is to be a story of salvation, whether present or future, and if it is to be a story in keeping with the broad sweep of the ministry of Jesus of Nazareth, we can do nothing but reply to this kyriarch, '*We* do not know *you*'. This bridegroom cannot symbolize for us Jesus Christ, the liberator. Rather, this bridegroom symbolizes for us all kyriarchs who first make the rules, then use them to exclude others. 'They tie up heavy burdens, hard to bear, and lay them on the shoulders of others; but they themselves are unwilling to lift a finger to move them' (Mt. 23.4). Such kyriarchs 'lock people out of the sovereign realm of heaven. [They] do not go in [themselves], and when others are going in, [they] stop them' (Mt. 23.13, modified). Such 'Lords', whether ecclesiastical or secular, shut the door on those seeking liberation and wholeness.

If we allow the closed door to be the final word, we have accepted the *two way* paradigm which sees the world as a series of binary distinctions. The closed door is the symbol of final separation in this story. However, in Matthew's Gospel, the word 'door' (*thyra*) is to occur again at 27.60, where it refers to the door of the tomb of Jesus, shut after the crucified body of Jesus has been laid inside. But there, what seemed to have been shut permanently, with all hope gone, is found opened on the third day by the God of new hope. The shut door does not have the last word.

So too in my reading of this parable. The kyriarchal bridegroom of this parable may have shut the door in the face of those who did not conform, but the story of Easter gives hope that here, too, the door will be opened by God. If we search this parable for a symbol which can speak to us of Christ the liberator, it is there only in potential at present.

As we search for a symbol of Christ in this story, we can invoke the one who said 'I am the door' (Jn 11.9) to be present not as kyriarch but as liberator and to open the door to the marginalized, to those who are, like so many of us, the 'foolish'. Only if the closed door becomes an open one can it enable us to glimpse Christ as liberator in this story. If it remains shut, then Christ's presence is hidden among those on the outside.

'MAKING UP STORIES': A FEMINIST READING OF THE PARABLE OF THE PRODIGAL SON (LK. 15.11b-32)

Mary Ann Beavis

Fairytales endure because they spell out our hidden desires and our hopeful solutions. Their kings and queens and witches and ogres represent our mommies and daddies with their ultimate power to nurture or destroy us (Sylvia Fraser, *My Father's House*).[1]

Introduction

Including a chapter on the parable of the prodigal son is problematic in a book of feminist interpretations of parables about women, women's work and Sophia. No female characters, apart from the prostitutes (*pornai*) whom the younger son is accused of consorting with by his elder brother (Lk. 15.30), are mentioned in the story. Presumably, the family includes female members: mothers, grandmothers, daughters, sisters, wives, slaves—but they remain in the background, unmentioned and irrelevant. Nonetheless, a feminist interpretation of the parable could take several approaches:

- it could focus on the 'forgotten women' of the parable, the submerged female family members, and the effects on them of the father's premature division of the property, and of the younger son's defection and return.[2]
- the story could be rewritten as a tale of mothers and daughters, as

---

1. S. Fraser, *My Father's House: A Memoir of Incest and Healing* (Toronto: Doubleday Canada, 1987), p. 153.

2. Two interpreters who briefly acknowledge the effect of the family's troubles on the women of the family are R.L. Rohrbaugh, 'A Dysfunctional Family and Its Neighbours', in V.G. Shillington (ed.), *Jesus and His Parables: Interpreting the Parables of Jesus Today* (Edinburgh: T. & T. Clark, 1997), pp. 151-152 and B.B. Scott, *Hear Then The Parable: A Commentary on the Parables of Jesus* (Minneapolis: Fortress, 1989), pp. 109-11.

in Miriam Therese Winter's parable of the 'Delinquent daughter and her sister'.[3]

- even more provocatively, the story could be recast as an inter-change between a *paterfamilias* and an errant daughter, returning pregnant from a life of prostitution. Perhaps following from this, the role of prostitutes (v. 30) in the patriarchal social system of antiquity could be explored, and the parable could be compared with Lk. 7.36-50, the story of a 'sinful' woman who anoints Jesus.[4]
- the parable could be interpreted as implicitly undermining the patriarchal family, since, as R.H. Rohrbaugh has persuasively argued, this is an extremely dysfunctional family by ancient Mediterranean standards, with a weak and indulgent father and two outrageously unfilial sons.[5]

While all of these approaches have potential, another interpretation was suggested to me by an advertisement for a conference called 'Return to the Father's House: God the Father and Human Fatherhood' published in a recent issue of the conservative Christian journal *First Things*.[6] The ad features a drawing of an elderly, bearded, 'biblical'-looking man raptly gazing heavenwards while a child or youth embraces him, head buried in the patriarch's lap, presumably in an attitude of distress or repentance. Projecting between the child's head and the man's belly is a curved—and unfortunately phallic-looking—staff. The ostensible purpose of the picture is to portray an image of loving, forgiving fatherhood, but it is also disturbing. Presumably, the image and the conference title allude to the parable of the prodigal son.[7] The man in the drawing recalls the father of the parable, although he looks more like a grandfather or great-grand-father—a veritable 'ancient of days'—than the parent of two young men.[8]

3. M.T. Winter, *The Gospel According to Mary: A New Testament for Women* (New York: Crossroad, 1994), pp. 69-70.

4. On Lk. 7.36-52, see D.A. Lee, 'Women as 'Sinners': Three Narratives of Salvation in Luke and John', *Australian Biblical Review* 44 (1996), pp. 1-15.

5. Rohrbaugh, 'Dysfynctional Family'.

6. *First Things* 94 (June/July 1999), p. 51.

7. The phrase 'my father's house' (*ho oikos tou pateros mou*) is not actually used in the parable; the most memorable usages of this formula are found in Lk. 2.49, where the child Jesus refers to the temple as his (heavenly) father's house; and in Jn 14.2 ('in my father's house are many rooms'). See also Lk. 16.27; Jn 2.16. Lk. 15.18a reads: 'I will arise and go to my father'. The house (*oikia*) is mentioned in the parable in 15.25.

8. The two sons are invariably interpreted as being young, perhaps because the younger son appears to be unmarried.

In turn, the father of the illustration/parable represents God the Father–the patriarchal image of Godde that feminist theologians have repudiated, and that even the theologically conservative Pope John Paul II has criticized![9] More disturbing, however, are the sexual undertones of the graphic. While, superficially, the ad portrays a compassionate parent welcoming his errant child, on another level—not far from the surface—the child's abject pose, the position of his/her head, the patriarch's clasp, the man's vacant, ecstatic expression, the protruding staff are disturbingly suggestive of child sexual abuse.

While this interpretation of the advertisement is no doubt a far cry from the intent of the artist, or of the conference organizers, a reader familiar with the issues surrounding child sexual abuse—or someone who had experienced such abuse—might well find the image upsetting. As a feminist reader, I find myself with similar misgivings when I read the familiar, much-loved parable of the Prodigal Son. Although recent interpreters have shied away from the allegorical identification of the father with God and the son with the penitent sinner,[10] this *is* the way that the parable is usually interpreted in Christian preaching and teaching:

> The prodigal son, a fictional character in the parable, sinks to the depth of degradation through serious, habitual sin. Nonetheless, he is forgiven when he approaches his father, confesses his sin and asks for forgiveness. It is important to note that the father, who represents God the Father, comes out to meet him and rejoices wonderfully, showering his son with gifts and affection.[11]

Even Rohrbaugh, who rejects the simple identification of the father with God, admits the theological possibility that the father's actions can be symbolic of the actions of God.[12] Assertions that God can be interpreted in

9.   C. Andrews, 'Modernizing God's Image', *National Post* (January 20, 1999): 'Pope John Paul II recently announced that Catholics should abandon traditional patriarchal ideas about God. Speaking to pilgrims at St. Peter's, the Pope said God is "not be imagined as an old man with a flowing beard", and Christians must guard against envisioning God in human terms'.

10.   Rohrbaugh, 'Dysfunctional Family', pp. 142-43; K.E. Bailey, *Poet and Peasant and Through Peasant Eyes* (Grand Rapids: Eerdmans, 1983), p. 159.

11.   C.J. McCloskey III, 'Go, Sin No More', *Columbia* 79,4 (April 1999), p. 20. This interpretation of the parable is cited by McCloskey as favoured by Pope John Paul II. (*Columbia* is the magazine of the Knights of Columbus, a Catholic men's service organization.) The exegesis goes on to compare the father/God who forgives the erring son to the father/priest who welcomes the penitent to the sacrament of reconciliation.

12.   Rohrbaugh, 'Dysfunctional Family', p. 143 n. 1.

maternal as well as paternal terms,[13] or that fatherhood is merely a meta-phor for a God who transcends human, gendered categories, do little to ameliorate the overwhelmingly patriarchal impact of the image. From a feminist vantage point, the best such revisionist interpretations can do is gloss over patriarchal ideology with a veneer of 'love-patriarchalism', where the absolute authority of the kyriarchal father is upheld on the condition that it is tempered with love, and met with loving submission by subordinates.[14] The father, 'compassionate' (v. 20) though he may be, is only satisfied when the runaway son returns home to be absorbed back into the patriarchal 'house' (*oikos*, v. 25). No one thinks to ask why the younger son ran away, or what he was running away from.

E. Schüssler Fiorenza has called for a 'hermeneutics of proclamation' that requires biblical scholars, teachers and preachers to 'explore not only their own but also the cultural-religious locations of their audiences and adjudicate the impact or effects that their biblical interpretations have on such audiences, especially on those who credit the scriptures with divine authority'.[15] Prompted by my visceral response to the advertisement for

13. In the issue of *Columbia* cited in n. 10, above (the theme of this particular issue of the magazine is 'God the Father', and the cover boasts a painting of an ancient, bearded man and a dove!), the feature article (accompanied by a stained-glass image of a bearded patriarch) tries to soften the overwhelming masculinity of the metaphor: 'For those who question a too-masculine image of God, the catechism offers this: 'God's parental tenderness can also be expressed by the image of motherhood... We ought therefore to recall that God transcends human fatherhood and motherhood, although he is their origin and standard...' (M. Pable, 'Returning to the Father's House in Time for the Great Jubilee of the Year 2000', *Columbia* 79,4 (April 1999), p. 11. The theme of the issue was inspired by the papal proclamation of the year 2000 as the Year of God the Father.

14. The term 'love patriarchalism' was coined by G. Theissen to describe the inculturation of the radical early Christian ethic of love and equality (*agapē*) to the patriarchal social system of class differentiation, expressed in terms of domination and subordination. The blending of the radical love ethic with the patriarchal system leads to an ethos of the 'willing' acceptance of inequalities; those in dominant positions (fathers, husbands, overlords) treat their inferiors with 'love', and those under their 'care' respond with 'loving' submission. (G. Theissen, 'Itinerant Radicalism: The Tradition of Jesus Sayings from the Perspective of the Sociology of Literature', in N.K. Gottwald and A.C. Wire (eds.), *The Bible and Liberation: Political and Social Hermeneutics* [Berkeley: Radical Religion Reader, 1976], pp. 84-93). For a feminist critique of the concept of love patriarchalism, see E. Schüssler Fiorenza, *In Memory of Her: A Feminist Theological Reconstruction of Christian Origins* (New York: Cross-road, 1983), pp. 76-80.

15. E. Schüssler Fiorenza, *Sharing Her Word: Feminist Biblical Interpretation in*

the 'Return to the Father's House' conference described above, I shall base my interpretation of Lk. 15.11b-32 on its impact on an 'implied reader' with a history of child sexual abuse.[16] In taking this approach, I acknowledge that the 'reader' of my interpretation is a construct, based on narratives written by survivors of child abuse, and on social scientific research and feminist theological reflection on incest and child abuse.[17] I am also aware that I am 'reading against the grain' of the Lucan parable, which, in the gospel context, is told by Jesus to refute the criticism of 'Pharisees and scribes' that he receives 'sinners and tax collectors' (Lk. 15.1-2). The parable of the father and his two sons is placed after two other parables of losing and finding, the lost sheep (Lk. 15.3-7) and the lost coin (Lk. 15.8-10). Both parables are followed by 'morals' (*epimythia*) that specify that they apply to the joy in heaven over the return of a repentant sinner (Lk. 15.7, 10). The parable of the prodigal, a longer and more developed narrative than the previous two, is the climax of the triad, and makes the identification of the compassionate father with God, and the runaway son with the 'sinner', inevitable. For Luke, the postscripts added to the two previous parables foreshadow the meaning of the third: the father's joy over his son's return symbolizes the joy of the 'heavenly father' over the child/sinner who repents. Finally, I recognize that this is a much-beloved parable, and that an interpretation of the parable from the perspective of a survivor of child abuse may be considered irrelevant, offensive or perverse by some readers. Like children who 'tell on' their abusers, I may be accused of 'making up stories', like the young runaways interviewed by S. Butler in San Francisco:

> in most cases these young people, both male and female, had been abused by their fathers over the years. When they could no longer bear the degradation and were old enough to leave home, they tried to improve their situation by getting a new start somewhere else, but they usually ended up

Context (Boston: Beacon, 1998), p. 138.

16. Scott (*Hear Then the Parable*, p. 103) identifies three readers/audiences presupposed by the parable: the historical audience of Jesus, the audience of Luke's fictional world, and Luke's own 'implied readers'. The last category of 'reader/ audience', by extension, includes readers/hearers in our own time, with their multiple cultural-religious locations.

17. Here, I follow J. Manlowe's definition of incest as 'the sexual seduction, molestation, and/or rape of a child by any relative (blood, step, adoptive), trusted caregiver, or friend of the family' (Jennifer L. Manlowe, *Faith Born of Seduction: Sexual Trauma, Body Image, and Religion* [New York/London: New York University Press, 1995], p. 4).

as prostituted. When they were apprehended by the police, they told the truth about their background, hoping that the defenders of law and order would protect them, but they were only accused of making up stories and were sent back to their parents.[18]

The interpretation that follows does not purport to uncover the 'true' or 'original' meaning of the parable, the meaning intended by Jesus, or the meaning intended by Luke. Rather, informed by the skills of a professional biblical scholar, it attempts to read the parable from the perspective of an implied reader with the life experience of one of the runaways described above.

A Dysfunctional Family

Back and forth the princess paces, tearing her blond hair out by its roots. Wearing Arlene's scornful expression, the queen draws her scissors from her bodice. 'I didn't know it was possible to hate another person so much'.[19]

The parable presupposes a well-off Jewish household living in an agricultural village.[20] As Rohrbaugh and others have observed, by the standards of ancient Mediterranean village culture, the family of the parable is a troubled and chaotic one; a contemporary social worker would call it 'dysfunctional'.[21] In antiquity, it would have been extremely irregular for a son to ask for his inheritance before his father's death; by doing so, the younger son implicitly wishes that his father were dead.[22] In

18.   The reference is to S. Butler, *Conspiracy of Silence: The Trauma of Incest* (San Francisco: Volcano Press, 1978, 1996), as discussed by A. Miller: *Thou Shalt Not Be Aware: Society's Betrayal of the Child* (new edn; London: Pluto Press, 1998), p. 325.

19.   Fraser, *My Father's House*, p. 180.

20.   D.E. Oakman, 'The Countryside in Luke–Acts', in J.H. Neyrey (ed.), *The Social World of Luke–Acts: Models for Interpretation* (Peabody, MA: Hendrickson, 1991), p. 163.

21.   Rohrbaugh, 'Dysfunctional Family'; Scott, *Hear Then the Parable*, pp. 109-111; Bailey, *Poet and Peasant*, pp. 161-69.

22.   Rohrbaugh, 'Dysfunctional Family', p. 150; Scott, *Hear Then the Parable*, p. 111; Bailey, *Poet and Peasant*, p. 161-69; J.D.M. Derrett, 'Law in the New Testament: The Parable of the Prodigal Son', *New Testament Studies* 14 (1967), p. 59. According to Derrett, the only circumstance that could provoke a father to divide up his estate prior to his death would be to avoid squabbles after his death–a circumstance in itself that points to a troubled family. P. Perkins, however, asserts that 'Legal evidence shows that the initial division of property was possible. It was not an act of disrespect

a culture where the public reputation of a family (expressed in terms of 'honour' and 'shame') was a fundamental value, the son brings disgrace on his family by dishonouring his father not only in private but before his neighbours.[23] Moreover, in Jewish religious terms, he breaks the commandment to honour one's parents (Exod. 20.12).[24] Less obviously, the older son is little better. The parable states that the father 'divided his living' between the two sons (Lk. 15.12), and there is no indication that the elder objected.[25] The appropriate response from a loyal son would be a vigorous rejection of his share before his father's death.[26] The father appears to have two very shameless, unfilial and irreverent sons, who hold him in contempt, and have no qualms about exposing him to public ridicule. In short, they act as if they hate him.

Not only do the sons behave shamefully, but the father accepts their behaviour unquestioningly, and grants the younger son's outrageous demand. In Jewish tradition, fathers are warned not to hand over their property to anyone, wife, brother, friend or child (Sir. 33.19-23):

> While you are still alive and have breath in you, do not let anyone take your place. For it is better that your children should ask from you than that you should look to the hands of your sons… At the time when you end the days of your life, in the hour of death, distribute your inheritance (Sir. 33.21, 23, RSV).

To act otherwise is a stain upon one's honour (Sir. 33.22). Rabbinic teaching also decries any man who hands over his property to his children

for the father. The father did not have to consent' (*Hearing the Parables of Jesus* [New York: Paulist, 1981], p. 54). Perkins may be referring to the opinion of J. Jeremias that the situation depicted in the parable was not uncommon (*The Parables of Jesus* [New York: Charles Scribner's Sons, 1972], p. 129). Against this view, see Scott, *Hear Then the Parable*, pp. 109-111.

23. Rohrbaugh, 'Dysfunctional Family', p. 151, draws attention to the terrible impression the behaviour of the sons and their father would make on the villagers: 'Even if this shameful episode took place in private, it would only be a short time before the whole village knew what happened. Since nonconformity is seen as a threat, village gossip networks are very effective in spreading stories about those who break the rules'. According to Rohrbaugh, the village would quickly close ranks against the offending family, lest others should follow suit.

24. In Jewish enumeration, the command to honour one's parents is reckoned as the fifth commandment; in Christianity, it is often counted as the fourth.

25. See Bailey, *Poet and Peasant*, p. 168; Rohrbaugh, 'Dysfunctional Family', p. 151.

26. Bailey, *Poet and Peasant*, p. 168; Rohrbaugh, 'Dysfunctional Family', p. 151.

while he is still alive.[27] Rohrbaugh explains: 'In other words, the father who does not wait is a fool. He has given his place as head of the family to a son and thereby destroyed his own honour and authority'.[28]

The question of why the sons disdain their father so much that they would publicly humiliate him and his entire household, and why the father accepts such appalling conduct, is not answered in the parable, and is only cursorily discussed by most interpreters. Rohrbaugh explains that the parable is a kinship story about 'a generous, if somewhat erratic, father with his *two* rather difficult sons'.[29] D.O. Via opines that the parable begins with an apparently satisfactory home life—enough to draw the son back in the end—and that the father, if he has any faults, is over-indulgent and perhaps not solicitous enough of his older son's feelings.[30] In fact, for Via, the father of the parable 'points subsidiarily both to Jesus' historical conduct and to the nature of God'.[31] F.H. Borsch observes that the text of the parable does not even hint at the possibility that there was animosity between the son and the father, and speculates that the son's actions must have caused the father great pain.[32] C.A. Evans describes the son as ungrateful, sinful and degraded, with 'no concern for the well-being of his father (or family)'.[33] That is, commentators tend to assume that the father is over-indulgent, the younger son is spoiled and demanding, and the elder son is mean-spirited. An exception is J.D.M. Derrett, whose expertise in oriental law leads him to the conclusion that there was a serious rift between the father and the younger son: 'For a son to ask for a share while his father was in good health was a confession that the son could not live in that home'.[34]

A survivor of child sexual abuse would likely agree with Derrett, and guess that the younger son, and possibly the older brother, had been sexually molested by their father. Child sexual abuse inevitably arouses strong feelings of hatred and anger, which can finally be expressed only

27. *Baba Mezia*, 75b, cited by Rohrbaugh, 'Dysfunctional Family', p. 150 and Bailey, *Poet and Peasant*, p. 110.

28. Rohrbaugh, 'Dysfunctional Family', pp. 150-151.

29. Rohrbaugh, 'Dysfunctional Family', p. 143.

30. D.O. Via, *The Parables: Their Literary and Existential Dimension* (Philadelphia: Fortress, 1967), pp. 164, 172.

31. Via, *The Parables*, p. 173.

32. F.H. Borsch, *Many Things in Parables: Extravagant Stories of New Community* (Philadelphia: Fortress, 1988), p. 40.

33. C.A. Evans, *Luke* (NIBC; Peabody, Mass.: Hendrickson, 1990), p. 232.

34. Derrett, 'Law in the New Testament', pp. 105-106.

when the victim reaches an age when s/he can challenge the perpetrator.[35] Speaking of male victims,[36] M. Lew observes:

> Anger is an emotion that is reserved for those in power... He draws the logical conclusion that to be powerful, he must be angry. If only the powerful are allowed to be angry, he reasons, then only the angry can be powerful... In an attempt to counteract his feelings of vulnerability and impaired masculinity, the adult male survivor can end up feeling that his only protection lies in intimidating the world with a theatrical display of anger. This works, with varying degrees of success, in keeping potential abusers at bay. Unfortunately, it also keeps everyone else away, leaving the survivor angry...and isolated. This dramatization of anger seldom represents a pure emotion. It is more likely to be a protective mask, hiding what lies behind it (usually fear or sorrow).[37]

In ancient Mediterranean culture, asking for his share of the inheritance before his father's death would be a very effective way for a son to express hatred and anger in a way that would publicly shame the abuser without openly naming the offense. Whether or not the son/s would be consciously aware that their father had abused them is questionable, since many victims suppress their memories of incest for years.[38] Anger against the perpetrator may be stifled for a long time, finally erupting in distorted or displaced ways.[39]

What a boy or young man in a traditional Jewish household in antiquity would have made of the abuse if and when he was conscious of it is hard to say. While the Torah forbade homosexual relations between males (Lev. 20.13; 18.22),[40] there is no explicit prohibition of father–son incest or even of father–daughter incest.[41] In rabbinic legislation, the penalty of

---

35. E.S. Blume, *Secret Survivors: Uncovering Incest and Its After-Effects in Women* (New York: Ballantine, 1990), pp. 130-43.

36. Research on the prevalence of incest presents widely varying statistics, depending on various technical factors, and, especially, how incest is defined. Blume states (*Secret Survivors*, p. 27): 'estimates of female victims of incest range from 6% to 62%, while estimates for males vary from 3% to 31%'. Between 5% and 20% of perpetrators are estimated to be female' (pp. 29-30).

37. M. Lew, *Victims No Longer: Men Recovering from Incest and Any Other Sexual Child Abuse* (New York: Nevraumont Publishing Co., 1988), p. 73.

38. Lew, *Victims No Longer*, pp. Blume, *Secret Survivors*, pp. 80-83.

39. Blume, *Secret Survivors*, pp. 133-40.

40. See L.M. Epstein, *Sex Laws and Customs in Judaism* (New York: Ktav, 1967), pp. 135-38.

41. R. Westbrook notes that 'Undoubtedly, relations with a daughter were

death by stoning for homosexual activity did not apply to sex with a boy under the age of nine, since intercourse with a small child was not considered to be a sexual act under the law.[42] Since a high premium was placed on the virginity of daughters, it is possible that young sons would be targeted for incestuous relationships by fathers who did not want to damage their daughters' marriageability.[43] The kinds of confusion, shame, guilt, self-hatred and rage that would result from such relationships can only be imagined.

A survivor of incest would not be surprised that most interpreters of the parable 'side with the father' in supposing that the younger son is at fault. Victims of sexual child abuse are often discredited by authority figures. The most extreme example of this phenomenon is Freud's revision of his early 'trauma theory' that many of his patients' problems stemmed from being sexually abused by relatives as children, to the 'drive theory' that patients' supposed memories of incest are actually based on infantile sexual fantasies.[44] This theory obliges the therapist

> to regard everything patients tell about their childhood as fantasy and as their own desires projected onto the external world. Thus, in terms of the drive theory, parents do not actually abuse their children in order to fulfill their own needs but children supposedly fantasize this abuse, repressing their own aggressive and sexual desires ('instinctual drives') through the mechanism of projection as being directed against them from the outside.[45]

The tendency of family members, clergy and counsellors to deny or minimize the abuse or blame the victim is frequently reported by incest

---

prohibited, although this prohibition is missing from the biblical lists' ('Punishments and Crimes', *Anchor Bible Dictionary* [David Noel Freedman (ed.); New York: Doubleday, 1992], p. 549). Lev. 18.6-19 and Lev. 20.11-21 contain lists of prohibited relationships. For a feminist discussion of the Leviticus legislation on incest, see Manlowe, *Faith Born of Seduction,* pp. 61-62.

42. Epstein, *Sex Laws and Customs*, p. 136. However, such behaviour was subject to public flagellation (p. 136). Epstein does not specify whether both parties were beaten, or whether only the adult rapist was punished.

43. See Epstein, *Sex Laws and Customs,* p. 156, 164. Deuteronomy specifies that a bride found to be a non-virgin should be stoned (Deut. 23.19). The assumption is that the young woman has engaged in 'harlotry'; how many female victims of incest have suffered similar accusations in patriarchal societies that place a high premium on pre-marital virginity?

44. Miller, *Thou Shalt Not Be Aware*, pp. 3-4.

45. Miller, *Thou Shalt Not Be Aware*, p. 4. See also Manlowe, *Faith Born of Seduction*, pp. 11-13.

survivors. Dutch researchers A. Imbens and I. Jonker relate the case of Judith, a woman who had turned to her church for help:

> In her interview, Judith related how an assistant priest responded at the time: 'I realize that teenagers sometimes fantasize, but what you've told me is incredible. It's absolutely impossible that your father, who's done so much for the church, could do something like that. I mean, some teenagers tend to get carried away by their imaginations, but there's no way what you're telling me could be true. You've really got to get some help; this is out of hand. Your father does so much for the church. He would never do anything against the law'.[46]

On the basis of interviews with nineteen female incest survivors, researchers Imbens and Jonker found that the reactions of immediate family members and caring professionals ranged from 'a new rape [i.e., being raped by the confidant] to solidarity', and everything in between: 'We found disbelief and denial, minimization, blame, not recognizing the seriousness of the problem, no verbal response, and clumsy attempts to help (which were sometimes offensive)'.[47]

If the young man of the parable were conscious of having been abused, he would have had even less recourse against the perpetrator than twentieth-century women and men.[48] As a younger son in a patriarchal family system based on primogeniture, he would be entitled to two ninths of the estate, but would have been expected to stay at home and keep the land within the family.[49] Alienating his share of the property forever would be one of the most damaging blows to the family in the son's power.

---

46. A. Imbens and I. Jonker, *Christianity and Incest* (Minneapolis: Fortress, 1992), p. 277.

47. Imbens and Jonker, *Christianity and Incest*, pp. 143-44; see also pp. 144-152. The authors define incest as 'sexual abuse of children within the (extended) family. The term "sexual abuse within the extended family" refers to sexual contacts initiated by adults (father, stepfather, uncle, grandfather, a friend of the family, older brother), in which the wishes and feelings of the child with whom the acts are committed are not taken into account' (pp. 3-4). All the cases reported in this study were instances of father–daughter or brother–sister incest.

48. Although larger numbers of women suffer sexual abuse in childhood, there is a significant percentage of male victims. (Manlowe, *Faith Born of Seduction*, p. 10, quotes a figure of 38% for females and 10% for males within the patriarchal nuclear family; the statistic is based on a figure from the US Bureau of Justice.) While the majority of perpetrators are male, there are also women abusers. See also n. 36 above.

49. R.Q. Ford, *The Parables of Jesus: Recovering the Art of Listening* (Minneapolis: Fortress, 1997), p. 94; cf. Rohrbaugh, 'Dysfynctional Family', p. 152.

Rohrbaugh notes that previous interpreters have not taken enough notice of the fact that the father is 'suspect' because 'he gives in without protest or apparent necessity'.[50] An incest survivor might attribute the father's surprising passivity to the son's paradoxical sense of 'power' over the father. Some teen-aged survivors find strength in being able to threaten the perpetrator with exposure. Imbens and Jonker report that fifteen of the girls they interviewed were able to put an end to incestuous relationships themselves when they were between the ages of fifteen and twenty.[51] They tried to run away, asked for locks on their bedroom doors, found boyfriends:

> By this time, they are older and stronger; they have acquired more knowledge about and insight into their own situation through conversations with friends, or from books, radio, and television. Sometimes, talking with a girlfriend or family member gives that last encouraging push. Carol said, 'When I was about fifteen or sixteen I was better equipped to resist him. I started to realize that I had a certain power over him'. In six cases charges were brought against the offender, or the survivor threatened to bring charges, which resulted in the offender voluntarily committing himself to a clinic.[52]

However, resistance is not always effective, and perpetrators often refuse to accept a victim's attempt to end the incest, resorting to threats, psychological breakdowns, rages, scenes, bribes or punishments.[53]

The Runaway

Not only does the younger son ask for his share of the inheritance before his father's death, but he liquidates his share of the property immediately and leaves home (v. 13). Donahue explains that even if the younger son's request were legitimate, his subsequent behaviour is not:

> ...possession of his share did not give him rights to total disposal. He was allowed to invest the property and to use it to earn more income–an economic situation reflected in the parable of 'the Pounds' (Luke 19.11-27 = Matt. 25.14-30). He was forbidden, however, to jeopardize the capital. In a society with no benefits for the aged, the future of a parent was assured

---

50. Rohrbaugh, 'Dysfunctional Family', p. 151.
51. Imbens and Jonker, *Christianity and Incest*, p. 128.
52. Imbens and Jonker, *Christianity and Incest*, p. 128.
53. Imbens and Jonker, *Christianity and Incest*, p. 129.

only by retention of property within the family circle (cf. Jesus' criticism of corban [Mark 7.9-13], a gift of money to the temple rather than reserved for care of the parents). By dissipating the property, the younger son severs the bonds with his father, with his people and hence with God; he is no longer a son of his father and no longer a son of Abraham.[54]

Rohrbaugh points out that when the son sells off his portion of the land, the property is lost to the family forever, and the future of the family would be in jeopardy: 'no one would marry its sons or daughters, patrons would disappear, and the family would be excluded from the necessary economic and social relations'.[55] The youth further damages the family by moving away. The loss of a son would be an especially heavy blow to the mother, since sons are expected to stay at home to ensure her place in the family: 'Obviously he should maintain his father in his old age, but his presence means far more than that to his mother'.[56] Victims of paternal sexual abuse often blame their mothers more than their fathers,[57] even though many of the wives of abusers are sexually or physically abused by their husbands.[58] Contemporary women in this situation often feel that they have no way out, as J. Herman explains:

> Economically dependent, socially isolated, in poor health and encumbered by the care of many small children, these mothers were in no position to challenge their husbands' domination... No matter how badly they were treated, most simply saw no option other than submission... They conveyed to their daughters the belief that a woman is defenseless against a man, that marriage must be preserved at all costs, and that a wife's duty is to serve and endure.[59]

The mother of the runaway son would have even fewer resources for dealing with family abuse, or for protecting their children, than the women described by Herman. If the mother of this household fit the profile of the mother in an abusive family, her son's defection would make her position even less tenable.

54. J.R. Donahue, SJ, *The Gospel in Parable: Metaphor, Narrative, and Theology in the Synoptic Gospels* (Philadelphia: Fortress, 1988), p.154.
55. Rohrbaugh, 'Dysfunctional Family', p. 149.
56. Rohrbaugh, 'Dysfunctional Family', pp. 150-152.
57. Blume, *Secret Survivors*, pp. 137-138, 166-173.
58. Blume, *Secret Survivors*, pp. 165-166.
59. Judith Herman, *Father–Daughter Incest* (Cambridge, MA: Harvard University Press, 1987), no page cited, quoted in Blume, *Secret Survivors*, p. 170.

Teenage victims of incest often run away from home to escape the abuse.[60] Incest survivor[61] Sylvia Fraser remembers:

> for me the usual childhood reality was reversed. Inside my own house, among people I knew, was where danger lay. The familiar had proven to be treacherous, whereas the unfamiliar, the unknown, the foreign, still contained the seeds of hope.[62]

Tragically, teen runaways, especially those who have experienced the trauma of sexual abuse, are vulnerable to sexual exploitation, either through involvement in prostitution or in some other aspect of the sex trade (cf. the elder brother's accusation that his brother had been 'with prostitutes'; v. 30).[63] Runaways may seek to take control of their lives by utilizing their own sexuality:

> Raped and exploited in childhood, these survivors later take the reins of their own exploitation, deceiving themselves into believing that they now have control over their lives. Sometimes they merely become 'promiscuous', the label we use to describe women who are more sexual than we want them to be.[64]

Rohrbaugh interprets the reckless behaviour of the runaway as the often-repeated tragedy of dislocated peasants who 'blow all their money' when they immigrate to the city.[65] To a survivor of incest, the young man's flight to the city would 'make sense' as an attempt to escape his abuser,[66] and his 'abandoned living' (*zōn astōtōs*) might be interpreted as

60. Blume, *Secret Survivors*, pp. 179-180; R.N. Brock and S.B. Thistlethwaite, *Casting Stones: Prostitution and Liberation in Asia and the United States* (Minneapolis: Fortress, 1996), pp. 183-205.

61. Here, I use Manlowe's definition of victims and survivors: 'The term *victim* is used to identify the one who was sexually abused. The term *survivor* is used by those who prefer to see themselves as having survived sexual victimization' (*Faith Born of Seduction*, p. 4).

62. Fraser, *My Father's House*, p. 16.

63. Blume, *Secret Survivors*, pp. 180-182; Brock and Thistlethwaite, *Casting Stones*, 183-205.

64. Blume, *Secret Survivors*, p. 181.

65. Rohrbaugh, 'Dysfunctional Family', p. 153. The young man's taking a job as a swineherd indicates that he is in a city, since pigs were kept as urban livestock in antiquity; a swineherd would drive his herd into the forests and fields outside the town during the day, and return at night (E. Firmage, 'Zoology (Animal Profiles)', *Anchor Bible Dictionary* [D.N. Freedman (ed.); New York: Doubleday, 1992], p. 1130).

66. Imbens and Jonker cite the admiration for the child Jesus expressed by one of the incest survivors they interviewed, because he ran away from his parents in Lk.

the compulsive sexual activity of an incest victim:

> At worst, he may feel that the only person he can get close to is the one who is abusing him–and that the only possible intimacy is sexual... The abused child has no opportunity to learn to establish reasonable protective boundaries. Not having experienced safety, he cannot distinguish dangerous people and situations. He may throw himself into wildly perilous circumstances or, at the other extreme, refrain from daring any level of risk.[67]

The youth's 'attaching himself to' (v. 15) one of the townsmen once the money is gone would be consistent with this pattern of behaviour. The verb *kollaō* ('to glue together', 'to join together', 'to bind'), used in v. 15 to describe the youth's relationship to his new patron (*ekollēthē),* has the sense of 'to attach oneself closely to' when used with the dative of an object or person (*heni tōn politōn tēs chōras ekeinēs).*[68] However, interpreters of this parable have not previously noted the sexual overtones of this verb:

> we can see how *kollasthai* comes to be used for intimate association in the form of sexual intercourse. Thus we read in Mt. 19.5: *kollēthēsetai tē gynaiki autou.*[69]

The use of this verb suggests initial sexual contact, followed by rejection and degradation: 'Faced with the apparent choice between isolation and abuse, he may allow himself to be revictimized in order to be close to someone'.[70] For the young Jewish runaway, becoming 'attached to' a Gentile could be a way of expressing hostility to the ethnic group of his abuser;[71] ironically, his new patron further abuses him by requiring him to do a job disdained by both Jews and Gentiles.[72]

Interpreters often comment on the phrase *eis heauton de elthōn ephē* ('and coming to himself, he said...') that introduces the youth's decision to return home (v. 17). Via's existential-theological interpretation sees the phrase as suggesting 'a radical change in the self-understanding of the

2.41-51: 'Jesus stood up when he was twelve years old and left his parents. He stood up in the temple and started to preach. He went his own way, according to his own nature and his own spirit. I really identified very strongly with that' (*Christianity and Incest,* p. 40).

    67. Lew, *Victims No Longer,* p. 100.
    68. K.L. Schmidt, '*kollaō perikollaō*', *TDNT* III, p. 822.
    69. Schmidt, '*kollaō perikollaō*', p. 822.
    70. Lew, *Victims No Longer,* p. 100.
    71. Blume, *Secret Survivors,* p. ii.
    72. Firmage, 'Zoology', p. 1130.

prodigal... His coming to himself suggests that natural man [*sic*] can be aware of guilt and of the need for the restoration of fellowship with God, but he understands this in terms of law'.[73] The idea that this inner dialogue signifies a life-changing moment of repentance is commonplace in Christian interpretation.[74] However, Scott observes that the primary motivation for the son's decision to return home is his empty stomach, not moral repentance.[75]

On one level, the young man's dialogue with himself can be interpreted simply as a literary device found in other Lucan parables where the central characters 'speak to themselves' (Lk. 12.19; 16.3). However, an incest survivor might point out that abused children often block their memories of incest by some form of dissociative psychological mechanism:

> Many incest survivors refer to this separation as 'splitting'... I have often heard dissociation described as an out-of-body experience: 'I left my body and floated up to the ceiling', or, more simply, 'I could just feel myself slipping out of my body; therefore, it wasn't happening to me any more'. At the time of the trauma, many survivors make a conscious effort to separate from what was happening to their bodies.[76]

'Splitting' may result in a continuum of manifestations 'from a simple blocking trauma to fully developed multiple-personality disorder'.[77] The starving young man's frantic self-questioning (vv. 17-18) may be an expression of the 'craziness' felt by many abuse survivors;[78] but it can also be interpreted as a coping strategy. Therapist E.S. Blume describes an 'inner guide' that she has seen in many of her clients:

> The inner guide is not some other-world spirit or 'past life' guide, but an aspect of the incest survivor herself. This internal caretaker ensures that no matter how complicated or painful the incest survivor's outer life becomes, she protects herself enough to 'keep on keepin' on'.[79]

From this perspective, the son's plan to return home and ask to be hired as a paid servant (vv. 18-19) is not an act of humility or repentance, but a way of being fed while remaining at a remove from his father.

---

73. Via, *The Parables*, p. 173.
74. As noted by Rohrbaugh, 'Dysfunctional Family', p. 155.
75. Scott, *Hear Then the Parable*, p. 116.
76. Blume, *Secret Survivors*, pp. 83-84.
77. Blume, *Secret Survivors*, p. 84.
78. Blume, *Secret Survivors*, pp. 75-94.
79. Blume, *Secret Survivors*, p. 80.

Another feature of the parable—the eating motif—takes on new significance if the story is interpreted from the perspective of an incest survivor. Via notes the prominence of eating imagery throughout the story.[80] The land to which the prodigal emigrates suffers from a famine (v. 14); the youth is so hungry that he craves the carob-pods fed to the pigs, 'but no one gave him anything' (v. 15); the father's paid servants have plenty of bread while the son dies of hunger (v. 16); the father 'kills the fatted calf' for the returned son and holds a feast (v. 14); the elder son complains when he finds out that his father has put on a banquet for the prodigal (v. 27, 30), but has never given him as much as a kid (v. 29). Eating disorders and a preoccupation with food are often an outcome of child sexual abuse:

> The contemporary survivor's behavior with food reveals her desire to receive that which she felt was missing in her relationship to her parents, to God, and to herself. She both repairs and expresses her damaged self through her food conduct–overeating, binge-purging, chronic appetite policing, or not eating…what the survivor does with food corresponds to her history of being violated. She *enacts* the violence against her as she binges.[81]

The young man's 'sin' against heaven/his father (v. 18, 21)—namely, his father's sin against *him*—is mirrored in his starvation; his father's abusive 'love' is expressed in feasting. The young man's wish for the modest 'bread' of a 'hired servant' (v. 16) is a faint hope for survival.[82]

The Return

> She could tell us how her father used her sense of guilt to force her into silence, but had great difficulty telling us how she felt about it. I asked her, 'Can you name any passages from the Bible that made an impression on you, passages you experienced as oppressive or even passages you found inspiring?' Her reaction was, 'My father often told the story of the prodigal son. That's how he saw himself'.[83]

Imbens and Jonker do not specify how the speaker, Joan, who had been physically and sexually abused by her father, interpreted his references to

---

80. Via, *The Parables*, p. 165.

81. Manlowe, *Faith Born of Seduction*, pp. 85-86. On eating disorders in abuse survivors, including anorexia, bulimia, and compulsive over-eating, see also: Blume, *Secret Survivors*, pp. 151-156; Lew, *Victims No Longer*, pp. 103, 141-146.

82. Cf. Ford, *Parables of Jesus*, p. 104.

83. Imbens and Jonker, *Christianity and Incest*, p. 42.

the parable. Did he see himself as the prodigal in need of forgiveness by God, or, more likely, did he regard himself as the wronged patriarch of the parable, who loves and forgives his ungrateful child, always ready to welcome her home and resume their relationship? Perhaps, like some perpetrators, he bribed his victim with candy and treats, and regarded his sexual advances as signs of love (cf. Lk. 15.20b, 22), as Fraser's memoir illustrates:

> My daddy gives me candies. My daddy gives me chocolate-chip cookies. Of all the people in the world, I'm my daddy's favorite. *My daddy and I...*[84]

Fathers who perpetrate incest may be 'pillars of the community', who go to church regularly and appear to maintain high moral standards:

> Twice every Sunday my family drives to St. James' United Church in my daddy's secondhand Ford-with-a-running-board. I wear white stockings and carry my Dionne Quintuplet handkerchief with a nickel tied in one corner. That is for the collection. My father and three other gentlemen carry the silver plates tramp tramp tramp up to the altar where Reverend Thwaite blesses them, 'Thank you, Fatherrr, forrr yourrr bountiful blessings'. He means God.[85]

Blume notes that incest may take place within 'model families', and that abusive fathers are often respected teachers or community leaders.[86] Families in which the father is a perpetrator are usually rigidly patriarchal, 'characterized by a power imbalance wherein a father wields absolute authority over a relatively powerless wife and children'.[87] Paternal power is maintained through threats and fear, and other family members collude to keep their secret 'behind closed doors'. Other perpetrators may be perceived as weak and ineffectual by their peers, but maintain the status of 'the man of the house' within the family, where patriarchal privilege is invoked to dominate the weaker members of the household psychologically and sexually.[88] In either case, the common denominator is the

---

84. Fraser, *My Father's House*, p. 5.
85. Fraser, *My Father's House*, p. 4.
86. Blume, *Secret Survivors*, p. 34.
87. Blume, *Secret Survivors*, p. 34.
88. Blume, *Secret Survivors*, pp. 35-36. C.R. Bohn notes that 'incestuous fathers are often surprised to learn that they have broken the law since they believe that sexual access to their children is their right. One legal scholar has noted that sexual abuse is actually not prohibited by law, merely regulated. Since only violence that involved another man's property is prohibited, incest and other forms of domestic violence are often considered within acceptable norms' ('Dominion to Rule', in J.C. Brown and

'Christian' norm of the patriarchal family, 'the father's house', where man's authority over women and children is a given.[89] In identifying with the father of the parable, perhaps Joan's father was asserting his status as authoritarian patriarch with unquestioned rights over his family. Perhaps this perpetrator interpreted the parable to mean that Joan should 'return' to him and submit like a dutiful child. Otherwise, she would be 'lost' to him, like the son in the parable (Lk. 15.24, 32).

To an incest survivor, the young man's return home would be ominous, as would the father's elation at his return. Several commentators have noted that the father's over-enthusiastic reception of his son would have been unworthy of the head of a respectable family in antiquity:

> As Bailey has pointed out, in the Mediterranean world, *old men do not run*. It is not only shameful (ankles show), it also indicates lack of control. They *certainly* do not run to meet or welcome anyone, and especially not their children.[90]

Rohrbaugh speculates that the father makes such a public display of welcoming his son in order to repair the family's damaged status in the village.[91] If Rohrbaugh is correct, the implication is that the father's delight at the son's return is as much motivated by self-interest as by compassion; the show of affection, dressing the son in fine clothing, the banquet, are all ways of impressing the village, with the hope that the family will once again be accepted as 'respectable', i.e., as a family where the patriarch is in control.[92] It is significant that, from the father's perspective, the runaway son has been not just 'lost' but 'dead' (vv. 24, 32). As psychiatrist Alice Miller observes: 'the restoration of harmony is being celebrated here only at the price of the son's acquiescence in his father's definition of everything that separated his son from him as "death" '.[93]

C.R. Bohn [eds., *Christianity, Patriarchy, and Abuse: A Feminist Critique* [New York: Pilgrim Press, 1989], p. 109).

89. See Bohn, 'Dominion to Rule', pp. 105-116; R.R. Ruether, 'The Western Religious Tradition and Violence Against Women in the Home', in Brown and Bohn, *Christianity, Patriarchy and Abuse*, pp. 31-41; and S.A. Redmond, 'Christian "Virtues" and Recovery from Child Sexual Abuse', in Brown and Bohn, *Christianity, Patriarchy and Abuse*, pp.70-88.

90. Rohrbaugh, 'Dysfunctional Family', p. 156, citing Bailey, *Poet and Peasant*, pp. 180-82.

91. Rohrbaugh, 'Dysfunctional Family', p. 157.

92. Rohrbaugh, 'Dysfunctional Family', pp. 157-58.

93. Miller, *Thou Shalt Not Be Aware*, p. 204.

The son's plan to ask for a relatively 'safe' place in his father's household as a hired servant is quickly thwarted by his father, who interrupts the young man's rehearsed speech:

> I shall get up and go to my father and I will say, 'Father, I have sinned against heaven and before you. I am no longer worthy to be called your son. *Make me one of your paid servants'* (vv. 18-19).

> And the son said to him, 'Father I have sinned against heaven and before you, and I am no longer worthy to be called your son...' *But the father said to his slave, 'Quickly* bring out the best clothing and put it on him, and put a ring on his finger and sandals on his feet' (vv. 21-22).

From this point on, the son is silenced, absorbed back into the paternal household.

One of the few interpreters who sees the son's return and the father's welcome as unwholesome is clinical psychologist R.Q. Ford.[94] Ford interprets the son's flight as an attempt to gain adult autonomy, and his irresponsible use of the inheritance as an unconscious desire to return to a state of childish dependency: 'the son has unconsciously striven to reach this point; he has steadily and systematically destroyed every resource other than his father'.[95] The father, in turn, is smothering and 'all-giving', promoting sustenance and childlike obedience, but not autonomy: 'The father is not going to focus on what the son wants; the father will persist in using his son for his own needs'.[96]

From the perspective of an abused child, the return to the father's house holds the danger that the pattern of abuse will be repeated. The father's emotional reaction to the sight of his son, his embrace and tender kisses can be interpreted as a nurturing, 'maternal' response,[97] but also as a sexualized response (cf. Song 1.2; 8.1; 2.6; 8.3). In the novel *The Sweet Hereafter*, the teenage daughter, Nichole, who has been molested by her father since she was small, returns, disabled, from the hospital to find that her father has completely refurbished her room, a sign of his 'fatherly' love:

> My room. Daddy had walled most of it in an installed baseboard heating units, had even built a small closet in one corner, and had carpeted it nicely. One whole wall was still windows, and I could see the yard and the woods

94. Ford, *Parables of Jesus,* pp.90-106.
95. Ford, *Parables of Jesus*, pp. 102-103.
96. Ford, *Parables of Jesus*, p. 106.
97. Ford, *Parables of Jesus*, p. 105; Scott, *Hear Then The Parable*, p. 117.

> beyond. Mom had made white chintz curtains. There was a single bed and a
> new dresser and a worktable Daddy'd made from a door…there was a new
> picture of Jesus that I knew Mom had put up; she'd no doubt left the old
> one upstairs to keep track of Jennie.[98]

Nichole's reaction is to ask for a lock on the door.[99] Victims of incest are
vulnerable to repeated abuse in adulthood, by others or by the perpetrator.
Manlowe cites the case of a female survivor, Haddock, who 'claimed that
if her father wanted her to have sex with him today, she could not say no:
"I couldn't refuse him today if he made a pass at me because of the kind of
power he still holds over me"'.[100] A male incest survivor, Philip, aged
thirty-nine, recalls hopefully arranging a meeting with his father:

> I called out to him and was immediately launched into a frenzy of broken
> French/English and tears. He rushed to his car to get his camera and insisted
> that a passerby take a picture of us together. He was laughing, crying and
> quite out of control. I became outwardly more and more reserved, while
> inwardly overwhelmed and frightened.[101]

Shortly afterward, the father tried to force his son to have oral sex:
'Grabbing the back of my neck and twisting it sharply downward toward
him, he said he thought I called because I wanted to get together again to
do it'.[102] What message would Haddock or Philip derive from the account
of the father's warm reception of the 'prodigal' son? Perhaps they would
agree with Ford's conclusion that neither the father nor the son will
change for the better: 'The son will continue with devotion to agree to
self-destruction. The father will continue to smile down on the inexpres-
sible loneliness of a son who must forever remain his child'.[103]

The Elder Brother

In his time and culture, the older brother's angry reaction to the younger's
return is more appropriate than the father's: the younger man has let down
his family by selling their land, and disgraced them in the eyes of their
community. A survivor of incest might see the jealousy of the elder
brother as the reaction of a sibling in a family where the father had a

98. R. Banks, *The Sweet Hereafter* (San Francisco: HarperCollins, 1991), p. 164.
99. Banks, *The Sweet Hereafter*, p. 165.
100. Manlowe, *Faith Born of Seduction*, p. 41.
101. Lew, *Victims No Longer*, p. 118.
102. Lew, *Victims No Longer*, p. 118.
103. Ford, *Parables of Jesus*, p. 106.

'special', 'secret' relationship with one child, where the younger son was singled out as a 'favourite':

> *Now when daddy plays with me I keep my eyes tightly scrunched so I can't see. I don't want his pennies or his candies or his cookies. Mostly I leave them by the pillow while he swallows me. I hold my breath to keep from crying because daddy won't love me love me love me.*[104]

While some perpetrators abuse more than one child, others choose one for a 'love' relationship. Blume observes that

> Often incest comes with special favors. The siblings of a child victim of incest might endure beatings that she is spared. Or she might receive gifts that are better than those given her siblings.[105]

Like the younger son, the elder is silenced by his father, who addresses him not as the respected heir but as his 'child' (*teknon*, v. 31a). Although the inheritance has already been divided (v. 12), the father asserts that all that is his (the father's) is the older son's. The son remains an heir to a depleted estate, answerable to his father, and burdened for life with a penniless younger brother, who, the father reminds him, is his—the elder brother's—responsibility (v. 32). The *status quo* is preserved, the family's 'status' in the community is restored in the eyes of the celebrating villagers (vv. 24-25); the 'dysfunctional' family is back under the control of the father. 'Joan's' abusive father, who saw himself as the father of the parable, would approve. From the perspective of an incest survivor, the parable offers scant hope for healing of the abusive patterns that prompted the younger son to leave in the first place.

Is A Liberating Interpretation Possible?

This chapter opened with a quotation from Sylvia Fraser, an incest survivor, on the nature of fairy tales, which, she suggests, are powerful because 'they spell out our hidden desires and our hopeful solutions'. Their characters, kings, queens, witches, ogres represent our parents 'with their ultimate power to nurture or destroy us'.[106] Fraser, as a pretty blond-haired little girl, was often seen as a fairy-tale princess by the grownups in her life, but grew up feeling that she was really 'Satan's Child'.[107] This

---

104. Fraser, *My Father's House*, p. 11. The italics are Fraser's.
105. Blume, *Secret Survivors*, p. 111.
106. Fraser, *My Father's House*, p. 153.
107. Fraser, *My Father's House*, pp. 211-217.

parable, with its father and two sons, is noted for its evocation of an ancient folktale motif from many biblical stories where younger sons prevail over elder brothers, as in the stories of Cain and Abel, Ishmael and Isaac, Jacob and Esau, Joseph and his ten older brothers, Jesse's youngest son David.[108] It is also widely held to be the most interpreted and best beloved of the parables of Jesus.[109] Donahue notes of the parable that

> Its drama has enchanted believer and nonbeliever. It has been a subject for great painters (Dürer/Rembrandt), dramatists (Tudor dramatists, Gascoigne), choreographers (Balanchine), musicians (Prokofiev, Britten), novelists (Gide), and philosophers (Nietzsche). A variety of approaches—existentialist, Jungian, Freudian, structuralist—have vied to enrich its meaning.[110]

The story has not only been elaborated by theologians and artists, but it finds frequent expression in popular culture, as this quotation from M. Lew suggests:

> Recently, I watched a program of animated cartoons that were made in the 1940s and 1950s. The themes of these cartoons were surprisingly similar. A youngster (human or animal) strayed from the protection of home and family. In the course of his explorations, he found himself in danger (from the forces of nature or evildoers) only to be rescued at the last minute. The rescuer was usually the youngster's mother, although sometimes the father, both parents, another relative, or family pet played a part. The information conveyed to the child viewing the film was strong and unequivocal: Safety is with the family. Obey the rules. Do what your parents tell you. Stay with what is familiar.[111]

In fact, as Lew's words suggest, the parable differs decisively from the Old Testament tales in that rather than making his way in the world by his wits, skill or virtue, the younger son only 'wins' when he *fails* in his bid for independence, and humbly returns to his father's house, admitting that he has 'sinned' (vv. 18, 21).

As stated earlier, I do not offer this interpretation of the parable of the prodigal son as the 'only' one or the 'right' one. Families sometimes *do* suffer from recalcitrant children, and longsuffering parents must sometimes muster great reserves of compassion and forgiveness to maintain family harmony. No doubt this parable has encouraged estranged children

---

108. Ford, *Parables of Jesus*, p. 134; Perkins, *Hearing the Parables*, 53-54.

109. Donahue, *The Gospel in Parable*, pp. 151-152; Rohrbaugh, 'Dysfunctional Family', pp. 142 n. 1.

110. Donahue, *The Gospel in Parable*, pp. 151-152.

111. Lew, *Victims No Longer*, p. 31.

to re-establish contact with their parents, and parents to accept peace offerings from their children. In families where abuse is not an issue, these behaviours may be healthy and constructive. However, experts on child sexual abuse warn that 'forgiveness' can be a trap for survivors. Children who have been abused often mistakenly believe that *they* are at fault, and are the ones who must be 'forgiven'.[112] Well-meaning advisors may encourage the survivor to 'forgive' an unrepentant perpetrator—a step which should only be taken if the survivor *wants to*, and then only if the perpetrator has genuinely changed.[113] Here, the voices of two survivors, both of whom cite the evangelist's gloss on the parables of Lk. 15 (vv. 7, 10), are instructive:

> The church is for sinners and criminals, not for little girls doing their very best. 'The angels rejoice for that one sinner who repents in the last minutes of his life...[more than for] the ninety-nine who were good their entire lives. So there'll be more rejoicing for him up in heaven than for me when I get there?' (Margaret). The offender knows that too. After first trying to deny everything, he says: 'I have sinned, but that doesn't matter because my redeemer will grant me forgiveness' (Ellen). When she runs away from home or breaks the taboo on speaking out, the offender is consoled. The minister visits him. The prison chaplain teaches him to pray. The sexologist and the psychiatrist nod sympathetically and believe his pathetic story: He is sorry, he will never do it again; his feelings of love just got out of hand, or his daughter seduced him; he had problems at work, or with alcohol abuse.[114]

On this interpretation, even when the perpetrator is exposed as an abuser, he (or she) is welcomed by the 'heavenly father' with open arms. To explain to these women that they simply don't 'understand' God, or the bible, or the parable in the 'right' way–that the father of the parable is not like their fathers, but good, like God, and that the son is really a sinner and not a victim–would simply be to reinforce their victimization.[115]

My purpose in offering this interpretation is not to denigrate one of the most beloved parables in the Christian bible, or to suggest that it be removed from the biblical canon. However, this chapter may illustrate in a

---

112. Manlowe, *Faith Born of Seduction*, p. 65.

113. Manlowe, *Faith Born of Seduction*, p. 66.

114. Manlowe, *Faith Born of Seduction*, p. 163.

115. Imbens and Jonker, *Christianity and Incest*, p. 279, report that incest victims are often told by pastors that they don't understand the 'real' nature of the church, God, and the church's teachings, which, in their experience, have discounted them and protected their abusers.

graphic way how the identity and experience of readers can radically
affect how such a text is interpreted, and that some readers might *never* be
able to see this text, whereas others like it, as liberating or life-giving. As
J. Schaberg remarks, for feminist readers the bible is fraught with internal
contradictions, oppressive and liberating traditions (and aspects of
traditions); the ability to decide on what is the 'true word of God' resides
in women's—that is, human–experience.[116] It is in this spirit that I offer an
alternative parable—or more accurately, 'exemplary story'[117]–loosely
based on Sylvia Fraser's autobiographical novel, *My Father's House: A
Memoir of Incest and Healing*:

> A certain young woman ran away from her father's house to a new city.
> She went to college, married, divorced. She became successful, and many
> people knew her name. But she was full of sadness, anger and shame, and
> she didn't know why. Sometimes she starved herself, sometimes she ate too
> much, to punish herself for the pain and emptiness she felt inside.
>
> One day, she came to herself and remembered that her father had abused
> her. She learned to believe these memories. She realized that she had no
> reason to be ashamed, and that her father had sinned against her! The evil
> spell that had possessed her was broken, and now she could be free.
>
> When her father died, she returned to the house that had been his. She told
> her mother what her father had done to her. Her mother believed her, and
> apologized for pretending not to see, for not protecting her. She tenderly
> embraced her daughter, weeping, and from that day on, the daughter and
> her mother became closer.
>
> I tell you, the angels of Godde rejoice more over one innocent person who
> survives than over the repentance of the sinners who have abused them!

116. J. Schaberg, *The Illegitimacy of Jesus: A Feminist Theological Interpretation of the Infancy Narratives* (San Francisco: Harper & Row, 1987), p. 8.

117. The exemplary story is a subgenre of the parable, and is defined as a specific case that illustrates a general principle (M. Boucher, *The Parables* [Wilmington: Michael Glazier, 1981], p. 20). In this case, the story of the girl serves as an example of survival after a childhood marred by incest.

II

PARABLES OF WOMEN'S WORK

PATCHED GARMENTS AND RUINED WINE: WHOSE FOLLY?
(MK 2.21-22; MT. 9.16-17; LK. 5.36-39)

Pheme Perkins

Introduction

The sayings pair about the folly of patching an old garment with unshrunk cloth or putting new wine in old skins served to confirm Jesus' words concerning piety, discipleship and fasting in the synoptic tradition (Mk 2.21-22; Mt. 9.16-17; Lk. 5.36-39). Luke's variant makes the application explicit by labeling the response a 'parable' (v. 36a).[1] However, Luke appears to subvert the tenor of the sayings pair by adding a third saying in which a taste of aged wine stifles any desire for the new (v. 39). The *Gospel of Thomas* 47 provides evidence for a different configuration of sayings in which all three, drinking vintage wine, pouring new wine into old skins, and patching garments, have no connection with the fasting controversy. Instead they are linked to sayings about the impossibility of serving two masters (Lk. 16.13; Mt. 6.24). *Gospel of Thomas* also shifts the order of the set so that the aversion to new wine created by drinking the vintage leads off the group, followed by the need to match wine and skins. Patching the garment brings up the rear in what appears an incoherent variant, putting an old patch on a new garment. Even commentators who presume that *Gos. Thom.* 47b represents a more primitive stage of tradition than the synoptics, admit that this saying has botched the image.[2]

---

1. A common stylistic insertion in Luke's gospel (12.16; 14.7; 15.3; 18.9; 20.9, 19; J.A. Fitzmyer, *The Gospel According to Luke I-IX* [Anchor Bible 28; New York: Doubleday, 1981], p. 599).

2. S.J. Patterson, *The Gospel of Thomas and Jesus* (Sonoma, CA: Polebridge, 1993), p. 42; earlier treatments of the sayings group used agreement of Matthew and Luke against Mark in defense of complex theories of synoptic relationships (e.g., P. Rolland, 'Les prédécesseurs des Mc. II,18-22 et parallèles', *Révue Biblique* 89 [1982], pp. 370-405).

If one rejects the assumption that *Gos. Thom.* is prior to Luke,[3] then patching a new garment may be an attempt to fix the absurdity of Luke's variant, cutting up a new garment in order to patch an old one (Lk. 5.36).[4] Similar confusion attends the saying about new wine and wineskins. Mark adds an explanatory, 'rather new wine into new wineskins', at the end of verse 22.[5] The clause is likely correct in its comment on what people do, but not for the reason implied by the image of bursting skins in the saying. Wine was not fermented in skins, but in ceramic or wood containers.[6] The process which might cause a skin to burst would have been completed before 'new wine' was stored in other containers.[7] But there is a way to spoil 'new wine': by placing it in old containers, using containers which contaminate the wine with the flavor of their previous contents or material used to make them leakproof. Wine from vessels treated with wax soured. Those which once held vinegar were said to be less harmful than those that had contained sweet wine or mead.[8] This commonsense observation emerges in Mark's 'and the wine is destroyed', a loss that is quite

---

3.   G.J. Riley ('The Influence of Thomas Christianity on Luke 12.14 and 5.39', *Harvard Theological Review* 88 [1995], pp. 229-35) claims to demonstrate the influence of Thomas tradition on Luke. His argument relies on the dissonance between Lk. 5.39 and Lk. 5.36-38. He is forced to conclude that the patent absurdity of the patch saying in *Gos. Thom.* 47 is irrelevant to the reader, who is to take the whole series in *Gos. Thom.* as an affirmation of the value of the old. Riley considers this variant as 'humorous overstatement' (p. 234).

4.   *Gos. Thom.* may not derived from Luke directly, since its version of the drinking vintage wine saying omits the evangelist's explanatory phrase, 'for he says the old is good' (J. Dupont, 'Vin vieux, vin nouveau (Luc 5,35)', *CBQ* 25 [1963], pp. 295-98).

5.   R.A. Guelich, *Mark 1-8.26* (Word Biblical Commentary 34A; Dallas: Word, 1989), p. 114. The evangelist probably received the sayings about the cloak and the wine as a pair and edited them to emphasize the new teaching of Jesus (Mk 1.27; p. 115).

6.   As recognized by commentators on Job 32.19, who emend the unvented wineskin, likely to burst, to an unvented wine jar. The metaphor of the speaker's bursting belly has been transferred to the wine container, thus leading to the substitution of skins for the jars in which wine would have been fermented (see J.E. Harley, *The Book of Job* [NICOT; Grand Rapids: Eerdmans, 1988], p. 432 n. 15).

7.   See the discussions of wine-making in J.W. Humphrey, J.P. Oleson and A. N. Sherwood, *Greek and Roman Technology: A Sourcebook* (London and New York: Routledge, 1998), pp. 156-57 and L. Adkins and R.A. Adkins, *A Handbook to Life in Ancient Rome* (New York: Oxford University Press, 1994), p. 326.

8.   Humphrey, *Greek and Roman Technology*, p. 157.

independent of any tearing on the part of the skins. To return the saying to the 'tearing' which the evangelist takes as the key link between the cloak and wineskins, Mark tacks on 'and the skins'.

Matthew smooths over the awkwardness of Mark's formulation with a simple, 'they are destroyed' and then adds to the phrase about using new skins, 'and both are preserved'.[9] Luke remains closer to Mark's wording. The new wine tears the skins. Luke substitutes the verb *ekchythēsetai* ('it is poured out') for *apollytai* ('it is destroyed') and uses the latter with the skins as subject.[10] *Gos. Thom.* 47 has symmetrical sayings in which the mismatch between old and new creates the difficulty.[11] New wine tears old skins.[12] Old wine ruins new skins. But does it? Only on the presumption that the new skins were to be used for new wine at some future point. The alterations exhibited in the variants suggest that none of the sayings in this group represents an established proverb in the oral tradition. Nor was the referent of the sayings clear to the evangelist. Each clarification or reformulation generates new difficulties.

Most interpretations depend upon the synoptic context of these sayings to provide a referent for the 'old' in a Jewish piety that led people to reject the 'new' discipleship initiated by Jesus.[13] Some scholars have suggested that there is no authentic Jesus tradition behind this group of sayings.[14]

9.   C.E. Carlston, *The Parables of the Triple Tradition* (Philadelphia: Fortress, 1975), p.15; D.A. Hagner, *Matthew 1-13* (Word Biblical Commentary 33A; Dallas: Word, 1993), p. 242.

10.   Effectively transferring the emphasis on what is lost from the wine to the skins, much as Matthew has done (so J. Nolland, *Luke 1-9.20* [Word Biblical Commentary 35A; Dallas: Word, 1989], p. 249).

11.   Riley ('Influence', pp. 233-34) argues that all the sayings in *Gos. Thom.* advocate the superiority of the old over the new.

12.   In Coptic, the torn skins (*nnoupōh*) and the tear (*oupōh*) in the new garment echo each other. The sayings might have been reformulated in the translation.

13.   Hagner (*Matthew*, p. 244) interprets 'new wine' as obedience to Jesus' interpretation of the Torah. That reading attaches to Matthew's remark that both wine and skins are preserved. W.D. Davies and D.C. Allison (*The Gospel According to St. Matthew* [Vol 2: VIII-XVIII ICC; Edinburgh: T. & T. Clark, 1991], p. 115) see Matthew as a modification of Mark's view that the sayings describe an end to the pious practices of Jesus' opponents. Rather, Matthew wishes to affirm that elements of the old can be saved. Dupont ('Vin', pp. 287-292) traces the history of applying the one who drinks vintage wine, first to the disciples of Jesus and later to the Pharisees.

14.   For example, Carlston, *Triple Tradition*, p. 128. Carlston argues that there is no coherence between the 'new' in-breaking of God's reign found in authentic parables of Jesus and the old/new dichotomy in these sayings.

They should be treated as secular maxims that have been reformulated by each author. Others agree that the original application of the sayings in the teaching of Jesus cannot be recovered from the tradition as we have it, but assume that there must have been such.[15]

Are these sayings proverbs familiar to Jesus' audience? Their instability suggests not. A negative judgment on new wine in contrast to vintage appears in Sir. 9.10. A possible metaphor of unvented, fermenting wine bursting a new wineskin is found in Job 32.19. In the latter, unvented fermentation can burst the new skin. The author presumes that new wine will be put in fresh containers as a matter of course. So wine images may be common enough for a speaker to generate maxims that sound like proverbs.[16] Horace's epistles contain several such sayings which appear to be the poet's own formulations. 'When a jar is unclean whatever you fill it with soon goes sour', or the variant, 'A jar retains for years the smell with which it was tinged when new'.[17] Or a passage sometimes cited as a parallel to Lk. 5.39 in which the poet pleads with the emperor on behalf of his poetry, 'If poems like wine improve with age, will somebody tell me how old a page has to be before it acquires value?'[18] Though the last may be easily seen as a request for patronage, the jar sayings lack further meaning until they are applied in a particular situation.

However, Horace's maxims invoke details of ordinary experience, as does Lk. 5.39. Jesus' sayings about patched garments and spoiled wine or burst wineskins do not fit everyday experience. Their awkwardness raises a methodological question concerning the parables and maxims of Jesus.

---

15. For example, Davies and Allison, *Matthew*, pp. 115-17. A. Kee ('The Old Coat and the New Wine: A Parable of Repentance', *NovT* 12 [1970], pp. 13-21) rightly insists that scholars drop incompatibility as the assumed meaning and attempt to situate the sayings within the teaching of Jesus. Since the danger of loss is evident in both sayings, he proposes treating the sayings as parables of crisis, a summons to decisive action in view of the imminent coming of the Kingdom (pp. 19-20). However, as they stand, these sayings do not depict decisive actions, but patently foolish ones.

16. Aristotle instructed rhetoricians to produce maxims that had the appearance of proverbs as a means of persuasion (*Rhetoric* ii.21; iii.17). Since proverbs carry the authority of ancient witnesses (*Rhetoric* I.15), such maxims could substitute for formal proof. Given the authority of proverbs in oral cultures, use of the form to create proverb-like maxims would have been a common method of impressing an audience or winning a contested point.

17. Horace, *Epistles* 1.2 lines 54-70.

18. Horace, *Epistles* 2.1 lines 34-35. For other related variants in classical authors, see Dupont ('Vin', p. 286 n. 2).

Are they, in fact, derived from astute observation of ordinary life among Galilean peasants? In which case, variants of the sayings that best reflect what archaeology and social history can tell us about that life should be privileged over the obvious misfits in the variants.[19] If the parables of Jesus involve elements of imaginative or poetic fictionalizing in order to introduce a reality that is not ordinary or commonsense, then the hermeneutical principle of matching parable with social world should not be employed.[20] The task is even more difficult when the 'parables' in question take the form of aphorisms or maxims which by design represent actions that no one would engage in. Lk. 5.39 remains an oddity, since its 'no one' behaves as anticipated, not as the extraordinary fool presumed in the previous pair of sayings. Nor do we have any secure indicators for the gender of persons engaged in mending garments or storing wine. Again, Lk. 5.39 is an exception. Its subject is marked as both male and of a privileged social class by the mere fact of drinking and appreciating vintage wine.[21]

Who Is the Fool? A Woman or the Poor?

Turning to the paired sayings, the mismatch assumes actions which lead to ruin rather than preservation.[22] The 'no one' of the introduction suggests a formal comparison to proverbs about the foolish or the simple. Wisdom

---

19. J.S. Kloppenborg ('Some Comments on the Parable of the Tenants [Mk. 12.1-12; *Gos. Thom.* 65] in the Light of Papyrus Vineyard Leases', paper delivered at the Society of Biblical Literature Annual Meeting 1999; Abstract in *AAR/SBL Abstracts Annual Meeting 1999*, Boston MA, p. 395) used fidelity to documented lease agreements as an argument for the priority of *Gos. Thom.* 65 over Mk 12.1-12. If the parable was not formulated to correspond with agricultural practices, then the correspondence could have been an adjustment of an odd set of circumstances to the familiar by later tradition.

20. See the discussion of parables as 'poetic fictions' in C.W. Hedrick (*Parables as Poetic Fictions: The Creative Voice of Jesus* [Peabody: Hendrickson, 1994], pp. 27-34). Hedrick argues that interpreters should not jump outside the parables as narratives to the world to which they are supposed to refer. Rather, parables work on the imagination of persons who enter the world as they construe it.

21. See Horace's warning to a friend to bring good wine since that to be served by the host is of mediocre quality (*Epistles* 1.5 lines 3-5).

22. So Kee observes, 'From this re-reading of the parable one point emerges. Not old versus new, but the *danger of loss*... The point of the parable is that through thoughtless and ill-considered action there is danger of loss' ('Old Coat', p. 19).

belongs to those who manage a craft, or in the case of women, a household, well.[23] Though proverb collections often address elite males in the service of the court, they also include elements of folk wisdom. The practical wisdom and probity of the poor or women can be invoked as a rebuke to the presumptions of an elite audience.[24] The bicolon form employed in Prov. 10.31 often opens with a humorous or absurd image as in Prov. 11.22: 'Like a gold ring in a pig's snout is a beautiful woman without good sense' (NRSV). One-line folk proverbs may have been expanded to produce sayings of this form.[25] The sayings we are considering have an underlying two-clause form. 'No one' plus description of the absurd action, followed by a clause noting the consequence of the action ruled out in the first clause. Our written variants show further expansions that attempt to resolve difficulties with the initial images.

The contrast between patching an old cloak with unshrunk cloth (Mk 2.21; Mt. 9.16) and destroying a new one to patch the old (Lk. 5.36) shifts from a possible error due to stupidity or negligence to the implausible.[26] Like the gold ring in the pig's nose, this shift might have occurred at the oral level, assimilating the aphorism to sayings with a humorous or absurd opening colon.[27] Can cultural information provide possible interpretations for the subject of such actions? Are we to think of the fool as a poor worker, perhaps even a slave? Or are we to imagine a woman who may also be uninstructed, poor or a slave? Though Kee rightly notes that the opening should draw shouts of derision from Jesus' audience, he assumes without argument that male village tailors see one of their own as the subject.[28]

23. Managing the craft or household well is a fixed topos of Ancient Near Eastern wisdom. See Richard J. Clifford, *Proverbs* (Louisville: Westminster John Knox, 1999), p. 8.

24. As in the ancient Egyptian proverb attributed to Ptahhotep, 'Good speech is more hidden than the emerald, but it may be found with maidservants at the grindstones' (cited in Roland E. Murphy, *Proverbs* [Word Biblical Commentary 22; Nashville: Thomas Nelson, 1998], p. xxi).

25. Clifford observes: 'It is interesting to note that most of the poetic artistry (assonance, wordplay, humor) is found in the first colon of the bicolon. One can perhaps infer that, in some cases at least, old folk proverbs were artistically extended and given new depth by the addition of the second colon' (*Proverbs*, p. 19 n. 28).

26. Dupont, 'Vin', p. 297.

27. The shift is commonly attributed to Luke's editorial work, matching the loss of what is new in the garment case to the loss of new wine (so Dupont, 'Vin', p. 297).

28. Kee, 'Old Coat', p. 20.

Papyri testify to the commercial importance of textile production in Egyptian workshops.[29] Boys and girls, both freeborn and slaves, were apprenticed to the trade between the ages of 10 and 13.[30] Thus the 'no one' in our aphorism might distinguish an adult tradesperson from the child apprentice. Clothing manufacture also had taken on commercial importance and involved families as well as workshops in the trade.[31] Though not restricted to women, textile industries have the largest number of women's names associated with them.[32] Skilled female slaves who had been freed might establish themselves as owners of a wine shop or a workshop involved in weaving or dying textiles.[33] Consequently, the 'no one' of our aphorisms might be either female or male. The reference to 'wineskins' rather than jars seems inappropriate for the proprietress of a *thermipolium*. Transferring new wine into old containers which corrupt its flavor might be typical of a tiny shop at the bottom of the market. Similarly, patching old garments reflects the needs and activities of the poor, not the rich.

Turning from the public market to the household, the sayings also point toward the margins. A son writes home to his mother who is making him a garment with a purple border. Another mother informs her son that she could not find the 'Spartan style garment' he had requested, so she can send only 'a worn out Pergamene one'.[34] No patches are mentioned but the worn cloak may require such. A husband in Xenophon's Socratic

---

29. Humphrey, *Greek and Roman Technology*, pp. 356-357.

30. N. Lewis, *Life in Egypt under Roman Control* (Oxford: Clarendon Press, 1983), pp. 134-35.

31. In a letter to Zenon (ca 256 B.C.), a family specializing in making women's clothing seeks to relocate (quoted in Jane Rowlandson [ed.], *Women and Society in Greek and Roman Egypt. A Sourcebook* [Cambridge: Cambridge University Press, 1998] #201). Plautus satirizes the mob of persons who make different clothing items and textiles at the rich man's door seeking to collect what is owed (*Pot of Gold*, pp. 505-22; in Humphrey, *Greek and Roman Technology*, p. 366).

32. S.B. Pomeroy, *Women in Hellenistic Egypt* (New York: Schocken, 1984), p. 171.

33. E. Frantham *et al.*, *Women in the Classical World: Image and Text* (New York and Oxford: Oxford University Press, 1994), p. 268. There is little evidence for how women were trained in crafts. Slaves were expected to engage in home wool-working when they had no other duties (p. 270). Marriage contracts which require husbands to provide suitable clothing indicate that clothing was produced outside the home (Pomeroy, *Women*, pp. 93-94).

34. With the purple border, Rowlandson, *Women*, #109; the worn cloak, #97.

dialogue, *Estate Manager*, boasts about how well he has trained his wife. When she married at 15, the girl had seen female slaves required to spin wool and knew how to turn wool into a cloak (7.3-6). Having trained her to manage everything in the household, the husband no longer has to spend time indoors. Such training did not involve viticulture or wine production, activities supervised by the husband or his male slave manager. But it did require proper storage of goods inside the household, including the wine in appropriate cool rooms (9.4). When his wife remarked that her activities are worthless, since it is her husband who brings in the goods to be stored, he replied that his efforts would be useless without hers. He caps the argument with a proverb, 'Don't you see how those who pour water into a leaky jar, as the proverb puts it, are pitied for their useless effort' (7.36).

A household in which garments are patched or wine stored in skins, rather than appropriately marked leak-proofed jars,[35] must be nearer the poverty line than Xenophon's estate owner. Horace's poor boatman carries a skinful of sour wine (*Satires* 1.5 line 15). By contrast, the rich praetor Tilius journeys to Tivoli with servants carrying a commode and wine cask bringing up the rear (*Satires* 1.6 line 105). Local consumption involved local products of little distinction.[36] Given the low quality wine and vinegar drunk among the poor,[37] corruption of taste by an old container seems hardly possible. However, loss, whether of wine, its container or a worn cloak, becomes more severe for such persons. A mistake means more than punishing a young or inept slave, apprentice or wife. The family

35. After fermentation, wine in Egypt was stored in ceramic containers, usually leak-proofed with pitch. Wine that was not going to be drunk immediately had the year marked on the jar (Lewis, *Life in Egypt*, p. 125). There is no evidence for the concept of vintage years, though aging was know to improve wine as long as the containers were air-tight and not contaminated by other substances (see J. Davidson, *Courtesans and Fishcakes: The Consuming Passions of Classical Athens* [New York: St Martins, 1998], p. 41). Macrobius observes that the best wine comes from that in the middle of the fermentation vessel since that on top has been in contact with air and that on the bottom has its taste compromised by sediments (*Saturnalia* 7.12.13- 16, cited in Humphrey, *Greek and Roman Technology*, p. 156).

36. Davidson, *Courtesans and Fishcakes*, p. 41. Onomastica from Egypt list as many as forty types of wine from 'new wine' down to the dregs, a cheap old wine, 'such as servants might drink' (T. Hare, *Remembering Osiris: Number, Gender and the Word in Ancient Egyptian Representational Systems* [Stanford: Stanford University, 1999] p. 155).

37. Adkins, *Handbook*, p. 343.

might lose something necessary to its survival once the cloak is more torn than before, the wine spilt and the skins burst.

Horace satirizes another type of fool, the stingy rich man. Such persons refuse to open their old wine until it has soured, so that someone with a huge supply of fine wine drinks vinegar (*Satire* 2.2-3). Taken down the social scale, the stingy person may wear a much repaired cloak or insist on using old vessels, even old skins, to the detriment of the final product. In this context, foolish action follows upon a weakness of character that the audience joins in mocking.

For the two sayings in our group, no causes for folly are attested. The fool is masked by Jesus' use of the negative 'no one' as subject of the actions imagined. Only class, not gender or status (slave or free), mark the actor. S/he may be someone encountered in the market, cramped in a small shop or among the village poor. What s/he might lose through carelessness or the necessity of poverty is never specified beyond the items noted: an old garment, old wineskins, and ordinary, local wine.

Conclusion: Application and Missing the Point?

Are the variants of these sayings employed by the evangelists no more than misapplied words of Jesus, as Kee suggests?[38] Despite his reputation as champion for women and the poor, Luke's version has moved these sayings furthest from both groups. Old wine only drives out taste for the new (Lk. 5.39), if it is a vintage familiar to the affluent. When the poor drink old wine, it is sour, spoiled, or the dregs of the vat. For such persons, new wine would always be preferable. Similarly, in what household or workshop is the absurdity of cutting a patch from a new garment conceivable? Only that of the rich, satirized for the hoards of cloth and garment sellers found at their gates. Some foolish slave or apprentice might pull such a stunt. The mother labouring to sew a cloak with a purple border for her son or the one who can only find a worn cloak to send her son would not even have the means. As we have seen, such households would not have wineskins about. Their wine would have been carefully stored in cool rooms. Luke has not changed the imagery of that saying but may have understood its focus to be on folly which leads to the loss of new wine, not that of the skins.[39]

The socio-economic shift implied in the first and third sayings presents a

38. Kee, 'Old Coat', p. 13.
39. Dupont, 'Vin', p. 297.

new possibility for interpretation. The internal dialogue which the evangelist adds to the comment on the superiority of old wine in verse 39 is a characteristic literary device.[40] Since Luke designates these sayings 'parables' (v. 36), this element should be compared to the internal deliberations of such familiar Lucan characters as the prodigal son (Lk. 15.17-19) and the rich fool (12.17-29). The rich fool thought to guarantee himself a life of ease by hoarding, an example story that Luke applies to teaching about greed (12.15). We have seen that Horace satirizes the stingy, who keep vintage wine so long that it sours, or refuse to drink the good wine in their cellars. Luke has not developed the image of the man drinking old wine into a narrative, but provides a suggestive signpost. He assumes that readers will view the vintage wine-drinker as a rich fool. Similarly the absurdity of cutting a patch out of a new garment can be read as a satirical observation. No one but the absurdly rich would do such a thing. Luke's ability to satirize the hopeless blindness of the rich emerges full-blown in the parable of the rich man and Lazarus (Lk. 16.19-31).

Commentators correctly assume that Luke intends to elicit a consistently negative response from the audience in these three sayings, but have preferred allegorizing identifications of old and new to the literary category of satire. These identifications are generated by the need to see the sayings as comment on or resolution to the question of why Jesus' disciples are not fasting like those of John the Baptist and the Pharisees (5.33-35). Does social satire apply to that situation? The folly of the rich cannot apply to disciples of the Baptist, whose ascetic praxis was contrasted with the eating and drinking of Jesus and his followers (Lk. 7.31-35). But the controversy also involved disciples of the Pharisees. Lk. 16.14-15 attributes love of money to the Pharisees. It causes them to mock Jesus.[41] Luke often uses asides to unmask the pretense of those who

40. Dupont, 'Vin', p. 298 n. 41. Good's attempt to argue that Luke should not be read in light of Mark but as advocating a transformation of the old into what is 'new', that is, fulfilled in Jesus, depends upon reading this addition as Luke's defining comment on the whole pericope (R.S. Good, 'Jesus, Protagonist of the Old in Luke 5.33-39', *NovT* 25 [1983], pp. 19-36). This reading fails to consider the literary possibility that Luke is reporting the internal dialogue of his character.

41. On the Pharisees as lovers of money and honour in Luke, see H. Moxnes, *The Economy of the Kingdom: Social Conflict and Economic Relations in Luke's Gospel* (Philadelphia: Fortress, 1988), pp. 146-48. The evangelist has created this literary picture of the Pharisees by inserting the commentary on their love of money (16.14) into a collection of miscellaneous sayings. Lk. 16.13 comments on the impossibility of serving two masters. In *Gos. Thom.* 47, the sayings about the vintage wine-drinker, the

attempt to pass as righteous or worthy of honour.[42] The challenge comes not from disciples of John the Baptist and the Pharisees directly, but from others, a 'they' who observe the conduct of the various groups of disciples.[43] The parables are addressed to that 'they' (v. 36). If one reads the challenge as an attempt at dishonouring Jesus by contrasting his disciples with the others, then satire is an appropriate response. Luke may not be concerned to establish relationships between traditional piety and that of Jesus' disciples, positive or negative. Rather he uses the aphorisms to unmask Jesus' opponents as no better than rich fools.[44]

As we have seen, the other variants of the paired sayings on a patched garment and ruined wine emerge from the social experience of the lowly, not the rich. Taken apart from the debate over fasting, they represent stupid mistakes which result in a disastrous loss. If Mark and Matthew understood the aphorisms as defending Jesus' new teaching on piety,[45] then the application has no link to the tragedy of folly and loss. The lowly social origins of persons who might be driven to patch an old garment with unshrunk cloth, perhaps picked up off the workshop floor, or to ferment wine in old skins, may be invisible to the evangelists. Or, if the audience does pick up on the social location of these activities, it serves to discredit

new wine, and the patched cloak are linked to that saying. Perhaps Luke found the saying about the vintage wine drinker at that position in his version of Q and relocated it to substitute this explicit condemnation of the Pharisees.

42. Lk. 10.29; 14.7; 18.9; 20.20. 'These asides are usually not observations of visible facts; rather, they give information about the hidden motivations and forces that make people behave the way they do' (Moxnes, *Economy*, p.147).

43. Lk. 5.33 omits Mark's somewhat unclear statement, 'The disciples of John and the Pharisees were fasting and they came and they said to him, 'Why do the disciples…?' for the simpler, 'they said to him'. The reader is less confused about who posed the question, but left to infer that the questioners must have been observing the practice of the two groups. He has added a note that the disciples of the Baptist and the Pharisees engage in frequent fasting while Jesus' disciples 'eat and drink' (Fitzmyer, *Luke*, p. 594).

44. This literary reading supports Hahn's argument that Lk. 5.39 is directed against the attractiveness (*chrēstos*) of the teaching of the Pharisees ('Die Bildworte vom neuen Flicken und vom jungen Wein [Mk 2,21f parr]', *EvTh* 31 [1971], pp. 373-75).

45. Carlston, *Triple Tradition*, pp. 127-28. Mark may imply that fasting is acceptable but an indifferent matter (Carlston, *Triple Tradition*, p. 129). Incompatibility is highlighted by Mark's addition, 'they put new wine into new skins' (Mk 2.22; Guelich, *Mark*, p. 114). Matthew's desire to affirm the Christian rendering of inherited forms of piety emerges in the addition, 'and both are preserved' (compare Mt. 5.17-20; 13.52; Davies and Allison, *Matthew*, pp. 114-15).

Jesus' opponents by comparing them with the despised poor. But tragedy is not absent from the context. The bridegroom's 'being taken away' leads his disciples to fast (Mk 2.20). If Jesus' death is the consequence of foolish adherence to an understanding of piety by the opposition, then the tragic note in these aphorisms has not been lost completely.

As persons at the margins, the persons sewing or storing new wine may be women or men, slaves, even children hired out as apprentices. The aphorisms themselves don't say. As a figure of social satire, Luke's vintage wine-drinker is almost certainly a wealthy male. Since the aphorisms have been applied to a conflict over honour, status and piety that concerns male religious teachers and their disciples, the tendency of the tradition has been to read the subjects of the aphorisms as males. Lacking other clues, a first-century audience probably did the same. Our analysis suggests that pursuing questions of class rather than gender opens up possibilities of reading these aphorisms that had been suppressed once the fixed readings of old versus new, Jewish versus Christian, 'the others' versus 'us' had taken hold. Scholars who deny any link between these aphorisms and Jesus' images of the kingdom rightly reject that sedimented dualism as an appropriate representation of Jesus' vision. Admittedly, it has not been possible to pursue a new reading from within the gaps, silences and dynamics of the texts. We have relied upon social history and Roman satirists for clues to another context in which such maxims refer to folly and loss, whether among the poorest or the rich. In either version, the evangelists establish a distance between the listening audience and the imagined actors. No one takes the part of fool...except those whose ignorance is equivalent to that of the terrified young apprentice or new wife.

WOMEN'S WORK IN THE REALM OF GOD (MT. 13.33; LK. 13.20, 21; GOS. THOM. 96; MT. 6.28-30; LK. 12.27-28; GOS. THOM. 36)

Holly Hearon and Antoinette Clark Wire

Introduction

One of the characteristics associated with the parables of Jesus is the use of images from everyday life. The parable of the bakerwoman (Mt. 13.33// Lk. 13.21/ Gos. Thom. 96) and the teaching of the 'lilies of the field' (Mt. 6.28-29// Lk. 12.27/ Gos. Thom. 36) draw on images from the everyday lives of women. Indeed, these two particular images describe activities that consumed the lives of many peasant and slave women in antiquity because spinning and baking were central to the household economy. They continue to consume the lives of women today in many parts of the three-fourths world. Thus the worlds of women, past and present, are alive in these two images. Each is made of threads spun by different hands, but woven into a single cloth.

Spinning and baking were activities often carried out in the company of other women. Therefore it is appropriate that this chapter be authored by two women who have collaborated on several occasions. We share in common our location as middle-class, white women who hold advanced academic degrees and teach in Christian seminaries. Although we both are members of the Presbyterian Church (USA), Holly teaches at an institution sponsored by the Christian Church (Disciples of Christ). Both denominations support the ordination of women and Holly has been ordained to the ministry of word and sacrament, while Anne has assumed a number of leadership positions within the church. It is not surprising, therefore, that we scrutinize early Christian texts for evidence of women's initiative and leadership. We are separated from one another by our age and life experiences. Anne grew up in China, where her parents were missionaries. Holly grew up in the Pacific western region of the USA Anne has children and a grandchild; Holly has none. These differences lead us to consider the different life situations of women in antiquity.

Our social locations remove us far from women whose survival is based on the production of food and clothing. Yet daily, when we cook or clean our homes, we are reminded of women we have known all over the world and in our own country who live by the work of their hands. We are each aware of how the way we live our lives and the choices our representatives in Congress make impact the lives of these women. We carry this awareness into our interpretation of Christian texts.

Methodology

In examining the parable of the bakerwoman and the 'lilies of the field', we will undertake a feminist analysis. At a basic level, a feminist analysis of the Second Testament highlights the presence of women in the text in order to demonstrate the presence of women in the Jesus movement and early Christian communities. We attempt to go beyond this level in two ways: first, we seek not only to highlight the presence of women in early Christian communities, but to demonstrate ways in which women were central to the life of these communities, and often were leaders within them. Second, we try not only to locate women leaders, but to identify how they shaped our earliest witness to and about Jesus.

In order to pursue these goals, we employ five strategies.[1] (1) we work to re-construct the sociohistorical world of women through an examination of literary and archeological remains; (2) we examine the variant readings of texts for references to women, women's work and women's reality; (3) we undertake rhetorical analyses of the texts in order to hear women shaping debates within early Christian communities; (4) we attempt to uncover the androcentric ideology which pervades these early Christian texts and their interpretations by commentators; (5) we engage the text as active readers, resisting androcentric language and patriarchal social structures while lifting up challenges to those systems that offer good news to women then and around the world today.

The Need for a Feminist Interpretation

The sayings which are the focus of this chapter illustrate well the need for feminist interpretation. The parable is generally identified as the 'parable of the leaven'. This title obscures the presence of the woman in the

---

1. We draw here on the strategies outlined by E. Schüssler Fiorenza in her book *But She Said* (Boston: Beacon, 1992), pp. 21-40.

parable.[2] She remains hidden for many interpreters who focus entirely on the leaven: 'Leaven has power to transform into something new while maintaining continuity with the old'.[3] 'The Kingdom is like leaven, which, once hidden, cannot help but leaven the whole due to its active ingredients'.[4] 'The Kingdom of Heaven is not like the leaven, but the prepared risen dough'.[5] Each of these interpreters ignores the agency of the woman.[6] But Mt. 13.33 reads: 'The Kingdom of heaven is like yeast that *a woman took and mixed in* with three measures of flour until all of it was leavened'. Without the woman there is no parable. The *Gospel of Thomas* highlights this by bringing the woman to the fore: 'The kingdom of the father is like [a certain] woman. She took a little leaven, [concealed] it in some dough and made it into large loaves'.[7]

The teaching of the 'lilies of the field' offers another example: 'Consider the lilies of the field, how they grow; they neither toil nor spin, yet I tell you, even Solomon in all his glory was not clothed like one of these' (Mt. 6.28). Though the only person actually mentioned is Solomon, the lilies are being compared to women who spun wool and who toiled to provide the household with clothing. Thus women are present in the text, although never named. Yet because they are not named, most commentators make no reference to women or women's labour.[8] Feminist interpreters emphasize the presence of women in these sayings and hear what others have not.

---

2.   A similar argument may be made with the 'Parable of the Mustard Seed'. So titled, the agency of the sower is overlooked. We will, therefore, refer to this parable as the 'Parable of the Mustard Sower'.

3.   D.E. Garland, *Reading Matthew* (New York: Crossroad, 1995), p. 151.

4.   J.A. Fitzmyer, *The Gospel according to Luke X–XXIV* (New York: Doubleday, 1985), p. 1019.

5.   J. Jeremias, *The Parables of Jesus* (New York: Charles Scribner's Sons, 1972), p. 102.

6.   S. Praeder, *The Word in Women's Worlds* (Wilmington: Michael Glasier, 1988), p. 22; L. Schottroff, *Lydia's Impatient Sisters: A Feminist Social History of Early Christianity* (Louisville, KY: Westminster/John Knox Press, 1995), p. 87.

7.   Quotations from the *Gospel of Thomas* are taken from the translation by T.O. Lambdin in *The Nag Hammadi Library* (ed. James M. Robinson; HarperSanFrancisco, rev. edn, 1990).

8.   E.g., J.B. Green, *The Gospel of Luke* (Grand Rapids: Eerdmans, 1997), p. 493; L.T. Johnson, *The Gospel of Luke* (Collegeville, MN: Liturgical Press, 1991), pp. 199-202; Fitzmyer, *Gospel According to Luke*, pp. 977, 979; S. Ringe, *Luke* (Louisville: Westminster/John Knox, 1995), pp. 178-79.

Archaeological and Literary Evidence of Baking and Spinning

Spinning and bread-making were essential contributions to the household economy in the world of antiquity.[9] It is helpful to consider the economic condition of the majority of people inhabiting the world of the first century CE. The model constructed by Lenski of the relationship among classes in agrarian societies reveals that the majority of the population in the ancient world consisted of peasant farmers.[10] In a subsistence economy, survival depended upon the contribution of the entire household.[11] Spinning, wool-working, weaving and bread-making, under these conditions, were essential tasks carried out by women. In households where there were slaves, these tasks would have fallen to female slaves.[12]

Archaeological remains indicate that the average dwelling consisted of a room roughly 4.5 by 4.5 metres which might be divided into two or three living spaces.[13] This dwelling was built into a courtyard shared with other family dwellings, some of which might belong to relatives.[14] The court-yard provided a communal living space and much activity took place out-of-doors, including grinding meal and the baking of bread.[15] Smaller ovens, made of clay, could be transported between the indoors and out-doors, as weather permitted.[16]

9. J.R. Wegner, *Chattel or Person? The Status of Women in the Mishnah* (Oxford: Oxford University Press, 1988), p. 77.

10. G.E. Lenski, *Power and Privilege: A Theory of Social Stratification* (Chapel Hill: University of North Carolina Press, 1984), pp. 266, 284.

11. D.A. Fiensy, *The Social History of Palestine in the Herodian Period* (Lewiston, NY: Edwin Mellen, 1991), p. 93; S. Guijarro, 'The Family in First Century Galilee', in *Constructing Early Christian Families*, ed. H. Moxnes (New York: Routledge, 1997), p. 46; Lenski, *Power and Privilege*, p. 270.

12. Praeder, *Word in Womens' Worlds*, 18; *m. Ket.* 5.5; Xenophon, *On Household Management*, 7.6; quoted in M.R. Lefkowitz and M.B. Fant, *Women's Life in Greece and Rome: A Source Book in Translation* (Baltimore: Johns Hopkins University Press, 1992), p. 197.

13. Fiensy, *Social History of Palestine*, p. 126; Guijarro, 'The Family in First Century Palestine', pp. 50, 52.

14. Fiensy, *Social History of Palestine*, p. 124; Guijarro, 'The Family in First Century Palestine', p. 52; S. Safrai, 'Home and Family', in *The Jewish People in the First Century, Vol. 2: Historical Geography, Political History, Social, Cultural and Religious Life and Institutions* (ed. S. Safrai and M. Stern; Philadelphia: Fortress, 1976), p. 729.

15. Fiensy, *Social History of Palestine*, p. 127; Safrai, 'Home and Family', p. 730.

16. Safrai, 'Home and Family', pp. 738, 739. G. Dalman, *Arbeit und Sitte in*

Both bread-making and spinning served as occasions for women to gather together. The *Mishnah* describes how three women work with the dough–one kneading it, another rolling it out, while the third bakes.[17] A similar image is found in Q which describes two women grinding meal together [Mt. 24.41//Lk. 17.35]. Plutarch, in his treatise *Moralia,* tells of women singing songs together while they grind at the mill.[18] The communal act of making bread suggests that a large quantity may have been produced at any one time. L. Schottroff notes that a recipe found in her mother's and grandmother's cookbook called for 30 kilograms or 66 pounds of rye flour.[19] She recalls that bread was often made for more then one family, thus accounting for the large quantity of dough.[20] E. Carles, a peasant who grew up in the Alps of France, similarly recalls how the community gathered together to bake large quantities of bread which had to last them through the winter.[21] Safrai, in his description of the household economy in Judea, indicates that bread was baked once a week.[22] Thus the 'three measures of flour' mentioned in the parable do not necessarily represent an extraordinary amount.

Spinning was also a communal activity. In Ovid's *Metamorphoses,* women tell stories to pass the time as they 'ply their household tasks, spinning wool, thumbing the turning threads, or keep close to the loom'[23] It was the responsibility of women to produce clothing, rugs, curtains, and other woollen goods for the entire household. Wool-working was apparently hard on the hands. Soranus, in his instructions to midwives, cautions them to abstain from working wool as it will make their hands hard.[24] This suggests that, although a task associated with women, it was also task associated with class—i.e., with those who could not afford slaves to whom they could assign the work.

Anything produced in excess of household needs could be sold as a

Palästina, Vol. 4: *Brot, Öl und Wein* (Hildesheim: Georg Olms, 1964), pp. 29-140 and figs. 9-30.

17. *m.Pesah* 3.4.

18. Plutarch, *Moralia* 157E.

19. Schottroff, *Lydia's Impatient Sisters*, p. 80.

20. Schottroff, *Lydia's Impatient Sisters*, p. 80.

21. E. Carles, *A Life of Her Own* (New York: Penguin, 1992), pp. 15-17.

22. Safrai, 'Home and Family', p. 740. However, Praeder says that bread was produced daily (*Word in Women's Worlds*, p. 12).

23. Ovid, *Metamorphoses* 4.32-42.

24. Soranus, *Gynaecology* 1.3-4, quoted in Lefkowitz and Fant, *Women's Life in Greece and Rome*, p. 266.

means of supplementing the household income.[25] The goods produced by women or slaves belonged to the head of the household and any income gained from the sale of these goods accrued to his wealth.[26] An exception to this was if the wool belonged to the woman. In this case, clothes she made for herself, even if she employed her husband's slaves, belonged to her.[27] The *Mishnah* also states that if a husband provided his wife with no money for the running of the household, then her earnings belonged to her.[28] Despite these exceptions, the labour of women did not have a direct, positive impact on their own economic condition. Their labour largely benefited the head of the household, who both consumed the goods produced by women and received the income from their labour.

The Rhetoric of Work

In the world of antiquity, work was divided along gender lines and predicated on the model of the patriarchal household. Women's work belonged to the private sphere of the household; men's work to the public sphere of the *polis* or fields.[29] That this was not strictly the case is revealed by inscriptions and literary remains that identify women as fisherwomen, gladiators, grocers, bakers, vendors of a variety of goods, and scribes.[30] Despite this evidence of 'crossing over', the prevailing rhetoric neatly divided the labours of men and women into two separate and distinct spheres.

Among the work associated with women, spinning and bread-making stand out. According to the *Mishnah,* a woman was obligated to perform seven kinds of labour for her husband: grinding flour, baking bread, doing the laundry, preparing meals, feeding the children, making the bed, and working in wool.[31] Sources from the Greco-Roman world illustrate the emphasis given to spinning and wool-working as virtues of a well-

25. S. Appelbaum, 'The Social and Economic Status of the Jews in the Diaspora', in S. Safrai and M. Stern (eds.), *The Jewish People in the First Century*, II, p. 681.

26. *m.Ket.* 5.9; 6.1; *Digest* 24.1.31.

27. *Digest* 24.1.31; quoted in Lefkowitz and Fant, *Women's Life in Greece and Rome*, p. 116.

28. *m.Ket.* 5.9.

29. T. Ilan, *Jewish Women in Greco-Roman Palestine* (Peabody: Hendrickson, 1996), p. 185; M.B. Peskowitz, *Spinning Fantasies: Rabbis, Gender, and History* (Berkeley: University of California Press, 1997), pp. 50, 66.

30. See Lefkowitz and Fant, *Women's Life in Greece and Rome*, pp. 214, 220-24.

31. *m.Ketub.* 5.5.

mannered woman and obedient wife. Xenophon, for example, comments in his treatise *On Household Management* (7.6): 'Aren't you satisfied that [your wife] came knowing only how to take the wool and produce clothes and seeing how the spinning was distributed to women slaves?' A tomb inscription from the first century BCE reads: 'Praise for all good women is simple and similar…still, my dearest mother deserved better praise than all others since in modesty, propriety, chastity, obedience, wool-working, industry and loyalty she was on equal level with other good women'.[32] For women, diligence in spinning and wool-working was believed to reflect virtue in all good things.[33] It also kept them at home and, presumably, safe from all sources of shame.[34]

While spinning was a task restricted solely to women, men did take up weaving as a trade.[35] Herodotus in the fifth century CE describes Egyptian women as buying and selling and men staying home and weaving unlike 'all the other men'.[36] However, men who did so were considered suspect. By engaging in women's work they blurred the lines that distinguished one gender from another and, as a result, revealed their own weakness of character.[37] Similarly, while professional bakers tended to be men, it was not considered a respectable profession.[38]

From this brief overview we may pause to conclude that these two sayings, the parable of the bakerwoman and the 'lilies of the field', are images drawn specifically from the life experience of women in the world of antiquity. They were tasks often carried out by women in the company of other women, in the house or shared courtyard. Living conditions were such that privacy would have been a rare privilege. While spinning and wool-working were considered virtues for all women, it was nonetheless women from the peasant classes, servants, or slaves who carried out the bulk of this work.[39] While both the *Mishnah* and Greco-Roman sources indicate that women who owned as few as three slaves could pass these

32. CIL 6.10230.
33. Peskowitz, *Spinning Fantasies*, p. 104.
34. Peskowitz notes that, ultimately, spinning and weaving could neither ensure moral character or protect women (*Spinning Fantasies*, p. 70).
35. Peskowitz, *Spinning Fantasies*, p. 50.
36. Herodotus, *History* 2.35; Peskowitz, *Spinning Fantasies*, p. 92.
37. Peskowitz, *Spinning Fantasies*, pp. 66, 68.
38. Praeder, *The Word in Women's Worlds*, p. 17.
39. R.J. Allen, *Rabbinic Passages to Help Interpret the Parables* (Storytellers Companion to the Bible 9; Nashville: Abingdon, forthcoming), p. 50; Praeder, *The Word in Women's Worlds*, pp. 18-19.

tasks off to them, the majority of women would have been responsible for carrying them out themselves.[40] Thus these passages not only draw on, but would have spoken directly to women living a marginal economic existence as well as slaves whose existence was predicated on the good will of their owners. Further, they describe ordinary tasks, day-to-day tasks, yet tasks that were both necessary to the household economy and met essential needs for food and clothing. For such tasks to be identified with the activity of God calls attention to God's identification with the economically marginal—specifically, women whose work was exploited by the patriarchal household. It also describes the activity of God in terms that cross gender boundaries, and reveals God as one who provides for the household of humankind.

The Texts and Their Variant Readings

We can assume that in the ancient mediterranean Jesus' sayings were first passed on orally, with their tellers adjusting the words to suit different hearers. We will return to these primary oral tellers in the conclusion. But our earliest access to the baking and spinning sayings comes about 60 CE, when a collection of Jesus' sayings were made, whether in oral or written form.[41] This 'Sayings Source' (or Q for *Quelle* = source) can be reconstructed from Matthew and Luke's common passages that they have not drawn from Mark, their major source. We find here a collection of wise sayings and prophecies of judgment and salvation from John the Baptist, from Jesus, and from their followers who continued to challenge town after town to hear. When our two sayings are heard within this whole collection, we can see what they meant to one very early group who continued to tell them.

A second collection of Jesus' sayings called the *Gospel of Thomas* also includes both our sayings (*Gos. Thom.* 36 and 96). Although this collection may well be later than Matthew and Luke, it does not follow their wording or their order sufficiently to prove literary dependence on them. We will therefore take up this second sayings collection before turning to

40. Praeder, *The Word in Women's Worlds*, p. 18.

41. A defense of Q as an oral source is found in R.A. Horsley and J. Draper's *Whoever Hears You Hears Me* (Harrisburg, PA: Trinity, 1999). The more widely held thesis of Q as a written source of Matthew and Luke is summarized by J.S. Kloppenborg in *The Formation of Q: Trajectories in Ancient Wisdom Collections* (Philadelphia: Fortress, 1987), pp. 42-51.

Matthew and Luke. The *Gospel of Thomas* provides many sayings not in
the canonical texts, including some with gnosticizing interpretations, and
at the same time gives different forms of some traditions found in Matthew
and Luke. Especially interesting is the fact that the Coptic *Gospel of
Thomas* which survives in full is apparently the translation of a Greek
original, yet the few Greek fragments that have been found are not clearly
the sourse of the Coptic. The saying on anxiety survives in both Greek and
Coptic and each will be considered independently since we do not know
which is earlier.

Matthew and Luke tell the parable of the bakerwoman identically (Mt.
13.33//Lk. 12.27), except that Luke compares the yeast to the 'Kingdom of
God' and Matthew to the 'Kingdom of Heaven'. This parable is paired in
each text with the 'parable of the mustard sower', probably reflecting Q
described above. Yet the mustard sower appears without the bakerwoman
in Mark, and they are unrelated in the *Gospel of Thomas*, making clear that
they also circulated independently.[42]

Only very minor differences exist between Matthew and Luke in the
lines about spinning (Matthew's 'lilies of the field' vs. Luke's 'lilies';
Luke's collective third person vs. Matthew's third person plural of the
verb 'grow'.) But each gives rise to interesting variants when they are
copied. In Matthew, the original hand of the uncial manuscript *Sinaiticus*
reads, 'Consider the lilies of the field, how they neither card wool, nor toil
nor spin'.[43] Looking at the Greek, it is easy to see how such a variant
could have arisen: a change of three letters renders *auxanousin* as *ou
xenousin*.[44] Yet it is interesting that a similar variant reading appears in
the Coptic *Gospel of Thomas*. Carding is a stage in preparing wool for
spinning, in which the fleece is combed out into a mass of fibre. This
suggests that 'they neither toil nor spin' was heard by someone as a
reference to different stages of cloth production and was changed to 'do
not card nor spin', or the latter was generalized into the former.[45]

42. C. H. Dodd, *The Parables of the Kingdom* (New York: Charles Scribner's
Sons, 1961), p. 154; Fitzmyer, *Gospel According to Luke*, p. 1018.; Jeremias, *Parables
of Jesus*, p. 146; B.B. Scott, *Hear Then the Parable* (Minneapolis: Fortress, 1989),
p. 323.

43. The state of the manuscript makes the verification of this reading impossible.

44. T.C. Skeat considers the variant reading to be the original ('The Lilies of the
Field' *ZNW* 37 [1938]: p. 212).

45. See Glasson, 'Carding and Spinning in Oxy. Pap 655', *JTS* 13 (1962), pp. 331-
32. On the complex interwoven textual traditions, see J.M. Robinson and C. Heil,

In Luke, the uncial manuscript *Bezae Cantabrigiensis* as well as some of the Latin versions read 'Consider the lilies, how they neither spin nor weave'.[46] Are later copyists looking for a double description of women's work here to balance men's 'they neither sow nor reap, they have neither storehouse nor barn'? These variant readings from the Gospels of Matthew, Luke and Thomas give a fuller description of women's work and leave open the possibility that we are hearing in them traces of the voices of women who knew what it was to card wool and spin and weave. As we have already seen, these tasks filled up the lives of many women and the communal nature of the tasks made them occasions for story-telling. The variant readings, as well as the presence of the passages in two collections of Jesus' sayings, may offer evidence of women shaping the teachings of Jesus.

Engaging the Rhetoric of the Texts

The Q Sayings Source of Matthew and Luke exhibits a certain narrative and thematic coherence when it is read in three acts, and the references to spinning and baking prove themselves to be strategically placed.[47] In the first act, John the Baptist introduces Jesus and Jesus introduces John. Both the desert ascetic and the village favourite are shown to be prophets who vindicate the Wisdom of God, who has sent her children to challenge their generation to repent, receive God's inheritance and bear fruit (Q 3.3-7.35).[48] The second act tells how those who respond and are in turn sent

'Zeugnisse eines schriftlichen griechischen vorkannonischen Textes Mt 6,28b Sinaiticus*, P. Oxy. 655 I 1-17 (*EVT* 36) und Q 12,27', *ZNW* 89 (1998), pp. 30-44.

46. T.C. Skeat considers the variant reading to be the original ('The Lilies of the Field', p. 213).

47. We assume a sequence for Q close to that of Luke because Matthew reorders sayings material into sermons. For a tentative reconstruction and translation of Q, see the indented portions of A.C. Wire's article 'The God of Jesus in the Gospel Sayings Source', *Reading from this Place. 1. Social Location and Biblical Interpretation in the United States* (ed. F.F. Segovia and M.A. Tolbert; Minneapolis: Fortress, 1995), pp. 277-303. For the relevant Greek texts of Matthew and Luke see F. Neirynck, *Q-Synopsis: The Double Tradition Passages in Greek* (Leuven: University Press, 1988).

48. We translate 'God's kingdom' as 'God's inheritance' because the focus is not on God's ruling, but on God's giving people the right to the land and the living it can provide them (Wire, 'God of Jesus', p. 281). Q 3.7-7.35 refers to the common Sayings Source passages of Luke and Matthew that are the basis of their common material between Lk. 3.7 and 7.35.

out meet the same rejection as did John and Jesus, and they are afraid (Q passages in Lk. 9.57-12.34). Jesus assures them: the truth will out and God's Spirit that cannot be blasphemed will speak through your mouths to defend you. This assurance comes to a climax in an extended argument from God's care for nature on the grounds that if God provides for those who do no work, how much more will God provide for you:

> Therefore I tell you, don't worry about your life and what you will eat, nor about your body and what you will wear. Is life not more than food and body more than clothing? Look at the crows, for they neither sow nor harvest nor gather into barns, and God feeds them. Are you not worth more than they? Which of you by worry can add one inch to your life span? And why worry about other things? Notice the lilies how they grow—they neither labour nor spin, but I tell you, Solomon in all his glory was not dressed up like one of these. If God so clothes the grass in the field—here today and tomorrow thrown into the fire—how much more you, you faithless ones! So don't ask what you should eat or what you should drink, for all the world's nations seek these things and your Father knows you need them. But seek God's inheritance and these will come as a bonus (Q 12.22-31).[49]

Here, the crows that God feeds are being compared with men who sow, harvest and gather into barns to supply the family's food, while the lilies are compared with women who labour and spin to supply the family's clothing.[50] The division of tasks along gender lines reinforces the cultural rhetoric of gender spheres.[51] This rhetoric is reinforced by the reference to Solomon, since women, and very often slave women, provided the raiment for kings, although they carried out this task anonymously. At the same time, by describing God as the one who clothes both the grass and humankind, a correlation is created between the work of God and the work of women.[52]

49. Reconstruction and translation of Q here and elsewhere are taken from Wire, 'God of Jesus'. This is the conclusion *a minore ad maius* from an event that occurs in less likely conditions to its sure occurrence where the conditions are good. This argument called *qal wachomer* is by tradition one of Hillel's seven hermeneutical principles and is much used by Paul as in Rom. 5.6-10, 15-17; 11.24.

50. This is further suggested in the *P.Oxy.* 655 rendition that reads 'card and spin' (see below).

51. Although neither man nor woman is actually named in the passage, the tasks described correspond to the division of labour described by the rhetoric of work in antiquity.

52. One could argue that by giving credit to God for clothing humankind, the

Even as the passage maintains the division of labour according to gender, it assumes parallel subsistence work by men and women, and the multiple verbs in each case show that this work is heavy and continuous. The opening exhortation and closing epithet, 'Don't worry…you faithless ones', charge them with working anxiously without trust in God. If God cares for crows worth so much less than men, and God dresses the lilies beyond any woman or even Solomon in glory—though they die daily—God will surely feed and clothe them. The final instruction is not that they stop work and pray God to provide but that they work at seeking God's inheritance and their needs, which, God well knows, will be supplied too. Clearly the non-stop work which ties peasant men and women to field and house is being challenged by the necessity of representing God from town to town, where food and clothes come as a bonus to those who go out provoking people to welcome God's inheritance by feeding them.

In the final act of the Sayings Source, Jesus presents the shock that God's inheritance is given to those without resources (Q passages in Lk. 12.39 to 19.30). The section begins and ends with parables warning the privileged who think they can continue with business as usual. At the centre is his announcement of the great reversal: the owner locks out the entitled, the host welcomes those off the streets. The last will be first and first last. This announcement begins with a double definition:

> God's inheritance is like a mustard seed that a man threw in his garden, and it grew and became a tree, and the birds of the sky sheltered in its branches.

> God's inheritance is like yeast that a woman took and hid in fifty pounds of flour until it was completely leavened (Q 13.18-21).[53]

God's inheritance is compared here to a seed thrown in a yard and yeast hidden in flour. The intention of the persons who act is apparently not parallel. The verb 'throw' can be used for intentional broadcasting of seed (cf. Mk 4.26), but one would hardly broadcast a single seed. So the point

---

agency of women is undercut. It is a matter of how one receives the statement that 'But if God so clothes the grass of the field…will God not much more clothe you?' (Mt. 6.24//Lk. 12.28). The same problem does not arise with respect to the male-gendered activity of working in the field since no mention is made of God sowing and reaping. Rather, the text simply states, with respect to food and drink, that God 'knows you need all these things' (Mt. 6.32//Lk. 12.30).

53. We use 'man' to translate the Greek *anthrōpos* because the next sentence provides a female counterpart. Standing alone the term is better translated 'person' and could refer to a woman and her kitchen garden.

here seems to be that an invisible discarded seed can fill the sky with birdsnests. In contrast, the yeast 'that a woman took and hid in fifty pounds of flour until it was completely leavened' is very intentionally handled. Yet the parallel early lines in the two stories put the stress not on a contrast between a lucky man and a provident woman but on God's inheritance being like both seed and yeast in that the situation is reversed and so much comes from so little. In the village setting, fifty pounds of flour was not so much an exceptional quantity to prepare at one time for baking—an oven once heated would be used repeatedly as the story below suggests—but it is wondrous that the woman can press the flour in which she has hidden away the yeast until it is completely leavened and set for transformation. In each case, the results are not just large but life-giving: shelter for birds of the sky, food for people of the earth. This makes the stories a joy to hear, a vindication and celebration of life such as we also find in the story of the impoverished Rabbi Hanina ben Dosa's wife, who lived during the first century CE in a town near Nazareth:

> His wife was used to heating the oven each time the Sabbath was coming and putting something in it to make smoke because of her shame. She had this bad neighbor who said, 'I know very well they have nothing! What is all this?' She went and banged on the door and Hanina's wife was ashamed and went in to a dark corner. A miracle was done for her so that her neighbor saw the oven full of bread and the trough full of dough. She said to her, 'Hey you! Hey you! Bring a paddle because your bread is about to burn!' She said to her, 'I just went in for that'.[54]

With the same assurance, the woman of the Sayings Source has hidden away her yeast and pressed it through fifty pounds of flour to reveal the shock of God's inheritance reversing circumstances and giving life. These parables of Jesus need to be read in light of recent research by D.E. Oakman, W. Herzog, and V.V. John. They argue that the seed and the yeast are not concrete images of an abstract reality but are concrete evidence of God's provision of food and shelter, which are the most basic content of the inheritance God offers.[55]

54. *b.Ta'an.* 24b-25a.
55. D. Oakman links Jesus' parables to the agricultural systems of his time in *Jesus and the Economic Questions of his Day* (Lewiston/Queenstown: Edward Mellen, 1986), pp. 95-139. Herzog provides the methodology and broader social and political framework for this kind of analysis in *Parables as Subversive Speech: Jesus as Pedagogue of the Oppressed* (Louisville, KY: Westminster/John Knox, 1994), pp. 40-73. For a food-production reading of the seed parables see V.J. John, 'Nature in the

Other versions of Jesus' sayings on anxiety and on leaven appear in the *Gospel of Thomas*. In this text, each saying is listed as a separate item headed by 'Jesus said' or 'his disciples said'. Therefore each saying must interpret itself, except where several share a common syntax or theme.

Explicit reference to spinning has disappeared from the Coptic *Gospel of Thomas,* which gives only a single sentence on anxiety:

> Jesus said, 'Do not be concerned from morning until evening and from evening until morning about what you shall wear' (*Gos. Thom.* 36).

This is followed by:

> His disciples said, 'When will you become revealed to us and when shall we see you?' Jesus said, 'When you disrobe without being ashamed and take up your garments and place them under your feet like little children and tread on them, then [will you see] the son of the living one, and you will not be afraid' (*Gos. Thom.* 37; cf. 21).

It appears that clothes are seen not as necessities that God provides, but ornaments, defenses or resources that cause fear and need to be divested. This suggests that a longer saying on anxiety has been limited to anxiety about clothing and then cut short in order to be reinterpreted in this way.

But a Greek fragment of the *Gospel of Thomas* found among the *Oxyrhynchus Papyri* preserves a longer telling of this saying that can be reconstructed as follows:

> '[Jesus says, 'Do not be concerned] from morning [to late nor] from evening [to] morning, not [about] your [food], what [you will] eat, [nor] about [your clothing], what you [will] wear. [You are far] better than the [lilies] which [do not] card nor [spin]. Not having any garment, what [will you put on], you too? Who might add to your stature/lifespan? He will give you your garment' (*P. Oxy* 655. l. 1-17).

The opening line shows a tie to the Coptic *Gospel of Thomas* tradition, the remainder to elements found in the Sayings Source and Matthew, but this composition is distinct. Although the reference to food comes first, clothing is made the primary focus, provoking Jesus' question about what they will wear when unclothed and his response that God will supply their garment. If the intervening question concerns their lifespan, clothing may

Parables of Mark: An Inquiry into the Use of Nature Images in Mark Chapter 4 with special Reference to their Significance for Ecological Concerns', Ph.D. Dissertation at South Asia Theological Research Institute of Serampore College, P.B. 4635, Bangalore, India.

signify the spiritual body they will need when the physical body decays (cf. *Gos. Thom.* 21, 1 Cor. 15.35-58; 2 Cor. 5.1-10). But it could also signify God supplying daily needs. Since we have so little of the Greek *Gospel of Thomas*, the saying should probably be interpreted in this simpler way.

The conclusion is implied if not developed that if lilies are so dressed, who do not work, then surely working people will be dressed, and this becomes the basis of Jesus' assurance. Most interesting is the reference to carding. Because carding and spinning are understood in the Roman East as women's work even when done by men, the fact that only the example from women's work survives here could suggest women hearers. They hear: 'you (who card and spin) are far better than lilies who do not card and spin'. In the *Gospel of Thomas* the group of disciples does at least include women (*Gos. Thom.* 22, 61, 114), which supports the possibility of such a reading. In any case, women who card and spin are sufficiently integral to the lives of the readers of the *Gospel of Thomas* that an argument from such work is expected to be persuasive.

The story of yeast appears only in the Coptic *Gospel of Thomas* (96). It is separate from the mustard seed story (*Gos. Thom.* 20) and followed instead by a story about a woman who loses her meal while carrying it home (*Gos. Thom.* 97).[56]

> Jesus [said]: 'The Kingdom of the father is like [a certain] woman. She took a little leaven, [concealed] it in some dough, and made it into large loaves. Let him who has ears hear'. Jesus said, 'The kingdom of the father is like a certain woman who was carrying a [jar] full of meal. While she was walking [on the] road, still some distance from home, the handle of the jar broke and the meal emptied out behind her [on] the road. She did not realize it; she had noticed no accident. When she reached her house, she set the jar down and found it empty' (*Gos. Thom.* 96-97).

Here the Kingdom is not compared to the yeast, as it is in the Sayings Source, but to the woman, perhaps accentuating her initiative in taking the leaven and making the loaves. Yet the second story speaks of a deed done unawares. Some interpreters contrast the two stories, one leading to gain, the other to loss, because the second woman 'did not know' and 'had not noticed'.[57] But both sayings begin 'The Kingdom of the Father is like a

56. The following story in the *Gospel of Thomas* about the man preparing to kill another man (*Gos. Thom.* 98) is less closely aligned and cannot be discussed here.

57. For example, T. Zöckler in *Jesu Lehren im Thomas Evangelium* (Leiden/ Boston/Köln: E.J. Brill, 1999), pp. 196-97.

woman who...', making contrast unlikely. The stories could both be showing the dissemination of so little so far, whether or not the woman knows it.

In the bakerwoman saying, the most distinctive element is the double reference to size. 'She took a little leaven, [concealed] it in some dough, and made it into large loaves'. This should be heard alongside the similar stress on what is large in several *Gospel of Thomas* parables. The wise fisherman found in his net 'A fine large fish. He threw all the small fish back into the sea and chose the large fish without difficulty' (*Gos. Thom.* 8). Though the mustard is 'the smallest of all seeds...it produces a great plant and becomes a shelter for birds of the sky' (*Gos. Thom.* 20). And the shepherd whose 'largest' sheep went astray searched it out and 'he said to the sheep, "I care for you more than the ninety-nine"' (*Gos. Thom.* 107). So similarly the woman who exhibits the kingdom not only can be confident that the large will come from the small, but she actively chooses to conceal a little yeast in dough and make it into large loaves. The change in size speaks of the ample food that God provides, but in the context of the *Gospel of Thomas* as a whole there is also a challenge to choose the great value of a life guided by Jesus' words. There may also be a promise here, as well as elsewhere in the *Gospel of Thomas* (5, 6, 32, 107, 109), that what is hidden will invariably become manifest.

The *Gospel of Thomas* begins, 'These are the secret words which the Living Jesus spoke' and it does not ask that we choose a single meaning for each secret word. We may be intended to hear Jesus' parable about the woman who took a little yeast as a kind of bell that resounds with multiple tones. Though the saying ends with the refrain addressed to a masculine reader, 'Whoever has ears let him hear', the ringing of multiple tones calls us who are women to hear our own work held up, our hidden powers become manifest, and our choice loaves treasured.

When our sayings appear in the Gospels of Matthew and Luke, they retain the focus on God's provision of food and shelter for those who trust in the inheritance God offers. Yet they do so within a narrative rather than as part of a collection of sayings. Within the narrative, the sayings become speech acts of the character Jesus as he teaches crowds and disciples and challenges the behavior of other characters–in particular, the Pharisees. As speech acts, the sayings further a plot. This presents a different kind of referential field for each saying.

In Q, the saying about the lilies of the field is strategically placed following a saying about being sent out into the world. In Luke, it follows a saying about laying up treasure in heaven (Lk. 12.13-21), while in Matthew it follows a saying about choosing between God and mammon (Mt. 6.24). The evangelists shift the focus away from serving God by going out into the world proclaiming God's inheritance to serving God by seeking God's kingdom above all else. In this context, the saying demands a less radical action, calling instead for something closer to a change of attitude. The risks involved for receiving God's inheritance are less high in Matthew and Luke.

In both Gospels, the saying is addressed to disciples. However, the disciples do not represent the same character group in each Gospel. In Matthew, the disciples are the twelve [men] (Mt. 10.1-4; 28.16), while in Luke the disciples are a larger group of followers, distinct from the apostles, and inclusive of both men and women (Lk. 24.33). This would seem to suggest that Matthew downplays the role of women even further by confining the narrative audience to the disciples. However, the narrative audience is not the sole referent for how this saying is heard within the context of each Gospel, as will be shown below.

The 'lilies of the field' saying contains the only reference to spinning in the Gospels of Matthew and Luke, but each has an additional reference to toiling [*kopiaō*]. In Luke, Jesus stands on the shore of Lake Gennaseret and calls out to two fishermen, suggesting that they let down their nets. One of them, Simon, replies, 'Master, we have toiled [*kopiaō*] all night long but have caught nothing. Yet if you say so, I will let down the nets' (5.5). Heard in conjunction with this passage, the women's labour takes on the feel of endless hours of toil—like fishermen who have been out all night long. But this echo distracts from the fact that spinning is women's work, and may have led some copyist to exchange the word 'toil' for 'weave'. Were there some women who were determined that the full scope of women's labours be honoured?

In Matthew, the second use of the word *kopiaō* is found in 11.28: 'Come to me all you that are weary [*kopiaō*] and are carrying heavy burdens, and I will give you rest'. What English translates as 'weary' would be heard in Greek as 'those exhausted from their toils'. Here, 'toil' or 'labour' is not gender-specific, but inclusive of both men and women. Although Matthew's text, like Luke's, combines the more ambiguous term for labour, *kopiaō*, with the image of spinning, the lack of specificity is not quite so strained. In 11.28 both men and women are invited to take on Wisdom's yoke and have their burdens lifted from them.

The parable of the bakerwoman follows the parable of the mustard sower in both Gospels. As with the previous text, these two parables reflect the rhetorical division of labour on the basis of gender: the bakerwoman performs work associated with women while the sower of mustard seed performs work associated with men.[58] In the Gospel of Luke the parables are linked with 'and again' [*kai palin*], whereas in Matthew each is separate and the second simply called another parable [*allēn parabolēn*].[59] Yet there is a common echo. Birds nesting in branches and loaves of bread speak of basic needs of food and shelter being met.

Although these two parables follow one another in both Matthew and Luke, they are located in quite different contexts within each Gospel. In Luke, they are linked to the healing of the woman who had been bent over for eighteen years. The connective 'therefore' (*oun*) suggests that they serve as interpretive comments on that narrative.[60] In this context, the parable of the bakerwoman seems to reflect the in-breaking of the reign of God, here identified by an act of liberation that echoes the words spoken by Jesus earlier in the Gospel that he has come to 'set the captive free'.[61] Heard together, the story of the woman set free and the parable of the bakerwoman describe not only the acts of God on behalf of a woman, but the acts of God manifested in the hands of a woman as she deftly massages the leaven into the bread.

The parable also is linked to an earlier passage in Luke through the repetition of the word 'leaven' (*zymē)*. In 12.1 we read, 'Meanwhile, when the crowd gathered by the thousands, so that they trampled on one another, he began to speak first to his disciples, 'Beware of the leaven of the Pharisees, that is, their hypocrisy'. In the story of the woman bent over for eighteen years, Jesus calls the ruler of the synagogue who chastises him for healing the woman a 'hypocrite'.[62] If we read on in ch. 12, we see that the passages are further linked: 'Nothing is covered up that will not be uncovered, and nothing secret that will not become known. Therefore whatever you have said in the dark will be heard in the light and what you have whispered behind closed doors will be proclaimed from the house-

---

58. A.-J. Levine, 'Matthew', *The Women's Bible Commentary* (ed. Carol A. Newsom and Sharon Ringe (Louisville: Westminster/John Knox, 1992), p. 258; Schottroff, *Lydia's Impatient Sisters*, p. 85.

59. Mustard also was grown in family gardens within the courtyard compound and in such cases may have been tended by women.

60. Green, *Gospel of Luke*, pp. 526, 519; Johnson, *Gospel of Luke*, p. 213.

61. Johnson, *Gospel of Luke*, pp. 214-15.

62. The word 'hypocrite' occurs only 4 times in Luke: 6.42; 12.1, 56; 13.15.

tops' (12.2-3). This coming revelation refers to the hypocrisy of the Pharisees mentioned in v. 1. In ch. 13, the 'Parable of the Bakerwoman' demonstrates how, like the leaven of the Pharisees, the leaven which is the reign of God will not remain a secret, but become known. The contrast here is not simply that of leaven vs. leaven; it is also between a woman who, in the patriarchal world of antiquity signifies one without power or resources, and the male religious leaders of that day.[63] This contrast echoes another theme in Luke: 'God has brought down the powerful from their thrones, and lifted up the lowly' (1.52).

In the Gospel of Matthew, the parables of the mustard seed and the Bakerwoman fall in a sequence of seven parables.[64] All but one of these is introduced as a parable of the kingdom. The parables are framed by a conversation in which Jesus tells the disciples, 'to you has been given to know the secrets of the kingdom of heaven'. Thus, while Jesus speaks to the crowds in parables which they do not understand, the disciples have the parables explained to them by Jesus. Since the disciples seem to be limited to the twelve in the Gospel of Matthew, this is not a situation in which the followers of Jesus as a whole are granted understanding while those who do not follow Jesus are not. Rather, a particular group among the followers of Jesus is granted special knowledge, and it is these eleven men (Judas having since dropped out) who are later instructed to 'teach all that Jesus has commanded them'.

Although the 'parable of the bakerwoman' is not directly linked to the

---

63. Much has been made of the use of 'leaven' as a metaphor for evil. Unquestionably, this usage dominates Biblical texts, as well as other texts from the world of antiquity (e.g., Exod. 12.15-20; 13.3-10; 23.18; 34.25; Lev. 2.11; 6.17; 10.12; Deut. 16.3-4; Hos. 7.4; Mt. 16.5-12; Lk. 12.1; I Cor. 5.6-8; Gal. 5.9; *b.Ber.* 17a; Pliny, *Natural History* 18.26; Plutarch, *Roman Questions* 289F). However, a closer inspection of the references from the First Testament reveals that a number of these cluster around particular ritual contexts: Passover (Exod. 12.15-20; 13.3-10; Deut. 16. 3-4), the Blood Offering (Exod. 23.18; 34.25), and the Grain Offering (Lev. 2.11; 6.17; 10.12). In contrast, three positive references to leaven found in the First Testament also cluster around ritual contexts: the Thank Offering (Lev. 7.13; Amos 4.5), and the Elevation Offering (Lev. 23.17), which is associated with the festival of the first fruits. This raises the question of whether the 'leaven' referred to in the 'Parable of the Bakerwoman' should be heard in connection with the Thank Offering and the Elevation Offering, both of which celebrate the bounty of God's earth for the benefit of humankind.

64. Of the seven parables, only the parable of the bakerwoman presents a woman as the main character (Levine, 'Matthew', p. 257).

parable of the mustard seed, there does seem to be an implicit connection. This is indicated by the structure of this section:

Parable of separation   13.24-30 (the wheat and the tares)

Two short parables: 13.31-32 parable of the mustard seed
                            13.34 parable of the bakerwoman

Explanation of the parable of the wheat and the tares 13.34-43

Two short parables.   13.44 parable of the treasure hidden in the field
                            13.45 parable of the pearl of great price

Parable of separation 13.47-50 (the catch of good and bad fish)

This structure suggests that the parable of the mustard seed and the parable of the bakerwoman should be read as a pair, just as the parable of the treasure and the parable of the pearl should be read as a pair. The latter both focus on seeking something of great value. Matthew's rendering of the parable of the mustard seed states that the seed is the smallest of all seeds, but grows into the largest of shrubs and becomes a tree. This would suggest that the parable of the bakerwoman similarly is a story about insignificant beginnings resulting in exponential growth. Within this context, the focus is on the power of the leaven rather than the action of the woman.

The structure also suggests a connection between the parable of the bakerwoman and the parable of the treasure hidden in the field. In fact, these two parables are linked with the interpretive interlude by the repetition of the verb 'to hide' (*kryptein*) found in all three passages (vv. 33, 35, 44). In all three, that which is hidden refers to the kingdom of heaven: in the parable of the bakerwoman it is the leaven which permeates the whole; in the parable of the treasure it is the treasure for which a person will sell all; and in the interpretive interlude (13.34-43), it is that 'which has been hidden from the foundation of the world'—within the context of ch. 13, 'the secrets of the kingdom of heaven' (13.11). Set side by side, these texts serve as commentary on one another. Like the treasure, that which has been hidden from the foundation of the world is that which should be sought above all else (see also 6.19-21, 33). Like the leaven, that which has been hidden from the foundation of the world has, nonetheless, been active, leavening the whole of creation. To these readers, there is irony in discovering that the 'secrets of the kingdom of heaven' have been revealed to twelve men (the disciples), yet in one instance describe the activity of God in terms of the labour of a woman.[65]

The action of the woman seems to take on greater significance when the parable of the bakerwoman is viewed in relation to another chiastic structure within the Gospel of Matthew.[66]

A	13.33	parable of the bakerwoman and the leaven
B	14.13-21	feeding of the 5000
C	15.21-28	Canaanite woman ('crumbs from the table')
B'	15.32-39	feeding of the 4000
A'	16. 5-12	leaven of the Pharisees and Sadducees

As in the Gospel of Luke, the parable of the bakerwoman is linked to Jesus' warning against the leaven of the Pharisees and (Matthew adds) Sadducees. For the author of Matthew, the contrast is between the leaven of the bakerwoman, which signifies the kingdom of heaven, and the leaven of the Pharisees and Sadducees which 'locks people out of the kingdom of heaven', as Jesus' accuses them in Mt. 23.13.

But this is not all. These two pericopes frame three other narratives which incorporate the image of bread. Two of these narratives involve a miraculous feeding of the 5,000/4,000 men (much expanded by mentioning the 'not to mention' women and children) while in the third, a Canaanite woman claims the crumbs from the table so that her daughter may be healed. In each of these three narratives, individuals, and women in particular, are blessed by the bounty of God's table. Within this context, the parable of the bakerwoman becomes an illustration of God who 'gives us this day our daily bread' (6.11).[67] Here the focus of the parable becomes the woman who leavens dough sufficient for the feeding of multitudes with crumbs left over, even for those who seem farthest removed from God's reach. The bounty of her table is a symbol of divine providence.[68]

---

65. Such ironic moments are found elsewhere in Matthew: Peter's mother-in-law serves (*diakoneō*), while Peter is exhorted to serve yet fails to do so; the mother of the sons of Zebedee is present at the crucifixion while her sons, who promised to drink the same cup that Jesus drank, have fled.

66. We are building on a chaism observed by E. Wainwright who links the feeding of the 5,000/4,000 with the story of the Canaanite woman ('Matthew', in *Searching the Scriptures, Vol. 2: A Feminist Commentary* [ed. E. Schüssler Fiorenza; New York: Crossroad, 1994], p. 651). We have extended the structure by one more level, drawing on the reference to leaven of the bread/leaven of the Pharisees and Sadducees in 16.5-12 and the leaven of the whole [loaf] in 13.33.

67. Schottroff, *Lydia's Impatient Sisters*, p. 86.

68. Exod. 16.4; Wisd. 16.20; 2 Bar. 29.8 (Allen, *Rabbinic Passages*, pp. 51-52).

Engaging the Text as a Reader

If we were to imagine ourselves, for a moment, as women in antiquity gathered with the other women in the courtyard to bake bread and spin our wool, how might we retell these teachings of Jesus? Perhaps we would lift up the tedious labours that make up our day as illustrations of God's interaction with the world. We might comment on a bakerwoman God who knows how to work the leaven into the whole loaf so that it is leavened evenly. We might praise a God who identifies Godself with those who labour and toil.

As we engaged in further conversation, we might begin to re-vision ourselves differently: not as exploited workers in the patriarchal household, but as the hands of God who promises a new economy for the household of God. As bakerwomen, we work the leaven which is the well-being of creation and that challenges the leaven which corrupts. Drawing out our threads, we spin an economy of abundance where no one lacks. And when we are tired from our toils, we rest in the arms of the wisdom of God.

Listening to these sayings today, a contemporary story shows how powerfully they continue to live in the work of women and girl-children:

> Goli, a 9 year old Iranian girl with sweater sleeves rolled up above her bony elbows, mixes dough from flour and water. She has measured twenty double-handfuls of wheat flour into a basin, and she had gotten Fateme to help her. Making dough and baking bread requires the strength and experience of a woman. But Goli, a helper to her mother at this chore for a long time, has baked alone before this summer, and, anyway, what choice is there? Barely enough bread was left for the morning meal... Fateme pushes one knuckled fist into the dough, then the other, in and out, just as Goli does on her side... When they have covered all the dough with their knuckles, they fold half of it over the other half and punch it down again... Slowly the dough is turning smooth, sticking to itself rather than to the hands and the basin. Goli decides it is done... [She] pats the dough into a tray and covers it with heavy sacking. The dough will rest here overnight. Early tomorrow, Goli will roll the breads on her mother's heavy oak board and bake them on the griddle. It will take all morning, but perhaps her uncle's wife will help her.[69]

69. E. Friedl, 'Moonrose Watched Through a Sunny Day', *Natural History* 8 (1992), pp. 43-44.

The Woman Carrying a Jar of Meal (*Gos. Thom.* 97)

Kamila Blessing

Introduction

The woman carrying a jar of meal may well be the residue of one of the most ancient traditions of Jesus' sayings. It is one of only three parables that appear only the *Gospel of Thomas*, and one of six that appear only in the extracanonical literature.[1] It is thus potentially a rare witness, independent of the canonical Gospels, to the sayings of Jesus. Thus Logion 97 bears considerable importance. Unfortunately, the scholarly literature contains very few interpretations of this parable. Therefore it is of interest not only as a parable involving a woman, but as virtually uncharted territory among Bible-related literature.

The parable, in translation from Coptic, follows:

> Jesus said: The kingdom of the [Father] is like a woman carrying a jar full of meal. While she was walking [on a] distant road, the handle of the jar broke (and) the meal poured out behind her on the road. She was unaware, she had not noticed the misfortune. When she came to her house, she put the jar down (and) found it empty.[2]

In what follows, this paper discusses the date of origin and the parable's context in *Thomas* as a whole. Then, beginning with previous interpretations, it discusses the possible meanings of this story. Intertextual relationships will prove helpful in the interpretation.

---

1. The definition of 'parable' varies among scholars. For purposes of this paper, we adopt the definition: a parable is a story with a beginning, middle, and end (however abbreviated), as opposed to metaphorical language or an aphorism, similitude, or example story.

2. B. Blatz, 'The Coptic Gospel of Thomas', in W. Schneemelcher (ed.), *New Testament Apocrypha* 1: *Gospels and Related Writings* (Louisville, KY: Westminster John Knox Press, 1991), p. 128. The term 'Father' does not appear in the Coptic text. It is inferred by the translator from the parallel introductory phrases of the parables on either side of it (Logia 96 and 98).

Date

The *Gospel of Thomas* is variously dated to the mid-second century,[3] mid-to late first century,[4] or even before the letters of Paul (pre-50 CE).[5] The Coptic version has been dated as late as the third century CE.[6] Various factors, however, have led to a consensus dating the tradition recorded in Logion 97 to the first century. For example, the Jesus Seminar judged Logion 97 as probably original to Jesus. Among their reasons are the following. Although the term 'parable' is never actually used in *Thomas*, Logion 97 bears the typical grammatical structure of the Synoptic parable. It begins with a datival phrase, 'like a woman' followed by a relative clause, '[who was] carrying a jar'. Yet it contains no elements that are likely to result from later redaction–in particular, no allegorical or other interpretive statements added to the main story. The phrase 'The king-dom…is like' is of course associated with parables in the New Testament. Most scholars agree that Jesus did actually teach using parables and did often use parables to describe the Kingdom of Heaven. It is for these reasons that Logion 97 is often considered a rare extracanonical window onto the original teachings of Jesus.

Logion 97 in the Context of Thomas

The parable of the empty jar participates in several themes and forms of the entire *Gospel of Thomas*. This section will address *Thomas* as Wisdom literature, but not necessarily gnostic; its concern with the (spiritual) Kingdom; and its use of the parable to convey the special knowledge of the Kingdom. Since the Kingdom in 97 is likened to a woman, this section will also ask in what way the parable participates in the gospel's con-ceptuality of women generally.

3.   Blatz, 'Coptic Gospel', p. 113.

4.   W.D. Stroker, 'Extracanonical Parables and the Historical Jesus', in C.W. Hedrick (ed.), *Semeia* 44: *The Historical Jesus and the Rejected Gospels* (1988), p. 98; K. King, '"Kingdom" in the Gospel of Thomas', *Forum* 3 (1987), p. 49.

5.   J. Jeremias suggests that it may be an original parable of Jesus. Jeremias, *The Parables of Jesus* (New York: Charles Scribner's Sons, 2nd rev. edn, 1972), p. 175 n. 12. King, 'Kingdom', p. 72, says that the type of asceticism in *Thomas* is possibly this early; in contrast to the strict Gnostic dualism between world and spirit (Kingdom).

6.   King, 'Kingdom', p. 49.

Wisdom and Gnosticism

Thomas is considered by most scholars to be Wisdom literature, particularly because of the emphasis on knowing vs. not knowing. Having certain special knowledge leads to the Kingdom; not having it bars the way. As *Gos. Thom.* 1 says, 'he who shall find the interpretation of these [secret] words [of Jesus] shall not taste death'. Despite the use of the word 'secret' in the beginning verse, however, the gospel does not in general dwell upon the secrecy of the desired knowledge, but only on its hiddenness and discovery. Thus, in this respect the overall thrust of *Thomas* is not gnostic. Logion 97 reflects the Wisdom aspect in that its story turns upon the woman's awareness. It states twice that she is unaware of her loss; and she discovers the loss only after it is complete. It is noteworthy that unlike gnostic literature, but like most of the rest of *Thomas*, in 97 the knowledge is not secret, but only hidden.

The particular type of ethic, an ascetic one, also is not gnostic. According to King,

> The *Gospel of Thomas* sees the world, on the one hand, *positively* as the place of wisdom: 'The kingdom of the father is spread out upon the earth and [it is just that] men do not see it' (*Gos. Thom.* 113);…on the other hand,… 'If you do not fast from the world you will not find the kingdom' (*Gos. Thom.* 27.1)… In *The Gospel of Thomas*, it is therefore not the world itself that is evil, as in the sharp dualism of later Gnosticism. Evil is instead seen as anything that distracts one from the spiritual quest.[7]

Consistent with this orientation, the woman in Logion 97 might learn something of the Kingdom through her worldly possessions and what becomes of them.

The Kingdom

The Kingdom is a major concern of the gospel. The conceptuality of the Kingdom is, however, very different from that in the canonical gospels. It is not a historical Kingdom as in the Hebrew prophets, and it is not centred upon the second coming of Jesus. A living Jesus speaks–thus giving authority to the words of this gospel–but he speaks as a 'dis-embodied oracle'.[8] According to Miller, 'The Kingdom is located neither in time nor in space, but in experience'.[9] Thus the *experience* of the woman who loses

7. King, 'Kingdom', p. 72.
8. B.F. Miller, 'Study of the Theme of "Kingdom", The Gospel According to Thomas: Logion 18', *NovT* 9 (1967), p. 52.
9. Miller, 'Study', p. 52.

her jarful of meal is, importantly, the very locus of the Kingdom in some way. It is noteworthy that her experience is couched in the most ordinary terms, of obtaining food, carrying, walking, arriving home–activities with which any reader might identify. Therefore the reader also may participate in the Kingdom of this gospel, no matter what the reader's time, place, or culture.

However, the parable in *Gos. Thom.* 97 presents problems in respect of the Kingdom as well. According to King, in *Thomas*, the Kingdom is composed of people who are wise persons of understanding, who have access to 'mysterious and effective power for transformation' (e.g., Logion 96, the leaven) and for overcoming their enemies (Logion 98, the person who slew a powerful man). Members of the Kingdom are 'morally good persons, who seek and find what is truly worthy of love', that is, who participate in the community that constitutes the Kingdom.[10] The woman is apparently not very effective in the one thing she is doing. Yet, as will be shown, there is a mysterious power at work in this parable, a power that is intended to involve the reader in the Kingdom community.

Thomas's *Use of Parables: Their Literary and Psychological Force*
This brings us to the logion as one of the parables of *Thomas*. *Thomas* contains fourteen parables, all but three having parallels in the synoptic gospels. Besides having the typical grammatical structure, these parables also bear the typical literary and psychological structure of the synoptic parable. Parables that contain the basic elements of a story tend to share certain characteristics. Among these elements, those that appear in Logion 97 are the most essential: the appeal to common experience (bringing home meal); the use of absurdities and ambiguities of the story (such as the loss being due to the broken handle); and particularly the abrupt ending.[11] New insights into the effect of the parable on the reader have come from recent research into its psychological nature. Such research has demonstrated that the characteristic elements of a parable are virtually the same as those of a therapeutic story–that is, the story used in therapy that

10. King, 'Kingdom', p. 58.
11. For a good list of these basic characteristics, see S. McFague, *Metaphorical Theology: Models of God in Religious Language* (Philadelphia: Fortress Press, 1982), pp. 2-15. C.W. Hedrick, 'Parables and the Kingdom: The Vision of Jesus in Fiction and Faith', *Society of Biblical Literature Seminar Papers* 26 (1987), p. 381, points out the degree to which the entire *Thomas* both invites and propels the reader to provide the ultimate meaning for such stories.

actually primes the client for a deep, inner change.[12]

The psychological research further shows that when these elements are present, the reader or hearer is blocked in making the ordinary cognitive responses. Thus, while the person is still wondering how a broken handle can result in the loss of the meal, a new problem is presented–how the woman could go all the way home from the 'distant' road without realizing her loss. Then comes the abrupt ending, which cries out for resolution. Literature on parables and that on the therapeutic story both show that, faced with such a story, the reader/hearer is emotionally propelled to provide that resolution for herself. Since the usual cognitive responses are blocked, the way is open–for just a moment–for an entirely new type of response, one that may lead to real inner change. What better way to propel the reader to new levels of insight, new wisdom, and the Kingdom?

Thus there is real reason to expect that a parable such as 'the empty jar' will produce the effect that is the declared intention of the entire gospel: to prompt in the reader the new awareness of the hidden knowledge that will lead to eternal life.

The Woman in Thomas

Finally, the woman in *Gos. Thom.* 97 is often thought to be an example of what the Kingdom should not be, specifically because she is a woman. This type of interpretation results from other sayings in the gospel, particularly the closing logion (114): 'Women are not worthy of the life. Jesus said: Look, I will lead her that I may make her male, in order that she too may become a living spirit…For every woman who makes herself male will enter into the kingdom of heaven'. This saying and others like it, however, are part of a conceptuality of the Kingdom as a return to the primordial state–the androgynous being who was created in the image of God. Upon closer inspection of this gospel, all sexuality is decried as the source of the fall of humankind (which of course occurred in the Genesis account only after there were male and female). This concept parallels Paul's statement (Gal. 3.26-28): 'You are all sons of God through faith in

---

12. K. Blessing, 'Luke's Unjust Steward Viewed from the Window of Psychiatrist Milton Erickson', Annual Meeting of the Society of Biblical Literature, Psychology and Biblical Studies Group, Washington, D.C., Nov. 23, 1993; based on McFague, *Metaphorical Theology*, pp. 2-15; and M. Erickson, 'The Confusion Technique in Hypnosis', in E.L. Rossi (ed.), *The Collected Works of Milton H. Erickson on Hypnosis*, I (New York: Irvington Publishers, Inc., 1989) pp. 258-91.

Christ Jesus...There is neither Jew nor Greek, slave nor free, male nor female, for you are all one in Christ Jesus'. Like Paul, *Thomas* does not intend to eradicate or ostracize the physical woman but to emphasize, although differently, the preeminence of the spirituality of the believer over all else. Another parallel occurs in Philo, who considers the female a symbol of that which is earthly, and the male, of that which is spiritual and intellectual. All people are to strive for what he calls the virginal state, undefiled by worldliness. For Paul, the requirement is belief in Jesus; for Philo, it is a philosophical orientation. The distinctiveness of *Thomas* is that the return to the primordial, pre-fall state depends upon discernment of the hidden knowledge which the gospel reveals to those who have 'ears to hear'.

Thus the woman in Logion 97 should not be seen as a negative example of the Kingdom simply because she is a woman. This parable is one of many examples in the gospel of the type of spirituality that brings man *or* woman into the Kingdom–the primordial image-of-God-like state. In just what way this parable demonstrates such spirituality is the subject of the remainder of this paper.

Interpretation of the Empty Jar

The Problem
It will already be evident that this story resists interpretation; it does so in several ways. The unlikely detail of the meal being lost because the handle had broken is at least distracting. The formal ending of the story (the last verse) is frustrating. This woman not only suffers loss but fails to be at all aware of it until it is too late. The double acknowledgment of her unawareness makes the bitterness of her experience palpable: 'She was unaware, she had not noticed the misfortune'. Finally, the lack of a true resolution gives the impression that something is missing. The lack of a real ending is disconcerting. What is the consequence of the loss? What does it mean? Thus the parable leaves the reader as well as the woman in a state of unknowing. The reader herself is left with something of an 'empty jar'.

Not the least of the difficulties is the enigmatic representation of the Kingdom as a person who suffers unrecoverable loss, rather than as one who receives reward or fulfillment. According to King, 'it is not surprising to find parables of foolish and wise persons, a stock theme in wisdom literature, treated under the rubric of kingdom' in *Thomas*. But how is it that the Kingdom can be likened to both? King articulates the major conundrum of this parable: 'What is surprising is likening the kingdom to ignorant/foolish persons'.[13] Jeremias interprets the parable as 'a warning against false security'[14]–hardly an image of the Kingdom. Scott notes this difficulty in a particularly incisive way: in 97, the Kingdom is 'identified with loss, with accident, with emptiness, and with *barrenness*'. He continues: 'if the kingdom is represented as a home, it is [here] the woman's side, in ancient Jewish culture, the side of shame and of the unclean'.[15]

In view of these considerations, King concludes, 'Of course it is possible to take the Gospel of Thomas seriously and believe that the Kingdom is like (or is composed of) persons who are foolish, who out of ignorance spill their meal...But I think until we can put a less humorous construction on Thomas' words, it is best to leave this parable out of consideration'.[16] Thus Logion 97 presents either a dead end or a challenge for the most astute interpreter.

Positive Insights into the Parable
Nevertheless, several scholars have offered insights into the parable. According to Montefiore, the interpretation centers on the imperceptible loss of the meal. However, he goes on to note that in respect of the woman's lack of knowledge, it is like the parable of the man casting seed (Mk 4.26-29). In the Markan parable (v. 27, NIV), 'Night and day, whether he [the farmer] sleeps or gets up, the seed sprouts and grows, *though he does not know how*'. Even though he is unaware and ineffectual in creating the growth, he has the gratification of reaping the harvest. According to Montefiore, Logion 97, by analogy, represents the coming of the Kingdom, imperceptible to people until it is revealed.[17] Thus, after Montefiore's interpretation, the import of the woman's unknowing state is reversed. It is a message about the Kingdom in relation to human ability to comprehend it. (Recall that the physical meal and its possession are not necessarily the point.)

Scott sees the double meaning but disagrees about the ultimate signifi-

13. King, 'Kingdom', p. 58.
14. Jeremias, *Parables*, p. 175 n. 12.
15. B.B. Scott, 'The Empty Jar', *Forum* 3 (1987), p. 78. Emphasis added.
16. King, 'Kingdom', p. 58 n. 19.
17. H. Montefiore and H. Turner, *Thomas and the Evangelists* (SBT 35; Naperville: Alec R. Allenson, 1962), p. 71.

cance of the story. He writes that the parable operates on two levels.[18] The first level is the obvious, the loss of the meal. The second level–rather than resolving the tension–increases it. This parable, according to Scott, represents a reversal of the story of the widow of Zarephath (1 Kgs 17.8-16). In that story, the prophet Elijah asks the widow to make him a cake from her very last bit of meal, despite the ongoing famine. Upon complying, she finds that her supply of meal becomes endless. Rather than starving to death, she and her child live indefinitely from it. Clearly this bounty results from divine intervention. In alluding to this text, Logion 97 creates a scandal, according to Scott. The Kingdom is not identified with divine intervention, but with 'divine emptiness'. This parable thus 'attacks and subverts the myth of the appearance of God', and *God* (not just the woman) is identified with the unclean. The only way this can be a representation of the Kingdom is an indirect one, by analogy with Jesus' association with the outcast.[19]

Is the Kingdom like the woman in being empty and ineffectual, or in remaining unaware until the appointed time? Even these thoughtful interpretations leave the reader wondering. However, these scholars do point the way to an avenue of interpretation that may yet prove fruitful: the implications of intertextual relationships.

Intertextual Clues in The Empty Jar

In relating the parable to that of the man planting seed and to the story of the widow in 1 Kings, the above interpretations are making use of intertextuality. In fact, other parables such as the Good Samaritan (Lk. 10.25-37), the treasure found in the field (Mt. 13.44), and the leaven (Mt. 13.33; Lk. 13.21; *Gos. Thom.* 96) have also been likened to the parable of the empty jar. The intertextual allusions of Logion 97 encompass a much larger corpus of biblical material, however. Before exploring them further, it is necessary to make clear what is meant by 'intertextuality' when dealing with a text of late antiquity.[20]

Usually, 'intertextuality' refers to the interconnectedness of two

18. Scott, 'Empty Jar', p. 78.
19. Scott, 'Empty Jar', p. 79.
20. Cartlidge presents a very good summary of this subject. D.R. Cartlidge, *'Combien d'unités avez-vous de trois à quatre?* What Do We Mean by Intertextuality in Early Church Studies?', in D.J. Lull (ed.), *Society of Biblical Literature Seminar Papers* (Atlanta: Scholars Press, 1990), pp. 400-11.

documents by quotation, allusion, or influence. There are two basic sources of intertextual reference: influence manifested by the work of the author of the document, whether consciously or unconsciously; and connections perceived by the reader, whether created by the author or not. In regard to late antiquity, intertextuality does not refer exclusively to written documents. What we think of as a literary genre—the parable, for instance—existed both orally and textually. If a tradition was written down, it was for the purpose of reading aloud in the community. Many documents such as *Thomas* use these references to reflect the particular theological and social issues faced by the community in which each was transmitted. Thus interpretation of Logion 97 must relate in some way to the concerns of the *Thomas* community–specifically with the Kingdom and its fulfillment.

Finally and perhaps most important, even word-for-word agreement does not necessarily indicate literary dependence as such. Many traditions and texts existed in the 'ambient culture' and would be accessible–or in the 'back of the mind'–for the bearer of the tradition. Therefore connections such as those described here do not prove direct influence among the texts as we have them, but may nonetheless be of considerable importance.

Without attempting to be exhaustive, we can identify at least two parabolic themes in 'the empty jar'. The first is that of loss/finding; the second is that of planting/growing. Both of these themes are found in non-parabolic texts as well. Both themes are also related to the Wisdom concern with the hidden vs. the revealed.

Themes of Loss

The theme of loss in the synoptics is an obvious place to begin in approaching the meaning of Logion 97. The synoptics address different kinds of loss. The parables of the lost coin (Lk. 15.8-9) and the lost sheep (Mt. 18.12-13; Lk. 15.3-6) present the image of a woman and a man respectively who leave all to find the one that is missing. Both are given with interpretations to the effect that God rejoices over one who is lost and found again (that is, one who repents). The prodigal (Lk. 15.11-32) presents a similar theme; here, the 'lost' returns on his own. In these cases, loss is undoubtedly negative and to be corrected; abandonment of God is portrayed as God 'losing' one of God's own. Notably, the implication is that God does the correcting.

The 'hidden treasure' (Mt. 13.44) contains an implicit loss by the former owner of the field in which the treasure was found. Unlike Matthew, *Thomas* 109 makes the loss explicit and dwells upon it. Like Logion 97, 109 has two statements that the owners did not know (in this case, about the buried treasure). Thus they did not know that, in selling the field, they had lost the treasure. In *Thomas* (unlike Matthew), the new owner has already bought the field before he discovers the treasure; it is upon plowing it that he finds it. Apparently, the father, then the son who inherits the field, have failed to plow it. Thus the implication is that the one who works the field finds the treasure and also has the hidden revealed to him.[21] This links the Wisdom theme of hidden/revealed knowledge with the loss/finding theme of the synoptics. Again, it would appear that loss is negative–except that Logion 110 enjoins the one who 'has found…and become rich' to renounce the world. Thus finding is denounced also. It is only the discerning of the hidden that is valued, a subtle distinction left to the reader's inference.

To return to the empty jar, this parable also overlays the themes of loss vs. finding and hidden vs. revealed knowledge. From *Thomas'* variation on the synoptic parable of the hidden treasure, it is evident that the woman's loss of the physical meal, while unfortunate, is not the point. It is the revelation of previously hidden knowledge–which indeed she has before the end of the story. Further, if the synoptic assessment of loss is any indication, it is God who rectifies loss, specifically loss of one of God's own from the Kingdom. The woman in Logion 97 may simply have been 'set up' both for a moment of revelation, and for a yet uncompleted intervention by God. If this is the case, then Scott is incorrect that the parable represents a subversion of God's intervention. The intervention is left as a question mark, a possibility; at least, it is not explicitly contravened.

There are two other, non-parabolic, intertextual connections on the theme of loss, specifically related to emptying and filling. The first is the image of being 'poured out' (Logion 97, 'the meal poured out behind her on the road'). In the Bible, very few and particular things are ever 'poured out'. Apart from wrath (several times in Jeremiah) and love (Rom. 5.5), all other references–the great majority–are to the related subjects of offerings to and by God, and the offering of life itself. Offerings to God include sacrifices poured upon the altar or as a libation or other symbolic sacrifice. Offerings (gifts) from God include rain, symbolically equivalent to life; and the Holy Spirit, either poured out directly upon the believer or

21. Stroker, 'Extracanonical Parables', pp. 107-108, discusses this element of Logion 109.

symbolized by anointing with oil. The expected (grieving) sense of life being poured out is referred to in Job 30.16; Ps. 22.14; 79.3; 106.38. However, this simpler theme is combined with that of offerings to God in the very striking Phil. 2.17. There, Paul writes, 'I am being poured out like a drink offering on the sacrifice and service coming from your faith'. The pouring out represents both Paul's literal sacrifice of his life for the Gospel and the offering of life made by the conversion of the people to whom he writes. Finally, Paul's statement is not unrelated to the most important pouring-out in the New Testament, Mk 14.24 (cf. Mt. 26.28; Lk. 22.20): Jesus says at the Last Supper, 'This is my blood of the covenant, which is poured out for many' for salvation. Thus it is no small thing for an ancient tradition to present Jesus addressing the subject of 'pouring out'.

Does this symbolism have anything to do with the pouring-out in the empty jar? First of all, as stated by Scott, the elements of a parable, and this one in particular, are multivalent. Of course the meal is lost in the simple, frustrating sense; however, the meal *offering* was a powerful and central image in Israel. Further, bread and that from which it is made are generally considered to be symbolic of life itself, as is made explicit throughout John 6 (the 'bread of life'). Logion 97 thus contains pointed sacrificial imagery–that is, for the reader who has ears to hear (or eyes to see) it. The fact that the woman initially was unaware of the pouring-out does not diminish this. It is upon the completion of the 'sacrifice' that the hidden is revealed to her, as if by divine plan–even though on the surface it seems wrong that she comes to awareness of the loss only after the meal is irretrievably gone.

Add to this the importance of the phrase 'on the road', and the loss can no longer be simply a human accident. It is when she is walking 'on the road' that the woman has made sacrifice of a symbol of her life. Throughout the history of Israel, God reveals Godself when the people are *bĕderek*–on the way, often translated 'on the road'. For example, nearly all of the uses of this term in Exodus have this meaning, as well as many instances of it in Deuteronomy (e.g., 3.1; 5.33; 8.2). John's gospel makes a point of the disciples seeking to be 'on the way/road' with Jesus. In Jn 14.4-6, Jesus says, 'You know the way to the place where I am going'. Thomas replies, 'We don't know where you are going, so how can we know the way?' Jesus replies, 'I am the way'; the way is then set in apposition to the truth and the life. For God's people to be on the road is symbolically to be walking in the way of Jesus, living his life and death. Thus the woman in *Gos. Thom.* 97 can be seen as a disciple of the Lord.

Like John's Thomas, she is walking in the Lord's way, *without under-standing*. Only later, she suddenly realizes (in both senses) the sacrifice and offering that she has made. This interpretation accords with Monte-fiore's statement that the poured out meal is the imperceptible coming of the Kingdom. In this understanding, her 'sacrifice' and her coming to realization–action and knowing together–bring her into the Kingdom. That is why the Kingdom is like a woman who has lost her jar of meal.

Another empty/full paradigm has to do with the jar or vessel, often symbolic of the womb, the woman, or the people of God who are receptive to God's Spirit. This subject is summarized by Fehribach in relation to the Samaritan woman (Jn 4.4-42).[22] Fehribach demonstrates that the vessel is symbolic of the woman or of God's people by making explicit the allusion of this image to such texts as Prov. 5.15-18; Cant. 4.12; Jer. 2.1-15. In the context of the Samaritan woman, the point is that it does not matter whether her dipping bowl is full or empty of the physical well water. What matters is that she, as the vessel of the Lord, has room for the living water (the Spirit, eternal life) that Jesus offers to her. To put it another way, she is incapable of filling her jar in a way that is meaningful for the Kingdom until she is given the previously hidden knowledge of Jesus. Once she knows him as Messiah, she brings this knowledge to the rest of the Samaritans, with the result that all of them believe in Jesus. Thus she has borne many children for the Lord. Meanwhile, apparently she never does fill the physical jar. Jn 4.28 says, 'Leaving her water jar' (not, 'leaving her water'), she went back to the town to tell the people all about Jesus. The Samaritan woman forgets the whole jar. However, she is herself filled, so that she will never have to draw and fill again, spiritually. Like the widow of Zarephath, she is given perpetual food/drink/life–beginning with her state of unknowing and her empty physical vessel.

The woman in Logion 97 is no different; the implications are the same. It does not matter whether the jar is full or empty of the physical meal. What matters is that the woman/vessel/symbolic jar is filled with knowledge–in *Thomas*, knowledge that somehow relates to the Kingdom. What this knowledge is–beyond the simple loss of the meal–is not stated explicitly in 97. It is a direct invitation to the reader to supply or discern that critical knowledge for herself. Several other intertextual allusions will aid in that discernment here.

22. A. Fehribach, *The Women in the Life of the Bridegroom: A Feminist Historical-Literary Analysis of the Female Characters in the Fourth Gospel* (Collegeville, MN: Liturgical Press, 1989), pp. 52-58.

Themes of Planting/Growing

The meal in Logion 97 suggests grain, and several scholars have likened 97 to the parable of the leaven (Mt. 13; Lk. 13; *Gos. Thom.* 96, just before the empty jar). Grain, planting, growing, and leaven are all related by the fact that something small grows into something large without the knowledge or action of the human agent. Among the extensive references to planting and growing are the parables of the man scattering seed (above) and the sower (Mt. 13; Mk 4; Lk. 8; *Gos. Thom.* 9). Of course, the metaphor of planting and sowing is everywhere–including the story of the Samaritan woman. Fehribach shows that the interlude in that story concerning the harvest (Jn 4.31-38) relates to the Samaritan woman's 'sowing' the seed of the knowledge of Jesus among the Samaritans: she says that this passage alludes to Jer. 2.2-3 and other texts that portray God's people as the first fruits of God's harvest. Thus the Samaritan woman is a symbolic bride for Jesus as God's people are God's 'bride'. The disciples (Jn 4.37-38) are about to reap what 'others' (the Samaritan woman in particular) have sown; in other terms, they will gather the children she has borne for Jesus.[23] By analogy, admittedly a loose one, the woman in Logion 97 has scattered the seed of the Kingdom/the bread of life. Anyone who goes by the same road may find it.

While this analogy may seem weak, it becomes stronger when we consider the parable of the sower. If the woman is so unknowing (in the most derogatory sense)–she is no less so than the sower. The sower, clearly known to the writer of *Thomas*, scatters three-quarters of the seed in places where it cannot possibly grow. If anyone is unknowing in the (surface) sense of true stupidity or irresponsibility, it is the sower. Yet the sower scatters for a purpose–so that anyone and everyone (all of the soil) can have access to the seed (the word). If some of the seed is eaten by birds or other animals, perhaps it will be indirectly replanted in another place; but it is all worth it for the sake of the Kingdom. The woman of Logion 97 is no less stupid, but also no less self-sacrificial and no less comprehensive in her scattering. If she and her scattering are an image of the Kingdom, it is in this way: she allows for the food of the Kingdom to be spread out for the entire world. In that lies her own Kingdom living– especially if it is done unselfconsciously, in the way, in the ordinary course of life. In this the Kingdom, and the woman's action, is like love. It cannot really be one's own until it is given away. But love cannot be measured out in the giving; real love is given freely, with abandon, as that

23. Fehribach, *Women*, pp. 56-58.

of a woman for her first-born child–or that of God for the Kingdom. Thus the meal itself, as previously observed, is not the critical element. The critical element is for the reader (perhaps along with the woman) to see in what way the knowledge of the Kingdom is to be used, a way that is paradoxically unlike the ordinary ways of the world.

Finally, there is one more theme of emptiness that is alluded to by Scott when he uses the term 'barrenness'. While he sees this as a negative characterization of the Kingdom, in fact it may be the most positive of all. While it is not well known, there is a prophetic theme of the barren woman that runs throughout the Bible and all of the Judaic literature at least up to the time of the Bar Kochba revolt (c. 135 C.E.). Barrenness, of course, refers to a woman's failure to bear children, and in biblical cultures is usually the worst thing that can befall her. However, the distinctive Hebrew and Greek terms used in the Bible for 'barren' are strictly reserved for a special group of women. These are the women who are destined to bear the special child who will perpetuate the people of God (the Kingdom).[24] These women, Sarah, Rebekah, Rachel, and the mother of Samson in particular, do in fact perpetuate the people of God physically and spiritually. Note that the biblical women who are so designated are *forever* associated with the term and the concept of that kind of barren-ness. Their first children are explicitly said to be born by the intervention, and through the salvation-plan, of God. The other type of non-fruitful-ness—a desolate, non-arable land (or a woman mourning her lost children)—is always designated by other terms. The consistency of the linguistic pattern has been documented by Blessing.[25] Thus the ancient Judaic literature and the New Testament carefully distinguish two kinds of barrenness.

The significance for *Gos. Thom.* 97 is not in the use of the exact terms–since the logion exists only in Coptic–but rather is in the strength of the two cultural images of the fruitless woman. On the surface, the woman in Logion 97 is, metaphorically, the unacceptable kind of barren. She has simply lost her 'fruit' (in this case, the meal). A woman who represents this type of fruitlessness (desolation) cannot possibly represent the Kingdom. However, there hovers over this surface image the powerful one

24. There is only one exception in the Bible (Job 24:21), using the term as part of common language.

25. K. Blessing, 'Desolate Jerusalem and Barren Matriarch: Two Distinct Figures in the Pseudepigrapha', *Journal for the Study of the Pseudepigrapha* 18 (1998), pp. 47-69.

of the women who are described using the special terminology that
prophesies God's intervention. If the woman whose jar is empty is to be
like the Kingdom, and if she also represents barrenness, it must be the
divine-intervention type of barrenness. She is 'remembered' for her empty
'vessel' for one of two reasons: she is destined to give birth to the
Kingdom people in some way, or she has just done so. The realization/
revelation that the reader is to see in the woman in *Gos. Thom*. 97 is this:
she has just scattered (a symbol of) the Kingdom–a trail leading down the
road to it, though the ultimate 'destination' is not yet seen.

Actually, in Logion 97, the woman is both desolate and barren (the
victim of hopeless loss and the recipient of divine intervention). It is for
the reader to have ears to hear and eyes to see, and to resolve the meaning
of the story. The resolution may be to recognize the tension between the
two types of emptiness. The point is that it is up to the wise person to
discern which type of woman enters and perpetuates the Kingdom, and
then to apply the new understanding to her own life. The message of the
parable is then that the believer must become much more alert for the quiet
working of the Spirit in her life. Since the woman in the context of the
parable represents the people of God ('the Kingdom...is like' her), this
message of course applies to the male reader as well.

Conclusions

The parable of the woman who has lost her meal represents the Kingdom
in a number of important ways. First, it very likely tells us something that
Jesus really did teach about the Kingdom. Second, in being multivalent,
the parable demonstrates the predicament of one who is seeking the
Kingdom as represented in *Thomas*: a state of unawareness is contrasted
with a state of awareness (presumably, of something about the Kingdom).
The woman–seen in the context of the Wisdom ethos of this gospel–is
foolish and empty, but also very fruitful indeed for the spread of the
Kingdom. Not the least of her fruitfulness is in being Kingdom-like
herself. She is so by unwittingly and unselfconsciously demonstrating the
way in which a Kingdom person must walk, and the way in which she
must use her worldly goods in order to be a member of the Kingdom. It is
a way that, not surprisingly, is at odds with the world per se. Very
possibly, like the Samaritan woman, she has borne children for the
Kingdom. This woman has symbolically placed a biblical and cultural
symbol of life in their path.

Finally, the parable is prophetic; it accomplishes what it speaks. The very frustration evident in some scholars' conclusion that it cannot be interpreted bears witness to the pressing psychological and spiritual need of the reader somehow to supply that meaning. In the midst of this tension, if the reader comes to the knowledge of the way in which a member of the Kingdom should walk, she has accomplished the purpose of this gospel: to discern a part of the hidden knowledge that leads, ultimately, to eternal life.

THE LANGUAGE OF MOTHER WORK IN THE *GOSPEL OF THOMAS*: KEEPING MOMMA OUT OF THE KINGDOM (*GOS. THOM.* 22)*

Kathleen Nash

May her breasts satisfy you at all times;
may you always be intoxicated by her love (Prov. 5.19).

There will be days when you will say:
blessed is the womb that has not conceived,
blessed are the breasts that have not given milk (*Gos. Thom.* Logion 79).

Jesus saw little ones nursing. He said to his disciples: 'These little ones nursing are like those who enter the <Father's> kingdom'. They said to him: 'Then we shall enter the <Father's> kingdom as little ones?'

Jesus said to them: 'When you make the two into one, when you make the inside like the outside and the outside like the inside; when you make the above like the below; when you make the male and the female into a single one, so that the male will not be male and the female will not be female; when you make eyes in place of an eye, a hand in place of a hand, a foot in place of a foot, an image in place of an image, then you will enter [the <Father's>] kingdom'.[1]

* A 1999 summer stipend from the Le Moyne College Faculty Research and Development Committee supported research for this paper. Mary Ann Beavis has been a solicitous and considerate editor. Paul Goggi listened and challenged through months of talk about mothers, fathers, and little ones; his hope kept me writing. Jennifer Glancy, Mary Ann Keenan, Mary MacDonald, and Nancy Ring, Le Moyne colleagues, also contributed in numerous ways. Thank you all.
    1. R. Valantasis, *The Gospel of Thomas* (Routledge: London, 1999), p. 95. In this paper I follow Valantasis and the Scholars Version of the Gospel of Thomas in R.J. Miller (ed.), *The Complete Gospels* (Sonoma: Polebridge Press, 1992). The pointed brackets contain words implied in the original text and suppled by the translator of the Scholars Version.

Introduction

A root metaphor in the *Gospel of Thomas* is the act of 'making two into one'. The select few who accomplish this feat may enter the Kingdom of the Father; they discover new power and authority. They are no longer born of woman. They reject their biological parentage to become sons of the Father. They are reformed as infants within the sayings of the gospel. The Father's word, his will, shapes them. The path to the Kingdom presumes a certain asceticism that creates a new subject, a new identity.[2] While that identity is spiritual, 'so that male is no longer male, and female no longer female', discourse about the Kingdom, about those who may enter it, is gendered as male. The Kingdom, already present to the Thomas-Community,[3] is the Father's domain. Woman as mother is exiled. The Father makes no place for her in the Kingdom. Woman may become a living spirit only if she makes herself male (Logion 114) and accepts a male consciousness.

I argue that, in the *Gospel of Thomas*, the act of gaining the Kingdom, being saved, is a harsh and violent process for women, amounting to psychic rape, a lobotomy of the female self.[4] In Logion 114, for example, Jesus announces he will make Mary 'worthy of life' by making her male; he does not consider that she may, indeed, have a spiritual self, her self-knowledge as 'the woman Mary, female daughter of Eve'.[5] He carves out an interiority for her and fills it with a consciousness. Once Peter announces that Mary should leave because, as a female, she does not

2.   Valantasis, *Thomas*, pp. 10-12. For background on asceticism relevant to the *Gospel of Thomas*, see S. Griffith, 'Asceticism in the Church of Syria: The Hermeneutics of Early Syrian Monasticism', in V.L. Wimbush and R. Valantasis (eds.), *Asceticism* (New York: Oxford University Press, 1995), pp. 220-45; for a full discussion, see S.J. Patterson, *The Gospel of Thomas and Jesus* (Sonoma, CA: Polebridge Press, 1993), pp. 196-214.

3.   Throughout this paper, I use the terminology 'Thomas-Gospel' and 'Thomas-Community' found in B. Lincoln, 'Thomas-Gospel and Thomas-Community: A New Approach to a Familiar Text', *NovT* 19 (1977), pp. 65-76.

4.   My reading of the text has little in common with other feminist interpretations of this gospel, especially their readings of Logia 22 and 104; for example, J J. Buckley, *Female Fault and Fulfillment in Gnosticism* (Chapel Hill: University of North Carolina Press, 1986); Valantasis, *Thomas*, pp. 95-96, 194-95.

5.   A. McGuire, 'Women, Gender, and Gnosis in Gnostic Texts and Traditions', in R.S. Kraemer and M.R. D'Angelo, W*omen and Christian Origins* (New York: Oxford University Press, 1999), p. 278.

deserve life, her options are limited. Her femaleness can be forced to the margins of the Kingdom, or she can submit to the sea-change Jesus offers. Either way she does not act or choose for herself; she is acted upon. If she does remain in the Kingdom, seeking her own subjectivity, she threatens the stability established by the 'Law of the Father'.

To examine the language of what I call 'mother work'—pregnancy, birth, and breastfeeding—in the Thomas-Gospel, I combine some historical critical methodology with an analytic narrative approach that searches for ways to incorporate feminine voices into the text in order to counter masculine constructs masquerading as the 'truth' about woman. The resulting analysis is, admittedly, uneven and awkward since there are many 'truths' about women, no combination of them reducible to one. Julia Kristeva's work on the intersections of literary theory and psychoanalysis influences my reading of the *Gospel of Thomas*. In her consideration of some of the legal material in the Book of Leviticus, Kristeva listens to 'the linguistic subject of the biblical utterance', a subject who, she discovers,

> is not at all neutral and indifferent like the subjects described by modern theories of interpretation, but who maintains a specific relationship of *crisis, trial,* or *process* with his God.[6]

This subject is the text's narrator, with a stake in the outcome of the text because the act of discourse, which produces the text, also creates his identity. In the book of Leviticus, the speaking subject delineates 'the precise limits of abjection (from skin to food, sex, and moral codes)';[7] he creates pairs of opposites by marking the boundaries between, for example, inside and outside, female and male. In literature as in psychoanalysis, the subject becomes a speaking being through abjection, the repression or silencing of the 'other', who threatens the order that speech creates. Because identity is shaped within such an order, the abject necessarily threatens the speaker as well. Kristeva notes that the breakdown of the Levitical system brings 'the abject collapsing back in on the prophet as speaking subject and on the people of Israel as a whole'.[8]

---

6. J. Kristeva, *New Maladies of the Soul* (tr. R. Guberman; New York: Columbia University Press, 1995), p. 117.

7. Kristeva, *Maladies*, p. 118.

8. This discussion depends heavily on T. Beal ('Opening: Cracking the Binding', in *Reading Bibles, Writing Bodies: Identity and the Book* [eds. T.K. Beal and D. M. Gunn; London: Routledge, 1997], pp.1-11). Beal provides a particularly lucid application of Kristeva's approach to texts in his provocative reading of Mic. 1.8-9.

In the Thomas-Gospel, the repudiation of the world, typified in the abjection of the Mother, creates the boundary between Kingdom and world. In this Kingdom, woman loses both voice and identity. My goal in this essay is to find voices for 'the secret movement, the breaking, the torment, the unexpected'[9] speech of the female abject in the *Gospel of Thomas.*

Some Initial Observations

If an organizing principle, other than the intermittent *mot crochet*, guided the placement of sayings in the *Gospel of Thomas,* it remains as elusive as the meaning of the gospel itself.[10] While an earlier version of the gospel based on sayings of the apostle James may have circulated in Jerusalem before his martyrdom in 62 CE, a later author reworked and completed the Thomas-Gospel in eastern Syria, perhaps around Odessa, at the end of the first century CE. The gospel may represent a polemic against a more centrist Christian sayings tradition connected with the synoptic gospels.[11] Other suggested functions include: instructions governing an individual's passage through several stages of initiation into the Thomas-Community;[12] guidelines for socialization into a settled community;[13] preparation for baptism and safeguard against spiritual *ennui*;[14] legitimation of itinerant prophets, preachers, and teachers and the radical moral vision they advocated;[15] a manual for creating a new subjectivity and arriving at true self-knowledge.[16]

When I first discovered the *Gospel of Thomas,* I tried to read it as if I

9. Beal, 'Opening', p. 4.

10. For a discussion of the relationship between the form and the order of the sayings, see S.J. Patterson, *The Gospel of Thomas and Jesus* (Sonoma, CA: Polebridge Press, 1993), pp. 94-102. Patterson comments: 'The order of Thomas' sayings is motivated not by an elaborate theological system, gnostic or otherwise. Rather, its organizing principle is the very pragmatic technique of using catchwords to link successive sayings together' (p. 110).

11. Patterson, *Thomas and Jesus*, pp. 118-20. For a current survey of proposed dates, see Valantasis, *Thomas*, pp. 12-21.

12. Lincoln, 'Thomas-Gospel', pp. 67-68.

13. K. King, '"Kingdom" in the Gospel of Thomas', *FFNT* 34 (1987), pp. 48-97, cited in Patterson, *Jesus and Thomas*, pp. 48-97.

14. D.R. MacDonald, *There is No Male and Female: The Fate of a Dominical Saying in Paul and Gnosticism* (HDR 20; Philadelphia: Fortress Press, 1987).

15. Patterson, *Thomas and Jesus*, pp. 196-214.

16. Valantasis, *Thomas*, pp. 10-12.

were its ideal reader. I set aside disbelief and suspicion, fantasized myself into a 'little one' marked for the Kingdom; I was determined to glimpse that true self the gospel promised. Before long, I abandoned this project; the self, if it was there, had little interest in showing up to satisfy my curiosity. Now I come to the Thomas-Gospel again, this time as a 'problem reader', suspicious and cautious, sniffing out silences and plotting to fill them. I still hear the narrator's masculine voice, carving out more and more space for the sons of the Father, laying down boundaries, imposing order.

In the gospel, only three women speak. To understand more about the disciples, Mary asks Jesus to describe them, so he compares them to children, a category he assumes she understands (Logion 21). More boldly, Salome asks Jesus to identify himself when she finds him at her table; when he admits his equality with the Father, she declares, 'I am your disciple' (Logion 61).[17] A nameless woman calls out a blessing on the womb and breasts that nurtured Jesus, but Jesus blesses barren wombs and dry breasts, challenging this woman's ability to interpret her experiences (Logion 79). At the margins of the text, though, I hear sounds, coming from the borders of the Kingdom, in search of voice and subject. Pre-verbal, chaotic, they howl and swell with rage. My reading tries to coax these sounds into speech, to discover and reclaim what is lost when the Kingdom is secured.

Other essays in this collection discuss parables from the *Gospel of Thomas* in which the author has Jesus describe Kingdom by appealing to works of women—a woman 'hiding' leaven in dough to make more bread (Logion 96), a woman carrying home a jar full of meal, trailing its contents behind her (Logion 97). Further sayings refer to woman's work located in and on the female body—the labour of pregnancy, birth, and breast-feeding. To construct a context for reading Logion 22 with its talk of nursing babies or little ones and 'making male and female into a single one', I analyze the language of mother-work in Logia 15, 46, 79, 99, 101, and 105. In order to create and maintain an identity for the Kingdom of the Father, the narrator represses desire for and fear of the Mother. He creates opposition between Mother and Father, between world and Kingdom. He makes woman into the likeness of the world, thereby legitimating her exclusion from the Father's Kingdom unless she makes herself male. He builds the Kingdom on top of the Mother to contain her, but the part that is not-mother lurks at the edges of the Kingdom.

17. For a full discussion of problems associated with this saying, see Valantasis, *Thomas*, pp. 138-40.

The Language of Mother-work in the Selected Sayings of the Thomas-Gospel

The Thomas-Gospel uses a range of phrases to refer to the work of birthing, nourishing, and legitimizing babies: 'born of woman', 'not born of woman' (Logia 15 and 46); 'nursing babies' (Logion 22); 'womb that bore...and the breasts that fed...(Logion 79); 'mother' (Logion 99); 'mother and father', 'child of a whore' (Logion 105). Although the Coptic text of Logion 101 is damaged, a likely reconstruction yields '[father] and mother' and 'my mother...but my true [Father?]...'.

In Logion 15, one not born of woman is 'our Father', meriting worship and honor:

> Jesus said: 'When you see one who was not born of woman, fall on your faces and worship. That one is your Father'.[18]

A related saying, Logion 46, provides a rabbit-hole, labeled 'becom[ing] a child', through which the reader can escape the consequences of being woman-born and attain superiority over John the Baptist:

> Jesus said: 'From Adam to John the Baptist, among those born of women, no one is so much greater than John the Baptist that his eyes should not be averted. I have also said: Whoever among you becomes a child will know the Kingdom and will become superior to John'.[19]

This saying moves from a 'before' time (from Adam to John the Baptist) to an 'after' time (from Jesus onward), the temporal location of the Thomas-Community. Those 'born of woman' belong to this inferior Adam-to-John time, with John as its best exemplar. Jesus, however, inaugurates a new temporal dimension, 'the Kingdom', with whoever 'becom[es] a child' as its only exemplar. This Kingdom time is present and available to the Thomas-Community.[20] Those who are chosen to recognize and know this Kingdom have the work of interpreting the gospel's secret sayings; in this way, the reader lays aside the consequences of being 'woman born', that is, escapes mortality and death. The narrator sets woman's birth work in opposition to 'knowing the Kingdom' and places 'becoming a child' in opposition to 'born of woman'. The fruit of woman's womb is a physical being whose future is death. Study of the *logos* within the Thomas-Gospel does what woman cannot do; it brings forth a spiritual being who will never feast on death (Logion 1).

18. Valantasis, *Thomas*, p. 81.
19. Valantasis, *Thomas*, p. 122.
20. Crossan, *The Historical Jesus*, p. 262.

In Logion 15, 'one not born of woman' is the Father, whom the disciples should immediately recognize. Perhaps they have accomplished the work of replacing physical eyes with a single, spiritual eye (Logion 22). Perhaps the ability to recognize the Father comes with true self-knowledge. Within, the disciples discover the gospel's secret; they are the image of Jesus who is himself the image of the Father, the son of the Living One. In a real sense, 'it takes one to know one'.

If the Thomas-Community happens to agree with Paul that Jesus is 'born of woman, born under the law' (Gal. 4.4-5), then, in light of Logion 15, he cannot be the Father. At the same time, if he is 'born of woman', then, according to Logion 46, John the Baptist ranks ahead of him. A dubious reading, I admit. An alternative interpretation, more congruent with the gospel as a whole, is that the living Jesus whom the community knows is, in fact, the transformed woman-born Jesus, now a living spirit. This transformed Jesus is uncreated *logos*, the eternal s*ophia,* of the one God whom Jesus knows as the Father. This reading may be more questionable than the interpretation it purports to replace. It does, however, relate to 'the single one' of Logion 22 and the 'living spirit' of Logion 114 (discussed below) 'The Father' is, then, the divine One manifested as the living Jesus whose presence quickens the Thomas-Community.

Pushing the envelope to the extreme, 'the Father' may also be another name for the new consciousness forming within readers as they study and perform the sayings in the Thomas-Gospel. Having become little ones, they enter the Kingdom and possess it as it possesses them. As living spirits, they are one with Jesus who is one with the Father. They see beyond the physical to recognize the Father in their encounters with each other. Greeting one another becomes an act of spiritual worship.

The Kingdom in the *Gospel of Thomas* is the domain of the Father, a world of absolutes whose meaning brooks no challenge. For those who master it, this meaning confers identity and relieves them of 'the agonized joy of self relation, of self-creation, of self-observation in the bizarre and facinating process of relating to what constitutes the self as subject'.[21] While women, as well as men, can become little ones and enter this Kingdom, there is no place for women as mother. Woman as mother is physicality, plurality, pushed to the margins of the Kingdom. Her energy, necessarily repressed and controlled, maintains its borders and preserves

21. P. Huntington, *Ecstatic Subjects, Utopia, and Recognition: Kristeva, Heidegger, Irigaray* (Albany: State University of New York Press), p. 4.

stability.[22] At the same time there is more to woman as mother than the Kingdom can contain; this excess is a force that 'dissolves identity' and reveals what this society censures',[23] a *jouissance* or bliss that resists turning 'the human drive for meaning…into another "religion" ' or value system by mastering meaning and finding a passage through it in order to articulate a new disposition,[24] a new Kingdom as it were. Logion 79 reveals the potency of such *jouissance*:

> A woman in the crowd said to him: 'Blessed the womb that bore you and the breasts that fed you'. He said to her: 'Blessed are those who have heard the word of the Father and have truly kept it. For there will be days when you will say: "Blessed the womb that has not conceived and the breasts that have not given milk" '.[25]

This unnamed woman's shout disrupts Jesus' hold on the crowd; it diverts attention from his words and introduces a new subject, the femaleness that created and nourished him. Speaking from a masculine perspective, the woman identifies the mother in pieces, by those body parts that determine woman's worth in a patriarchal society: lactating breasts and a fertile womb. In the eyes of the narrator, neither the speaker nor her subject has the interior unity that merits a personal name. Woman, the 'sex that is not one', cannot participate in the kingdom as long as she remains not-one and woman.

The female speaker is the narrator's pawn; she does not bless the breasts and womb of Jesus' mother because they possess innate value. She acknowledges them for their yield, a son. She recognizes that these breasts and womb have served some man well; the male child is their *raison d'être*, the one connection the narrator allows between woman and life. Through the birth of a son, a woman acquires blessedness, a state she cannot achieve for herself.

The speaker may also be honoring her acquired blessedness, the son whose birth redeems her socially. She may be congratulating all mothers

22. E. Grosz, *Sexual Subversions: Three French Feminists* (Sidney: Allen and Unwin, 1981), pp. 71-78.

23. J. Kristeva, 'Women Can Never be Defined', in E. Marks and I. de Courtivron (eds.), *New French Feminisms: An An thology* (New York: Schocken Books by arrangement with University of Massachusetts Press, 1980), p. 138.

24. J. Kristeva, *Revolution in Poetic Language* (trans. M. Waller; New York: Columbia University Press, 1984), p. 51.

25. Valantasis, *Thomas*, p. 158.

on jobs well done.[26] Perhaps she subscribes to the 'old wives' tale' that, along with his mother's breast milk, the nursing child takes in personal traits so that a good mother, even a 'good-enough mother', deserves some credit if the little one matures into a good man.[27]

This woman, then, praises what a man might praise: the womb and breasts that produce a son for him, the womb and breasts whose power he fears. Woman's perspective on mother-work is absent. Some women consider it a blessing; others do not. If this woman and the mother she praises could escape the narrator's control, they might describe their pregnancies as disorienting, empowering, fulfilling, maddening. One might acknowledge she felt as if she were a stranger to her body, sharing its inside space with a tenant she could not control.

> It stirred inside me. Could I control its movements with my will?… I was not myself. And not for a brief passing moment of rapture, which men, too, experience, but for nine watchful quiet months… Then it was born. I heard it scream with a voice that was no longer mine.[28]

The other might describe mother-work as 'immediate and inescapable contact with the sources of life, death, beauty, growth, corruption…central to the main issues of life, relevant to great art',[29] the threshold of spiritual connections with the universe, enormous spirituality, and profound creativity. Protesting the unnamed speaker in Logion 79, they might also cry out together:

26. Valantasis, *Thomas*, pp. 158-59.
27. The philosopher Favarinus urges one of his followers to insist that his wife breast feed their infant son: 'Why in heaven's name corrupt that nobility of body and mind of the newborn human being, which was off to a fine start, with the alien and degraded food of the milk of a stranger? Especially if the person you use to supply milk is…from a foreign and barbarian nation, or if she is dishonest, or ugly, or immodest, or unchaste, or a drinker… The disposition of the nurse and the quality of the milk play a great role in character development; the milk is, from the beginning, tinged with the father's seed, and affects the baby from the mother's mind and body as well'. (M. Lefkowitz and M. Fant [eds.], *Women's Life in Greece and Rome: A Source Book in Translation* [2nd edition; Baltimore: The Johns Hopkins University Press, 1992], no. 250). In no. 251, a young mother gives her criteria for a wetnurse: '…a modest woman, inclined neither to drowsiness nor to drunkenness so she can make the best judgments about how to care for children appropriately' (3rd/2nd century BCE, Italy).
28. Cited in Adrienne Rich, *Of Woman Born: Motherhood as Experience and Institution* (New York: Bantam Books, 1981), p. 161.
29. Alicia Ostriker, quoted in U. LeGuin, 'The Hand That Rocks the Cradle Writes the Book', *New York Times Review of Books* (January 22, 1989), p. 36.

Mothers, what have you taught me?... Mothers, you have taught me that a
woman is as good as her womb. If she bears, her sons will place a standing
marker where she has died. And if she is barren, she is not part of the Old
Testicle. Mothers! Sarai! Rivka! Lea! Rahel! You have taught your
daughters that women fight for the penis of a man. Who named you my
mothers? Who names this a matriarchy?[30]

Antiphon by antiphon other voices would reply: 'Overwhelmed are we
whose wombs bring forth child after child, without our choice or consent'.
Another: 'No! Delighted, we are delighted that so many children open our
wombs!' And another: 'Shamed, because we open too soon, blood and
despair pooling in our beds, without our permission or consent'. And
others: 'Grateful, dizzy with relief, because our daughters, our sisters, can
'protect' (!) themselves, can determine what happens within their bodies'.
And others still: Silence.

Jesus quickly reasserts control. In his view, physicality, a woman-born
husk, must be worn away by the discipline of doing the Father's will. He
repudiates the experience of constricting uterine walls, the push through
vagina into sensuality—physical birth—in order to become a little one
who knows the Kingdom. His sayings, collected in the Thomas-Gospel,
provide a way for readers to duplicate this experience and stomp on their
connections to the mother (Logion 21). Cursed, then, is the womb that
gives birth, the breasts full of milk. Blessed is woman who, like man,
cannot bring forth physical life.

The Kingdom subverts what the world values; it delights in reversals of
identity. Logion 99 continues this subversion in its declaration that the
Kingdom rejects the basis on which the world determines relationships
and social order: the bloodlines that determine familial bonds, member-
ship, social status, and inheritance rights.

The disciples said to him: 'Your brothers and your mother are standing
outside'. He said to them: 'Those here who do what my Father wants are
my brothers and my mother. They are the ones who will enter my Father's
Kingdom' (Logion 79).[31]

Ignoring their desires and choosing the Father's will draw the Thomas-
Community into a relational network based on volition, not on the
sensuality of flesh and blood. Jesus redefines his brothers as those who

30. E.M. Broner, *Her Mothers* (Bloomington: Indiana University Press, 1985), p.
168.
31. Valantasis, *Thomas*, p. 158.

belong to his Father in the Kingdom and his biological mother as the Father who rules that Kingdom. Jesus' spiritual family comes together as its members obey the Father; spiritual activity, pleasuring the Father by doing what he wants, replaces the sexual activity of pleasuring the biological father by bringing forth a son.

The theme of the superiority of spiritual familial relationships probably continues in Logion 101; although it has several lacunae that make interpretation difficult, it describes contrasting behaviour toward two sets of parents, perhaps biological parents, representative of the World, and a spiritual parent, representative of the Kingdom.

> a. Whoever does not hate [father] and mother as I do cannot be my disciple]. b. Whoever does [not] love [father and] mother as I do cannot be my disciple. c. For my mother [...], but my true [...(SV: mother)] gave me life (Logion 101).[32]

The saying provides some criteria for becoming a disciple. When a disciple imitates Jesus, the disciple's identity is transformed; by doing what Jesus has done, he acquires Jesus' identity. This logion mandates love for one set of parents because 'my true [...] gave me life' and hatred for the other because 'my mother [...]'.

Sentence (a) and sentence (b) have similar structures: the subject of each one is a negative relative clause; the predicate of one is the antonym of the other: 'Whoever does not hate [father] and mother as I do...', 'Whoever does [...] love [father and] mother as I do...'; each sentence has the same predicate, 'cannot be my disciple'. A likely reading:

> Whoever does not hate [father] and mother...cannot be my [disciple].
> Whoever does [not] love [father and] mother...cannot be my disciple.[33]

Its interpretation is more difficult. The phrase 'father and mother' in each sentence may refer to the same biological pair; the predicates, 'does not hate', 'does not love', as a word pair, may mean the entire range of human emotions. Disciples, like Jesus, maintain an attitude of emotional detachment or indifference toward parents and, by extension, toward other family relationships. On the other hand, the saying may contrast different sets of parents, biological parents with spiritual parents; the spiritual parents may be a metaphor for the Thomas-Community as a whole or, perhaps, pairs of community members who instruct newcomers.

32. Valantasis, *Thomas*, p. 181.
33. Valantasis, *Thomas*, p. 181.

The final sentence of Logion 101 is difficult to reconstruct. While the two disjunctive clauses appear to have a parallel structure, key words are missing:

> For my mother [...],
> but my true [...] gave me life.

The synonymous parallelism in the first half of the saying makes 'mother' a reasonable choice for the lacuna in this last line. This would, however, make the saying unique in a gospel where feminine language and imagery are not associated with life or truth. In the Thomas-Gospel, women are not part of the Kingdom. While other materials from the Nag Hammadi collection use feminine imagery to depict the deity or deities who bring redemption and life,[34] the Thomas-Gospel uses male or non-gendered, but not feminine language: e.g., Kingdom of the Father, 'neither male nor female'. As a metaphor, 'true [mother]' identifies life-giving agent or process of transformation. For the Thomas-Community, one candidate for such an agent or process is the Thomas-Gospel with its assurance that 'whoever discovers the meanings of these sayings will not taste death' (Logion 1). The Thomas-Gospel and the community gathered around it would be the womb from which those 'born of woman' come forth as 'little ones'. Following this train of thought, the parallel of the 'true [mother] gives life' becomes 'the mother [gives death]'. This interpretation also associates feminine language with life. A final possibility is to read the last line as 'my true [Father] gives life', consistent with other sayings in the gospel. I prefer this reconstruction, but I have not been successful in finding other support for it. The saying first urges hatred toward earthly, biological parents and love for 'the Father' under the metaphor 'mother and father'; then the speaker provides motivation for these emotions, breaking up the 'mother and father' metaphor so the 'earthly mother' brings death and the 'true [Father]' gives life.

Logion 105: Jesus said:

> 'Whoever knows father and mother
> will be called the child of a whore...'[35]

34. Streete, 'Women as Sources of Redemption and Knowledge in Early Christian Traditions', in Kraemer and D'Angelo, *Women and Christian Origins*, pp. 330-54.

35. Valantasis, *Thomas*, p. 185. J. Schaberg (*The Illegitimacy of Jesus: A Feminist Theological Interpretation of the Infancy Narratives* [San Francisco: Harper and Row, 1987]) argues that this saying preserves an early tradition about the illegitimate birth of Jesus of Nazareth.

parallels other sayings that juxtapose the perspective of the Kingdom and the perspective of the world. Genealogy automatically locates individuals within a social system, independently of their achievements or character. More opportunities are available to the son or daughter of the 'right' family. In a patriarchal world, the 'right' family name, the 'right' father's name, usually works, in different degrees, to the advantage of sons and daughters. The 'wrong' family name brings few social or personal benefits.

'Knowing mother and father' means knowing where and to whom one belongs. The phrase may also function as a metaphor for unquestioning acceptance of parental beliefs and values.[36] 'Children of a whore' is a prime example of having the wrong parentage with the wrong values, at least from the perspective of the Thomas-Gospel. Those who 'know mother and father' know the world and are ignorant of the Kingdom. The Thomas-Community wagers its life that the opposition between Kingdom and world has already been resolved in favour of Kingdom. Those who know the Kingdom are 'children of the Father'; those who know the world are, from the Kingdom's perspective, 'sons of a bitch', children of a whore, of woman born.

To a world under the Father's gaze, a whore is a renegade, an outlaw; a cunt who knows her price and has it in hand before she spreads her legs. She is a threat to the Father's name and the social order it supports. Where do the children of a whore belong in a social system constructed on paternal bloodlines? More important, how does this woman constructed as whore know herself? How does she name herself? Does she call herself 'whore' or woman, woman with a child, a 'single mother'? A woman loving herself, loving other women? A woman who must repeatedly reclaim her integrity, destroying children bred in rape?

> 'Telling you. I am telling you, small girl Sethe', and she did that. She told Sethe that her mother and Nan were together from the sea. Both were taken up many times by the crew. 'She threw them all away but you. The one from the crew she threw away on the island. The ones from more whites she also threw away. Without names she threw them'.[37]

Does she call herself a woman doing the best she can with what she's got, buying a future for her babies out of the coinage of her flesh? Who are the children of a whore? How do children live with such a label, even though

---

36. Also, Valantasis, *Thomas*, p. 186.
37. T. Morrison, *Beloved* (New York: Plume, 1988), p. 62.

they may know they are well loved and, in cold places, still remember the warmth of a loving gaze? Do they search the faces of strange men of a certain age, looking for some resemblance?

The *Gospel of Thomas* and the Kingdom it creates resist these questions. It can recognize a whore when it sees one—any man who will not disown flesh to become a living spirit; any woman who rejects symbol systems that turn female experience, mother-work into metaphors and metonyms to represent the imperfect, the death dealing, the non-spiritual and the irrational; anyone who does not repudiate blood and genealogy to know the Kingdom.

Logion 105 constructs those who identify with the world, not the Kingdom, as 'children of a whore'. In contrast, Logion 106 labels those who 'make the two into one' as the family of a new 'Adam' with the power to reconfigure the universe.

Jesus said:

> a When you make the two into one,
> b you will become sons of Adam...
> c and when you say, 'Mountain, move away from here!',
> d it will move![38]

The temporal clauses (a) and (c) are clear enough, and the Coptic text of the whole saying is complete. The temporal clauses are parallel in several ways. Clause (a) refers to an internal, spiritual transformation, unseen and invisible; clause (c) describes an external, physical change, seen and visible. In clause (a), the subject itself creates change by doing; in clause (c), the subject creates change by issuing a command. Clause (c) is, in a sense, an outcome or consequence of clause (a), the manifestation of a spiritual state of being.

The Coptic for the phrase translated here as 'children of Adam' has been interpreted in different ways. One depends on Philo of Alexandria's interpretation of Genesis 1-3. Philo distinguishes between a primordial Adam, a spiritual Adam who its image, and the physical Adam, the spiritual image now clothed in a body. 'To make the two one' is to unite the spiritual Adam with the uncreated primordial Adam.[39] A second interpretation describes the earthly creature formed from wet clay and the God's living breath as an androgynous being, a third gender, for whom a young, pre-sexual child serves as a metaphor. With the creation of woman,

---

38. Valantasis, *Thomas*, p. 186.
39. See discussion in MacDonald, *No Male and Female*, pp. 26-30.

sex and gender appear. When its rib is removed, the androgynous being becomes man and woman, later Adam and Eve. 'To make one' is to reconstitute the androgynous Adam as a third gender.[40] This happens at the level of the individual, when the lower, inferior, female aspect of the soul is integrated into the higher, superior male aspect so that the rational masculine controls the emotional feminine.[41] It may also happen at the level of community, when males learn to see females as male, and females learn to see males as females. A third interpretation views the Kingdom and the world as two opposing subjectivities; the community members study and perform the sayings of the Thomas-Gospel, which offers the community the ability to understand and perform the sayings in the gospel, so that the subjectivity of the Kingdom grows strong and the subjectivity of the World disappears.[42]

Each of these interpretations illumines a different perspective on Logion 106. I am inclined to translate '*adam*' as the proper name 'Adam' and to interpret it as a metaphor with two references. 'Adam' is, from the perspective of the gospel, a figure like the one Paul identifies as bringing life into the world (Rom. 5) and whom the Thomas-Community would recognize as the 'living Jesus'. 'Adam' would also signify the physical Adam of Genesis 1-3, through whom sin entered creation. Here, 'family of Adam who is Jesus', 'Adamites', as it were, are the true family of Jesus within the Kingdom. The physical Adam heads a genealogy 'born of woman' with all its limitations. The spiritual Adam is Jesus, the living presence whom the Thomas-Gospel mediates. He is the first member of a new genealogy, the 'little ones' born of the gospel.

The Thomas-Gospel becomes, then, a sort of sacrament that effects this transformation. 'To make the two one' is not simply to stumble onto the reality that to know oneself is to acquire the identity of Jesus; it is to experience this identity as spiritual union with Jesus, the son of the Living One. The *Gospel of Thomas*, which eschews the body, ironically embodies the means to the unitive experience that drove Didymos Jude Thomas to create the gospel in the first place.

---

40. W. Meeks, 'The Image of the Androgyne: Some Uses of a Symbol in Earliest Christianity', *HR* 13 (1974), pp. 165-208.

41. E. Castelli, '"I Will Make Mary Male": Pieties of the Body and Gender Transformation of Christian Women in Late Antiquity', in J. Epstein and K. Straub (eds.), *Body Guards: The Cultural Politics of Gender Ambiguity* (New York: Routledge, 1991), p. 32.

42. Valantasis, *Thomas*, pp. 6-12.

In Logion 106, 'children of Adam' is synonymous with 'not born of woman' and 'becoming little ones'. The gospel establishes a spiritual universe in which the Living One assumes the life-producing function of the Mother and establishes the symbolic order associated with the Father. The body 'born of woman' and obstacle to the Kingdom is left behind. Those who know the Kingdom have become sons of the spiritual Adam, who is the Father's Son.

The Language of Mother-Work in Logion 22

> Jesus saw some little ones nursing. He said to his disciples: 'These little ones nursing are like those who enter the <Father's> kingdom'. They said to him: 'Then we shall enter the <Father's> kingdom as little ones?'

> Jesus said to them: 'When you make the two into one, when you make the inside like the outside and the outside like the inside; when you make the above like the below; when you make the male and the female into a single one, so that the male will not be male and the female will not be female; when you make eyes in place of an eye, a hand in place of a hand, a foot in place of a foot, an image in place of an image, then you will enter [the <Father's>] kingdom'.[43]

The Coptic original is an impressionistic description, short on details: Jesus saw some little ones taking milk. The reader viewing the scene from Jesus' perspective sees what Jesus sees and more: women cradling little ones—some offer nipples, cracked and encrusted, to tiny mouths that grab and pinch; others shudder with delight as they feel the sucking of the babies' tugs even in their wombs. The reader may slip into the text among the listeners and gaze back at this Jesus, wondering whether he notices the women whose breasts the infants are sucking, wondering whether he or his narrator knows that

> The act of suckling a child, like a sexual act, may be tense, physically painful, charged with cultural feelings of inadequacy and guilt; or, like a sexual act, it can be a physically delicious, elementally soothing experience, filled with a tender sensuality.[44]

Does he see with a different eye than the female reader sees? Does he have the right language to frame questions? Without that language, how does he know there are questions to be asked? Does he think to say, 'The Kingdom

---

43. See n. 1. Like the Scholars Version, Valantasis translates the Coptic as 'babies' [nursing]. I use a less interpretive translation, 'little ones'.
44. Rich, *Of Woman Born*, p. 18.

is like women breastfeeding little ones'? 'The Kingdom is like mothers whose breasts leak milk when their babies cry'? What does he know about such mother work?

While examples of woman's work reveal some aspect of the Kingdom in other logia, in Logion 22 the narrator's point of reference is 'nursing babies', probably male babies, at that. Here 'nursing' describes the work of the little ones, not the work of woman. For the narrator, nursing, like pregnancy, happens to woman; she is not its subject.[45]

The question the disciples ask—Babies? Be/come little ones to enter the kingdom?–echoes the incredulous and ambiguous reaction of Nicodemus to Jesus' pronouncement that he must be born again, from above (Jn 3.4).[46] Jesus does not hear the question his disciples are asking: 'What are you talking about?' The disciples lack the self-knowledge to frame such a query, to admit their ignorance. In shame-based cultures like those of the Mediterranean basin, few men would tolerate being compared to a child or a baby. Comments like 'You are such a baby!' or 'That remark is so childish' are intended and heard as insults. Most cultural codes value mature conduct, even in children, and often penalize the failure to 'act your age'; 'child's work' is frequently 'child's play'. Yet, the Kingdom values the state of being a child. In the gospel it is a metaphor for humility and freshness, for innocence and malleability;[47] the little ones represent a spiritual unity, neither male nor female, one in the midst of the world's many. Children are also easily controlled, at the mercy of the caregiver, their behaviours readily dictated by promised reward or threatened punishment. The reader prays for a Father whose unconditional love for 'little ones' outweighs his desire for order.

The author expands the 'nursing babies' comparison with language that is dense and difficult.[48] 'Becoming little ones' is a metaphor for achieving the subjectivity or self-consciousness synonymous with entering the Kingdom. The Thomas-Gospel outlines the work that produces and maintains this new identity, the Father's work, through which the members of

45. Grosz, *Sexual Subversions*, p. 78.

46. R.E. Brown, *The Gospel According to John* I-XII (AB 29; Garden City, NY: Doubleday, 1966), p. 130.

47. Crossan, *Historical Jesus*, pp. 266-69.

48. For a survey of interpretations, see, e.g., B. Gärtner, *The Theology of the Gospel of Thomas* (London: Collins, 1961), pp. 217-29; Valantasis, *Thomas,*, pp. 95-96; A.F.J. Klijn, 'The 'Single One' in the Gospel of Thomas' *JBL* 81 (1962), pp. 271-78; MacDonald, *No Male and Female,* pp. 46-48.

the Thomas-Community recognize their real identity.

The language of image links Logion 22 and Gen. 1.26-27, the creation of *'ādām* as image of God, one image, manifest in creation as male and female.

> Then God said: Let us make *'ādām* in our image, after our likeness... So God created *'ādām* in his image, in the image of God he created him; male and female he created them (Gen. 1.26-27, RSV).

Recovering or recreating this image means becoming little ones, making the transition from physical being to spiritual being. Because materiality is the birthright of those 'born of woman', this transition is performed on the level of language in every saying in the Thomas-Gospel that repudiates or devalues woman and woman as mother. The Kingdom is the father's space, established out of the struggle to impose his law upon the mother's powerful mystery. This project is nearly successful; only the not-mother aspect of woman escapes its control, pooling at the borders of the Kingdom and remaining there until it must remind the Kingdom, with one of the many flavors of death, that the Kingdom owes its existence to the power of an 'other'.[49]

The Thomas-Gospel deals with the mother by, in a sense, burying her under the Kingdom. It offers faithful readers the experience of union with the Living One so they become children of the Father marked for life, once they give up their identity as children of the Mother marked by death.

Greek and Hellenistic philosophers attest that such a unitive spiritual experience is possible. The soul can escape its physical limitations by drawing inward, out of the world of the senses. According to Plotinus:

> [t]he soul sees God suddenly appearing within it, because there is nothing between: they are no longer two, but one; while the presence lasts, you cannot distinguish them. It is that union which earthly lovers imitate when they would be one flesh. The soul is no longer conscious of being in a body.[50]

Conclusion

> Simon Peter said to them: 'Make Mary leave us, for females do not deserve life'. Jesus said: 'Look! I will guide her to make her male, so that she too may become a living spirit resembling you males. For every female who makes herself male will enter the Kingdom of heaven (Logion 104).[51]

49. This discussion is based on Grosz, *Sexual Subversions*, pp. 70-81.
50. Plotinus, *Ennead* 1.6.7.5-7. Cited in MacDonald, *No Male and Female*, p. 24.
51. Valantasis, *Thomas*, p. 194.

I imagine Peter pounding a table or stamping his foot when he demands that Mary be sent away. No one, not even Jesus, disputes his view that 'females do not deserve life'. In his reply, Jesus ignores Peter's reasoning and offers a solution: Mary may remain, and he will 'make her male', so she can become a 'living spirit', resembling 'you males'. In fact, any woman who makes herself male can follow Mary into the kingdom.

This solution is part of the gospel's agenda, to establish unity. Those called into the Kingdom share a single identity, one consciousness, that of Jesus himself (Logion 108). Males can make themselves like little ones. Mary, the titular female, requires additional assistance. If, as Peter maintains, women do not deserve life, they do not possess the potential to receive it; they cannot change their condition unless some one intervenes on their behalf. Logion 114 describes the work that must be done upon women so they can enter the Kingdom.[52]

I indicated earlier that the Thomas-Gospel perceives women as flesh inside and out, with no inner space, no interiority. That assertion requires some modification in light of Logion 104. On the biological level, woman does possess internal physical space, a vagina and a womb, elastic enough to receive the penetrating penis or the gestating fetus and stretch (be stretched?) to accommodate shifts in size. From her perspective, woman may see herself as an active subject in sexual intercourse, pregnancy, and birth; she opens her body to envelop the penis, to seize and hold it. From his perspective, and the perspective of most cultures, the male sees himself as the subject of this act, plowing into the female body stretched beneath him as an agriculturalist plows the field stretched out in front of him. Metaphorically, then, Jesus 'plows' Mary with his 'word' to make her male; he fills her with the ability to do the work of males in the Thomas-Community. Once Mary acquires this male subjectivity, she can do the work of males: interpret the sayings of the Gospel and understand its secrets so that, like them, she can know the kingdom.

This two-part transformation of the female may occur symbolically in two related liturgical rituals, the ritual of the 'bridal chamber'[53] and the

---

52. Because it suggests a misogynist attitude, considered foreign to the gospel's worldview, Logion 114 is sometimes regarded as a later addition to the gospel, meant to modify and dilute the inclusivity of Logion 22. I agree with the view that Logion 114 addresses the innate inferiority of the female by first making her male so she at least has the potential to transform herself into a 'little one' worthy of the Kingdom. See, e.g., McGuire, 'Women, Gender, and Gnosis', pp. 278-82.

53. The meaning of 'bridal chamber' is controverted; it may not refer to a ritual at

ritual of baptism. In the 'bridal chamber' (Logion 75), a ritual that may be necessary only for female candidates, Mary receives the *logos* of the gospel that makes her male. I am not suggesting a *hieros gamos* or some other cultic sexual activity, but a ritual whose symbols and script represent the transformation of female into male. Baptism, on the other hand, is the ritual for both men and women. Although the Thomas-Gospel does not refer directly to baptism, interpreters do find allusions to the sacrament in the gospel (Logion 21).[54]

E. Castelli, however, bases her reading of Logion 114 on Philo of Alexandria's commentary on Genesis 2. She recalls that in *Questions and Answers about Genesis,* Philo takes 'female' to represent the soul's inferior elements, which, through creation, have become separated from its superior 'male' elements. The female aspect of the soul must be brought together with the male elements in a process Philo calls 'progress': ' [t]he giving up of the female by changing [it] into the male, since the female is material, passive, corporeal, and sense-perceptible, while the male is active, rational, incorporeal, and more akin to mind and thought'.[55] Thus, Mary must first transcend her passivity, physicality, and sensibility so that her masculine qualities rule her and she can begin the work of 'becoming a little one'. Once woman becomes male, she surrenders her status as 'other' and is no longer a threat to the Kingdom and its order.

Anne McGuire explains the process in another way. Since Logion 114 equates such categories as 'worthy of life', 'living spirit', and entering the Kingdom, with the category, being male, Jesus' action, 'making Mary male', reverses the process of woman's creation described in Genesis 2. Woman is formed from a rib of the genderless being created as 'living spirit' and enlivened by the divine breath (Gen. 2.7). The process that creates woman creates man at the same time. To escape death, woman and man must be made one again so that together they constitute the original living spirit.

The juxtaposition of Logion 114 with Genesis 2 and Philo's commentary on it is an important insight. Castelli may, however, overplay the similarities she discovers. If her reading is correct, Logion 114 is the only

all, but to the Thomas community with whom Jesus the bridegroom is present when the gospel is interpreted and understood (Logion 104). 'Bridal chamber' then functions as a metaphor, as 'the Kingdom' does. See, for example, Valantasis, *Thomas*, pp. 153-54.

54. Castelli, ' "I Will Make Mary Male" ', p. 32.

55. Philo of Alexandria, *Questions and Answers in Genesis II.49*, cited in Castelli, ' "I Will Make Mary Male" ', p. 32.

saying in the Thomas-Gospel in which the self is constructed of positive, 'male' qualities and negative 'female' qualities. The worlds created by these three texts do indeed intersect, but the point of this intersection is not the construction of the self. The three texts account for the duality of male and female as a consequence of creation and the collapse of that duality into a primordial One. The three texts also reflect the decisions to privilege one element of the male/female word pair as 'superior', to describe that element in gendered male language, and to make it a physical image of the spiritual One who is the Kingdom.

Final Observations

The reading I have presented in this paper does not describe the socio-historical reality of the Thomas-Community, nor does it discuss the roles women played in whatever model of governance the 'community' may have had. It does not consider whether women, like men, traveled from church to church as itinerant preachers and teachers, wearing masculine clothing, their bodies flattened into masculine bodies through fasting.[56] It has, however, considered the language and imagery the narrator uses to construct the Kingdom within the Thomas-Gospel. That language concerns Father and son/s. The language the narrator uses to construct the world is generally gynocentric. Those born of woman are at home in the world, blind to the spiritual reality of the Kingdom among them; children of a whore, they are whores themselves. They do not know their true identity, that they are spiritual beings, created as the image of God. Physically alive, they are corpses from the perspective of the Kingdom. To gain the knowledge that brings life, they must forsake their bodies, formed from and within woman flesh, so they can be born again as children of the Father, living spiritual beings who no longer fear the death of being swallowed up by the Mother.

To make this happen, the narrator has the Father, the Alpha male, establish a new order, the Kingdom, on the body of the Mother, to impose boundaries on her so she cannot engulf his domain. As much as the male

56. Patterson, *Thomas and Jesus,* pp. 210-14. C.W. Bynum, (*Holy Feast and Holy Fast: The Religious Significance of Food to Medieval Women* [Berkeley: University of California Press, 1987]); Castelli, '"I Will Make Mary Male"', pp. 29-49; and G. Cloke (*This Female Man of God: Women and Spiritual Power in the Patristic Age, AD 350-450* [London: Routledge, 1995]), among others, relate this motif of 'female becoming male' to ascetical practices prescribed for women by male spiritual directors through the 15th century.

desires the Mother, that much more is he afraid that, unless he controls her, her mystery and otherness will draw him back into her body. The Kingdom is the symbolic order of the Father, a masculine space whose entry passage is the language, the *logos* of the gospel. This passage leads to life; only those who deserve life have access to it: males reborn as spiritual beings, women who suffer the macabre transformation into males so they, too, can be reborn. Too high a price for this woman to pay. In the company of others, she stands outside, near the margins, listening, creating, plotting.[57]

57. Lurking in my imagination is the 1991 film, *The Rapture* (written and directed by M. Tolkin). Midway through the film, its main character, Sharon, found God, sought his forgiveness, and turned from sexual promiscuity to a life lived under the will of God. Now, after trusting God absolutely and finding him lacking, she refuses to confess any love for this God to join husband and daughter in heaven, following the end of the world. Instead, she chooses to remain alone, outside heaven, unwilling to forgive God for his betrayal of her and his failure to ask forgiveness.

WHO IS THE FAITHFUL STEWARD? LUKE 12.41-45[*]

Deborah Core

When I was a youngster and already a budding leftist, I was always troubled by the annual fuss over *A Christmas Carol*. Everyone loved it, except me. Why was I, well, a Scrooge, when it came to this almost universally loved classic of the holidays? The fact is, I was always bothered by Scrooge's 'redemption', or rather, not by his redemption so much as the nature of his newfound charity and support of poor, long-suffering Bob Cratchitt. Because Scrooge repents and reforms, Cratchitt and his family are saved. Justice is not the issue. Cratchitt is saved only because Scrooge now *feels* that he was unkind and wants to be better. The conscientious reader (or viewer of the many film versions) might well ask, But what if Scrooge had changed back again? What if the Spirits' good work of one night did not last, and Scrooge's charitable impulses were to fade? Poor Bob would find himself again huddled over his one little coal, and Tiny Tim would grow thin and die. Seen through the light of Christian theology, Scrooge's story is a traditional one of repentance and change. Through the agency of Marley and the spirits, Scrooge once was lost but now is found, and now found as charitable and fatherly.

Scrooge's world changes—but 'the' world does not. In Dickens' senti-mental tale, personal reform is all that matters. I myself would rather have trusted Cratchitt's future to a strong labor union than to Scrooge's con-tinued good will. The system which allowed the powerlessness and oppression of Cratchitt was unchanged by the Spirits, and is in fact unchallenged by Dickens. While Scrooge exerts his patriarchal (or, as E. Schüssler Fiorenza would term it, *kyriarchal*)[1] ways differently, he is still clearly the patriarch, the overlord lording it over Cratchitt, first hinting

---

[*]   I am grateful to Dr. Jane McAvoy of Lexington Theological Seminary for her very helpful thoughts on an earlier version of this essay.
    1.   E. Schüssler Fiorenza, *But She Said: Feminist Practices of Biblical Interpre-tation* (Boston: Beacon Press, 1992), p. 8.

at firing him and then commanding him to build up the fire before they discuss his raise.

While close analysis of the politics of *A Christmas Carol* may seem to be attacking a butterfly with a cannon, the enormous popularity of the tale, re-told in dozens of versions, makes a corrective analysis worth doing.[2] Contemplation of this little icon of a tale raises a number of complex ethical issues. What is the relationship between personal reformation and social change? Does massive social change reduce the need for personal redemption? If we value the individual, of course we must argue for the importance of the individual's will, purpose, and power to change. Yet if we value the larger society and the powerless within it, we must value perhaps more highly that social change which imposes, usually by law, some justice for the powerless, change that turns the world upside-down.

Here parables might be able to help us. The story-work of the parable overall has been described by Brawley as allowing readers to 'identify with characters and events…when the second shoe drops, the parabolic world to which they have already committed themselves inverts… The shoe not only falls, it also fits'.[3] Parables tell stories which implicitly shape a Christian understanding of the world. Central among these are the most beloved Lucan parables, which are often tales of the world turned upside-down, the powerless enfranchised, the valueless treasured. In the most famous of these, a powerful father not only welcomes his worthless son home but runs out to meet him, and a despised religious outsider is recognized as superior to the religious hierarchy in the practice of compassion. And if some parables do not show the values of the world inverted, they may instead offer, at least, as Reid says, 'puzzling stories that could turn a person's world upside down'.[4] Such parables may affirm women's reading of scripture and offer good news to the downtrodden. Such parables make it easier to read scripture as upturning the status quo

2.   We can probably learn a great deal about cultural values by contrasting the two most loved and re-visited Christmas 'parables', *A Christmas Carol* and *It's a Wonderful Life*. In the former, a powerful, self-satisfied man realizes the good he could have done, while in the latter, a less powerful man realizes the good he did do. One is confronted with his death, while the other, more frighteningly, is confronted with never having been born. Supernatural agency awakens each to the truth about his life.

3.   R.L. Brawley, *Text to Text Pours Forth Speech: Voices of Scripture in Luke–Acts* (Bloomington: Indiana University Press, 1995), p. 28.

4.   B. Reid, *Choosing the Better Part? Women in the Gospel of Luke* (Collegeville, MN: Liturgical Press, 1996), p. 169.

and foreseeing a society in which power 'has nothing to do with control over one another' and 'is shared rather than being consumed'.[5] Power may become, not 'power-over' but 'mutual empowerment' and 'the ability to make a difference'.[6] With visionary parables, it is easy to believe, with Phyllis Trible, that 'redemption is already at work in the text'.[7]

But then there are the others. Luke 12.41-45, the parable[8] of the just and unjust stewards, is a middle-world story, a brief tale of an all-powerful lord (*kyrios*) who observes, rewards, and punishes, who functions in a stratified world full of dichotomies which the parable apparently endorses and encourages. Power, traditional power, imposed from on high by the *kyrios*, is used to punish the unjust steward, who has used *his* power to oppress those beneath him. Proper use of traditional kyriarchal power, *not* the diminution of such power, is the substance of the message. God, as Ruether has shown, is judging and 'wholly other', a 'disconnected and all-powerful male', and humankind's posture is one of total dependence; such a vision proposes social structures as un-reformable.[9] Schaberg has written that the gospel of Luke reveals 'an unrelieved tension…between the ideal and the accommodation'.[10] This parable is a case study of such tension. The parable of the just and unjust stewards provides a Christian glimpse into the world of *Realpolitik*, where reform within the system is the best that one may hope for.

Most traditional interpretation of this parable revolves around the role of the steward. Christian theology and praxis have adopted 'steward' as a shorthand description of proper use of resources, and 'Stewardship Sunday' traditionally marks an appeal for funds (and sometimes 'time and

5.   M. McBride, 'Power', in L. Isherwood and D. McEwan (eds.), *An A to Z of Feminist Theology* (Sheffield: Sheffield Academic Press, 1996), p. 183.

6.   L. Isherwood and D. McEwan, *Introducing Feminist Theology* (Sheffield: Sheffield Academic Press, 1993), p. 149.

7.   P. Trible, 'Eve and Miriam: From the Margins to the Center', in H. Shanks (ed.), *Feminist Approaches to the Bible* (Washington: Biblical Archeological Society, 1995), p. 8.

8.   Not all exegetes agree that Lk. 12.42-46 even comprises a parable. Hedrick, for example, argues that there are not enough 'semantic markers' for these verses to be labeled as a parable. See C.W. Hedrick, *Parables as Poetic Fictions: The Creative Voice of Jesus* (Peabody, MA: Hendrickson Publishers, 1994), p. 11 n. 19.

9.   R.R. Ruether, *Women and Redemption: A Theological History* (Minneapolis: Fortress Press, 1998), p. 185.

10.   J. Schaberg, 'Luke', in C.A. Newsom and S.H. Ringe (eds.), *The Women's Bible Commentary* (Louisville, KY: Westminster/John Knox Press, 1992), p. 278.

talent' as well as 'treasure'). This parable and its implicit praise of dividedness fits nicely with our unfortunate, even tragic, tendency toward dualism instead of mutuality and relationality. Here stand the two stewards, or rather (as the parable actually suggests) one Dr. Jekyll-and-Mr. Hyde steward, using his paternalistic power either well or badly, being either rewarded generously or punished harshly himself. In his study *The Steward: A Biblical Symbol Comes of Age*, D.J. Hall claims that steward-ship is an appropriate and positive image, because it 'encapsulates the two sides of human relatedness, the relation to God on the one hand and to…creatures of God on the other'.[11] The problem with Hall's reading is that 'relatedness' is not the main issue; power is. Traditional readings of this parable, as with so much of scripture, ignore its fundamental accep-tance of an unacceptable reliance upon power over mutuality. Hall's middle-world reading of the steward's role is only one example of a selective understanding of the parable. B. Reid's excellent study of women in Luke has only one reference to this parable, and again the focus is carefully chosen: she comments that 'alert and hardworking servants are blessed',[12] a reading which allows an understanding that the virtuous are rewarded. Is it correct to assume that such a teaching exists in scripture overall? If we privilege such a reading, what are we to do with the image of the slaves who were beaten and starved by the unjust steward?

It is significant that the distribution and the denial of food should be the markers, respectively, of the good steward and the unjust steward; as many scholars have noted, food in Luke's gospel plays a major role, and attending banquets or talking about them occupies much of the Lucan Jesus' time. As du Plessis points out, banqueting is in fact a common Lucan signal of 'eschatological fulfillment'.[13] In this case, however, ban-queting is not even discussed. The good steward simply distributes the food, whereas the bad steward does not, saving it (apparently) for his solitary gorging—the very opposite of a banquet with shared food and drink. 'Food' here is *sitometrion*, a word unique to this passage, meaning 'food ration or allowance'[14] or literally, a 'measure of grain'.[15] (In

11. D.J. Hall, *The Steward: A Biblical Image Come of Age* (Grand Rapids: Eerdmans, rev. edn, 1990), p. 26.

12. Reid, p. 71.

13. I.J. du Plessis, 'Reading Luke 12: 35-48 as Part of the Travel Narrative', *Neot* 22 (1988), p. 228.

14. C.A. Evans, *Saint Luke* (Trinity Press International Commentaries; Phila-delphia: Trinity Press International, 1990), p. 536.

Matthew's version of the parable, 24.45-51, *trophen,* a more common word, is used.) Luke's use of *sitometrion* may be intended simply to raise the level of language,[16] but the unusual word heightens not only the language but the sense of what the steward, even the just one, is all about: for him, whether it is distributed or withheld, food is a thing to be measured, doled out. How far this measuring-out is from the plenty of the banquet!

The rhetoric of this parable resonates with dividedness, even 'binary oppositions'.[17] Du Plessis has noted that Peter's question in v. 41 divides the whole discourse,[18] and furthermore, his question itself encourages divisiveness: it posits an 'us and them' world-view, with an elite of disciples over against a larger body of believers. In fact, everything in this parable is divided, and divided by power: the social classes of lord, steward, and lower slaves. Even the description of food takes on the quality of the divided, the partial, the stinted, the measured-out. The parable is perhaps an appropriate foregrounding to vv. 51-53, in which Jesus claims to be bringing division, not peace on earth.

The fate of the evil steward reflects this theme of divisiveness. The steward has cut himself off from his proper rule in life, and so his just punishment is further cutting-off. When the lord-*kyrios* appears to set things aright, his justice is swift and silent: he 'will cut him in pieces and assign him a place among the faithless'. This final verse has occasioned much comment—one may well wonder, if the servant is cut to bits, what his 'place' or 'portion' (*meros*) matters. It seems that the verse works to double the appropriate punishment–having cut himself off from his right duties, the steward is twice 'cut' by the lord: first cut in two and then cut out of the chosen, excommunicated. Having failed to act faithfully with the portion he was to distribute rightly, now ironically he is given his 'right' portion.

Such is the penalty for those who have been accorded power and have failed to act justly. But they have also recorded another failure: they have failed to watch. Their bullying, beating, and starving of their fellow-

15. L.T. Johnson, *The Gospel of Luke* (SacPag; Collegeville, MN: Liturgical Press, 1991), p. 204.

16. Johnson, *Luke*, p. 204.

17. P.J. Hartin, 'Angst in the Household: A Deconstructive Reading of the Parable of the Supervising Servant (Lk 12.41-48)', *Neot* 22 (1988), p. 381.

18. J.G. du Plessis, 'Why Did Peter Ask His Question and How Did Jesus Answer Him? Or: Implicature in Luke 12: 35-48', *Neot* 22 (1988), p. 318.

servants is predicated upon the master's delay, and upon their own failure to be alert and hard-working. In the pericope (12.38) just before this parable, preparedness is rewarded, not just by the giving of more possessions, but by the lord's girding himself and serving the alert servants. But in this parable, the just steward is simply given more, while the emphasis falls on the punishment of the unjust steward. We see an active degrading of the moral flow of the passage; just a few lines earlier (v. 34), the injunction 'where your treasure is, there will your heart be also' has been offered, a much more visionary and positive proclamation. But by v. 44, the vision of this discourse has declined to a point where more possessions, more treasures *on earth,* are the great reward of the 'just' steward.

It's interesting to note that the text hints at allowing the reader's assumption that the lord-*kyrios* bears some responsibility in the unjust steward's evil: it is, after all, the lord who delays in returning, and his delay allows or perhaps even encourages the unjust steward's selfish actions! Is his delay a test?[19] If we read it as such, the parable becomes the more troublesome, in that the fate of the weak is, Job-like, tied to the whim of a mercurial lord.

Who is to be prepared? What does it mean to be prepared? Peter asks whether or not the preceding parable is for everyone or just for 'us'. Exegetes have traditionally understood the question to relate to the leaders of the Lucan church community: they are the ones to be prepared and responsible. But the Lucan author has Jesus respond with another parable. Du Plessis argues that Peter's question itself is a 'sign of deficient discipleship, which equals unpreparedness'.[20] And indeed it is interesting that Peter should be at the centre here: Peter, who trumpets his readiness (*hetoimos*) to die with Jesus, and who of course is not ready at all. A feminist appraisal of 'readiness' must question the underlying assumption that an end is coming in which all will be set right and that one's own concern is to be on the proper side when the end comes. 'Readiness' must be instead an on-going condition that looks to the daily and not to the end, to a lord's arrival. The good steward has been *pistos* and *phronimos*, faithful and wise—that is, faithful to his master's interest, and wise in his own. He has doled out food on the right schedule, and his behavior

---

19. C.A. Evans and J.A. Sanders read this parable as relating to Deut. 13.1-5, an account they label as 'time tests the faithful'. See their *Luke and Scripture: The Function of Sacred Tradition in Luke–Acts* (Minneapolis: Fortress Press, 1993), p. 121.

20. du Plessis, p. 320.

certainly outranks that of the other steward. Nonetheless, this portrait of 'readiness' lacks virtue.

There are three levels of humanity in this parable: the powerless slaves, the steward, and the lord together create for the reader a 'triangular relationship'.[21] When he is first named, the steward is *oikonomos*, a butler in charge of the household. The domestic power of such a person, though unfamiliar to most of us today, cannot be understated. In traditional upper-class households, the steward or butler would have almost unlimited power over the rest of the servants, acting as the father of the family 'below stairs', with the other servants as children under his care. He could reward or punish, answering only to the owner of the house. In Luke's parable, the steward, left unsupervised, initially uses his power responsibly, providing for those beneath him, and his behavior earns him even more power and possessions when his lord returns and finds him 'at work', doing whatever he needs to do to forward the activities of the household.

The second scenario, however, shows a different outcome. The steward first notes that the lord is not around—he himself needs to be watched—and then he bullies or beats those beneath him and finally destroys any sense of unity by violating the Lucan ethic of banqueting—he eats (perhaps the very food intended for the others) and gets drunk. Now the text describes him as *doulos*, a slave, instead of *oikonomos*, a steward: he is perhaps now seen as a 'slave' to his passions who has thus abdicated his proper stewardship. As his label has changed, so has that of the fellow-servants, who are now made to appear more child-like and vulnerable by the designation *pais* and *paidiskē*.

All is set right, in the oppositional logic of the parable, by the lord-*kyrios*. Unlooked for, he appears and dispenses judgment, asserting (at least implicitly) the right of the least powerful to be treated fairly. It is interesting to note that the characters' labels are changed as their role changes: the steward is first *oikonomos* but then *doulos*; the fellow servants are initially *therapeiai*, but then *paides* and *paidiskes*—boy-and girl-servants—as they become more powerless, or rather, as their true powerlessness makes them more victimized. Only the designation of the lord, *kyrios,* remains the same, his unchanged label reflecting his unchanged powerful nature. In Matthew's parallel verses, the steward is always simply *doulos* and the fellow-servants *syndouloi*; the first gospel's

---

21. H. Moxnes, *The Economy of the Kingdom: Social Conflict and Economic Relations in Luke's Gospel* (Philadelphia: Fortress Press, 1988), p. 63.

account, then, seems to lack some of the shades of meaning which complicate the Lucan version.

The body in this parable is more object than subject. The unjust steward indulges his own body, eating and drinking to excess, but the bodies of the servants are beaten and starved. When the lord returns, he pays back the unjust steward by punishing *his* body, cutting him in two and casting him out. The text does not show a restoration of concern for the bodies of the abused servants, because the emphasis of this tale is on punitive justice for the abuser, not restorative justice for the abused.

To interpret this or any scripture passage through a feminist lens is to ask how the pericope may be understood as responding to God's constant call for a more just and loving world. This parable is a parabola, an arc on the cusp of change, punishing an abuser, yet not changing the world which allows abuse. It refuses to turn the world upside down but instead 'rights' the worst disorder in order to make it bearable. Do we find here revealed the God who desires to wipe every tear? 'All metaphoric language is tensive', says Kathleen Wicker, 'suspended between the "is" and "is not" of the metaphor'.[22] Here we find ourselves within the tension, desiring the 'is' of affirmation, yet recognizing the 'is not' of this parable.

Reading this and other troubling tales, who are we? Perhaps most of us will find ourselves in the hard-working servants who receive a blessing. We have paid a fair wage and even benefits to the nanny or housecleaner, and we are unfailingly respectful to such individuals. We work hard, and the blessings should be ours. Economically and educationally privileged, we believe ourselves to be using our power wisely and faithfully.

Few of us will see ourselves as the girl-servants, starved and beaten. For those who do find themselves in that role, it may be too abstract and distant to praise an eradication of traditional power; instead it is more immediately meaningful to praise the power of the unchanging lord-*kyrios* who rights the use of power. Working in a factory and abused by a shop-steward, would we not take great pleasure in the owner's finding out the steward's abuses and firing him? For this, we would praise the owner indeed. Seeing the abusive boss exposed and deposed would be some recompense, even without our knowing immediately what other recom-pense might come to us. In the same framework, we hear of the victim's

22. K.O. Wicker, 'Teaching Feminist Biblical Studies in a Postcolonial Context', in E. Schüssler Fiorenza (ed.), *Searching the Scriptures: A Feminist Introduction* (New York: Crossroad, 1993), p. 374.

family who gain closure by watching the execution of their loved one's killer.

But this vision cannot be all. Human though it undoubtedly is, from Miriam's and Mary's songs of triumph of the lord-*kyrios* drowning Pharaoh's army and casting down the mighty from their thrones, such emotion cannot be the end of the story. Like the parable of the just and unjust stewards, the celebration of solely punitive justice must always represent a partial economy, a stinted and measured-out version of the great banquet for which the human community yearns.

III

JOHANNINE METAPHORS OF MOTHER AND BRIDE

The (Pro)creative Parables of Labour and Childbirth (Jn 3.1-10 and 16.21-22)

Kathleen Rushton

In this exploration of Jn 3.1-10 and 16.21-22, I shall concentrate on the latter.[1] This does not mean that attention will not be given to 3.1-10. Indeed, one pericope informs the other. Interpretative traditions may have marginalized and obscured 16.21-22. However, this parable centres on a woman, a woman in childbirth. Therefore, the language and imagery of human generation according to the female principle could not be denied as has been the case in interpretations and translations of 3.1-10 and related birth imagery (1.12-13; 7.37-39; 19.34). In a feminist reading of this gospel, Jn 16.21 functions in the Johannine symbolic universe to highlight a tradition of theological meaning-making of the death-glory of Jesus and of discipleship (cf. the grain of wheat [12.24] or the shepherd [10.15]). I aim to demonstrate that birth imagery is not just 'in' this gospel but is an integral part of its theological agenda.

Elsewhere I have argued extensively that this metaphor evokes sets of association related to the arenas of natural birth (γυνή, τίκτω, γεννάω, τὸ παιδίον), Johannine theological themes (ἦλθεν ἡ ὥρα αὐτῆς, ἄνθρωπος, εἰς τὸν κόσμον) and the LXX (λύπη/λυπέω, θλῖψις, χαρά/χαίρω).[2] The language and imagery of human generation according to the female principle makes meaning not only intratextually but intertextually. Through the transformative image of Jn 16.21, the Isaian 'daughter of

---

1. I acknowledge Dorothy Lee who was to have written this chapter. On learning that I was about to submit a PhD related to this topic, Dorothy declined and thereby facilitated my contribution to this project.

2. See my 2000 doctoral thesis, 'The Parable of Jn 16.21: A Feminist Socio-Rhetorical Reading of a (Pro)creative Metaphor for the Death-Glory of Jesus', School of Theology, Griffith University, Brisbane, Australia. I confined my investigation to birth imagery, as opposed to pursuing the implications of motherhood inherent in this imagery. This chapter is influenced also by that somewhat artificial delineation.

Zion' is the paradigmatic suffering one evoked in certain strands of the Johannine death-glory of Jesus.

I shall suggest that the parable of 16.21 and the explanation of v. 22 existed in an extended form in the storytelling of the Johannine communities. As it is found in the Fourth Gospel, John 'got it wrong' by reducing that story to one sentence.[3] Although 'John' may well have done a particular disservice in obscuring this tradition, by a stroke of brilliance the shapers of the text recorded its core in the trope of a metaphor. Additionally, the metaphor is further enhanced because the story is written in the genre of *paroimia* or parable.[4] This parable genre, particular to Jesus in the gospel traditions, strengthens the potential of story to enshrine the activities of God theologically. In the activity of the human person, in this case a woman, her body and (pro)creative potential evoke a strong female biblical figure. A feminist theory of parables and a theory of metaphor will enable possible remnants to be gathered and an imaginable telling of the story to be sketched.

1. *The Ethics of Reading a Birth Parable*

A birth image is read from a multiplicity of perspectives which are as various as each woman and her culture. A plurality of meanings result from factors arising from race, gender, class, sex, religion or culture. One's social location and the interpretation that issues from it is no less rhetorical than the text itself. I am influenced by my Anglo-Irish Pakeha cultural heritage, educational and religious background.[5] Further, I approach a birth image which evokes female experience and issues of reproductive politics as one who has not been involved directly in the actual process of giving birth.

The appropriation of a birth metaphor for feminist purposes needs to be critiqued.[6] Further, the present-day reader is well aware that the choices,

3.   For this suggestion I am indebted to David Jobling and participants in the Bible and Critical Theory Seminar, University of Queensland, Brisbane, 21 September 1999.

4.   On Jn 16.21 as a parable in the Synoptic sense, see C.H. Dodd, *Historical Tradition in the Fourth Gospel* (Cambridge: Cambridge University Press, 1963), p. 386 and pp. 369-73. On *paroimia*, see K. Dewey, '*Paroimiai* in the Gospel of John', *Semeia* 17 (1980), pp. 81-90.

5.   'Pakeha' designates a Person from Aotearoa-New Zealand whose cultural origins are other than indigenous Maori, and in particular, one of European descent.

6.   On the uncritical feminist appropriation of symbols, see M. Peskowitz, 'Roundtable Discussion: What's in a Name? Exploring the Dimensions of What "Feminist

well-being and amenities that facilitate birth for some women has a counter face.[7] Even the birth of a longed-for child may be fraught with ambivalence. For an alarming number of women, childbirth is dangerous for both themselves and the infant. 'Joy' does not necessarily follow. Particularly for young women, childbirth may be the result of lack of information and choice, poverty, exploitation, sexual and cultural violence. Hazards arise from fertility control, or lack of it, and the low priority given to diseases affecting women. Oppression and domestic violence afflict women world-wide.

Philosopher S. Ruddick draws a distinction which enables me to confine this discussion to 'birth' and to challenge stereotypical presuppositions. For Ruddick 'maternal thinking', which is her deconstruction of instinctive 'mothering', is a morally anguishing program of learned behaviour.[8] If, according to Simone de Beauvoir, 'One is not born, but rather becomes, a woman',[9] then according to Ruddick, '[n]either a woman or a man is born a mother; people become mothers in particular historical and social circumstances'.[10] A birthgiver engages in 'a social, adoptive act when she commits herself to sustain an infant in the world'.[11] Ruddick suggests that the work of a birthgiver is not compromised if, with care, she passes to others the responsibility for the infant she has birthed. However, that possibility must not deny that women and men have very different connections to human birth. Although ambivalent responses may accompany birth, it is 'a physically innovative act' creating a new life.[12] Birth, an undeniably female event, enshrines 'symbolic, emotional and ultimately political significance' in a philosophical tradition that privileges mind over body, idea over matter, 'the word over the bloody, shitty, mortal flesh'.[13]

Studies in Religion" Means', *JFSR* 11 (1995), pp. 111-15. For a history of childbirth which shows that this original source of female power was relegated to a role of passive suffering and the archetypal female experience of childbirth, see Adrienne Rich, *Of Woman Born: Motherhood as Experience and Institution* (New York: Norton, 1976), pp. 129-55.

7. See, Rich, *Of Woman Born*, pp. 156-85.

8. S. Ruddick, *Maternal Thinking: Towards a Politics of Peace* (London: Women's Press, 1990), p. 49.

9. S. de Beauvoir, *The Second Sex* (New York: Vintage, 1974), p. 301.

10. Ruddick, *Maternal Thinking*, p. 52. On childbirth as 'a culturally produced event', see, Rich, *Of Woman Born*, pp. 177- 79.

11. Ruddick, *Maternal Thinking*, p. 51.

12. Ruddick, *Maternal Thinking*, p. 49.

13. Ruddick, *Maternal Thinking*, p. 48.

2. *A Feminist Theory of Parables*

L. Schottroff advocates that the crucial question to be asked of any theory of parables is 'how it assesses the parable's 'image' *theologically*' because parables concern 'the relationship of God to the world, or more precisely, of God to creation'.[14] Schottroff elaborates criteria to counter current parable theory which is part of wider theological thinking which renders women invisible and which does not see women's activities as an object of theological reflection.[15] She advocates that feminist theologians must develop a theory of parables 'in which feet once again touch the ground of reality' because the parables 'speak of social reality'.[16]

> The two levels of the parables—the human world or creation and God's reign—both are spheres of God's action in creation... In the parables creation is a window through which God's action in the world can be seen; creation is the place in which God's actions may be experienced.[17]

In other words, the parable of Jn 16.21 must be understood in its historical context to determine how the social realities evoked in its metaphor convey insight into divine action in two arenas, namely, the human world or creation, and God's reign. I shall outline how a theory of metaphor assists in breaking open the worlds of this image.

3. *Attention to Metaphor*

Jn 16.21 is essentially a metaphor, as is the birth image in 3.1-10. Therefore, the point of this interpretation is not whether it is arguable that Jesus is the 'daughter of Zion' on the cross and all that a literal interpretation of such a trajectory may suggest. The aim of this study is to be very clear about the nature of metaphor in this gospel. Consequently, I am not arguing that the male body of Jesus is pregnant and giving birth on the

14. L. Schottroff, *Lydia's Impatient Sisters: A Feminist Social History of Early Christianity* (trans. B. and M. Rumscheidt; Louisville, KY: Westminster/John Knox Press, 1995), p. 51. Italics hers. For her theory of parables, see pp. 51-57.

15. R. Bultmann, *The History of the Synoptic Tradition* (trans. J. Marsh; Oxford: Basil Blackwell, 1963), p. 198, claims that the images of parables are neutral. Therefore, God and the world are juxtaposed. In this scenario, the woman giving birth (Jn 16.21) is an interpretative aid. For a critique of 'the scandalous disturbance of the commonplace' theories, see Schottroff, *Lydia's Impatient Sisters*, pp. 51-54.

16. Schottroff, *Lydia's Impatient Sisters*, p. 52.

17. Schottroff, *Lydia's Impatient Sisters*, p. 53.

cross as the 'daughter of Zion'. Similarly, in construing the metaphorical power of the metaphor of the grain of wheat parable, one does not argue that Jesus is literally a grain of wheat in his death-glory.

J.M. Soskice offers a working definition which sees metaphor as a linguistic 'figure of speech whereby we speak about one thing in terms which are seen to be suggestive of another'.[18] Metaphor brings to expression that which cannot be brought to expression in literal speech. It enables new meaning and 'suggests new categories of interpretation'.[19] Metaphors rely on an underlying model or models. In this instance, the word 'model' follows Soskice's definition: 'an object or state of affairs is said to be a *model* when it is viewed in terms of some other object or state of affairs'.[20] For example, when the concept of birth is used as a frame on which to develop an understanding of the death-glory of Jesus or discipleship, then birth is the model. However, when human persons are spoken of as being born as children of God, then one is speaking metaphorically on the basis of the birth model.[21]

With these understandings in place, the 'interanimation' theory of metaphor, as advanced by Soskice, may now be outlined. Metaphor is a form of language use that is essentially linguistic, for it involves speaking of some thing in terms suggestive of another.[22] There is an interanimation of terms. For Soskice metaphor has a 'unity of subject-matter…yet draws on two (or more) sets of associations, and does so,…by involving the consideration of a model or models'.[23] Each metaphor involves at least two different sets of associations, not two subjects.[24] Networks of associations surround the particular *terms* of a metaphor creating interanimation between the associations. Further, at the secondary level, 'metaphorical construal is characterized by its reliance on an underlying model, or even a

18. J.M. Soskice, *Metaphor and Religious Language* (Oxford: Clarendon Press, 1992), p. 15.

19. Soskice, *Metaphor*, p. 62.

20. Soskice, *Metaphor*, p. 55.

21. Soskice, *Metaphor*, pp. 55, 50-51.

22. As Soskice, *Metaphor*, p. 18, explains: 'A metaphor may prompt us into non-linguistic recognitions and comparisons, but of equal if not greater importance are the linguistic associations to which it gives rise…one goes beyond the bare utterance into a network of implications, it is not so much that one goes beyond words, but one goes beyond the words one is given…while the implications of a metaphor may go beyond the utterance, they are not necessarily extra-linguistic'.

23. Soskice, *Metaphor*, p. 49.

24. Soskice, *Metaphor*, pp. 49-51.

number of models'.[25] Context is limited to textual elements but includes experience, the socio-cultural context and the interpretative tradition.[26] This understanding of metaphor converges with a view of intertextuality and reading in which many texts, both literary and socio-cultural, intersect in the shaping of readers and readings.[27]

In the light of the above, it is appropriate now to sketch how this theory will enhance the interpretation of Jn 16.21. This metaphor evokes several sets of associations which gravitate around the three arenas of natural birth (γυνή, τίκτω, γεννάω, τὸ παιδίον); the LXX (λύπη/λυπέω, θλῖψις, χαρά/χαίρω); and Johannine theological themes (ἦλθεν ἡ ὥρα αὐτῆς, ἄνθρωπος, εἰς τὸν κόσμον). Each of these terms, while suggesting a set of associations, does not have a meaning in itself but 'as a complete utterance in a context of uttering', which is the Fourth Gospel.[28] Each of the sets of associations is reliant in various ways on an underlying model of birth. Further, sets of associations arise from socio-cultural inter-textuality within the Greco-Roman world. This theory of metaphor, as we shall now see, is a theoretical tool to show how 'the ordinary experience' and 'the social reality' of the woman giving birth in the parable is the arena for insight into divine action in the human world or creation and in God's reign.

4. *The Parable of John 16.21*

a. *Sets of Association with Natural Birth—'Ordinary' Experience*
Commentaries and articles on Jn 16.21 enable a reader to gauge the gendered nature of this parable in the history of interpretation. The obvious word for the female person (γυνή) and the verb used to describe her activity (γεννάω) illustrate this. There is a surprising lack of acknowledgment of the γυνή. The woman and her body all but disappear. Embodiment as the site of human activity which theologically images God's activity is unacknowledged. To borrow an expression usually applied to Jesus, her flesh is not incarnated in the theological discourse of

25. Soskice, *Metaphor*, p. 49.

26. Soskice, *Metaphor*, pp. 137-38, 150-59.

27. E.M. Wainwright, 'Rachel Weeping for Her Children: Intertextuality and the Biblical Testaments–A Feminist Approach', in A. Brenner and C. Fontaine (eds.), *A Feminist Companion to Reading the Bible: Approaches, Methods and Strategies* (Sheffield: Sheffield Academic Press, 1997), pp. 456-57.

28. Soskice, *Metaphor*, p. 53.

biblical interpretation. An astonishing number of scholars interpret this parable without any mention of 'the woman' whose 'ordinary activity' of childbirth is the metaphor of the parable.[29] A transfer takes place to emphasize the 'birth of a child' with no mention of a woman at all.[30] Numerous interpretations accent the pains of childbirth with or without reference to the agency of the woman.[31] Others focus on a theme which the metaphor suggests, e.g., grief or joy.[32] Yet others make no mention of the woman herself, for she is 'the mother'.[33] Some interpretations do, of course, focus on the woman herself.[34]

Further, the gendering of birth imagery in this gospel and its often obscured nature in English translations, hinges on the verb which is translated as 'is born' in 16.21 (NRSV). The term γεννάω encompasses both a father's begetting and a mother's giving birth'.[35] References tend to emphasize that this term is usually predicated to a male.[36] In the LXX, this verb translates the Hebrew root *yld* (ילד), which likewise embodies generation from both male and female perspectives.[37] This word is used to refer to the relationship of God and the people (Deut. 32.18; Isa. 1.2; Ezek. 16.20 and Prov. 8.25). The LXX translates these instances with γεννάω. The application of γεννάω to female generation elicits comments like 'is also, but rarely, used of the "bearing" of children by a woman'.[38]

29. For example, G.S. Sloyan, *John* (Interpretation; Atlanta: John Knox, 1988), p. 194.

30. For example, M.C. Tenney, 'The Gospel of John', in F.E. Gaebelein (ed.), *John-Acts* (EBC 9; Grand Rapids: Zondervan, 1973), p. 159, 'painful birth of a child'.

31. For example, Dodd, *Tradition*, p. 369, uses the title 'The Pains of Childbirth'.

32. For example, W. Howard-Brook, *Becoming Children of God: John's Gospel and Radical Discipleship* (The Bible and Liberation Series; New York: Orbis, 1994), pp. 351-352, uses a title, 'Grief Will Become Joy'. He has the following translation: 'But when she has become a parent [*gennesē*]'.

33. G.H.C. MacGregor, *The Gospel of John* (London: Hodder and Stoughton, 1928), p. 301, refers to the 'mother's 'time'.

34. For example, J. Lieu, 'The Mother of the Son in the Fourth Gospel', *JBL* 117 (1998), p. 71.

35. A. Kretzer, 'γεννάω', *TDNT* 1, p. 244; cf. F. Büchsel, 'γεννάω', *TDNT* 1, p. 665.

36. LSJ, vol.1, p. 344, points out that this verb is used 'mostly of the father'. For ancient sources in which γεννάω is found predicated to women, see BAGD, p. 155.

37. On English translations for the verb *yld* (ילד) see, M.P. Korsak, 'Genesis: A New Look', in A. Brenner (ed.), *A Feminist Companion to Genesis* (FCB 2; Sheffield: Sheffield Academic Press, 1993), pp. 43-44.

38. J.H. Bernard, *A Critical and Exegetical Commentary on the Gospel According*

Obviously, Jn 16.21 is one of those 'rare' occurrences which denote generation from the female principle which is commonly translated in biblical references as 'give birth', 'bring forth',[39] 'bear',[40] 'give birth to (perhaps conceive)',[41] and 'that which is born of'.[42] Up to the point of Jn 16.21, the reader has encountered the word γεννάω in the distinctively Johannine way in which it is employed to express the relationship between God and all God's children (1.13; 3.3, 5, 6; 8).[43]

In the image, the experience of a woman in childbirth is evoked through the words ἡ γυνή, τίκτῃ, γεννήσῃ and τὸ παιδίον. These may evoke the often prolonged hours of tortuous pain and distress which precede the onset and actuality of childbirth, along with the bodily realities of the breaking of waters, birth contractions and loss of blood. However, these are not stated overtly. This mirrors the Johannine theological presentation of the death of Jesus, which is expurgated of the humiliating, bloody, messy, degrading aspects which mark the violent death of a crucified criminal. Theological and rhetorical purposes also overlay the birth image of Jn 16.21. The insertion of the terms λύπη/λυπέω and θλῖψις (along with χαρά) jolts the reader to search for new meanings.

b. *Sets of Association with the Septuagint–Literary Intertextuality*
The approach employed here differs from the way in which biblical scholarship, following linear or diachronic literary and historical study, has focused on 'the use' of the Scriptures as a source (i.e., direct quotation, allusion or type) so as to interpret the life of Jesus and the theological understanding of his life in the texts of early Christian communities. For example, Jn 16.21-22 has been linked to Isa. 26.17ff. and 66.7ff., often

---

to St. John (2 vols.; Edinburgh: T. & T. Clark, 1928), p. 18. However, the ancient literature from which scholars draw such conclusions is androcentric and patriarchal, and written by male authors.

39. H.-J. van der Minde, 'γεννάω', *TDNT* I, p. 243; LSJ p. 344.

40. LSJ, p. 344; BAGD, p. 155.

41. B.M. Newman, *A Concise Greek-English Dictionary of the New Testament* (Stuttgart: Biblica-Druck, United Bible Societies, 1971), p. 36.

42. BAGD, p. 155.

43. These five instances are in the passive. This verb is never used in the Christian Scriptures to express the relationship between God and Jesus at the beginning of the latter's earthly life. Jesus is conceived of the Holy Spirit in Mt. 1.18 (εὑρέθη ἐν γαστρὶ ἔχουσα ἐκ πνεύματος ἁγίου). Ps. 2.7 is used in the context of resurrection (e.g., Acts 13.33) or the exaltation of Jesus (e.g., Heb. 1.5). Ps. 2.7 is a coronation image, not a conception one.

through the term θλῖψις. Alternatively, intertextuality enables one text to be read in the light of another to discover the relationships which are evoked by echoes, resonances, intersections and erasures.[44]

In 16.21, the λύπη and θλῖψις of the woman are transformed into χαρά. The reader of this gospel would notice that λύπη (vv. 6, 20, 22) and the verb (v. 20) and θλῖψις (v. 33) are particular to the discourse of ch.16. The late first-century reader would probably notice that it is highly unusual to associate λύπη/λυπέω with childbirth as depicted by τίκτω and γεννάω. Further, her familiarity with the LXX would alert her to biblical traditions surrounding the term θλῖψις. New arenas of meaning are evoked when this parable is read intertextually with a feminist retrieval of the literary figures of the woman of Gen. 3.16 and the Isaian 'daughter of Zion'.

i. *The Woman of Gen. 3.16.* A strand of biblical scholarship recognizes that Gen. 2.4b-3.24b functions as a parable (*mašal*) or 'a wisdom tale'. Consequently, it belongs to the category of speculative wisdom which ventures into the paradox of suffering and the harsh realities of life.[45] Within this agenda, 3.16 is significant for it holds the key to feminist claims that this wisdom tale/parable is not a sin/fall story. Gen. 3.16 may be regarded fruitfully as part of a myth of human maturation (Gen. 2.4b-3.24b).[46]

44. Wainwright, 'Rachel Weeping', p. 459.

45. C. Meyers, 'Gender Roles and Genesis 3.16 Revisited', in A. Brenner (ed.), *A Feminist Companion to Genesis* (FCB 2; Sheffield: Sheffield Academic Press, 1993), p. 129, states that in 'format, technique (vocabulary and use of puns and double entendres), setting, characterizations and even 'plot', Gen. 3 follows the form of a parable or, perhaps more accurately a "wisdom tale"'. Cf. Job, Ecclesiastes and certain Psalms.

46. L.M. Bechtel, 'Rethinking the Interpretation of Genesis 2.4b-3.24', in Brenner (ed.), *Feminist Companion to Genesis*, pp. 116, 84-86; E. van Wolde, *A Semiotic Analysis of Genesis 2-3: A Semiotic Theory and Method of Analysis Applied to the Garden of Eden* (SSN; Assen: Van Gorcum, 1989), pp. 216-19, especially p. 218. U. Cassuto *A Commentary of the Book of Genesis, Vol. 1* (trans. by I. Abrahams; Jerusalem: Mages/Hebrew University, 1961), pp. 113-17. This is significant in so far as the death of Jesus in the Fourth Gospel is not about the expiation of sin, see J.T. Forestell, *The Word of the Cross: Salvation as Revelation in the Fourth Gospel* (AnBib 57; Rome: Biblical Institute Press, 1974; and G.R. O'Day, 'Johannine Theologians as Sectarians', in F.F. Segovia (ed.), *'What is John?': Readers and Readings of the Fourth Gospel* (SBL.S 3; Atlanta: Scholars, 1996), pp. 199-203.

The myth reduces woman and man to their essence, which is survival. Their respective roles are life-producing wife/mother/parent and worker (3.16), and life-sustaining farmer and father/parent (3.17-19). Gen. 3.16 is not a birth image. The Hebrew term הרון (*hērōn*), in the developed biblical vocabulary of human reproduction, refers to the period of pregnancy, not to childbirth.[47] In the LXX, λύπη is applied to both the woman (3.16) and the man (3.17). [48] This suggests that a semblance of equality exists between woman and man sharing the tasks of survival, even in that patriarchal text and world.[49] Its usage in v. 17 refers to the physical labour involved in the daily struggle for a livelihood. It is not so much physical work that is involved, but the concept of the unrelenting difficulty which accompanies this toil.[50] These lexical nuances speak directly of societal conditions of the period. The female's contribution is increased in terms of subsistence living and childbearing, while for the male are the unremitting hardships of agricultural life.[51] Bechtel sees their world as one in which 'salvation is...symbolized in terms of generations of progeny'.[52]

When the metaphor of the woman of Jn 16.21 is read intertextually with the woman of Gen. 3.16, the latter's symbolic 'bundles' are evoked. For the γυνή of the Genesis parable has 'multiple relatedness' to the other

47. This is illustrated when Jer. 20.17 is compared with other reproduction terms in vv. 14-18. On Gen. 3.16, see C. Meyers, *Discovering Eve: Ancient Israelite Women in Context* (New York: Oxford University Press, 1991), pp. 102-103 and in general, M. Ottosson, 'הרון', *TDOT* 3, pp. 458-61.

48. Meyers, 'Gender Roles', p. 130, translates 3.16b as: 'I will greatly increase your work and your pregnancies. (Along) with toil you shall give birth to children'. For a literary analysis, see P. Trible, *God and the Rhetoric of Sexuality* (London: SCM, 1992), pp. 126-28, who sets Gen. 3 within the sin/fall paradigm but accentuates equality.

49. This is not to suggest that equality exists between the woman and the man according to a feminist understanding.

50. Cf., Gen. 5.29 וּמֵעִצְּבוֹן/λυπῶν.

51. Meyers, 'Gender Roles', p. 139, categorizes three areas of activity: protection (through defensive or offensive military actions), production (subsistence: foodstuffs, shelter, clothing), and procreation (childbearing and childrearing). In the balance of labour, production has the greatest potential for gender asymmetry and the potential to rearrange traditional gender roles (cf. p. 123). Meyers, 'Gender Roles', p. 137 and *Eve*, pp. 47-71, dates Gen. 3 to the Iron I period. For a critique, see N. Steinberg, 'Review of *Discovering Eve: Ancient Israelite Women in Context*, by C. Meyers', *Critical Review of Books in Religion* (1990), p. 163.

52. Bechtel, 'Rethinking the Interpretation of Genesis', p. 112.

elements of the myth.[53] Therefore, in symbolic terms she is, for the most part, inseparable from the multiple relatedness of the maturation process which journeys through *'ādām/iššâ* and the associated symbols of the trees, the snake, garden, and water. The Johannine text itself echoes this multiple relatedness: the woman (16.21); the tree of the cross, i.e., the lifting up motif (3.14; 8.28; 12.32, 34) and the cross/tree itself (19.17, 18, 25, 31); the snake (3.14);[54] the situating of the death-resurrection of Jesus in the garden (18.1; 19.41; 20.15);[55] and the prominence of water (19.34). All these feature in the Johannine depiction of the death-glory of Jesus.

ii. *Jn 16.21 and the 'Daughter of Zion'.* In a similar but different way, Jn 16.21 evokes and reinterprets the biblical traditions of the Isaian 'daughter of Zion'. Her story must be retrieved because this woman character is almost always unrecognized. In the seven times when she is named (Isa. 1.8; 3.16 [daughters]; 10.32; 16.1; 37.22; 52.2; 62.11), her identity is absorbed by the city of Jerusalem or the city of Zion. The term 'daughter of Zion' includes a female character who appears mainly in Isa. 40-66 and whose story may be traced through four main passages: 49.14, 21, 24; 51.17-52.2; 54.1-10; and 66.7-16.[56] Arguably there are others. These four, however, show a clear development from abandonment, suffering, fear, childlessness and loneliness to culminate in joy and fulfillment in the birth of her children. The vividness of the portrayal of the 'Daughter of Zion' as a character and her extent in the text is illustrated by a comparison with the four main 'servant' texts (42.1-7; 49.1-7; 50.4-9; 52.13-53.12). Sawyer goes as far as saying that the 'servant' has 'been studied almost to the

53. Bechtel, 'Rethinking the Interpretation of Genesis', pp. 95-98.

54. This refers to the son of man being lifted up as Moses lifted up the serpent in the wilderness. On Moses and the serpent, see K.R. Joines, *Serpent Symbolism in the Old Testament: A Linguistic, Archaeological, and Literary Study* (Haddonfield: Haddonfield Press, 1974), pp. 85-93.

55. N. Wyatt, "Supposing him to be the Gardener' (John 20,15): A Study of the Paradise Motif in John', *ZNW* 81 (1990), pp. 21-38; J. Lieu, 'Scripture and the Feminine in John', in A. Brenner (ed.), *A Feminist Companion to Hebrew Bible in the New Testament* (FCB 10; Sheffield: Sheffield Academic Press, 1996), pp. 235-37. The oppositional forces were screened out by the LXX παράδεισος (paradise; cf., Gen. 2.8, 9, 10, 15, 16) which suggests an enclosed park or pleasure ground rather than the Hebrew גן (garden). See Bechtel, 'Rethinking the Interpretation of Genesis', 94. The term in Jn 18.1 and 19.41 is κῆπος and 20.15 refers to a κηπουρός.

56. J.F.A. Sawyer, 'Daughter of Zion and Servant of the Lord in Isaiah: A Comparison', *JSOT* 44 (1989), pp. 89-107.

point of idolatry by Christian exegetes' while in contrast the 'daughter of Zion' as a parallel motif in the text of Isaiah is largely unrecognized.[57]

Like 'the servant', the 'daughter of Zion' is indeed an ambiguous character. Sometimes she is named as in 49.14.[58] Sometimes she is anonymous (54.1).[59] After ch. 40, both characters are addressed afresh and the passages in which their stories are told interweave, interrupted yet with continuity throughout the text. The first words of the 'daughter of Zion' are a response expressing doubt in the face of God's promise of triumph (Isa. 49.8-14): 'The Lord has forsaken me, my Lord has forgotten' (49.14). This parallels the 'servant's' expression of doubt in 49.4: 'I said, 'I have laboured in vain...spent my strength for nothing and vanity'. In 49.21 she complains: 'I was bereaved and barren...left alone'. In a similar but different way (v. 7), God speaks to the 'servant' as 'one deeply despised, abhorred by the nations; the slave of rulers'. However, God assures the 'daughter of Zion' that she is loved: 'Can a woman forget her nursing child...the child of her womb?' (v. 15). The 'servant' recalls that God 'called me before I was born, while I was in my mother's womb God named me' (v. 1). Kings and queens will bow down before the 'daughter of Zion' (v. 23) while the 'servant' is also assured (v. 7) that kings and princes will prostrate before him. Continuity and verbal parallels exist between the 'daughter of Zion' poem of 51.17-52.2 and the 'servant' poem of 52.13-53.12. Both are humiliated, afflicted, and then vindicated. Both will live to see their offspring grow up (66.7-9 parallels 53.10) and the nations will be affected by what happens (54.3 parallels 52.15).[60] It is, however, the remarkable differences between these two figures which suggest that the 'daughter of Zion' is 'the suffering one' in the Fourth Gospel.

I understand Jn 16.21 to be a Johannine re-interpretation of two female motifs, the barren woman tradition and the birth image tradition, which have been adapted and retold creatively in Israel's long religious history.[61]

---

57. Sawyer, 'Daughter of Zion', p. 93.

58. But Zion said, 'YHWH has forsaken me, my God has forgotten me'.

59. 'Sing, O barren one who did not bear'.

60. In 57.6-13 the 'daughter of Zion' is described as having become a harlot. There is a similar discordant parallel for the 'servant' in 43.22-28.

61. On biblical constructions of childbirth, see L.H. Lefkovitz, 'Sacred Screaming: Childbirth in Judaism', in D. Orenstein (ed.), *Life Cycle: Jewish Women on Life Passages and Personal Milestones*, Vol. 1 (Woodstock: Jewish Lights Publishing, 1994), p. 8; R. Lacks, *Woman and Judaism: Myth, History, and Struggle* (Garden City:

M. Callaway traces the motif of the barren woman from Genesis to Luke.[62] This tradition of the barren matriarchs—Sarah, Rebekah, Rachel, mother of Samson—focuses on the birth of a significant person, a son. The tradition changes with Hannah to focus on a people and reaches its fullness in the Isaian 'daughter of Zion'.[63] The third-person narrative gives way to the poetic literary form of an oracle of salvation which addresses the woman directly in the second person (e.g., Isa. 54.1-3). The shift is from narration to proclamation. My study of birth images in both testaments concludes that only that of the birth of the 'daughter of Zion's' children (Isa. 66.7ff.) and that of Jn 16.21 are birth images in the fullest sense—that is, a woman, mention of pain, childbirth, offspring, and joy at the birth. Jn 3.1-10 does not come into this category. Others are similes centred on pain or fear, a birth that is really adoption, or evoke some aspect of birth.

The Isaian reinterpretation of this motif in chs. 40-66 probably originated in the experience of the exile. This resonated with the situation of the Johannine communities who in the face of persecution projected their struggles back into the time of Jesus. The figure of the 'daughter of Zion' was particularly evocative in their situation. As a stereotypical woman, she is depicted as being subjected to being abused, humiliated, carried off and powerless.[64] While both the servant (41.14) and 'daughter of Zion' (51.12, 54.4) are told not to be afraid, very different imagery is evoked. The 'daughter of Zion' is invited to awaken, put on her strength, put on beautiful garments, shake herself from the dust, loose the bonds from her neck (52.1-2), sing, burst into song and shout, and enlarge the size of her

Doubleday, 1980), p. 148. On 'mother', see R. Adler, 'A Mother in Israel: Aspects of the Mother Role in Jewish Myth', in R. Gross (ed.), *Beyond Androcentrism: Essays on Women and Religion* (Missoula: Scholars, 1977), pp. 237-55; E. Fuchs, 'The Literary Characterization of Mothers and Sexual Politics in the Hebrew Bible', in A.Y. Collins (ed.), *Feminist Perspectives on Biblical Scholarship* (Atlanta: Scholars, 1985), pp. 117-36; and J.C. Exum, 'The (M)other Place', in Exum, *Fragmented Women. Feminist (Sub)versions of Biblical Narratives* (JSOTSS 163; Sheffield: Sheffield Academic Press, 1993), pp. 94-147.

62. M. Callaway, *Sing, O Barren One: A Study in Comparative Midrash* (SBLDS 9; Atlanta: Scholars, 1986).

63. Callaway, *Sing, O Barren One*, pp. 59-72, 77-81. See p. 64 where she remarks that 'Second Isaiah's use of the traditions of creation and exodus are universally recognized, his use of the traditions of the barren women have only been superficially noted.

64. See the fates of woman Babylon (ch. 47) and the daughters of Zion (3.18-26).

tent (54.1-4). These give a life-giving, even revolutionary dimension to the story, which contrasts with the servant who will be helped by God (41.13) to use 'strength to overcome adversity by brute force' as in 41.15.[65] While the 'daughter of Zion's' role is primarily domestic, and always dependent on her lord and master (as is the servant), she is portrayed as claiming her freedom and dignity.[66] Yet she is not subservient. She shakes her head defiantly. Perhaps the most telling difference is found in the climaxes of both stories. The last servant song climaxes with his sharing the spoils of war (53.12) and the creation of a new Israel, but is in predominately male imagery. God is portrayed as a powerful monarch imposing his authority on the world (43.15-17) or resembling a mighty warrior slaying the monsters of chaos (51.9-10). In contrast, the climax of the story of the 'daughter of Zion' (66.7-14) is framed by explicit references to the creation of a new heaven and a new earth (65.17; 66.22). This is preceded by the passage of 54.1-10, in which her extraordinary relationship with God culminates with the latter as her midwife.

The term θλῖψις/θλίβεω is a significant religious concept in the LXX.[67] In the oppression and affliction, the people of Israel constantly face θλῖψις and are aware of its significance in their history (e.g., Isa. 26.16; 37.3; 63.6 and 65.16). In the Psalms, the θλῖψις of the people, and especially that of righteous individuals or figures, has paradigmatic significance.[68] The 'daughter of Zion' is such a paradigmatic figure in Israel's sacred story. Her λύπη and θλῖψις are transformed into χαρά. These words in Jn 16.21 evoke this scriptural tradition. The actual word, θλῖψις, does not feature in the finale of the story of the 'daughter of Zion'. However, Schlier, when discussing paradigmatic figures in the psalms, infers that the 'servant of the Lord' of Isaiah is such a one but states that θλῖψις is not used in this connection in Job, '*nor does it appear at all in Is. 53*'.[69] The 'daughter of

---

65. Sawyer, 'Daughter of Zion', p. 104.

66. Isa. 52.1-2; 37.22 (tosses her head defiantly).

67. See, H. Schlier, 'θλῖψις/θλίβεω', *TDNT* 3, pp. 140-43. The literal sense of the verb denotes 'to press', 'squash', 'rub', 'hem in' (p. 143). The figurative sense as used in the LXX according to J. Lust, E. Eynikel and K. Hauspie, *A Greek-English Lexicon of the Septuagint* (2 vols.; Stuttgart: Deutsche Bibelgesellschaft, 1992, 1996), p. 206, is 'to compress', 'oppress', 'afflict', to be distressed', while the noun denotes 'oppression', 'affliction', 'anguish'.

68. E.g., the θλῖψις of the righteous. Ps. 33.19; 137. 7; 36.39; 49.15; 76.2; God hears their prayer and delivers them from distress: Ps. 9.9; 31.7; 33.6, 17; 36.39-40; 53.7; 58.17.

69. Schlier, 'θλῖψις/θλίβεω', p. 142 n. 2. Italics his.

Zion' is, indeed, in good company. She is the paradigmatic 'suffering one' evoked in the image of the woman in childbirth and enables new insight into the death-glory of Jesus and discipleship in the Fourth Gospel.

c. *Sets of Association with Johannine Theological Themes–Intratextuality*
The poetic and symbolic function of Jn 16.21-22 may be explored further by examining the phrases 'her hour has come' (ἦλθεν ἡ ὥρα αὐτῆς) and 'into the world' (εἰς τὸν κόσμον). The rhetorical effect of these two distinctively Johannine phrases is that by the time the reader encounters this parable, a number of associations have been made intratextually with other theological understandings.

The first matter which would be clear to a late first-century reader is that the meaning of the phrase ἦλθεν ἡ ὥρα αὐτῆς is not traceable to any contemporaneous Greek expression for the approaching time of childbirth as its English translation might suggest. In secular Greek, the ὥρα of a woman seems to be the bloom of her youth.[70] The quest for the significance of ἡ ὥρα in 16.21, then, must be found in relation to its other occurrences in this gospel and its association with ἦλθεν. Dodd holds that ὥρα with a personal genitive of possession is 'sufficiently unusual for its frequent employment by this writer to constitute a stylistic idiosyncrasy'.[71] This means that this variation with the female pronoun ἡ ὥρα αὐτῆς (must be interpreted in relation to ἡ ὥρα, or ἡ ὥρα αὐτοῦ (or ἡ ὥρα). These are employed to prefigure my/his/the 'hour' when Jesus will be 'lifted up' or 'glorified' and his work 'accomplished'.[72] The phrase ἦλθεν ἡ ὥρα αὐτῆς evokes very similar phrases which function as a constant refrain throughout the gospel associated with the death-glory of Jesus. There is, however, a remarkable difference. In 16.21 the pronoun is feminine.

A second phrase, εἰς τὸν κόσμον, also suggests that 16.21 is integrally part of the Johannine theological agenda.[73] The phrase εἰς τὸν κόσμον,

70. Dodd, *Tradition*, p. 371; Gerhard Delling, 'ὥρα', *TDNT* 9, p. 676; See Xenophon, *Hist. Graec.*, 2.1, 1 which refers to ὥρα as the time of the greatest bodily fitness in human life, 'the bloom of youth'; Philo, *Vit. Moses* 1.297; *Spec.* 1.103. Also Josephus, *Ant.* 1.200; 3. 275.

71. The only other example in the Christian Scriptures is Lk. 22.53. Dodd, *Tradition*, p. 371, attests that it is not used in LXX or Philo. See his comments on other ancient sources.

72. 2.4, 5.25, 28; 7.30; 8.20; 12.23; 13.1; 16.2, 4, 21, 25, 32; 17.1. This combination is found only in Mk 14.41 and Mt. 26.45.

73. 1.9; 3.17, 19; 6.14; 9.39; 10.36; 11.27; 12.46; 16.28; 17.18 (2x); 18.37. See, N.H. Cassem, 'A Grammatical and Contextual Inventory of the Use of κόσμος in the

with the verb ἔρχομαι, is predicated only to Jesus or the one who is understood to be the Messiah (1.9; 3.19; 6.14; 9.39; 11.27; 12.46; 16.28; 18.37). The combination of ἔρχομαι and εἰς τὸν κόσμον is found with φῶς, stressing that Jesus is the light who has come into the world (1.9; 3.19; 12.46). This phrase and verb are employed to relate the perception that Jesus is the Messiah (6.14; 9.39; 11.27; 16.28). These four instances suggest that 'coming into the world' is a technical term for the prophetic or messianic mission. This notion is also found when the phrase plus the verb ἀποστέλλω 'to be sent into the world', is used of Jesus' mission (3.17; 10.36; 17.18). Again in 17.18, this combination records Jesus' handing over of his mission to the disciples. Thus rhetorically the phrase εἰς τὸν κόσμον of Jn 16.21 is drawn intratextually into the theological ambiance which this phrase enjoys in the symbolic universe of this gospel.

The rhetorical function of Jn 16.21 has been enhanced by exploring some aspects of its literary intertextuality with the scriptures and its intratextual Johannine associations. The socio-cultural world also shapes a literary text and its readers. This is context of the social reality or 'ordinary activity' of the parable.

d. *Socio-Cultural Intertextuality*
Glimpses of childbirth practices in the first and second centuries CE are found in the only two surviving sources which provide detailed information about midwifery and obstetrical practices in the ancient world. The layman Pliny the Elder, whose *Historia Naturalis* reports mainly on the practices of folk medicine, and the medical practitioner Soranus, whose *Gynecology* is a medical treatise, most likely cover the range of maternity care available.[74] These texts contemporaneous with the Fourth Gospel enable a brief overview of women's labour as birth-givers and as midwives.

V. French concludes that the vast majority of women were cared for most probably with the methods and medications described by Pliny.[75]

Johannine Corpus with Some Implications for a Johannine Cosmic Theology', *NTS* 19 (1972-1973), pp. 83-84.

74. V. French, 'Midwives and Maternity Care in the Roman World', in M. Skinner (ed.), *Rescuing Creusa: New Methodological Approaches to Women in Antiquity* (*Helios* Special Edition 13.2 1987), p. 69. There is 'a rather scant' bibliography on this topic, see pp. 80-81.

75. French, 'Midwives', p. 80. The medical practices recommended for Jewish women would be categorized under folk medicine according to the evidence of S.

Treatments held to be efficacious could be taken internally by mouth before or during labour, or after delivery.[76] Other remedies are recommended to be placed on the woman's body, especially in the vaginal area to relieve pain[77] or to withdraw the infant.[78] The placebo effect of many of these treatments should not be underestimated. The range of care was person-centred and attentive to the woman, who most likely was in the familiar environment of her home and in the care of female relatives.[79] If she could afford one, there would be a midwife.

The writings of both Strabo and Diodorus Siculus preserve a rare glimpse of a rural woman whose engagement in hard work and the urgency to earn money records her as having given birth to her baby in the fields. The following is from Strabo's account.

> [A]nd while at work in the fields, sometimes, they turn aside to some brook, give birth to child, and bathe and swaddle it...Charmoleon... narrated to him [Poseidonius] he had hired men and women together for ditch-digging; and how one of the women, upon being seized with the pangs of childbirth, went aside from her work to a place nearby, and, after having given birth to her child, came back to her work in order not to lose her pay; and how he himself saw that she was doing her work painfully, but was not aware of the

Safrai, 'Home and Family', in S. Safrai and M. Stern (eds.), *The Jewish People in the First Century: Historical Geography, Political History, Social, Cultural and Religious Life and Institutions* (CRI 2; Assen: Van Gorcum, 1976), pp. 764-66. On childbirth in Jewish circles, see Tal Ilan, *Jewish Women In Greco-Roman Palestine: An Inquiry into Image and Status* (TSAJ 44; Tübingen: J.C.B. Mohr/Paul Siebeck, 1995), pp. 116-19. Ilan points out that Jewish law equates helping a woman in childbirth with saving a life.

76. To relieve the pains of labour a drink sprinkled with powdered sow dung was suggested. By drinking sow's milk with honey childbirth is eased, while a drink of sow's milk itself refills the drying breasts of nursing mothers; see *Historiae Naturalis* (*HN*) 28.77.250.

77. *HN* 28.27.102-103, records that fat from hyena loins produce immediate delivery for women in difficult labour. Placing the right foot of hyaena on the woman brings about an easy delivery, but the left foot causes death. *HN* 30.44.129-30 refers to a snake's slough which is tied to the loins as an armlet to make childbirth easier. The feather of a vulture may be placed under a woman's foot to help delivery.

78. See *HN* 28.77.251, where fumigation with ass's hoofs hastens delivery, so that even a dead foetus is extracted. *HN* 30. 143. 123 records that the afterbirth of a bitch which had not touched the ground was placed on the thighs of the woman.

79. In Aristophanes (257-180 B.C.E.), *Women in the Assembly (Ecclesiazsae* 526-34), the heroine accounts for her early morning absence by informing her husband that she had to hurry out during the night to help a friend who had gone into labour.

cause till late in the day, when he learned it and sent her away with her wages; and she carried the infant out to a little spring, bathed it, swaddled it with what she had, and brought it safely home.[80]

The fact that the woman in both accounts persists in working, indicates that the compassion she eventually experienced was probably not the norm. Pregnancy, and, in particular, the time away from work for childbirth threatened not only her wages but her employment.[81] Economic demands deprived her, and presumably other poor women, of the solidarity and expertise of other women which usually surround childbirth. Reading Jn 16.21 beside this glimpse of a poor first-century rural woman suggests the strength and hardship of the lives of the vast majority of women in the Greco-Roman world–a world away from idealizing a birth image.

Soranus outlines potentially more enlightened practices that were possibly available to a small number of wealthy elites.[82] A description of childbirth and an array of requirements are found in his instructions for a midwife in the case of a normal delivery.[83] Aspects of his account are verified by visual depictions of the period which show a woman positioned on a birth stool or chair attended by a midwife and her assistant(s).[84] Soranus' descriptions of nooses to extract an infant who could not be born

80. Strabo, *Geogr.* 3.4.17. Translation from H.L. Jones, *The Geography of Strabo* (vol. 2; London: Heinemann, 1949), p. 113; Greek text, p. 112. Cf. Diodorus Siculus, 4.20.1. Poseidonius was a Greek philosopher born c. 135 B.C.E. See also, Schottroff, *Lydia's Impatient Sisters*, p. 99.

81. On women's agricultural work, see W. Scheidel, 'The Most Silent Women of Greece and Rome: Rural Labour and Women's Life in the Ancient World', *Greece and Rome* 42 (1995), pp. 210-13, especially p. 211.

82. For example, Soranus did not subscribe to the theory of the wandering womb, see M.R. Lefkowitz and M.B. Fant, *Women's Life in Greece and Rome: A Source Book in Translation* (2nd edn; Baltimore: John Hopkins University Press, 1992), p. 256; and M.R. Lefkowitz, *Heroines and Hysterics* (London: Duckworth, 1981), pp. 12-25; French, 'Midwives', p. 80.

83. *Soranus' Gynecology*, II, 67-70b (trans. with an Introduction by Owsei Temkin; Baltimore: John Hopkins University Press, 1991), pp. 70-79. For the Greek text see, Paul Burguière et al. (eds.), *Soranos d'Éphèse: Maladies des femmes* (vol. 2; Paris: Les Belles Lettres, 1990), pp. 4-9.

84. From a tomb in the necropolis of Isola, near Ostia (Museo di Ostia; Foteca Unione); see Lefkowitz and Fant, *Women's Life in Greece and Rome*, pp. 166-67, plate 13; Ivory relief from Pompeii (mus. Naz., Naples, No. 109905) and Marble relief from Silvestro Baglioni collection, see French, 'Midwives', pp. 77-78. For a fragment from a sarcophagus showing a baby immediately after delivery (DAI Neg. No. 42-101), see S. Dixon, *The Roman Mother* (London: Croom Helm, 1988), plate 7.

alive point to the complexity and danger of birth. His writings may indeed be prescriptive, but a profile of a skilled, demanding female profession of midwifery emerges.[85] The midwives were usually slaves or freedwomen.[86] There were male doctors, but childbirth was the domain of mothers and midwives whose skills and practice were transferred orally and by example throughout generations.[87] Therefore, the usual socio-cultural reality of the image of the woman in childbirth cannot be contemplated as a lone woman.

These glimpses from ancient male writings contemporaneous with the Johannine text offer some insight into the 'ordinary' activity of women which is the criterion by which the theological significance of the parable of Jn 16.21 must be gauged. This also enabled the retrieval of female practitioners, the midwives, those slave women and freedwomen whose domain was to care for a woman amidst the hope of wellbeing and under the shadow of the dangers that accompany childbirth.

5. *Gathering Together the Remnants*

In its essence, the metaphor at the core of the parable of Jn 16.21 is a transformative image. The woman brings new life through her suffering and childbirth. This 'ordinary' experience is layered with terms evocative of the relative equality that woman and man share in the hardship of life in Gen. 3.16-17. This intimates that female and male disciples share the tasks of Johannine discipleship. The transformative story of the paradigmatic suffering one, the 'daughter of Zion', evokes new Johannine nuances in the long tradition of storytelling that has seen this motif reinterpret the interplay between suffering and joy in new historical circumstances. She evokes the birth of the people in the context of the new creation. In the Johannine symbolic world, the phrase 'her hour has come' evokes the nuances that associate this with the coming of Jesus Messiah. The phrase

85. S.B. Pomeroy, *Goddesses, Whores, Wives, and Slaves: Women in Classical Antiquity* (London: Random House, 1975), pp. 191-92. For the qualities and skills, see Soranus, *Gynecology*, 1.3-4, in Temkin, *Soranus' Gynecology*, pp. 5-7. Greek text in Burguière, *Soranus*, vol. 1, pp. 5-8.

86. See inscriptions in Lefkowitz and Fant, *Women's Life in Greece and Rome*, p. 267, no. 377.

87. Pomeroy, *Goddesses*, p. 84; A. Rousselle, *Porneia: On Desire and the Body in Antiquity* (trans. Felicia Pheasant; Oxford: Basil Blackwell, 1988), pp. 24-26; Lefkowitz and Fant, *Women's Life in Greece and Rome*, p. 265.

'into the world' is evocative of God's loving presence entering the human story. In the Johannine world, symbolism functions at two levels. At the primary level, Jesus is the one who brings transformation by accomplishing the works of God. At the secondary level, this transformative image makes meaning of the situation of the Johannine disciples and their discipleship.

The four sets of associations evoked by Jn 16.21, and its explanation of v. 22, network with other sets of associations within the Fourth Gospel, thus forming networks of associations. The metaphor of Jn 16.21 relies on the underlying model of birth, which is a frame on which to develop an understanding of the death-glory of Jesus and for the Johannine Christians to develop an understanding of their particular situation.[88] Intratextually, the underlying model of birth forms a network of sets of associations with other Johannine birth images (1.12-13; 3.3-8; 7.37-38; 16.21; 19.34). Further, as an image of the death-glory of Jesus, Jn 16.21 creates interanimation with sets of associations surrounding the death-glory of Jesus in the Johannine construction of that event, e.g., the lifting up/exultation (3.14; 8.28; 12.32, 34) and 'the hour' (12.23; 17.1). In addition, Jn 16.21 forms networks of sets of association in which those associated with the death of Jesus merge with the life experience of the Johannine Christians in their first-century situation: the accomplishment of the works of God (4.34; 5.36; 17.4; 19.30); the coming of the Spirit (14.16, 25-26; 15.26; 16.7-11, 13-14); the mission to the world (4.31-38; 17.18; 20.21); and the gathering of the people of God (11.52; 12.20, 32; 19.25-27). Some sets of associations are suggestive of the Johannine disciples in particular: the transformation of understanding (2.17, 22; 12.16; 14.25-26; 16.12-13) and their suffering and persecution (9.22; 15.18-21; 16.1-4). How other dimensions of the strand of birth images participate in this symbolic world is illustrated by the parable of 3.1-10.

6. *The Parable of John 3.1-10*

A reader aware of the networks of associations evoked in 1.12-13, recognizes a female metaphor for God birthing as a mother suggested by γεννάω in the words of Jesus and Nicodemus in 3.3-8 (1.13, ἐκ θεοῦ

---

88. The fundamental structure of Johannine symbolic images is twofold. Images apply primarily to Jesus and then to discipleship, see C.R. Koester, *Symbolism in the Fourth Gospel: Meaning, Mystery, Community* (Minneapolis: Fortress, 1995), pp. 13-15.

ἐγεννήθησαν, 3.3, γεννηθῇ ἄνωθεν; cf. 3.5, 6, 7, 8). A late first century reading of Jn 3.3-8 could have been influenced by earlier Christian texts which drew on the oral traditions of a saying of Jesus.[89] It is significant that this female image is found in association with the only explicit mention of the metaphor 'the reign of God' (ἡ βασιλεία τοῦ θεοῦ) in the Fourth Gospel (3.3, 5).[90] Furthermore, this coupling of birth/children and entering 'the reign of God' is one of the few sayings of Jesus that is found in some form in the *Gos. Thom.* (22.2-4), the synoptics (Mk 10.14-15; Mt. 18.3; 19.14; Lk. 18.16-17) and the Fourth Gospel (Jn 3.3, 5).[91]

According to M. Sawicki, 3.3-8 is a fourth trajectory of a *basileia* metaphor which began with references to nursing babies in *Gos. Thom.* 22.[92] Its similarities to this possibly earliest extant version are notable for the motherhood metaphor is not suppressed. This aspect is concealed as trajectories of 'belongs' (Mk 10.14b; Lk. 18.16b; Mt. 19.14b), 'like a child' (*Gos. Thom.* 22.3; Mk 10.15; Lk. 18.17; Mt. 18.3), and 'hinder not' (Mk 10.14a; Lk. 18.16a; Mt. 19.14a) develop.[93] Here the synoptics use παιδίον. Viewing Jn 3.3-8 within this development is significant for three reasons. It demonstrates that female generative imagery for God's activity with humanity was present in the oral traditions of earliest Christianity, even going back to Jesus. Further, it indicates that female imagery for God

89. On the circulation of ancient Christian texts, see M.B. Thompson, 'The Holy Internet: Communication Between Churches in the First Christian Generation', in R. Bauckham (ed.), *The Gospel for All Christians: Rethinking the Gospel Audiences* (Grand Rapids: Eerdmans, 1998), pp. 49-70.

90. On the neglect of this female image, see S.M. Schneiders, 'Born Anew', *TToday* 44 (1987-1988), p. 194.

91. J.D. Crossan, *Sayings Parallels: A Workbook for the Jesus Tradition* (Philadelphia: Fortress, 1986), numbers 158 and 446; J.D. Crossan, 'Kingdom and Children: A Study in the Aphoristic Tradition', *Semeia* 29 (1983), pp. 75-95.

92. 'Jesus saw some little ones nursing. He said to his disciple, 'What these little ones who are nursing resemble is those who enter the kingdom' *(Gos. Thom.* 22). M. Sawicki, *Seeing the Lord: Resurrection and Early Christian Practice* (Minneapolis: Fortress, 1994), pp. 37-49, especially the diagram, 45, for her reconstruction of this tradition.

93. Sawicki, *Seeing the Lord*, pp. 36-50, especially 45 fig. 1. I. de la Potterie, ' "To Be Born Again of Water and the Spirit"–The Baptismal Text of John 3,5', in I. de la Potterie and S. Lyonnet (eds.), *The Christian Lives by the Spirit* (trans. Daniel V. Flynn; New York: Alba House, 1971), pp. 25-29, compares Jn 3.5 with Mt. 18.3 and parallels. For other commentators these parallels, see 24 n. 54. De la Potterie argues that ὕδατος belongs to a later edition of this verse.

was used contemporaneously in Christianity's Jewish religious matrix (e.g., Deut. 32.18). Johannine traditions continued this practice, which influenced its reinterpretations of God, Jesus and humanity. Finally, according to Sawicki, in the changed situations of the Christian communities '[w]hat "God's kingdom" meant had to change in tandem with changes in what "entering" the kingdom could mean and require'.[94] In the later Johannine trajectory, the possibility of hindrance emerges even to the point of nature posing a difficulty (3.4). Entry becomes 'entry-as-seeing' (3.3) while the womb takes on the dimension of water and spirit (3.5).[95] In the ambiguity of metaphorical evocation, the figurative sense of γεννάω may also suggest the birthing which occurs in the teacher–disciples relationship.[96]

For S. Schneiders, these totally ambiguous and irony-charged verses engage the reader in the multi-layered meanings in 3.3-8 and draw her into the community of believers.[97] Many commentators draw attention to the doubtful or double meaning of γεννηθῆναι ἄνωθεν. However, this phrase is part of a Johannine strategy used throughout the Gospel, and exemplified in 3.1-15, whereby 'image is superimposed on image, creating a literary ecosystem of metaphor'.[98] Similarly, van den Heever concludes that micro-metaphors must be understood macro-metaphorically.[99] In this passage, the metaphorical use of ambiguity is linguistic rather than narrative in that it 'feeds on the ambiguity of single words or phrases'.[100] Kysar demonstrates that in these 'stacked' and 'progressive' metaphors, the reader is 'systematically led to quest the resolution of the earlier metaphor in the next'. He posits that:

> BORN *Anōthen* TO ENTER THE KINGDOM OF GOD
> leads to
> BORN OUT OF WATER AND SPIRIT
> leads to

94. Sawicki, *Seeing the Lord*, p. 50.

95. Sawicki, *Seeing the Lord*, p. 45.

96. NL 13.48 and Büchsel, 'γεννάω', pp. 665-66.

97. Schneiders, 'Born Anew', p. 189.

98. R. Kysar, 'The Making of Metaphor: Another Reading of John 3.1-15', in F.F. Segovia (ed.), *'What is John?' Readers and Readings of the Fourth Gospel* (SBLSS 3; Atlanta: Scholars, 1996), p. 39.

99. G.A. van den Heever, 'Theological Metaphorics and Metaphors of John's Gospel', *Neot* 26.1 (1992), p. 94.

100. Kysar, 'The Making of Metaphor', p. 38.

SPIRIT IS LIKE WIND
leads to
THE SON OF MAN BEING LIFTED UP.[101]

In other words, the meaning of one of these, for example, γεννηθῇ ἄνωθεν, is found in its progressive association with other metaphors in the unit and is part of clusters of metaphors throughout the narrative which evoke the death-glory of Jesus and the nature of discipleship. For Kysar, such a phrase 'miniaturizes a single basic story'.[102] This is an innovative insight into how γεννηθῇ ἄνωθεν is resolved in this progressive cluster. However, Kysar does not recognize that this is part of a parable which evokes a female birth image for God.

7. Conclusion

The parables of women's 'ordinary' experience of labour and childbirth in Jn 3.1-10 and 16.21-22 are not just isolated pericopes in this gospel. They are woven into the very fabric of the theological meaning-making of the death and resurrection of Jesus, and Johannine discipleship. The metaphorical power of the birth metaphor demonstrates what S.S. Friedman has called 'a subversive inscription of women's (pro)creativity that has existed for centuries'.[103] The abridgement of this tradition which is strongly evocative of female experience is possibly attributable to two factors. First, J. Dewey shows how in oral cultures storytelling was the domain of all, including women.[104] At the stage of the writing of the traditions in gospel form, by usually educated male elites, women's storytelling was diminished and marginalized. A second factor is particular to the Fourth Gospel. Schneiders proposes that women influenced the writing of this gospel and were most likely members of the authoritative Johannine school.[105] In the period of uncertainty that preceded the Fourth Gospel's acceptance into the canon, the prominence of women was a feature which

101. Kysar, 'The Making of Metaphor', p. 39.

102. Kysar, 'The Making of Metaphor', p.39.

103. S.S. Friedman, 'Creativity and the Childbirth Metaphor: Gender Difference and Literary Discourse', Feminist Studies 13.1 (1987), p. 51.

104. J. Dewey, 'From Storytelling to Written Text: The Loss of Early Christian Women's Voices', BTB 26.2 (1996), pp. 71-78.

105. S.M. Schneiders, ' "Because of the Women's Testimony": Reexamining the Issue of Authorship in the Fourth Gospel', NTS 44 (1998), pp. 517-35.

seemingly aligned it with gnostic writings.[106] Additionally, from another perspective, the tradition of imaging the death-glory of Jesus as a woman in childbirth may well have been judged to diminish this gospel's acceptance in an increasingly patriarchal, wider Great Church. However, the Johannine women were influential. Meaning-making of the death-resurrection of Jesus and discipleship as evoked by the (pro)creative image of a woman in childbirth and its extensions in parable was integral to their traditioning. This strand was obscured but not deleted.

106. Schneiders, ' "Because of the Women's Testimony" ', p. 523. For a general overview, see G.S. Sloyan, 'The Gnostics' Adoption of John's Gospel and Its Canonization by the Catholic Church', *BTB* 26 (1996), pp. 125-32.

THE 'BRIDE' IN JOHN 3.29: A FEMINIST REREADING

Adele Reinhartz

In her introductory essay to *Searching the Scriptures: A Feminist Introduction*, E. Schüssler Fiorenza writes:

> Women's biblical studies have developed a dualistic hermeneutical strategy that is able to acknowledge two seemingly contradictory facts. On the one hand, the Bible is written in androcentric language, has its origins in the patriarchal cultures of antiquity, and has functioned throughout its history to inculcate androcentric and patriarchal values. On the other hand, the Bible has also served to inspire and authorize women and other nonpersons in their struggles against patriarchal oppression. Women's biblical studies today in one way or another still presuppose and seek to address this dual problematic…women's biblical heritage…is at one and the same time a source for women's religious power and for women's suffering.[1]

This description implies that 'women's biblical studies', and, by extension, feminist biblical criticism, have a dual purpose: to expose the androcentrism of the Bible, and to uncover the Bible's potential to aid in the liberative struggle of women and other oppressed people.

While most biblical texts permit the first of these tasks, many resist the latter. It is difficult, for example, to view Lev. 18.22 ('You shall not lie with a male as with a woman; it is an abomination'[2]) as a text that has liberative possibilities even apart from the long history of its use to justify homophobia. Other biblical texts may at first glance promise to be fruitful for a feminist liberative interpretation, only to have this potential evaporate under closer examination.

One such passage is Jn 3.29a, a brief figurative saying attributed to John

---

1. E. Schüssler Fiorenza, 'Transforming the Legacy of *The Woman's Bible*', in *Searching the Scriptures: A Feminist Introduction* (New York: Crossroad, 1993), pp. 5-6.
2. Unless otherwise noted, English translations of biblical texts are from the New Revised Standard Version.

the Baptist. This saying is embedded in a brief discourse set before John's imprisonment (3.24). The discourse is prompted by John's disciples, who complain that Jesus is baptizing and gaining many adherents (3.20). In his reply, John calls upon his followers to bear witness to the fact that he is not the messiah but the forerunner (3.28). He then declares: 'He who has the bride is the bridegroom. The friend of the bridegroom, who stands and hears him, rejoices greatly at the bridegroom's voice. For this reason my joy has been fulfilled' (3.29). Therefore 'he [Jesus] must increase, but I [John] must decrease' (3.30).

Because the saying contains the appealing female image of the bride, John 3.29 might seem like an excellent candidate for the dual hermeneutic strategy described by Schüssler Fiorenza. I will argue, however, that the saying in its present form permits the uncovering of androcentrism but provides no foothold for a feminist liberative reading.

The saying is described by scholars variously as a parable (Dodd, Lindars, Barrett, Brown),[3] a parable with allegorical traits (Schnacken-burg),[4] a metaphor,[5] or a comparison.[6] These descriptions all share a methodological implication, namely, that exegesis of the saying should begin by determining the referents of its terms—the bride, the bridegroom, the friend—within the Johannine narrative context. Because feminist biblical criticism includes a focus on the Bible's use of female images,[7] it seems appropriate to begin a feminist study of Jn 3.29 with an examination of the 'bride'.

This is not a straightforward task, however. Whereas it is obvious that John the Baptist, in uttering the saying, identifies Jesus as the bridegroom

3. C.H. Dodd, *Historical Tradition in the Fourth Gospel* (Cambridge: Cambridge University Press, 1965), p. 386; B. Lindars, 'Two Parables in John', *New Testament Studies* 16 (1970), p. 318; C.K. Barrett, *The Gospel according to St. John* (2nd edn; Philadelphia: Westminster, 1978), p. 222; R.E. Brown, *The Gospel according to John I-XII* (AB 29; Garden City, NY: Doubleday, 1966), p. 152.

4. R. Schnackenburg, *The Gospel according to St. John* (vol. 1; New York: Crossroad, 1982), p. 416 [translation of 1965 edition].

5. H.N. Ridderbos, *The Gospel According to St. John: A Theological Commentary* (Grand Rapids, MI: Eerdmans, 1979), p. 147 [translation of 1992 edition].

6. E. Trocmé, 'Jean 3,29 et le thème de l'époux dans la tradition pré-évangélique', *Revue des Sciences Réligieuses* 69 (1995), p. 13.

7. This focus is implicit in a broad range of books and articles from a feminist perspective; it is articulated explicitly, for example, by S. Ringe and C. Newsom in their introduction to the *Women's Bible Commentary* (exp. edn; Louisville, KY: Westminster John Knox, 1998), p. xxi.

and himself as the bridegroom's friend, the identity of the bride is elusive. Barrett argues that the bride is the church, a Christian image that develops from the Old Testament usage of the bride as a figure for Israel in relationship with God.[8] Ridderbos, on the other hand, argues that the church as the bride of Christ does not play a distinct role in this text, and should not be assumed in the metaphor.[9] These divergent conclusions suggest that any attempt to identify the bride, or to investigate whether in fact she can be identified, entails two steps: an examination of the biblical background to the metaphorical use of the 'bride' image, and a study of her role in the saying itself.

In the background of Jn 3.29 is the everyday situation of a wedding, at which the groom and bride are by definition the guests of honour. Scholars suggest that the bridegroom's friend of Jn 3.29 is the שׁוֹשְׁבִין who, according to rabbinic texts, assists in the wedding preparations and stands outside the door of the room in which the marital relationship is consummated.[10]

A significant number of biblical passages use nuptial imagery metaphorically to describe the covenantal relationship between God and Israel. The union between God and Israel is contractual, binding, and exclusive;[11] it has a sensual undercurrent as well as affective elements such as love and devotion. In the background of both the human marriage bond and its metaphorical application is the notion that marriage is a hierarchical relationship in which the male partner is dominant and the female subordinate. The male has authority and power over the female, whose role is to obey and submit to her husband.

All of these aspects are evident in the metaphorical use of nuptial imagery, which appears principally in the prophetic literature. In Isa. 54, Israel is provided with consolation and hope after destruction:

---

8.   Barrett, *Gospel According to St. John*, p. 222; Trocmé, 'Jean 3,29', pp. 15, 18.

9.   Ridderbos, *Gospel*, p. 147.

10.   So Schnackenburg, *Gospel*, p. 416; Brown, *Gospel*, p. 152. *Tosefta Ketuboth* 1.4 refers to the practice in Judah of having two 'friends' sleeping in the place where the groom and bride sleep, whereas in the Galilee this practice was not in place. *Tosefta* (ed. S. Lieberman; New York: Jewish Theological Seminary of America, 1955), p. 58 [in Hebrew]. See also 1 Macc. 9.39, which refers to the bridegroom and his friends, and *Mishnah Sanhedrin* 3.5, which mentions the groomsman as the definition of 'friend'.

11.   In its exclusivity, the covenantal relationship between God and biblical Israel departed from the human marriage paradigm, in which polygamy was permitted.

Sing, O barren one who did not bear; burst into song and shout, you who have not been in labor!…For your Maker is your husband, the LORD of hosts is his name; the Holy One of Israel is your Redeemer, the God of the whole earth he is called. For the LORD has called you like a wife forsaken and grieved in spirit, like the wife of a man's youth when she is cast off, says your God (Isa. 54.1, 5-6).

In Jer. 31.31-32, God promises that:

The days are surely coming…when I will make a new covenant with the house of Israel and the house of Judah. It will not be like the covenant that I made with their ancestors when I took them by the hand to bring them out of the land of Egypt—a covenant that they broke, though I was their husband, says the LORD.

The eschatological use of the wedding metaphor is also found in Isa. 61.10:

I will greatly rejoice in the LORD, my whole being shall exult in my God; for he has clothed me with the garments of salvation, he has covered me with the robe of righteousness, as a bridegroom decks himself with a garland, and as a bride adorns herself with her jewels.

The erotic potential of nuptial terminology is made explicit in Ezek. 16.8-14:

I passed by you again and looked on you; you were at the age for love. I spread the edge of my cloak over you, and covered your nakedness: I pledged myself to you and entered into a covenant with you, says the Lord GOD, and you became mine. Then I bathed you with water and washed off the blood from you, and anointed you with oil. I clothed you with embroidered cloth and with sandals of fine leather; I bound you in fine linen and covered you with rich fabric. I adorned you with ornaments: I put bracelets on your arms, a chain on your neck, a ring on your nose, earrings in your ears, and a beautiful crown upon your head. You were adorned with gold and silver, while your clothing was of fine linen, rich fabric, and embroidered cloth. You had choice flour and honey and oil for food. You grew exceedingly beautiful, fit to be a queen. Your fame spread among the nations on account of your beauty, for it was perfect because of my splendor that I had bestowed on you, says the Lord GOD.

The metaphor is worked out in the greatest detail in Hosea, which conveys the tumultuous relationship between God and Israel as it goes through marriage, infidelity, divorce, and finally, remarriage. God asks his children, Ammi and Ruhamah, to plead with their mother, his wife, that she cease committing adultery, 'or I will strip her naked and expose her as in the day she was born, and make her like a wilderness, and turn her into a parched land, and kill her with thirst' (2.3). After considerable punishment, however, God promises to 'allure her, and bring her into the wilderness, and speak tenderly to her…On that day, says the LORD, you will call me, "My husband", and no longer will you call me, "My Baal"…I will take you for my wife in faithfulness; and you shall know the LORD' (2.14, 16, 20).

In the New Testament, the nuptial imagery of God's covenant with Israel is transferred to the relationship between Christ and the church. For example, in 2 Corinthians, Paul laments:

> I feel a divine jealousy for you, for I promised you in marriage to one husband, to present you as a chaste virgin to Christ. But I am afraid that as the serpent deceived Eve by its cunning, your thoughts will be led astray from a sincere and pure devotion to Christ (11.2-3).

In its rendition of the household codes, Ephesians compares the relationship between human spouses to that between Christ and the church:

> For no one ever hates his own body, but he nourishes and tenderly cares for it, just as Christ does for the church, because we are members of his body. 'For this reason a man will leave his father and mother and be joined to his wife, and the two will become one flesh'. This is a great mystery, and I am applying it to Christ and the church. Each of you, however, should love his wife as himself, and a wife should respect her husband (5.29-33).

Most explicit is Revelation, which declares, ' "Let us rejoice and exult and give him the glory, for the marriage of the Lamb has come, and his bride has made herself ready; to her it has been granted to be clothed with fine linen, bright and pure"–for the fine linen is the righteous deeds of the saints'. (19.7-8). Rev. 21.2 identifies the bride as Jerusalem: 'And I saw the holy city, the new Jerusalem, coming down out of heaven from God, prepared as a bride adorned for her husband'.

The biblical background of the 'bride' image therefore shows a well-entrenched use of 'bride' as a metaphor for Israel (in the Hebrew scriptures), or the early church (in the Christian scriptures) in covenantal relationship with God. This background supports Barrett's interpretation of the 'bride' of Jn 3.29 as the church. Further support can be adduced from the Fourth Gospel as a whole. Since a wedding honours the union of bride and groom, the metaphorical use of wedding imagery also points to the union of God and the covenant people. Although this concept is not made explicit in the Fourth Gospel, it can be read out of the Johannine presentation of Jesus' relationship with his believers. For the Fourth

Evangelist, Jesus is God's Son and agent in the world; it is only through Jesus that humankind can have knowledge of God (1.18).

Among the variety of ways that the Gospel describes the relationship between the community and Jesus, also occur expressions of union, and in particular, the mutual indwelling between Jesus and believers. In the parable of the vine and the vinegrower (Jn 15), Jesus declares to his disciples:

> Abide in me as I abide in you. Just as the branch cannot bear fruit by itself unless it abides in the vine, neither can you unless you abide in me. I am the vine, you are the branches. Those who abide in me and I in them bear much fruit, because apart from me you can do nothing. Whoever does not abide in me is thrown away like a branch and withers; such branches are gathered, thrown into the fire, and burned. If you abide in me, and my words abide in you, ask for whatever you wish, and it will be done for you. My Father is glorified by this, that you bear much fruit and become my disciples. As the Father has loved me, so I have loved you; abide in my love. If you keep my commandments, you will abide in my love, just as I have kept my Father's commandments and abide in his love. I have said these things to you so that my joy may be in you, and that your joy may be complete (15.4-11).

Therefore to argue that the 'bride' of Jn 3.29 is the church is to claim that this image evokes the covenantal relationship between Jesus and the community of believers, which parallels, and, indeed, supersedes, that of God and Israel as described in the Hebrew Bible (cf. 1.17).

Barrett's identification of the bride of Jn 3.29 as the church is therefore plausible both with respect to its biblical usage and also within the Fourth Gospel. But does it make sense within the saying itself and its narrative context? Some scholars argue that such an identification is absent from or irrelevant to Jn 3.29. Lindars argues that while the 'bride' may have had some importance in the original parable, it has no relevance in its present context.[12] Dodd, like Ridderbos, cautions us not to press the details of the parable by asking who the bride is.[13]

This view is substantiated by an analysis of saying itself, in which the female metaphor as such is completely eclipsed. The saying sets up a chain in which the groom is defined in relationship to the bride and the

---

12. According to Lindars, the parable was originally spoken by Jesus and was transferred to John the Baptist by the Fourth Evangelist. Cf. Lindars, 'Two Parables', pp. 324-29; B. Lindars, *The Gospel of John* (Grand Rapids, MI: Eerdmans, 1972), p. 168.

13. Dodd, *Historical Tradition*, p. 386; cf. Ridderbos, *Gospel*, p. 147.

friend is defined in relationship to the groom. But this logical chain does not correspond to the relative importance of the referents. Rather, the syntax of the saying, in which male figures are the subjects of each of its clauses, draws the reader's attention to them, and away from the bride.

The eclipsing of the 'bride' contrasts with her prominent, if problematic, role in the biblical and New Testament passages surveyed above. But this dismissive treatment is remarkably consistent with a number of synoptic passages in which nuptial imagery appears. In Mk 2.18-20, for example, Jesus responds to the question of why his disciples refrain from fasting with a saying that is similar to Jn 3.29 but omits all reference to the bride: 'The wedding guests cannot fast while the bridegroom is with them, can they? As long as they have the bridegroom with them, they cannot fast. The days will come when the bridegroom is taken away from them, and then they will fast on that day'. Mt. 22.1-14 tells of the guests to a wedding banquet; Mt. 25.1-13 uses the term elsewhere translated as 'brides' but here understood as the 'bridesmaids' who await the groom upon his return from the wedding. Lk. 5.34-35 speaks of the fact that the guests should not fast while the groom is among them; here the guests seem to be the community. Lk. 14.7-11 refers only to the host and guest and does not speak of either the bride or the groom. Although these passages may arguably assume the presence of a bride, they do not focus on her identity, nor do they provide a vehicle for considering the relationship between God and church as do the other New Testament usages of nuptial imagery that we have considered above.

Thus far, our attempt at feminist interpretation of Jn 3.29 has taken a well-trodden path in the field of New Testament exegesis, by examining the usage of the 'bride' metaphor broadly within biblical literature, and specifically within this saying in its Johannine context. The results are clear: while the biblical use of the image suggests that its most likely referent is the church, the Johannine use of the image suggests that its specific referent is irrelevant. The image functions solely to identify and to rank the two male figures, namely, the bridegroom and his friend.

If the conventional exegetical strategies we have followed to this point contribute at all to feminist interpretation of this passage, it is only to underscore the androcentrism of the Gospel and of the metaphorical use of the 'bride' image within biblical literature. We can proceed further in our feminist exegesis of this passage only if we step outside the bounds of conventional exegetical method and attempt a more creative and playful approach to the text. That such an approach is appropriate for feminist biblical interpretation is articulated by Schüssler Fiorenza, who describes 'a feminist hermeneutics of creative actualization' that may entail rewriting biblical stories and a variety of other activities.[14]

We can propose two moves under this rubric, that parallel the procedure we have just completed. The first move focuses on the 'bride' image itself. As we have seen, the biblical background to this image presupposes an understanding of marriage as hierarchical: at her wedding, the bride enters an unequal relationship in which she is the subordinate partner. Let us now set aside the biblical use of the nuptial metaphor and, instead, read the 'bride' image in light of a contemporary view of marriage as an intimate relationship that is egalitarian rather than hierarchical. Let us say that at her wedding, the bride enters not into a submissive role but rather into a partnership of equals from which patriarchal authority and the expectations of obedience are absent. Biblical justification for such a view of marriage, if required, may be found in Gen. 1.27, in which male and female are created simultaneously, in the divine image, and are addressed together by God without differentiation. The second move builds on this egalitarian understanding of the 'bride' and 'groom' and suggests that the first clause of Jn 3.29 may be supplemented by a further statement that simply transposes its elements: If he who has the bride is the bridegroom, then she who has the bridegroom is the bride. From a feminist perspective, the question now becomes: what is the referent of 'bride' in this expanded form of the saying?

Our starting point is the sense of the verb 'have' (ἔχω) in this revised version of 3.29. The canonical form of 3.29 ascribes a narrow proprietary meaning to this verb that reinforces the understanding of the nuptial relationship as hierarchical. But adding the corollary broadens the meaning by implying mutuality: the bride and groom 'have' each other, that is, they have entered into an intimate union with one another. As we have already discussed, the Fourth Gospel supports the view of a union or intimate relationship between Jesus and the community. Although the relationship between Jesus and his followers is inherently hierarchical, like that of a shepherd and his sheep (Jn 10), it also has elements of mutuality. These emerge most clearly in the foot-washing scene (Jn 13), in which Jesus reverses the usual hierarchical relationship between master and servant by insisting that he wash his disciples' feet. As Jesus tells Peter,

14. E. Schüssler Fiorenza, *Bread Not Stone: The Challenge of Feminist Biblical Interpretation* (Boston: Beacon, 1984), p. 21.

who is discomfited by Jesus' behaviour, 'Unless I wash you, you have no share with me' (13.8).

But the 'bride' is not simply a collective image. Its very singularity entices us to look at the individual female characters in her light. Every female character in the Gospel of John, without exception, can be described as 'having' Jesus, that is, as being positively and intimately connected to him. The mother of Jesus has the knowledge of and confidence in her son's powers to relieve the wine shortage at the Cana wedding (2.3, 5), and she receives his consideration even as he is dying upon the cross (19.27). The Samaritan woman encounters Jesus privately at the well, receives his request for water to drink, and hears him acknowledge his christological identity (4.7, 26). Mary and Martha have Jesus' love (11.5) and the confidence to call upon him in times of need (11.3). Mary Magdalene has the privilege of being the first to see him in risen form (20.1-18).[15]

Not only do these women 'have' Jesus but they also become partners in his work. Jesus' mother sets the stage for the first of Jesus' signs at Cana by informing him of the problem and prompting the servants to obey him (2.3, 5). The Samaritan woman preaches to her fellow Samaritans and encourages them to come to Jesus (4.39). Mary and Martha provide the setting and perhaps also the encouragement for others to come to faith (11.45).[16] Mary Magdalene is commissioned by Jesus to be his messenger and in this role provides the first post-resurrection communication to the disciples (20.17-18).

But just as male imagery can be read too inclusively (for example, the 'brothers' of Jn 20.17 are sometimes referred to as 'brothers and sisters'[17]), so too can we use this female image as a lens through which to

15. On the erotic undertones in the relationship between Jesus and Mary Magdalene, see A. Reinhartz, 'To Love the Lord: An Intertextual Reading of John 20', in *The Labour of Reading: Essays in Honour of Robert C. Culley* (ed. F.Flack, R. Boer, C. Kelm, E. Runions; Semeia Studies; Atlanta: Scholars Press, 1999), pp. 46-69.

16. For a discussion of the leadership roles of Mary and Martha, see A. Reinhartz, 'From Narrative to History: The Resurrection of Mary and Martha', in *'Women Like This': New Perspectives on Jewish Women in the Greco-Roman World* (Atlanta: Scholars Press, 1991), pp. 161-84; E. Schüssler Fiorenza, *But She Said: Feminist Practices of Biblical Interpretation* (Boston: Beacon, 1992), pp. 51-76.

17. S.M. Schneiders, 'John 20.11-18: The Encounter of the Easter Jesus with Mary Magdalene—A Transformative Feminist Reading', in *What is John? Readers and Readings of the Fourth Gospel* (ed. F.F. Segovia; Atlanta: Scholars Press, 1996), pp. 161, 166.

examine a number of male characters. Certainly there are male figures in the Gospel who are either ambivalent about Jesus, such as Nicodemus (3.1-21; 7.51; 19.39), or act in opposition to him, such as Judas (6.70-71; 13.26; 18.3). The disciples, on the other hand, 'have' Jesus in the sense that they have some level of faith in him and build their lives around him. They not only follow him but also assist in the 'harvest' that is to come (4.34-38) and receive the holy spirit along with the power to remit or retain sins (20.22-23). Lazarus, like his sisters, has Jesus' love (11.3) and aids, albeit indirectly, in drawing believers to Jesus (12.9-10). The Beloved Disciple rests in Jesus' bosom at his final dinner (13.23); his privileged position is recognized by the other disciples (13.24). As the implied author of the Gospel (19.35, 20.24), he is instrumental in recording the signs and words of Jesus so that others may believe that Jesus is the Messiah and Son of God (20.31).

Most intriguing in this regard is John the Baptist, particularly as portrayed in Jn 3.26-30. In identifying himself as the friend of the bridegroom, the Baptist indicates that he acts towards Jesus as a groom's friend does towards the groom; specifically, he hears the bridegroom's voice, and rejoices when he does so. The exact meaning of 'hearing the groom's voice' is unclear. Some commentators think of the best man as waiting with the bride at her home and straining to hear the noise of the groom's procession; others suggest that what the friend hears is the conversation of the groom with the bride,[18] or the triumphal shout by which the bridegroom announces to his friends outside that he has been united to a virginal bride.[19]

Clarification of the Baptist's role can be gained by looking at two phrases, 'hearing him' (ἀκούων αὐτοῦ) and 'rejoice at his voice' (χαρᾷ χαίρει διὰ τὴν φωνήν). Hearing Jesus or his voice is a typically Johannine way of describing those who believe Jesus to be Messiah and Son of God. Hearing Jesus speak attracts Jesus' first disciples to him (1.3-51). In Jn 5.25 Jesus declares that 'the dead will hear the voice of the Son of God and those who hear will live'. Indeed, Jesus continues, the hour is coming when all who are in their graves will hear his voice (5.28). This concept is given graphic illustration within the Gospel narrative, when the dead man Lazarus, lying in his tomb, hears Jesus' voice calling his name and comes out (11.43-4). In his role as shepherd, Jesus calls his own sheep

18. Brown, *Gospel*, p. 152.
19. Schnackenburg, *Gospel*, p. 416.

by name; they follow him because they know his voice. The friend who hears the bridegroom is thus defined as his disciple.

The verb 'to rejoice' (χαίρω) occurs in eight other verses. In some cases it describes those who work together for the success of this divine mission, as in 4.36, in which the sower and the reaper of the divine harvest are described as rejoicing together. In 8.56 the reference is to Abraham, who is said to rejoice 'that he would see my day'. Jesus rejoices that he was not there when Lazarus died, so that you may believe (11.15); the world rejoices at Jesus' death (16.20). But primarily it defines the disciples' relationship with Jesus. This nuance, implicit in 4.36, is made explicit in 14.28, in which Jesus declares to the disciples, 'If you loved me you would rejoice that I am going to the Father'. In 16.22, he promises them, 'I will see you again and your hearts will rejoice'. The promise comes to fruition in 20.20, according to which the disciples rejoiced when they saw the Lord. Hence this phrase too defines John the Baptist as a disciple.

John the Baptist is therefore both forerunner and disciple. Like Mary, Martha, and Lazarus, he 'has' the bridegroom in close relationship with him. Like them, John contributes to the success of his mission, by bringing his own disciples to Jesus (1.35-37), disarming the discontent of his own followers (3.26-30), and, indeed, recognizing that 'he must decrease' (3.30). His joy is fulfilled with coming of the bridegroom, like the joy of the disciples when Jesus comes to them in the closed room (20.20).

To conclude: Reading Jn 3.29 in its canonical form underscores the androcentrism of the text; revising this saying by adding its mirror image that features the bride provides some opening for a feminist liberative reading by ascribing mutuality to the relationship between 'bride' (or disciple) and 'groom' (Jesus). This ascription allows us to view the individuals and the community as a whole as essential partners in Jesus' mission as understood in this Gospel. It also draws our attention in particular to the female figures as major players in this mission. This perspective may mitigate to some extent the androcentrism of the text in its canonical form.

But the focus on mutuality does not, in the end, liberate us entirely from the hierarchical elements in the relationship between Jesus and the women and men with whom he is united in partnership. In the final analysis, Jesus is the leader; they are the followers. He sets the agenda to which they must contribute if they are to be in intimate relationship with him. This situation is most evident in the figure of John the Baptist, who, on any reading of this passage, is subordinate to Jesus even as he contributes to his success, and not only accepts but also rejoices in this role. The question that this study leaves for feminist theologians is this: can there be true mutuality in the covenantal union between the individual or community and God, or must the human partners in that relationship come to accept, as the Baptist does, their subordinate position in the divine-human relationship?

IV

PARABLES OF WISDOM/SOPHIA

JESUS/HOLY MOTHER WISDOM (MT. 23.37-39)

Elaine Guillemin

Jerusalem, Jerusalem, the city that kills the prophets and stones those who are sent to it!

How often have I desired to gather your children as a hen gathers her brood under her wings, and you were not willing! See, your house is left to you, desolate.

For I tell you, you will not see me again until you say,
'Blessed is the one who comes in the name of the Lord'.[1]

Jesus' lament over Jerusalem, considered as a 'wisdom parable', raises several theological/methodological issues. Is it a parable of wisdom because Jesus speaks as Wisdom? Is Jesus identified with Wisdom? Does Jesus replace Wisdom? Questions such as these are related to the issue of 'Matthew's wisdom christology'.[2] In the past few years, however, reader–response studies have offered new insights into the complex question of wisdom in Matthew.[3] Taking my cue from reader-response approaches and from studies of gender in Matthew, I propose a feminist/literary reading of female imagery in the gospel.[4] The images include personified

---

1. All translations are taken from the NRSV.

2. For a review of the positions see W.D. Davies and D.C. Allison Jr, *A Critical and Exegetical Commentary on the Gospel According to St. Matthew, Vol. 2: Matthew XIX-XXVII* (ed. J. Emerton, C. Cranfield and G. Stanton; Edinburgh: T. & T. Clark, 1991), p. 295.

3. Reader-response criticism is an approach to literature which focuses on the reader and the reading process. See J.P. Tompkins (ed.), *Reader Response Criticism*. (Baltimore: Johns Hopkins University Press, 1980). For a reader-response approach to wisdom in Matthew, see especially, R. Pregeant, 'The Wisdom Passages in Matthew's Story', *SBL 1990 Seminar Papers* (Atlanta: Scholars Press, 1990), pp. 469-93.

4. This paper owes much to the seminal article of J.C. Anderson, 'Matthew: Gender and Reading', *Semeia* 28 (1983), pp. 3-27. Other studies I found useful include A.-J. Levine, *The Social and Ethnic Dimensions of Matthean Salvation History*

Jerusalem (23.37-39; 2.3), Rachel (2.18) and Jesus' foremothers (1.3, 5, 6, 16), Sophia (11.19) and the Queen of the South (12.42), and the mother hen (23.37).[5] All are female, some are maternal, and some are images of wisdom. These striking images both intrigue and trouble a feminist reader alert to the tension between the female imagery and its androcentric contexts and/or use. Many previous critical studies either ignore the female gender of Matthean wisdom images, fail to explore the significance of the female images qua female, or ignore the *effects* of the imagery on the reader. Drawn into the force field of these female/wisdom images, I endeavor first to recover their significance as female, and then to 'imagine' feminist readers' responses to the imagery.[6] This study is, in effect, a kind of salvage operation, an attempt to raise to the surface of our awareness a few of the many 'submerged female images' mentioned by the editor of this volume in her introduction.

W. Iser's theory of reading provides a useful analytical framework.[7] Iser is concerned primarily with the individual text and how readers relate to it. Iser makes clear that in order to understand the effects caused and the responses elicited by literary works, one must allow for the presence of a reader. He proposes the concept of the 'implied reader', a term which has its roots in the structure of the text, and is in no way to be identified with a real reader. Iser's implied reader refers to the active nature of the reading process which varies historically from one age to another. It designates a network of response-inviting structures which impel an actual reader to

(Studies in the Bible and Early Christianity, 14 (Lampeter: Edwin Mellen Press, 1988); E. Wainwright, *Towards a Feminist Critical Reading of the Gospel According to Matthew* (Berlin, NY: Walter de Gruyter, 1991).

5.　Jerusalem is a female personified being only in 2.3; 21.5; 23.37-39, although it is possible that it is she who is being addressed in 23.34-36. Only in 2.3b is Jerusalem grammatically a feminine singular and not a neuter plural. Rachel and the mothers are historical women whose stories are imported into the gospel via scriptural quotation. Sophia and the Queen of the South are wisdom figures. The mother hen has some connection to wisdom in the anterior tradition.

6.　J. Culler, *On Deconstruction: Theory and Criticism after Structuralism* (Ithaca: Cornell University Press, 1982), p. 67: 'To read and interpret literary work is precisely to imagine what a "reader" would feel and understand'.

7.　W. Iser, *The Act of Reading* (Baltimore: Johns Hopkins University Press, 1978); Iser, *The Implied Reader* (Baltimore: Johns Hopkins University Press, 1974). Iser's theory is useful because it makes it possible to analyze the experiences of real readers in relation to the conditions that have governed them, and to compare that response with those of others in an intersubjective dialogue.

grasp the text. Real readers respond to the role of the implied reader as they read. Part of this role is internal to the text and part external. The implied reader is both 'textual structure' and 'structured act'.[8]

It must be kept in mind that Iser's concept of the 'implied reader' focuses on the process or act of reading. He is not so much concerned with an actual, physical reader sitting in an armchair with a book in her/his hands, as with what 'happens' when a reader reads. Iser is interested in the phenomenon of the reading process itself. He wants to understand and explain how a reader creates meaning(s) as s/he interacts with the text. One way to describe Iser's implied reader as 'textual structure' is as the role (found within the text) which an actual reader must play when s/he begins to read. The role emerges from what any reader of a narrative encounters—that is, the (usually four) inter-related textual elements of plot, characters, narrator, and position marked out for the fictitious reader.[9] Iser's concept of the reader as 'textual structure', therefore, refers not to an actual reader, but rather to a virtual role offered to any reader. Iser's implied reader as 'textual structure designates the possibilities for meaning offered by a text.

The external part of the role of the implied reader is what Iser calls the implied reader as 'structured act'. An actual reader engages in the act of reading, that is, s/he actualizes the virtual role of the implied reader. As s/he occupies the shifting vantage points offered by the interaction between plot and characters, for example, s/he 'imagines' how these perspectives converge and meet, and thus s/he produces a meaning.[10] The meaning of the text is therefore, not a given, but is constucted by a reader. It should be noted that although actual readers must respond to the role of implied reader, different readers may respond differently (conceivably even by refusing to play the role). The result is what we have all observed; different readers may produce different meaning(s) from the same text. All, however, have responded to the role by fitting the various perspectives

---

8.   Iser's 'bi-functional' concept of the implied reader as an heuristic device allows him to move from text to reader in a sophisticated endeavour to grasp process. The composition and/or contribution of either half of the partnership is not always clear.

9.   Iser, *The Act of Reading*, p. 96, notes that the narrative texts need not always deploy the full range of these different orientations. Since in the Matthean text, the fictitious reader is addressed in 24.15, 27.8 and 28.15, passages not directly connected to the female images, I do not include the fictitious reader as one of the perspectives.

10.   Experiencing a text involves imagining the meaning, which is not given, but must be produced.

of plot, characters, narrator, etc., into a gradually evolving pattern in order to constuct a particular meaning.

For purposes of analysis, each of the two aspects of Iser's implied reader will be treated separately. In the first part of this paper, the female/wisdom imagery will be considered in terms of the role of the implied reader as textual structure. Where in the plotted story do the images appear?[11] Do they further the action? With which story characters are they associated?[12] From what point of view does the narrator present the imagery?[13] What view of the images is the implied reader encouraged to adopt? In a second step, I consider the implied reader as structured act, i.e., a real reader reading. In this case, one asks how a feminist reader reads an androcentric biblical text.[14] What emotional and/or intellectual effects might the female images have on a feminist reader?[15] How might she understand the (in)significance of the female imagery as it is presented? Although she is obliged to respond to the 'textual directions' given, she is also free to resist, to disobey these directions.[16] What alternative meanings might a 'resisting' feminist reader construct? Is her spiritual life nourished by the images? And how does her lived experience challenge or enrich her reading?

11. Matthew's gospel is considered to be a story. U. Luz, *Matthew 1-7: A Commentary* (trans. W.C. Linss; Minneapolis: Augsburg Fortress, 1989), p. 35; J.D. Kingsbury, *Matthew as Story* (Philadelphia: Fortress Press, 1986).

12. When I deal with the perspective of the characters, I want to clarify how the female imagery is linked to certain characters. Such use is justified because it helps me to see the imagery in relation to the various story characters. This is a deviation from Iser's use of characters' conversations with each other to reveal their perspectives.

13. Anderson, 'Matthew: Gender and Reading', p. 23 n. 55, 'The narrator [of Matthew] is undramatized, reliable, omniscient, and intrusive. He or she, in effect, serves as the implied author's voice. For all practical purposes their ideological viewpoints are identical'.

14. Feminist critiques of Iser and other reader-response approaches challenge their abstract theory which posits privileged readers, and call for the inclusion of gender and politics in interpretational theory. See P. Schweickart, 'Reading Ourselves: Towards a Feminist Theory of Reading', in E. Showalter (ed.), *The New Feminist Criticism: Essays on Women, Literature and Theory* (New York: Pantheon Books, 1985), pp. 17-44.

15. See for example, Anderson, 'Gender and Reading', p. 23: 'If the actual reader uncritically adopts the patriarchal worldview represented by the narrator and Jesus, she assumes a worldview which abridges the full humanity of female and male. The reading experience is destructive'.

16. Anderson, 'Gender and Reading', p. 8, 'Actual readers are free to accept or reject this [the narrator's] guidance but must respond to it as they read'.

Matthew's Androcentric Story

Before exploring the role of the female images in relation to the four perspectives outlined above, we should consider briefly the androcentric nature of Matthew's story, especially the sections in which the female imagery appears.[17] The story opens with the narrator's initial commentary in the form of a patrilineal genealogy (the women named are exceptions) which substantiates Jesus' patrilineal claim to the titles given to him in the superscription and locates him in salvation history viewed essentially as a male enterprise.[18] In the opening chapters, the plot is so structured that Joseph, not Mary, propels the action. Male characters predominate as King Herod and the Jewish authorities plot against the child, while Joseph cares for him, and the Magi worship him. Mary, although pivotal to the story, is a totally passive character. Personified Jerusalem is so closely associated with the male religious leaders as to be virtually identified with them. Rachel, a significant female personage, is imported from scripture only to point to the importance of a tragedy in the life of the main character, Jesus. Later in the gospel, the adult Jesus is associated exclusively with male characters in the story of his baptism and temptation, and is named beloved Son of a G*d imaged as Father. Predominantly male characters carry the action in the story of Jesus' public ministry.[19] Jesus teaches in parables, in which males invariably are the key figures (one exception is 13.33; cf. 25.1-13). The female images of Sophia and the Queen of the South (11.19; 12.42) emphasize the wisdom of the main character, the male Jesus, while the simile of the mother-hen (23.37) focuses attention on

17. I am indebted in large part to Anderson, 'Gender and Reading', and to A.-J. Levine, 'Matthew', in C.A. Newsom and S.H. Ringe (eds.), *The Women's Bible Commentary* (London: Westminster/John Knox Press, 1992), pp. 252-62, for the following.

18. A certain knowledge of the Hebrew Scriptures and therefore of the female images and of the foremothers' stories in the gospel, must be assumed on the part of Matthew's implied reader as 'textual structure'. It is also the case that any actual reader, ancient or modern, might play the role of the implied reader more or less competently, to the degree that they are/are not familiar with these scriptures.

19. Jesus chooses only male disciples. In Jesus' teachings as well as in narratorial comments, patriarchal marriage and inheritance customs are assumed (1.18-25; 5.31-32; 19.1-12; 21.33-43; 22.22-33, etc.). Women are never directly mentioned as part of Jesus' audience, as for example, in the Sermon on the Mount, which addresses its demands exclusively to men (5.28, 32). Neither does the narrator include women in the missionary focus of Jesus' preaching (14.21; 15.38).

Jesus' sentiments. Throughout the stories of Jesus' ministry, when women characters are mentioned they are usually not portrayed as equal in status to men ((9.18-19; 9.20-22), and inevitably appear in isolated and self-contained episodes. In fact, women characters function most often simply as foils for the disciples (26.6-13). In sum, Matthew's story contains and constrains women characters and images of women within the boundaries of a model that assumes male gender as the norm and ensures a sub-ordinate and auxiliary position even for extraordinary women and/or striking female imagery.

Female/Wisdom Imagery and 'the reader in the text'.

It will be useful at this point to remark briefly on the powerful rhetorical strategies used to introduce the female imagery into the story. A close reading reveals that all the female/wisdom images appear in either the narrator's commentary or in Jesus' words, in scriptural quotations or in allusions to scripture.[20] The images are inserted into the plot at key moments of conflict between Jesus and the Jewish leadership.[21] The strategic positioning of the images is a deliberate attempt by the narrator either to inform the reader of what is to come, or to educate her/him about aspects of Jesus' origins, identity and/or ministry. Jesus' foremothers (1.3, 5, 6, 16), for example, appear in the narrator's initial commentary in a genealogy.[22] Significantly, the foremothers are on the scene even before the story proper has begun.[23] Rachel (2.18) comes into the story via a direct quotation from the scriptures.[24] Jerusalem is mentioned both by the

---

20. Scripture quotations function as the most prominent means by which the Matthean narrator illumines for the reader significant aspects of Jesus' life and gives her/him interpretive directions for reading the gospel. These references to scripture serve to specify the real world which the narrative takes as its reference, i.e., the history of Israel as G*d's chosen people.

21. The images do not forward the action of the plot. Rather they illumine the significance of the events/characters with which they are associated.

22. Initial commentary is a powerful rhetorical strategy because it gives information about the attitudes, characters and narrative world projected for the reader, all of which influence the reader until new information comes along. See D.B. Howell, *Matthew's Inclusive Story. A Study in the Rhetoric of the First Gospel* (JSNTSup 42; Sheffield: Sheffield Academic Press, 1990).

23. The opening genealogy is expository material which provides necessary information concerning characters and events existing before the action begins. Its emphasis is strongly explanatory.

24. In this and in other quotations, we have the narrator's direct commentary, the

narrator and in Jesus' direct speech.[25] Sophia and the Queen of the South likewise appear in Jesus' discourse.[26] We now turn to each image viewed from the perspectives of narrator, plot and characters, that is, to the role of the implied reader as 'textual structure'.[27]

Personified Jerusalem (2.3, 4; 23.37-39)

The implied reader's understanding of personified Jerusalem is shaped by the perspectives of narrator, plot and characters, which, when taken together, yield a portrait of the personified city as Jesus' implacable opponent.[28] The narrator introduces the personified city as 'troubled', along with King Herod, at the Magis' news of Jesus' birth (2.3, 4).[29] The narrator's initial account of the conflict between Jesus and Jerusalem, Herod and the Jewish leaders functions proleptically, foreshadowing the hostility of the Pharisees towards Jesus which erupts publicly in ch. 9 and hardens into irreconcilable opposition in ch. 12. In ch. 21, Jesus' entrance and acclamation demand a response from Jerusalem, the 'Daughter of

most powerful vehicle, short of self-mention, that a narrator can employ to communicate his/her point of view to the reader and shape the reader's response. Howell, *Matthew's Inclusive Story*, p. 180, notes that commentary also provides clues to the author's view of reality: 'The presence of commentary...presupposes the existence of an agreed system of general cultural codes held by people outside the text'.

25. The use of direct speech increases immediacy between narrator and reader: '[When] an emphasis is placed on Jesus' speech, which is also a medium for the implied author's value system, Jesus addresses the implied reader together with the characters' (Howell, *Matthew's Inclusive Story*, p. 203). The device of direct address draws the reader into the narrative so that s/he feels s/he hears the words spoken as if spoken directly to her/him.

26. Each of these two figures appears at different points in the Matthean story. They are presented together because they are female, because both of them are associated with the concept of wisdom, and because both are introduced to speak of Jesus' righteous position in the face of opposition.

27. Because the images are related, there is some overlap in their treatment.

28. Jerusalem is mentioned in 2.1, 3; 3.5; 4.5, 25; 5.35; 15.1; 16.21; 20.17, 18; 21.1, 10; 23.37; 27.53. Although at times the inhabitants of the city may be favorable to Jesus, the personification establishes a distinction between the citizens and the city. Other personified cities hostile to Jesus include those in ch. 11, Chorazin, Bethsaida, Capernaum, and Tyre and Sidon. They are all classified as evil and unrepentant.

29. Davies and Allison, *Critical and Exegetical Commentary*, Vol. 1, p. 238, speak of 'the guilt of the capital, which is here personified. Broadly speaking, 'she did not repent' (11.20).

Zion', but the response is questioning rather than rejoicing.[30] In ch. 23, at the climactic point of the conflict between Jesus and Jerusalem, Jesus laments over her perversity, states the consequences she must endure for her hostility towards him, and declares that she shall not see him again until and unless she acknowledges 'the one who comes in the name of the Lord'.[31] The convergent negative points of view of both the narrator and the story character of Jesus toward 'murderous' Jerusalem emphasize to the reader the culpability of the personified city.[32] The image of Jerusalem poetically expresses and exposes to the reader the range and depth of murderous Jerusalem's malevolence toward Jesus throughout his ministry. Jesus ultimately declares (23.38) judgment on her house, deserted and desolate, in words which anticipate the tribulations of the eschatological discourse in ch. 24.[33]

Rachel (Mt. 2.18. [Jer. 31.15]) and the Foremothers (Mt. 1. 3, 5, 6, 16)

> A voice was heard in Ramah,
>   wailing and loud mourning,
>   Rachel crying for her children;
> and she would not be consoled, because they are no more.

An account of the genealogy of Jesus the Messiah, the son of David, the son of Abraham...and Judah the father of Perez and Zerah by Tamar...and Salmon the father of Boaz by Rahab, and Boaz the father of Obed by Ruth...And David was the father of Solomon by the wife of Uriah...

---

30. Davies and Allison, *Critical and Exegetical Commentary*, Vol. 3, p. 118, 'Was the beginning of Zech 9.9 ['Rejoice greatly, daughter of Zion] deemed inappropriate in view of Jerusalem's hostility and/or the destruction of Jerusalem in AD 70?'

31. Davies and Allison, *Critical and Exegetical Commentary*, Vol. 3, p. 320 n. 55, remark on the (Semitic?) solecism. They note the 'remarkable transitions in 23.37-39 from the address in the second person singular to the third singular, thence back to the second singular and finally to the second plural'. This grammatical feature suggests that Jesus is addressing in the person of the city, other individuals, conceivably the hostile Jewish leaders. But see 23.36, with its enlargement of prophetic condemnation beyond the scribes and Pharisees to 'this generation'.

32. The convergent perspectives of the narrator (2.3; 21.5) and Jesus (23.37-39) offer a double witness to personified Jerusalem's negative attitude toward Jesus.

33. Davies and Allison, *Critical and Exegetical Commentary*, Vol. 3, p. 322: 'Scholars have debated whether "your house" refers to the temple, to Jerusalem, or to the "house of Israel"...quite often...there are indiscriminate transitions from temple to city or vice versa, so that one may often speak of their identification'.

The narrator introduces Rachel, one of the most dramatic and mysterious female figures in Matthew's story, in an equally intriguing scriptural quotation.[34] The quote follows immediately the story of Herod's murder of the children of Bethlehem, but the application to the story is strained. There does not seem to be an exact correspondence between the story and the quote. How is Rachel the 'mother' of the murdered children? In what sense are the slaughtered babes Rachel's 'children'? What is the meaning of Rachel's tears? Will she weep forever? [35]

The gospel image of Rachel weeping for 'her' children functions as a metaphor, although the thing/idea/action to which/whom Rachel refers in the gospel is not made explicit.[36] By employing the metaphoric figure of Rachel, the narrator provides the conditions which invite and enable a reader to 'see' imaginatively more than what might otherwise be seen in a more prosaic passage. That more points to Rachel as a symbolic figure who suggests a direction, or a broad area of reference beyond herself. The reader is thereby encouraged to see in the poetic image of the weeping Rachel something new, something other than that presented.[37] A reader might intuitively identify Rachel as a representative mother, a 'stand-in' for the mothers of Bethlehem, for whose children she (by poetic license) grieves, but this is but one direction in which the image could be taken.

The significance of Jesus' foremothers and Mary (1.3, 5, 6, 16, 18-24; 2.11, 13, 14, 20, 21), who surround the image of Rachel in Matthew's

34. Most interpreters have found the text problematic. Generally it is assumed that the quotation refers to something more than can be derived from the words themselves, but there is no agreement on what that 'something more' might be. What is virtually certain, however, is that the quotation refers to more than what the text indicates on the surface.

35. Rachel in Jer. 31 is depicted as a transhistorical mother of Israel weeping over 'her' children, represented by the northern tribes who have been carried off into Exile. The passage is found in the 'Book of Consolation' (30-31) depicting a time when YHWH's love for his people would bring them back from afar and set them up in their own land, never again to be disturbed. Rachel personifies the afflictions of the northern kingdom. Within the context of consolation, YHWH responds to Rachel's grief with assurances of reward for her 'work' and hope for her future. Her children shall come back to their own country.

36. M.H. Abrams, *A Glossary of Terms* (3rd edn; New York: Holt, Rinehart and Winston, 1971), p. 61, 'in an implicit metaphor the tenor (the subject to which the metaphoric word is applied) is not stated, but is implied by the verbal context'.

37. C. Baldick, *The Concise Oxford Dictionary of Literary Terms* (Oxford/New York: Oxford University Press, 1990), p. 134: 'The use of metaphor to create new combinations of ideas is a major feature of poetry'.

gospel, is not spelled out.[38] Commentators have noted that the women mentioned in the genealogy do more than distinguish between clans or tribes, or between the children of concubines and those of wives.[39] They, like all those mentioned in the genealogy, give specific content to claims made about Jesus Christ, the son of David, the son of Abraham. The precise nature of that content (except for Mary) is never explained.[40] Their stories reveal that the situations of the five women in one way or another pose a threat to a male-centered society, and necessitate their being brought back under control.[41] This state of affairs is presented by the Matthean narrator as within the overarching plan of G*d (and an overall patriarchal framework).

In sum, the narrator gives ambiguous 'reading instructions' to the implied reader regarding the significance of Rachel and the mothers. While Rachel is imported from scripture in order to signal the meaning of the tragedy of Bethlehem, as a metaphorical figure she points to meanings beyond herself and even beyond the boundaries of Matthew's story. The mothers are important exceptions in a predominantly male-centered genealogy, and Mary, although passive, is at the same time a pivotal story character. A reader familiar with the mothers' stories and with the gospel as a whole is presented with a number of story strands with which to weave possible meaning(s). The many different conclusions offered in the history of interpretation of these verses is evidence of the way the role of the implied reader has been played out.[42]

38. The first, Tamar, is portrayed in Gen. 38 as an eminently righteous widow who, wronged by her kinsman, takes strong measures to bear children and ensure her survival. The second, Rahab, is described in Josh. 2 and 6 as a Canaanite prostitute who puts her faith in Israel's G*d, aids the Israelites' invasion of her land, and adopts the religion of Israel. Ruth is a Moabite woman left childless and alone except for her mother-in-law, Naomi, with whom she leaves her homeland to return to Israel, where she marries Boaz and gives birth to Obed. The fourth woman, wife of Uriah (2 Sam. 11-112; 1 Kgs 1-2) is taken in adultery by David who then kills her husband and takes her into his harem. She later gives birth to Solomon.

39. Levine, *Social and Ethnic Dimensions*, p. 59.

40. 1.16 is further developed by 1.18-25.

41. Wainwright, *Towards a Feminist Critical Reading*, p. 66.

42. Reasons given for Matthew's inclusion of the women include the following: they were sinners, foreigners, involved in 'irregular' marital unions, showed initiative in furthering G*d's plan, were models of faith, those who overcome obstacles created by men in authority, socioeconomically and cultically powerless, figures who critique patriarchy, etc., etc.

Sophia and the Queen of the South (11.19; 12.42)

The narrator introduces Sophia, or Wisdom personified, in Jesus' reply to the hostility of 'this generation' towards John and himself (11.19).[43] As has often been noted, the mention of Wisdom's 'deeds' (11.19) forms an *inclusio* with the 'deeds of the Christ' (11.2), which seems to indicate Matthew's equation of Jesus with Wisdom.[44] The works of Jesus are identical with the works of Wisdom. The narrator encourages the implied reader to understand that Jesus is vindicated by his, that is, Wisdom's works, referred to in vv. 2-6: 'the blind receive their sight, the lame walk, the lepers are cleansed, the deaf hear, the dead are raised, and the poor have the good news preached to them'. In terms of plot, 11.1-19 marks a turning point. Up until this point, the reader has learned of the words and works of Jesus, manifested in his public ministry. Now the issue becomes the *response* to Jesus, i.e., the answer to the question posed at the beginning of the chapter. Does the reader accept Jesus as the Coming One, i.e., the Messiah, or will s/he look for another? The response of story characters in this section, i.e., 'this generation' and the unrepentant cities, was negative, since they did not recognize his 'mighty works' (11.20-24).

In ch. 12, Jesus responds to the criticism of the Pharisees by justifying his disciples' conduct, challenges the Pharisees' understanding and interpretation of scripture and of Sabbath law, and confronts their attacks on his integrity. He ultimately refuses their demand for a sign and refers to the Queen of the South's coming judgment and condemnation of 'this generation' (12.42).[45] She, a royal figure, judges Jesus to be greater than Solomon. 'This generation' stands over against her, for it cannot bear testimony to Jesus as Messiah, even though it has a certain knowledge of the scriptures and of the law. Like her, it also tested a king, but, unlike her, could not see the truth of his identity. The personified cities, unrepentant and perverse, shall be cast down on the day of judgment by the Queen of

---

43. Sophia is a transliteration of the Greek word for wisdom, and a proper name for Wisdom as the female personification of G*d's self-manifestation in creation and in the history of Israel. Because Sophia as a proper name immediately suggests a person rather than a concept, I use this name interchangeably with Lady Wisdom or simply Wisdom.

44. Davies and Allison, *Critical and Exegetical Commentary*, Vol. 3, p. 264.

45. The Queen of the South appears in 1 Kgs 10 and 2 Chron. 9. She is a foreign queen with fabulous wealth who comes to test Solomon with hard questions. Solomon bests her by answering her riddles, and then sends her on her way.

the South who shall rise up to condemn them.[46] Sophia and the Queen of the South provoke the reader to reflect on the consequences of accepting or rejecting Jesus, whose works they justify and whose identity they recognize.[47]

The Mother Hen (23.37)

The reader meets in the mother hen image Jesus' first and only reference to himself as a maternal figure. The image emphasizes Jesus as mother, explains his attitude toward Jerusalem's 'children', and enlarges the image of Jerusalem to include the idea of motherhood. At the breaking point of the bitter conflict between Jesus and the Jewish authorities, Jesus laments Jerusalem's fate. The context is sheer poetry. Jesus' poignant lament opens with an apostrophe to personified Jerusalem.[48] He declares her to be a killer of prophets and hostile to those who are sent to her. He tells Jerusalem both of his longing to gather her children as a mother hen gathers her chicks under her wings, and of his chagrin that Jerusalem will not allow it. In v. 38, Jesus declares judgment upon Jerusalem, in dramatic contrast to his subsequent words of promise and hope in v. 39. A note of pathos emerges in his declaration that, as a consequence of her hostility, Jerusalem shall be left desolate, her house empty, her children gone. The passage ends with Jesus' declaration that she will not encounter him again until that day when she greets him with a blessing rather than with rejection.[49]

Verse 37, with its maternal imagery, stands as a middle term in the pericope (23.37-39), mitigating the severity of Jesus' previous condemnation of the city as killer of prophets, etc., and softening his subsequent words of judgment and warning. Jesus' use of the mother hen image also

---

46. D. Garland, *Reading Matthew: A Literary and Theological Commentary on the First Gospel* (New York: Crossroad, 1993), pp. 129-30, notes that the response of the Galilean towns up to this point has not been portrayed as negative, and that furthermore, they have not committed the great sins committed in Sodom. The severe judgment on them is because of the deadliest of sins, that of rejecting Jesus.

47. M.D. Goulder, *Midrash and Lection in Matthew* (London: SPCK, 1974), p. 334, sees the Queen of the South as a fitting feminine pair to the Ninevites.

48. Davies and Allison, *Critical and Exegetical Commentary*, Vol. 3., p. 320, 'The double vocative here adds...emphasis and pathos'.

49. P.S. Minear, *Matthew: The Teacher's Gospel* (New York: Pilgrim Press, 1982), p. 119, 'in vv. 37-39...the dominant notes are the love of the Messiah for this city, his grief over its blindness, and his undiminished desire for its salvation'.

enlarges the image of Jerusalem, for Jesus' comparison of himself to a mother hen and his mention of Jerusalem's children whom he would gather to himself implies that Jerusalem herself is a mother, albeit a 'bad mother' who will not allow her 'children' to find refuge under his wings. The opposition of malevolent 'Mother Jerusalem' to Jesus underscores his love for her and her children. Mother Jerusalem's hostility toward the adult Jesus is underlined by her abandoning her own children to a desolate fate rather than allowing them to be 'gathered' by him. [50] Mother Jesus' deepest feelings toward Jerusalem are those of compassionate desire, reluctant judgment, a deep tenderness, and a profound sorrow over her children lost to him.

In sum, the implied reader is guided to construct a particular under-standing of the significance of the female imagery by combining the per-spectives of narrator, plot and character. These textual structures influence the reader to adopt the particular view of the female imagery laid out by the perspectives. The narrator uses personification, metaphor and simile to draw the reader into the story, to encourage her/him to reflect upon the female images and even to imagine the images anew. In relation to plot, the female imagery does not so much further the action as illumine for the reader the meaning of the events. Female images appear at strategic points of conflict in the plot. The foremothers point to (unspecified) aspects of Jesus' origin and identity even before the story proper begins. Mary and Rachel, endangered and suffering mothers, are set against Herod and Jerusalem in the initial conflict between Jesus and his enemies. As the conflict escalates, Jesus justifies himself and his ministry by appealing to the witness of a justified Sophia and a wise and powerful Queen of the South. At the breaking point of the conflict, and on the eve of the passion, Jesus laments over a murderous maternal Jerusalem, and declares his longings for her welfare in the simile of the protective mother hen. The implied reader is encouraged to adopt the narrator's androcentric perspec-tive in which the female imagery is significant and yet insignificant. The female images are significant as witnesses to Jesus' origins and identity, to the righteousness of his person and ministry, to the depth of the hostility of Jesus' opponents, and to Jesus' reluctant judgment of and compassionate love for Israel. They are insignificant in that they are inserted into the story

---

50. The feminization of the city of Jerusalem is somewhat problematic for the reader because it raises the question of the nature of her malevolence. Is Jerusalem malevolent because she represents the Jewish leadership, or because she represents evil mothers?

simply as markers of Jesus' significance. The fullness of their meaning is curtailed, constrained and diminished within the boundaries of a story focused on male interests.

Female Imagery and the Reader as Structured Act

The point at which the textual structures begin to affect a reader is the moment when an actual reader starts to read, i.e., to assemble the textual perspectives.[51] The 'textual instructions' stimulate mental images by which the reader is drawn into the world of the text, and ultimately constructs meaning.[52] As text and reader merge in the process of reading, meaning emerges, not as an object to be defined but as an effect to be experienced. Reading Matthew's gospel has a profoundly damaging effect on an uncritical reader, for in it wo/men's experience and perspective are systematically assimilated into a male perspective considered as the norm.[53] A discerning feminist reader must therefore resist the textual directions, reject the story's androcentric perspective, and claim the freedom to construct an alternative story which mirrors back with symbolic exemplariness the patterns which underlie wo/mens empirical reality. S/he 're-visions', 're-interprets', and 're-constructs' the meaning of the images from a new direction, that of wo/men's lived experience.

I now describe one feminist reader's journey through Matthew's narrative world, in which she lingers at the refreshing oases of female imagery, discovers alternate routes, and arrives at a destination which is not yet the end of the road.[54] The 'reader' I propose is myself. In order to illustrate

51. A real reader who plays the role of the implied reader now must be allowed to bring to the text her/his knowledge and experience, i.e., what Iser, *Act of Reading*, pp. 36-38, calls the 'background to and frame of reference for the act of grasping and comprehending…as textual structures become transmuted through [the reader's] ideational activities into personal experiences'. As s/he reads, s/he remembers and expects, is surprised, mistaken, corrected, enlightened, etc.

52. Iser's notion of the image (a way of grasping reality) derives from his understanding of meaning not as an object which the reader attempts to define in relation to a particular frame of reference, but rather as the production of an interaction between the textual signals and the reader's acts of comprehension.

53. In this section of the paper, I follow E. Schüssler Fiorenza's use of the word 'wo/men' as a term inclusive of disenfranchised men, and indicative of the many differences among wo/men and within wo/man.

54. The destination is the attempt to 'press the tradition to the fullness of its meaning, and womanhood to the fullness of its being'. E.F. Genovese, 'For Feminist Interpretation', *Union Seminary Quarterly Review* 35, 1/ 2 (1979-1980), p. 5.

aspects of an imaginative reading process, i.e., what Iser calls the reader's 'wandering viewpoint', I treat the images not in the order in which they appear in the gospel, but in terms of their significance for this reader, who reads as a feminist in solidarity with feminist scholars and all wo/men engaged with the Bible as a witness to G*d's liberating power.[55] My journey is but one example of reading as a praxis which generates, albeit not without struggle, new significance for the imagery and a new world for wo/men readers. [56]

Mater Dolorosa

Rachel (2.18) and the Foremothers (1.3, 5, 6, 16)

Rachel's anguished cry echoes and re-echoes in memory and imagination down through years of reading Rachel (Jer. 31.15; Mt. 2.18) as a metaphorical figure, a trans-historical mother, who poetically mourns 'her children', whether the exiled tribes of Israel or the babes of Bethlehem. Rachel's personal drama points to metaphysical reality.[57] Her burial place in Ramah, on the border between Judah and Israel, lies between fixed places of human concourse in a 'no-man's land', the metaphysical space which her 'children' will cross on their way into exile.[58] A liminal figure, she meets them, as it were, at the border, the place where they move off into non-being, and responds to her children's pain at their point of dispersal. Rachel's longing love accompanies them even in their exile. In this she is an image of the compassionate grief of G*d, for, as Jeremiah reveals, YHWH is a mother who, like Rachel mourning her children, declares her divine sorrow for 'a darling child'. As Rachel mourns the loss of the fruit of her womb, so YHWH from the divine womb mourns the same child.[59]

Matthew's Rachel (2.18) weeps unceasingly and without hope: 'Directed to no one in particular, and hence to all who may hear, the voice of Rachel

---

55. I adopt the writing of the divine name espoused by Schüssler Fiorenza in order to communicate the inadequacy of our G*d language.

56. Schweickart, 'Reading Ourselves', p. 24: 'We cannot afford to ignore the activity of reading, for it is here that literature is realized as *praxis*. Literature acts on the world by acting on its readers'.

57. The following relies on A.G. Zornberg, *The Beginning of Desire: Reflections on Genesis* (New York: Doubleday, 1995).

58. Zornberg, *Beginning of Desire*, p. 375.

59. P. Trible, *God and the Rhetoric of Sexuality* (Philadelphia: Fortress Press, 1978), p. 170.

travels across the land and through the ages to permeate existence with a suffering that not even death can relieve...'[60] Conflicting images shape each other to create a new image of Rachel's infinite longing as an act which paradoxically engenders stubborn hope. Her children's absence is situated in the limited perspectives of this world, but her sense of 'what is not' engenders imaginings beyond the visible. These imaginings are the 'labour' of her tears, a labour of hope enacted in weeping. Rachel emerges in all her heroic complexity as a figure of tragic optimism; her holiness translates pain into strength; it intuits 'the strength within the pain, the coherence within chaos'.[61]

Rachel's resilient suffering forms a horizon against which to understand the five women who precede her in Matthew's story: Tamar, Rahab, Ruth, She-of-Uriah and Mary. Their suffering also generates hope and integrative energy, for despite their domestication within patriarchal structures, they challenge and transform conventional ideas about divinity, family structures, war, sexuality and marriage. The widowed Tamar, righteous, resourceful outsider, hungers for justice. Shrewd in act and ready in wit, she not only assures her survival, but also ensures her standing as marker of transition and agent of transformation. Tamar's clear moral vision enables Judah not only to see her as a person in her own right, but also to recognize his own obduracy, and thus his own relationship to G*d.[62] No G*d comes to Tamar's rescue, yet her very marginalization opens up an interpretative space for the presence of 'the [G*d] of Genesis, [who] is partial to marginal people...the god of the tricksters who uses deception to deal with the power establishment'.[63] Tamar's righteousness images the righteousness of a G*d partial to outsiders, situated in the 'in-between' of patri/kyriarchal authority structures. To see Tamar's face is to glimpse the face of this gracious G*d who rewards a woman's struggle with blessing (Gen. 32.10).[64]

60. Trible, *God and Rhetoric*, p. 40.

61. Zornberg, *Beginnings of Desire*, p. 214.

62. Zornberg, *Beginning of Desire*, p. 326-77.

63. S. Niditch, 'Genesis' in Newsom and Ringe (eds.), *Women's Bible Commentary*, p. 16.

64. M. Bal, *Lethal Love: Feminist Literary Readings of Biblical Love Stories* (Bloomington: Indiana University Press, 1987), pp.101-102, 'More than an easy moral victory, as most readings suggest, the tale represents a struggle, not yet won, not yet accomplished, but significant in that it demonstrates the dependency of each subject on the other'.

Against the horizon of the story of Tamar, I recognize Rahab, another liminal figure, who dwells in the city wall (Josh. 2.15), and who, as a tool of a warring Canaanite king, is used by both sides and is a potential victim of both. Seemingly trapped within the dynamic of male conflict, Rahab's steadfast love (Josh. 2.12) and faith enables her not only to escape the snares of violent men, but also to challenge the notion of the holiness of war.[65] Rahab puts her faith in a G*d of 'holiness' (Josh. 5.13), not a god of war. Her spiritual largesse, mercy and kindness reflect the qualities of the G*d in whom she has come to believe. She is truly a woman of G*d's shalom (Heb. 11.31).

Ruth, a poor, widowed foreigner, reflects the lovingkindness and stead-fast love of her 'sisters' and of her G*d. A strong woman, capable of acting in company with other women to preserve life and thus to ensure the future of the Davidic line, Ruth, like Rahab, practices mercy and kindness (Ruth 3.10). Her deeds prove her a woman of worth and a person in her own right. No G*d helps Ruth; rather the enduring bond between Israel and YHWH is modeled on the loving relationship between Ruth and Naomi. Female foreigners exemplify divine pity; 'the past loyalty of human beings is a paradigm for the future kindness of the divine being'.[66] The two women's loving care for each other finds an echo in the solicitude shown to them by the community of women under whose wings they ultimately find refuge (Ruth 4.14-17).

Against the background of women's stories of suffering and strength, She-of-Uriah appears as the most tragic. Encompassed by personal violence and national warfare, She-of Uriah is doubly victimized. Yet, against all odds, the violated and bereaved woman possesses the courage to mourn her murdered husband and her dead child (2 Sam. 11.26; 12.24). Grieving love engenders healing and new life, however scarred, for herself, for David, and for her future son, Solomon. In her radical suffering she also images the compassion of Israel's G*d, for like the other women in Matthew's story, her grief and her resilient love image divine pity (directed in the text toward David, cf. 2 Sam. 12.8, 9, 13).

The story of the last woman, Mary of whom Jesus was born, echoes the four preceding stories and introduces a new note. Mary, a marginal figure like the other women, conceives in an anomalous state outside of marriage (1.18). But despite the ultimate domestication of Mary and her unborn

    65. D.N. Fewell, 'Joshua', in Newsom and Ringe (eds.), *Women's Bible Commentary*, p. 63.
    66. Trible, *God and Rhetoric,* p. 170.

child within the confines of a (more or less) conventional marriage, her conception of Jesus remains a powerful critique of the androcentric point of view from which Matthew's story is told. Mary's role in the production of the Messiah is not only independent of human male patriarchal control, but is also blessed by a G*d who rejects the claims, powers, and structures of patriarchy. As with Rachel and the other mothers in the genealogy, Mary's sufferings and triumphs are intimately related to the grieving, loving and life-giving G*d of the marginal, the oppressed, the suffering and the powerless.

I remember and identify with these women's sufferings and strengths which I see repeated in women throughout history. I wonder how Matthew's story of Jesus, G*d's Messiah, fits into the pattern of our lives. I read on, expecting to find a Jesus sympathetic to and congruent with women's experience of reality and of G*d. I find him as son of Wo/man. Jesus, of the lineage of Rachel, Tamar, Rahab, Ruth, She-of-Uriah and Mary, is heir to their legacy of tenacity, courage in the face of suffering, righteousness, and mercy. Jesus, son of Rachel, weeps with her until her children return, i.e., until all understand with their heart and return to the Lord (Mt. 13.5); he will not cease to mourn until the blind see and the lame walk, the deaf hear and the dead are raised, and the poor have the gospel preached to them (Mt. 11.4-5); until all say, 'Blessed is the one who comes in the name of the Lord'. (23.39). We wo/men who follow Jesus, son of Rachel, share both his grief and his vision as together we listen and respond to

A voice…heard in Ramah/ Hiroshima, Salvador/ Women refusing comfort/
For their children are no more/ No garland of lovely flowers/ Can dispel the
ancient grief/ Or silence the anguished voices/ That abhor the war machine.[67]

I adopt the morality I find expressed in the person and vision of Jesus, son of the righteous outsider, Tamar for whom there was no place in society. Like the displaced Tamar, Jesus also acts righteously within a system with no place for him as son of David. Jesus urges John to 'do all that righteousness demands' (Mt. 3.15), i.e., to baptize him as a devout and observant Jew in a rite of repentance. Jesus urges his listeners to rely on G*d's righteousness (Mt. 6.33), castigates some for their unrighteousness (Mt. 12.37), and declares that only the righteous who practice mercy will go to eternal life (Mt. 25.37). Together, Tamar and Jesus, son of

---

67. C. Fulmer, *Cry of Ramah. Songs by Colleen Fulmer. Dances by Martha Ann Kirk* (Albany, CA: Loretto Spirituality Network, n.d.), p. 9.

Tamar, breach the narrative boundaries of the androcentric stories in which they are enmeshed to reveal the liberating power of an inclusively loving G*d, a G*d of greater righteousness who exceeds patri/kyriarchy.

I strive to be merciful in the power of Jesus, son of Rahab the merciful, who desired mercy, not sacrifice (Mt. 9.13), who showed mercy to those in need (Mt. 9.27; 17.15), esteemed it as higher than any law (Mt. 12.12) and taught his followers to do the same (Mt. 18.33).

I celebrate inclusivity with Jesus, son of Ruth the foreigner, she who recognized in the faith of foreign women, an astounding faith not found in Israel (Mt. 8.10; 15.28). This Jesus sets a place for Ruth, true Israelite and authentic daughter of the *basileia* (Mt. 13.38), together with Abraham, Isaac and Jacob (Mt. 8.11) at the heavenly banquet. Jesus, Son of Ruth, offers to Israel's leaders the maternal protection of G*d's comforting wings, the same blessed safety which his foremother sought and found in the company of the women of Israel.

I take courage from Jesus, son of She-of Uriah, who shared his tragic foremother's unspeakable and unspoken suffering as violated ones, brought to the brink of despair. Their silence before their persecutors (Mt. 27.12), their sadness and great distress (Mt. 26.37; 2 Sam. 11.26), their sorrow unto death (Mt. 26.38) was unrelieved by divine consolation (Mt. 27.46). Both turned their grief outward to lament not their own suffering but the fate of the innocent (Mt. 23.37). Both are *imago Dei*, images of a living and maternal G*d whose presence, even when darkly intuited in the mode of absence, offers new possibilities to the situation from within. Both show us a G*d who 'transforms suffering, not mitigating its evil, but bringing in inexplicable consolation and comfort'.[68]

I find my place in Matthew's narrative world and in my world of wo/men as I recognize and acknowledge Jesus, son of Mary. This Jesus is 'more' than the crowds—or we—can fathom; he gives offense because of his ordinariness, which in reality is the extraordinary that we miss because seeing, we do not perceive, and hearing, do not listen (Mt. 13.13) to the one who is G*d's son through Mary. I take my stand with this liminal Jesus, and together with Mary, the foremothers, and wo/men throughout the history of the world, claim space in the land 'in-between' patri/kyriarchal boundaries. Jesus, son of Wo/man, gathers us to himself in that blessed space wherein we discover G*d and ourselves as G*d's image.

---

68. E.A. Johnson, *She Who Is: The Mystery of God in Feminist Theological Discourse* (New York: Crossroad, 1992), pp. 267, 269.

The Deeds of Sophia

The Queen of the South and Sophia (11.19; 12.42)

I am drawn, at the mid-point of the gospel, into the story of the fabulously exotic figure of the Queen of the South (Mt. 12.42; 1 Kgs 10; 2 Chron. 9). In the scriptures, the foreign queen visits Solomon after he has chosen Wisdom over riches and honour (1 Kgs 3). The Queen tests Solomon with hard riddles (a form of Wisdom) which he answers, and then bestows on him immense riches and honour. As the story is told, she is ultimately bested by Solomon in a verbal sparring match and returns to her own home, perhaps after having bested Solomon by seducing him.[69] The story raises questions about the Queen as a Wisdom figure, and also about Jesus' words concerning her judgment and condemnation of 'this generation'. In the scriptural tale, the Queen poses Wisdom riddles to Solomon out of the store of her own vast knowledge and with a hermeneutic of suspicion (1 Kgs 10.1). She determines for herself whether in fact Solomon is as wise as he is reputed to be. Solomon's former dedication to Wisdom above honour and riches now seems somewhat compromised. Are honor and riches the true reward of Wisdom? It would seem that the Queen's wise and wily testing of King Solomon is best understood as a critique of Solomon's (and the narrator's) valuing of kyriarchal wealth and prestige.

In Matthew's story this same Queen rises up in judgment against a generation which rejects one even greater than Solomon, namely, Jesus (12.42). Like Solomon, 'this generation' does not recognize or possess true Wisdom, and therefore cannot recognize Jesus for who he is. The Queen of the South judges that Jesus is greater than Solomon because he is justified by his deeds, that is, Wisdom's deeds (11.19; cf. 11.2, 4-5). In truth, Jesus' care for the poor and the marginalized elevates him above even one of the greatest of Israel's kings, and makes of him a prophet of Sophia.

Jesus himself appeals to the witness of Sophia on his behalf. I am intrigued by Jesus' reference to the justification of Sophia by her deeds, for it conjures up the image, long known in the tradition, of Sophia as both beneficent and judgmental, one who tests and challenges human beings to live a life obedient to her, one who teaches virtue and gives good counsel. Her deeds are the deeds of Israel's G*d, for she is Israel's G*d in female

---

69. C. Camp, '1 and 2 Kings', in Newsom and Ringe (eds.), *The Women's Bible Commentary*, p. 102.

form.[70] Sophia, the female embodiment of Go*d's Wisdom and of the practical understanding of life, vindicates Jesus as preserver and restorer of life, compassionate healer, doer of merciful deeds which stand as judgment on those who reject him, and who in rejecting him, reject G*d's Wisdom.

As I read the gospel account, images merge. Present images are understood in the light of previous ones, and the latter are in turn shaped by aspects of the former. The image of the independent and resourceful Queen of the South merges with that of Wisdom (Mt. 11.19). The Queen of the South is 'Woman Wisdom, cast in narrative form'.[71] Sophia and the Queen's double witness to Jesus' justification through deeds of compassion encourages me to stand in solidarity with the two female Wisdom figures, one an image of the other and both paradigms of the Wisdom attributed to Jesus. Together with them, I acknowledge Jesus as Sophia's prophet. I accept Jesus as one who is known by Sophia/G*d, and who knows Her intimately, who reveals to wo/men what is hidden, and who invites us to take up his (Wisdom's) yoke and find rest in so doing (11.25-30).[72]

Holy Mother Wisdom

Jerusalem and the Mother Hen (23.37-39)
The first of these female images disconcerts a feminist reader. Matthew's astoundingly negative apostrophe to 'mother Jerusalem' (23.34-36, 37-39) is almost unprecedented in the tradition.[73] Jesus' words to 'mother

---

70. Johnson, *She Who Is*, p. 91: '...if the breadth of Sophia's activity in the wisdom literature is taken stringently into account...her actions in creation and salvation are obviously divine ones. What she does is already portrayed elsewhere in the Scriptures as the field of action of Israel's God under the revered, unpronounceable name, YHWH'.

71. C. Camp, '1 and 2 Kings', in Newsom and Ringe (eds.), *Women's Bible Commentary*, p. 102.

72. Davies and Allison, *Critical and Exegetical Commentary*, Vol. 2, p. 272, notes the intriguing parallels between Jesus and Sophia. Examples include the fact that only G*d knows Wisdom (Sir. 1.6-9; Bar. 3.32); only Wisdom knows G*d (Wisd. 8.4; 9.1-18); Wisdom reveals divine secrets (Wisd. 9.1-18; 10.10); Wisdom invites others to take up her yoke and find rest (Sir. 51.23-30 [cf. Prov. 1.20-3; 8.1-36]; 24.19-22; *Odes Sol.* 33.6-13, etc.

73. O. Steck, *Israel und das gewaltsame Geschick der Propheten* (WMANT XXIII; Neukirchen: Neukirchener Verlag, 1967), p. 227, 'Jerusalem ist in spätjudischer

Jerusalem' stand in sharp contrast to ancient Zion theology's emphasis on the idea of Jerusalem as a spiritual reality rather than simply a city. Within such a framework, while it is true that maternal Jerusalem was at times devastated, never is the 'mother' city herself guilty. Maternal and widowed Jerusalem weeps for her suffering children (Lam. 1.5, 6, 8, 11, 14, 16, 18). She is mother of the exiles (3rd Isaiah, Baruch, 4 Ezra). She is a mother comforting her children (Isa. 56-66, esp. 66.10-12). She is a desolate woman comforted by G*d (Bar. 4.11, 12, 16, 19, 20): 'Jerusalem is either weeping for her children who have been sent away in punishment for sin, or she receives them upon her breast. But in no case is Jerusalem as mother responsible for the destruction or guilty of sin'.[74]

Images now begin to coalesce and expand, to transform and be transformed. Jerusalem lamenting her children's sins, weeping that they must be punished, is like Rachel weeping for her children.[75] Jesus' maternal lament (Mt. 23.27-39) echoes Jerusalem's own lament, which in turn is a sister image of Rachel's cry of anguish (Mt. 2.18). Images of the fertile tears of Jesus' foremothers, of grief turned to life-giving deeds are recalled.[76] Lament gives way to warning and promise of redemption. Jesus' words of warning to Jerusalem parallel Jerusalem's words of instruction to her people (Bar. 4.18) when, very much like Sophia (Prov. 1–9) she comforts them with the assurance that their suffering is not meaningless, but is in the control of YHWH. Jerusalem is a good mother, unwilling to abandon her children, even to Jesus. She may yet comfort her children on the day that they welcome Jesus who comes as Sophia's prophet. I anticipate that day when the sorrowing woman, Zion, 'the mother of us all', is transformed into the beautiful city (4 Ezra 10.8), the

Tradition sonst nicht Subjekt des Ungehorsams und auch mit dem gewaltsamen Prophetengeschick nie betont verbunden...Auch im Rahmen der Vorstellung von Jerusalem als Mutter ist die Stadt nur Klgl 1.8.14.18 als Sünderin apostrophiert'.

74. Mary Callaway, *Sing, O Barren One: A Study in Comparative Midrash* (SBLDS 91; Atlanta: Scholars Press, 1986), p. 89: 'This is in contrast to the Jerusalem of Jeremiah, First Isaiah and Ezekiel, which is portrayed as a harlot and a hopelessly faithless wife'. She further notes: 'Jeremiah and Ezekiel had attacked the doctrine of the inviolability of Zion and had portrayed the city as polluted and faithless... Second Isaiah and Ezekiel used the ancient mythologies [the idea of Jerusalem as a transcendent reality] in a new *historical* way' (p. 90; emphasis mine).

75. Calloway, *Sing, O Barren One*, p. 82.

76. S.N. Kramer, 'BM 98396: A Sumerian Prototype of the Mater Dolorosa', *Eretz Israel* 16 (1982), p. 141, notes the archetypal character of the weeping Rachel, similar to the 'weeping goddess' figures whose tears bring life.

truly 'holy city' (Mt. 27.53). If Jerusalem as a religious idea in the past represented the beginnings of the world, the presence of the deity, and even life in Eden, she can also be understood and embraced as an image of every human mother of every age, who in turn images G*d as a mother suffering for the sake of her children, even lamenting their guilt, misfortune or loss, but always comforting them with hope for a better and brighter future.

The imagery comes full circle as Jesus speaks in the simile of the mother hen, of his longings to gather Jerusalem's children to himself. The mother-hen image gathers together the previous images of the mothers and foremothers, of Mother Jerusalem and of a maternal G*d to generate a final image of Holy Mother Wisdom. The image of the mother hen is used fairly often in the tradition to portray G*d. Sheltering wings conventionally depict various aspects of G*d's relationship to Israel; G*d's saving deeds in the Exodus, 'like an eagle...hover[ing] over its young' (Deut. 32.11); the shelter offered to proselytes (Ruth 2.12; 2 Bar. 41.3-4); G*d's protection of Jerusalem, 'Like birds hovering overhead, so the Lord of Hosts will protect Jerusalem' (Isa. 31.5); notions of G*d's protection from enemies, 'he will cover you with his pinions and under his wings you shall find refuge' (Ps. 91.4); G*d's steadfast love (Ps. 36.7); G*d as a source of joy (Ps. 63.7).[77]

The connection of the mother hen image with Wisdom is less obvious. Certainly Wisdom is portrayed in the tradition as maternal (Sir. 4.11; 15.2; Wisd. 7.12), and there are some references to Wisdom in terms of nesting. Wisdom makes as 'a nest' (Sir. 1.15) among human beings an eternal foundation where she will abide faithfully.[78] While there are no specific references in the tradition to the 'wings of Wisdom', some have found a relationship between Sophia and her sister, the Shekinah, or 'dwelling place' of G*d, and have noted the deep-seated nature of the metaphor of shelter in connection with the deity.[79] In any case, it is but a short imaginative step from the image of the wings of the protective mother hen to the persona of the winged Shekinah as presence of G*d, and thus to the

77. See also Ps. 17.8; 57.1; 61.4.
78. Prov. 16.16 LXX speaks of Wisdom's 'brood'.
79. C. Matthews, *Sophia: Goddess of Wisdom. The Divine Feminine from Black Goddess to World Soul* (Bath: Bath Press, 1991), p.115, notes that the Shekinah is associated with the emblems of the winged cherubim on the Ark of the Covenant, which in turn resemble images of the Egyptian Hathor with her outstretched and protecting wings.

image of the mother hen as image of Sophia/G*d. It would seem that Jesus, prophet of maternally protective Sophia/G*d who must threaten Jerusalem's children where he would bless, resembles no one so much as another prophet, the tender-hearted and anguished Jeremiah who could not save Jerusalem.[80]

Jesus, prophet of Holy Mother Wisdom, not only warns and judges her erring children, but also consoles and comforts them. The children of Jerusalem and of Jesus are not to remain tragically divided on his account. Rather, as Wisdom's children they are invited to live together under her protective and enveloping wings.

Reading means entering into the text to the extent that we are taken 'out of this world', and are thus able to see it and ourselves anew. In my reading of Matthew's female imagery, I have embraced the ambiguity, mined the silences for their treasure, and discovered the riches of wo/men as images of Holy Mother Wisdom. The end of my story of reading is but the beginning of continued dialogue with the gospel and with other readers so that this parable of wo/men's wisdom may become truly good news for us all.

80. M. Plath, 'Der neutestamentliche Weheruf uber Jerusalem', *Theologische Studien und Kritiken* 78 (1905): p.457.

THE ENIGMA OF THE YOKE: DECLINING IN PARABLES (MT. 11.28-30)

Edith M. Humphrey

> 'Come to me, all you that are weary and are carrying heavy burdens, and I
> will give you rest. Take my yoke upon you, and learn from me; for I am
> gentile and humble in heart, and you will find rest for your souls. For my
> yoke is easy, and my burden is light'. (Mt 11.28-30, NSRV)

The logion of Mt. 11.28-30 issues an invitation to rest; biblical scholars
have seized upon it and have found instead unending labour, speculation,
and controversy. The complex saying has been pressed into the service of
source criticism, since among the canonical gospels it is found only in
Matthew, while it also appears in *Gos. Thom.* 90 (among other later
sources). A lively debate continues as to its status as an actual saying of
Jesus, its possible presence in Q (in connection with Q 10.21-22), its
origin in other pre-Matthean sources or oral traditions, or its adaptation/
composition by Matthew for various polemical purposes. In the reconstruction of earliest christologies the passage has also played a key role,
understood by some as a telling moment in the development of Wisdom
Christology, when the image of Jesus in the sayings gospel ('an emissary
of Wisdom') was either intensified or corrected.

Again, debate has continued concerning the place of the logion within
the context of Matthew as the gospel stands: do these words function to
highlight the role of Jesus himself, to teach about discipleship, to combat
the Pharisaic focus upon Torah, to introduce the scribe Jesus and a new
interpretative approach to Torah? Finally, there are several mysteries
latent in the saying itself, in the areas of both form and content. Does the
saying display symmetry or not? Which Hebrew Bible, 'intertestamental'
or other echoes, reverberate here? Is there a paradox to be seen in the
bringing together of 'yoke' and 'rest'? What might 'yoke' and 'rest' mean
in terms of both denotation and connotation? And on it goes.

So much has been written on these issues that it would be pointless to
replicate those discussions here. However, for the purposes of this volume,

the passage is of particular interest because of its connection with the function and form of the parable. Only a few chapters beyond our passage, arguably within the same unit (Matthew's 'Galilean ministry'), the reader is given a commentary upon Jesus' *modus operandi:* 'Jesus told the crowds all these things in parables; without a parable he told them nothing' (13.32)[1]. Since the invitation of 11.28-30 is most certainly a word 'to the crowds', it is not much of a stretch to consider it as an example of parabolic, or at least enigmatic, teaching. Certainly the logion does not follow a common parabolic form, since its point of comparison is not transparent. Nor is an actual drama recounted, as is the case in the narratival parable; yet a potential drama is proposed as a course of action. Not much imagination, in fact, is required to transform these verses into a parable: 'The kingdom of heaven is like a weary labourer who came to one who was humble, took on his yoke, and found rest'.

But already in reformulating the words, I have tamed them, dispelling (perhaps incorrectly) the mysteries which tease. What exactly *is* the latent or suggested main point of comparison here? Is it a paradoxical comparison of 'yoke' and 'rest'? Then we must know what 'my yoke' means. Is Jesus being compared to Wisdom? Then the hearer must have a prior knowledge of the stories about personified/hypostatized Wisdom. Is knowledge being linked with humility? Then we will be led to connect the logion with the prayer that precedes it. Here is a tantalizing saying with numerous possibilities, placed aptly by Matthew in the context of allusive public teaching, rather than as special teaching to the disciples.

And yet, its form as an invitation and its connection with 11.25-27 suggest that at least some of 'all you' who listen may be transformed into those 'to whom the Son chooses to reveal'. As with the parables, the net is cast wide, and the possibility of collusion with the worldview of the speaker is intimated. What would happen, then, if we were to 'decline' these two complex verses as a set of four parables, so as to open up various potential readings? It is hoped that a set of parables generated from the logion may show different facets of the 'secrets' hidden and revealed therein, including the themes of 'my yoke', 'rest', 'learning', and 'humility', as well as the enigma concerning the speaker. En route, intertextual echoes, the immediate context in Matthew, and clues within the gospel as a whole will be considered, prior to a final consideration of this 'not-quite-parable' that continues to bemuse and beckon.

1.   The English translation used throughout is NRSV, unless otherwise noted.

Declension 1: Wisdom's Parable

The kingdom of heaven is like a scribe who searched diligently, high and low, for wisdom, adding burden upon burden to his back, and straining at the yoke while he quested; when behold, there unexpectedly was Wisdom preparing a table before him, inviting many of her servants to come, taste her delights, and rest.

Of the liaisons traced between our text and other works, the themes of wisdom literature and the words of Wisdom herself have been dominant. It is no doubt the spectre of Dame Wisdom, discerned in the shadows of our Matthean setting, who pleads most eloquently for the inclusion of this saying among these 'parables of women, work and wisdom'. A strong influence of her words upon Mt. 11.28-30 is evident, and has indeed been denied only by the most intransigent analysts.[2]

Connections to Proverbs and Sirach are most obvious in three of the key phrases in the logion—'Come to me', 'Take my yoke' and 'You shall find rest'.

'Come to me'

'You that are simple, turn in here!… Come, eat of my bread and drink of the wine I have mixed' (Prov. 9.4-5); 'Come to me, you who desire me' (Sir. 24.19); 'Come to her with all your soul' (Sir. 6.26); 'Draw near to me, you who are uneducated, and lodge in the house of instruction' (Sir. 51.23). The excision of these verses from their literary contexts, though instructive in showing their overtones in Matthew, obscures a feature of difference. In Proverbs and Sir. 24, it is personified (or hypostasized) Wisdom who issues the invitation; in Sir. 6, the teacher issues an invitation to Wisdom's joys in the third person. In Sir. 51, there is perhaps a commingling of agents, with the teacher issuing a personal invitation for students to enter the house of instruction. Is this Wisdom's house, the teacher's house, or are the two interchangeable? The human instructor speaks, yet in hearing this call at the conclusion of the book, the hearer may be led to recall more particularly the figure of Wisdom herself, who throughout Sirach has her own home, table, and refreshment to offer those

---

2. The centrality of the Wisdom motif, through not its presence, is questioned by J. Laansma, *I Will Give you Rest* (Tübingen: Mohr Siebeck, 1997) and W.D. Davies and D.C. Allison, *A Critical and Exegetical Commentary on the Gospel According to Saint Matthew* (2 vols.; Edinburgh: T. & T. Clark, 1988–1991).

who will draw near. This association of teacher and Wisdom is far more pronounced in Matthew, if the first-person logion is read in context as it follows 11.25-27. The most natural sequential reading is to absolutely identify the figures of 'teacher' (i.e., revealing Son) and Wisdom in Matthew, over against the close but subordinate identification of teacher with Wisdom in Sirach. Taken on its own, however, 11.28-30 is more ambiguous: the literate hearer may well identify 'me' as the voice of Wisdom, without immediately asking about the connection of Jesus to this host. This is the effect our first parabolic declension, which does not call attention to the identity of the narrator.

In the composed parable, Wisdom's profligate generosity is stressed, as in both Proverbs and Sirach, where her cry is made publicly, to any who will hear. Though Wisdom is traditionally characterized as liberal in her proclamation, the public quality of the invitation is not unmitigated. In both earlier texts, the recipients are defined by the overall literary context and inner-textual commentary: potential students or guests of Wisdom are those among the covenant people of God. In Proverbs, the ideal reader is the 'son' of 'Solomon'; in Sirach, the addressee is defined by the commentator. That is, immediately after Sirach's Wisdom lures with her 'fruits' and delicacies (24.19-22), we read 'all this is the book of the covenant of the Most High God, the law that Moses commanded us as an inheritance for the congregations of Jacob... It overflows...with wisdom... It runs over...with understanding... It pours forth instruction' (Sir. 24.23-27). Implicitly in Proverbs, and explicitly in Sirach, 'the children' of Wisdom (4.11) are those who respect the covenant—the 'simple' and 'uneducated', then, are those to whom Torah has been given, but who need to appreciate this gift more profoundly.

We see, then, in these pre-Matthean invitations, a tension between the free movement of Wisdom in the human realm, and her special connection with the covenant. This double tendency is seen in greatest relief in a later-written book of Wisdom, Baruch:

> [God] found the whole way to knowledge, and gave her to his servant Jacob, and to Israel whom he loved. Afterward she appeared on earth and lived with humankind. She is the book of the commandments of God, the law that endures forever. All who hold her fast will live, and those who forsake her will die. Turn, O Jacob, and take her; walk toward the shining of her light. Do not give your glory to another, or your advantages to an alien people. Happy are we, O Israel, for we know what is pleasing to God' (Bar. 3.35-4.4)

Is Wisdom one who 'lives with humankind' in general, or is she the special privilege of those who possess the 'glory' of Torah? Interpreters who view her second appearance ('Afterwards...') as a later Christian interpolation create a neater and more hegemonic text. However, to read Bar. 3.37 as an intentional reference to the Incarnation of the Word is hardly compelled by the text, which might be cashed out in a more general manner. On the other hand, to accept the text as it stands is to note that 'Baruch', along with other wisdom writers, struggled with the compatibility of Wisdom's characteristics—that she is both distinctive and all-pervasive. As the (probably) later author of Wisdom of Solomon was to put it: 'While remaining in herself, she renews all things' (7.27b). All these portraits of Wisdom speak from within the tradition of Israel, and without fail closely link Wisdom to Torah. Yet, through the celebration of Wisdom's extravagance, this constraint is at least potentially weakened.

In the end, the image that endures is that of a Wisdom who quests beyond Israel, even while she is linked inextricably with Torah. Her generosity and initiative remain startling: 'Wisdom...is found by those who seek her... because she goes about seeking those worthy of her, and she graciously appears to them in their paths' (Wisd. 6.12, 16). Our parable emphasizes the particularity of the addressee ('a scribe who searched diligently for wisdom') in a more marked way than does the logion itself. Mt. 11.28-30 preserves, at least partially, a tension through its juxtaposed description of those called (*pantes* with its universal appeal) *hoi...pephortismenoi*, perhaps alluding to those who nobly bear the yoke of Torah. Yet it is arguably the *pantes* that sounds the strongest note.

'(Take my yoke) and I will give you rest'

Wisdom, in her generosity, offers a rest to those who have also taken her dignified and worthwhile yoke. The command to take up the yoke is obscured in our declension, but its presence in Mt. 11.28-30 provides further confirmation of the logion's connection with earlier wisdom texts. Two passages in Sirach provide the most obvious allusions:

> Put your neck under her yoke, and let your souls receive instruction: it is to be found close by (51.26).

> My child, come to her like one who ploughs and sows, and wait for her good harvest... Put your feet into her fetters, and your neck into her collar. Bend your shoulders and carry her, and do not fret under her bonds... Her yoke is a golden ornament, and her bonds a purple cord (6.18-31).

Here, the teacher encourages his disciple to take up Wisdom's yoke, so that learning may occur. Whereas the invitation links instruction to the joys of eating and drinking, the yoke stresses the connection of labour and learning. The incompatibility of these two metaphors is perhaps less obvious in the diffuse Wisdom passages of Sirach than it is in our composed Matthean parable. For example, in Sirach the invitation to delights (ch. 24) is uttered by Wisdom herself, whereas the call to labour comes from the teacher. The paradox, however, is stronger in declension one, and completely unreserved in the Matthean logion, where the two themes of becoming slave (or beast of burden) and becoming guest sit side-by-side. (It must be admitted that the invitation to table is muted in the logion itself: our parable has made explicit the constellation of metaphors that are latent in the invitation.)

Finally, we should note that the 'rest' offered by Wisdom in Sirach comes at the end of the labour process: the yoke may fit just right, but there is still work to be done.[3]

It is probably inaccurate to project a 'paradox' back from Matthew into Sirach, since the tension is not supported by the story told in the earlier work. Rather, in Sirach the reader is told 'before the harvest, you must sow'. The connection in Sirach between yoke and rest is therefore sequential, rather than paradoxical. By contrast, Matthew's logion allows a true collision of pictures, as our parabolic 'declension' highlights. The sequence of the logion suggests that it is actually through the 'coming' to the speaker that burdens will be removed; yet it is also through the 'coming' that a yoke is assumed.

One problem which has emerged in contemporary study of this sapiential aspect is that of the relationship between Jesus and Wisdom, a question that takes a special shape in Matthew's gospel. Is Matthew's Jesus a representative of Wisdom, or a replacement for her? (Should we take special note, for example, of Mt. 11.19's 'wisdom is vindicated by her deeds' over against the possible implications of variants B2, C, D, L, Q, etc. and the Lucan 'by her children'?) Furthermore, if Jesus now takes Wisdom's place, is this a usurpation that forces a modulation of themes, so that the strong 'master–lordship–discipleship' complex of the gospel now obscures the 'alongside' immanent quality of Wisdom, as she had been presented in the traditional material? There is a potential dissonance

3.   Here I affirm the reading of Laansma, *I Will Give You Rest,* p. 200 over that of C. Deutsch, *Hidden Wisdom and the Easy Yoke: Wisdom, Torah and Discipleship in Matthew 11.25-30* (JSNTSup 18; Sheffield: JSOT Press, 1987), p. 36.

between a dominant and masterful Jesus (already introduced as 'the Christ' in 11.2 and the privileged 'Son' at 11.27) and the traditional feminine symbol/hypostasis of divine tabernacling–a collision particularly striking for contemporary readers.

However, lest we be overly romantic about an unassuming and egalitarian traditional Wisdom, let us remember that Wisdom is presented, or even presents herself throughout the traditional material as God's special confidante–at one point she even claims to have 'alone' scaled the heavens, and plumbed the abyss (Sir. 24.5-8). Both grandeur and humility characterize Wisdom, and find an echo in Matthew's presentation of Jesus. Nor need we overstress a male–female dissonance in Mt. 11.28-30, since the first person form of this logion allows Jesus to speak *in persona Sapientiae* without the awkwardness of directly attaching masculine pronouns to Wisdom's voice. (Again, the 'I' is allusive rather than unequivocal, and may thus be heard as prophetic rather than a clue to actual identity. This ambiguity is reflected in the ongoing scholarly squabble over whether Wisdom Christology is the point of the logion in Matthew, or not.)

While the echoes from wisdom books are very strong, the midrashic richness of the Dame Wisdom tradition, that is, its own close interconnections with other books and motifs, should serve as a warning against a monochrome reading of Mt. 11.28-30. J. McKinlay reminds us that 'the… Wisdom motif [provided]…imagery which had already been used to combine creation and salvation themes, and expanded further to express the rich giftedness of the Torah'.[4] Sequences in the biblical and intertestamental literature where Wisdom speaks or is described have ready-made links with important dramatic sequences in books like Exodus and Deuteronomy, thus recalling the figure of Moses, teacher and scribe. In the light of such a 'textured' background, it would be unwise to assume that Matthew's sole concern is to figure Jesus as Wisdom. It is of course possible that a New Testament author may have exploited only one of the possibilities provided by the nourishing traditions. However, explicit intentionality is not the sole criterion in an attentive reading of imagery; moreover, a limited intent is most unlikely in the case of a writer like Matthew who, after all, understood the scribe's role as that of a 'house-holder' who brings new and old out of the 'treasure'. We may therefore

---

4.   J.E. McKinlay, *Gendering Wisdom the Host: Biblical Invitations to Eat and Drink* (Gender Culture Theory, 4; JSOTSup, 216; Sheffield: Sheffield Academic Press, 1996), p. 180.

expect that Matthew's use of 'secondary' Biblical texts (i.e., those books that comment upon Torah) will provide examples of what has been called 'textual triple-exposure'[5] (i.e., Torah, Wisdom literature, Q or M or Matthew). While Laansma's case may be overstated,[6] his probing queries remind us that 'Wisdom speculation is [only] one of the possible tributaries of [Matthew's] thought'.[7] It could not be otherwise, given the tributaries that have already flowed into the Wisdom passages observed in Mt. 11, and given Matthew's own delight in many treasures. Since the Wisdom passages themselves hearken back to the figure of Moses, let us use the next two parabolic declensions to recall Moses, meek teacher and custodian of Torah.

Declension 2: Discipleship alongside a Humble Teacher

The Kingdom of heaven is like a wise and humble teacher who presented his yoke to keen students who were willing to learn from him. As they carried, they themselves learned gentleness and humility, and they were at rest.

This parable directs an understated polemic against arrogant teachers, though not necessarily a strong argument against the rigours of Torah per se. The yoke is one that the teacher has carried in his own turn—it is his lore—and which he now presents to his followers. Here is the voice of experience, coupled with an emphasis upon discipleship, an unassuming attitude, and transferable skills. In exploring this mutation of the Matthean logion, we will again detail the three statements, 'come to me', 'take my yoke' and 'you shall have rest'.

'Come to me'

The unassuming quality of the teacher predominates in this declension, muting the 'to me' of the logion. It is not the identity of the speaker that is highlighted, but the character. In this case, even a link with the illustrious Moses is surprisingly helpful, since the one who was the mediator of Torah is himself characterized as possessing exemplary humility (Num. 12.3; Sir. 45.4). These earlier traditions link Moses' humility to his

---

5. This is the term used by R. Hays to facilitate the reading Paul in *Echoes of Scripture in the Letters of Paul* (New Haven: Yale University Press, 1989), p. 78.

6. Laansma, *I Will Give You Rest,* 'Matthew is not particularly interested to give Wisdom her own chair at the table of his Christology', p. 208.

7. Laansma, *I Will Give You Rest,* p. 208.

intimacy with God, so that humility is understood, along with faithfulness, as foundational to Moses' consecrated role. Our present declension of the saying, however, is not directed towards an outright encomium of the master teacher, but instead highlights the teaching and the learning. It is just possible to read the logion itself in this way, if the 'me' is de-emphasized. In reading the logion not as 'Come to *me*' but rather as '*Come* to me' (i.e., 'to a teacher like I am...') a flavour of self-abnegation may be preserved, despite the first person pronoun.

'Take my yoke'

From this perspective, perhaps rest is to be understood as rest from one's own self-assertiveness. Here is the rabbinic model of taking on the yoke. Such a reading would place the logion squarely within the mainstream wisdom tradition of Proverbs. This is an everyday wisdom which emphasizes wise and healthy attitudes, and congruent actions, over against that other type of wisdom that could be characterized as dramatically subversive (e.g., Job) or mysteriously apocalyptic (e.g., Dan. 7-12). Far from view here is the impenetrable Wisdom of the abyss or the glorious Wisdom who alone has seen the heavenly throne (Bar. 3.29-31; Sir. 24.5-6)–those scenes in which the sapiential borders upon the apocalyptic or mystic.[8]

A logion of practical wisdom may seem to some rather bland, yet it matches a portrait of Jesus that has been urged on other grounds. Here we envisage the rabbi Jesus, that wise householder of God's wisdom sketched by G. Vermes,[9] or the sage (vs apocalypticist) depicted variously by B.

---

8. It is helpful to note the rich tradition of interpretation stemming from Deut. 30.11-14, in which various scribes and commentators, including Philo (*Post.* 84-85) expanded upon the original Torah verses in various ways. Some of the targumim (see especially *Neofiti Targum*) appear to be aware of mystical traditions, and employ commentary on these verses to underscore the danger of visionary exploits. See M. McNamara, *The New Testament and the Palestinian Targum to the Pentateuch* (AnBib 2a; Rome: Pontifical Biblical Institute, 1978), pp. 70-81 and A.M. Goldberg, 'Torah aus der Unterwelt? Eine Bemerkung zu Röm. 10, 6-7', *BZ* 14,1 (1970), pp. 127-31.

9. See G. Vermes, *The Religion of Jesus the Jew* (Minneapolis: Fortress, 1993), especially pp. 4-7 and 125-149, which offer a domestic picture of Jesus the rabbi. Vermes Jesus understands God as *paterfamilias* or landowner, and teaches, by means of many kingdom parables, the importance of human co-operation with God. Vermes does not deny the prophetic or eschatological aspects of Jesus' teaching, but downplays these, registering appreciation for the more egalitarian strands where Jesus resembles the rabbis.

Mack *et al.*[10] The word of the teacher is here typically detached from a larger view of his identity, and certainly from any gospel metanarrative which would give the words a sovereignty or urgency by virtue of speaker's accomplishments. Not surprisingly, this 'life-style' declension of the parable is closest in flavour to the version of the saying found in the 'sayings gospel' *Gos. Thom.* 90: 'Jesus said, "Come unto me, for my yoke is easy and my lordship is mild, and you will find repose for yourselves"'.

'And I will give you rest'

In harmony with this reading of humble instruction, Jesus' words 'I will give you rest' should be explicated by the parallel half of the saying, 'you shall find rest for your souls'. The commentator might be tempted, in fact, to go the source critical route, considering that Matthew has modified an earlier 'self-help' saying, more like that found in *Gos. Thom.* 90 ('rest for yourselves'), and enriched it with an explicit reference to the master teacher. At any rate, the emphasis is on the learning of the students themselves: the declension's wording 'they themselves learned' picks up on this facet of the original saying. Unlike the first declension, this version works best when it is understood in isolation from both its general and immediate literary context in Matthew. Certainly Mt. 11.25-28 (parallelled in Lk. 10) forbids an interpretation that sets aside the status of the speaker. To preface the yoke saying, as Matthew has done, with the so-called 'Johannine thunderbolt from the blue' is to insist that the question of Jesus' identity be asked.

Those intrigued by a Declension Two reading of the logion are thus likely to be those questing for a Jesus unencumbered by apocalypticism or prophetic claims, a Jesus (from this perspective) 'long obscured' by the gospel writer's christological concerns.[11] However, its emphasis, with

10. B. Mack, in *A Myth of Innocence: Mark and Christian Origins* (Philadelphia: Fortress, 1988) is perhaps best known for his iconoclastic picture of the 'lacklustre Jesus'. This is his own term, used subsequently in Mack, 'Q and a Cynic-Like Jesus', in *Whose Historical Jesus* (ed. W.E. Arnal and M. Desjardins; Studies in Christianity and Judaism 7; Wilfrid Laurier University Press, 1997), pp. 25-36. More recent contributions to this discussion have included F.G. Downing, 'Cynics and Christians, Oedipus and Thyestes', *Journal of Ecclesiastical History* 44 (1993), pp. 1-10; L. Vaage, *Galilean Upstarts: Jesus' First Followers According to Q* (Valley Forge: Trinity Press International, 1994); and J.D. Crossan, *The Essential Jesus: Original Sayings and Earliest Images* (San Francisco: HarperSanFrancisco, 1994).

11. This is not the place to debate the merits and deficiencies of various approaches to Jesus and history. The major thrust of this study has been to consider the logion

some 'finessing' could also be supportive of some readings of the gospel as well. G. De Virgilio,[12] for example, argues that Matthew puts forward a nonviolent model of messianism, and situates our text within a concentric structure which points to this theme. In a reading such as his, the question of Jesus' own identity is not dismissed, but is at least decentred by the key themes of humility, the inheritance of the land, and a messianism of peace. It might be asked, however, whether such perspectives do justice to the polemic edge of the gospel, a tendency which is surely latent in the logion under analysis. Our last two declensions move from the irenic to the argumentative.

Declension 3: A Parable about Torah

The kingdom of heaven is like this: A diligent servant continually bore the yoke of his master, carrying heavy loads for him and for all those who gave orders in his name, to the point of utter fatigue. Suddenly he met one who offered a new yoke, and as he began to carry, behold, the burden was light, and he found a new Sabbath rest.

'Come to me'

Whereas Declension One highlighted the relationship of the logion's speaker to the ineffable figure of Wisdom, and declension two subverted the question of the speaker's identity, this version works through comparison—a comparison of both and old and new situation, and of the yoke-giver with former masters. The advent of a new situation is signalled by the prefacing words 'The Kingdom of Heaven is like', a formula found frequently in the parabolic collections, and a concept introduced in Matthew as the dawn of God's rule (Mt. 4.16-17). This declension makes explicit a characteristic that the logion shares with many of the parables particular to Matthew (e.g., the sheep and goats, the ten virgins, the two

within the context of Matthew's gospel, rather than to ask about how the logion might be treated on the level of the historical Jesus. Certainly other portraits of Jesus, notably those involved in the 'Third Quest', would question a hellenizing view of Jesus, and would have not consider self-reference in itself to be a mark against use by Jesus. Here I use the term 'Third Quest' in line with its original description (and in contrast to other current methods), as put forward by N.T. Wright in S. Neill and N.T. Wright, *The Interpretation of the New Testament 1861-1986* (2nd edn; Oxford: Oxford University Press, 1988), pp. 379-403.

12. G. De Virgilio, 'La valenza teologica dell'espressione: 'πραΰς εἰμι καὶ ταπείνος τῇ καρδίᾳ'(Matthew 11, 29)', *Rivist Bib* 45,4 (1997), pp. 409-28.

sons, the unmerciful servant)—the use of vivid contrast to make its point. Implicit in the logion (but unavoidable in our declension) is the comparison of those who pile on burdens with the speaker, whose yoke brings relief. Later in the gospel, we will hear invective against those who 'shut the Kingdom in people's faces' (23.13) and who 'tie heaven burdens and put them on men's shoulders' (23.4).

Thus, this logion, as seen through our parabolic refraction, deftly prepares a ready-made and positive picture against which the reader is later induced to compare Pharisaic constraints. Ch. 12, which follows immediately, adapts two Sabbath controversy stories (cf. Mk 3.1-6) so as to demonstrate the 'mercy' of Jesus over against the stance of his interlocutors. This theme is intimated both by the scripture citation included in his preaching (Mt. 12.7/Hos. 6.6) and by an extended story (12.11-12) about the fallen sheep in the pit. The next sections of ch. 12 then link this characteristic of mercy with the recapitulated theme of humility (found earlier in our own logion), through reference to Jesus' healing, the injunction to silence (12.15) and the adapted citation of Isaiah's quiet and merciful servant (Mt. 12.28-21/Isa. 42.1-4). In this way, the gospel writer 'has his cake and eats it' at the same time: Jesus becomes the focus of wisdom and the true teacher of adherence to God's will, yet does not call attention to himself. Declensions 1, 2 and 3 merge. 'Wisdom' is vindicated not by her own claims—not by 'crying out' (although Dame Wisdom in fact does this in the traditional material), but by gracious invitation, by deeds and by her offer of a new yoke.

'Take my yoke'
This refraction of the logion also demonstrates the inter-relationships of 'yoke' symbolism with both Wisdom and Torah—relationships established long before this gospel was written. The book of Sirach, for example, gives a strong commendation of 'statutes' and 'commandments' (Sir. 6.37) immediately following the teacher's call to the yoke of Wisdom (6.24-29). The general connection of yoke and Torah is also a commonplace in the prophetic literature of the Hebrew scriptures, where the 'yoke' of the Lord is contrasted with the oppressive yoke of the nations (Jer. 2.20, 5.5). Pseudepigraphical books such as *2 Bar.* 42.3-5 and *2 Enoch* 34.1-2 extend this imagery, speaking about the disobedience of those who have rejected or cast away the yoke of the Lord, after first being subjugated to it. Likewise in the rabbinic writings, reference is made to 'the yoke of heaven' (e.g., *Sotah* 147b, *Sanhedrin* 111b) and 'the yoke of the Torah' (e.g., Pirke Aboth 13.5; Sanhedrin 94b).

As we have phrased our own parable, it is not clear whether the initial 'burdens' or 'loads' are themselves to be equated with Torah, or interpretations of this by those who give orders in God's name. Is the labour inevitably strenuous, or is it the *manner* of labouring that is the cause of grief? Another way of posing this question would be to ask whether the 'new yoke' is pictured as new because of its content (cf. *Barnabas* 2.6; *1 Clement* 15.17), or because of its easier fit? This lack of clarity is intentional, since it leaves open the place of the Torah for Matthew and his 'original' readers. How the original saying is read depends in part on whether the reader of the entire gospel privileges other pro-Torah sayings (such as the permanence of 'jots and tittles'), or the 'new Torah' of the Sermon on the Mount and the anti-Pharisaic polemic of ch. 23. Certainly Matthew intends his reader to see Jesus as a new Moses—but does he carry a new Torah, or a new hermeneutic for reading the old one?

'And I will give you rest'
In Matthew's Gospel, terms having to do with 'doing', 'wisdom' and 'rest' are frequently linked, and quite prominent. Indeed, a strong case can be made for reading 11.1-13.58 as a unit in which Jesus' 'wisdom and… deeds of power' (11.19; 13.58) are demonstrated 'in their cities', culminating in the ministry at Nazareth. (The sandwiching of episodes concerning the Baptist around this unit at 11.2-15 and 14.1-12 reinforces the structure.) The Wisdom motif is here enriched by its connection with Torah, a new Moses, and the fulfilled Sabbath rest. As has already been seen, two of six Matthean Sabbath controversies follow immediately after the logion. One of the effects of this sequence is that the promise of 'rest' in ch. 11 is actually expounded by Jesus' perspective on the Sabbath rest, as seen in the controversies of ch. 12.[13] Looking at the gospel as a whole, we can see that the Sermon on the Mount,[14] these controversies of ch. 12, and the extended discourse of ch. 23 represent 'Torah' and its new herald in Deuteronomic fashion—neither too hard nor too far away, but near to the humble (cf. Deut. 30.11-14).[15]

13. See also ch. 4 of J. Neusner, *A Rabbi Talks with Jesus: An Intermillenial, Interfaith Exchange* (New York: Doubleday, 1993). Here, he connects Mt. 11.28-30 with Mt. 12.

14. H.-D. Betz 'The Logion of the Easy Yoke and of Rest (Matt 11.28-30)', *JBL* 86 (1967), p. 24, argues that the saying is theologically consonant with the beatitudes.

15. This Deuteronomic injunction, in fact, was the basis of a hermeneutical tradition carried into various ancient commentaries, including the very Wisdom books

Among Torah precedents, we may also be directed to the Exodus narrative found immediately before the renewal of the covenant and the giving of the new tablets. Here the Lord promises the despondent but interceding Moses, 'My presence will go with you [presumably, throughout the desert], and I will give you rest [presumably, in the land]' (Exod. 33.14).[16] Despite the 'stiff-necked' behaviour which sparks this episode, the tenor of the Exodus passage is hopeful: Moses worries about his appointment to 'bring up the people' and fears that the people cannot be distinguished from other nations, but is reassured of God's presence with them (and with him). The sequence continues by speaking about 'knowledge' of God's name and divine mercy (33.17-20), and then culminates with the manifestation of God's glory (33.21-23). Within the immediate context of the Matthean logion we see similar concerns: visitation by God through messengers (11.1-19), stubbornness and repentance (11.20-24), revelation to whom God wills (11.25-27, cf. Exod. 33.17-19) and divine presence with God's people (12.15-20). The cumulative effect is to suggest that if the Baptist is greater than all messengers before, the deeds and words of the Son render him both greater than Solomon (12.42) and more intimate with God than Moses who knew the name, spoke to God 'mouth to mouth' but could not see the mysterious face. Matthew's Isaianic commentary on Jesus' mission at 12.18-21 suggests that 'rest' is at last offered both to the 'bruised reed' and to the Gentiles by this new (or 'last'?) Moses. Our third parable casts the logion's invitation to presence, yoke and rest in a positive light, but also adds a muted polemic against those who have made God and Torah inaccessible. The logion could be heard, however, in a less reserved manner: our final declension pulls out all the stops of argumentation.

Declension 4: Parable and Polemic

Once there were some stewards of a master's house who placed the master's load as well as their own heavy burdens upon the servants, keeping them outside of the household, fitting them with a chafing yoke and not lifting a finger to help. Then there was a strange labourer in their midst bearing an easy yoke, inviting others to be yoked with him. So they carried and found their rest from enemies in the land.

(e.g., Sir. 24.5-8; Bar. 3.29-30) which seem to have nourished the Matthean logion.

16. Davies and Alison, *Commentary*, vol. 2, pp. 283-87 argue that this is the major intertextual echo for the logion, rather than Sir. 51.23-7.

In listening (through the first three variations) for the connection of Mt. 11.28-30 with Wisdom and Torah, it has been difficult to hear the over-tones of another preliminary voice—that of the prophet, and in particular, Jeremiah. We are alerted to its presence by the echo 'you shall find rest for your souls' (Jer. 6.16) and also find, proximate to that phrase in Jeremiah, several of the themes which have emerged already in our study of the logion—concern for Torah (7.8-9), the call to mercy (7.5-7), discourse about true wisdom (8.8-9), and reference to the call of God (7.13). Behind the magnanimous 'come' does there reverberate a more plaintive and pointed jeremiad, a lament over faithlessness and a call to 'return'?

'Come to me'

Certainly the Matthean context sets the scene for this darker reading. It is not only the generation of marketplace children who issue unheeded calls—woes are declared on Chorazin, Bethsaida and Capernaum (11.20-24), ignorance is ascribed to Jesus' interlocutors 12.7, the present 'gene-ration' is likened to an empty house (12.43-45), and the 'family' of Jesus is pointedly reconstrued (12.46-50). The Exodus, from the perspective of its internal drama, looked forward to 'rest' in the land of promise. Jeremiah called for a 'return' to the Lord (3.14, 4.1) a condition of peace (4.1), and of God's dwelling with Judah (7.30); also envisaged are the guilty as fleeing from the coming of the Lord (6.1). Matthew writes from the perspective of 'fourteen generations [after] the deportation to Babylon' (1.17c), and looks still for the 'meek to inherit the land'—the exile, so to speak, is still in progress. The tree brings forth bad as well as good fruit (12.33-37), weeds have been planted in the crop (13.24-30, 36-43), and ears and eyes remain inoperative (13.10-15). For the Gentiles who come, there is a yoke to assume and learning to be done; for the generation to 'return', a yoke must be taken up again and learning renewed. For Matthew, this coming and possible return are all centred around the figure of Jesus, as our parable clarifies by pointing to 'the strange labourer in their midst'. Although this 'strange' one speaks with his own authority,[17] he is contrasted in Matthew with those who 'teach human precepts as doctrines' (15.9)—hence our declension, in which the stranger is con-trasted with those who lay their own burdens on the backs of the workers.

---

17. Neusner, *Rabbi Talks,* calls attention to such presentations of Jesus as a teacher 'who speaks not as sage nor as a prophet... [so] that at issue is the figure of Jesus, not the teachings at all' (pp. 30-31).

'Take my *yoke'*

Jeremiah also speaks of the yoke: 'Long ago you broke your yoke and burst your bonds, and you said, "I will not serve!"' (2.20); 'But they all alike had broken the yoke, they had burst the bonds' (5.5b). In a moment of crisis, the prophet called the south to 'stand at the crossroads and look, and ask for the ancient paths, where the good way lies, and walk in it and find rest for your souls' (6.26)—without such wisdom, burnt offerings would be rendered useless, and the divinely-ordered stumbling block would have its effect (6.20-21). The gospel writer understands the drama he is depicting to be of the same critical nature. Like the prophet, his narrative is studded with leaders who 'deal falsely' (cf. Jer. 6.13) and who assume peace, when there is none—his polemic, intimated here, builds through ch. 12 (see especially 12.14), increases through the entry into Jerusalem and the parable of the tenants (21.33-46), until it reaches its climax in ch. 23 with the cry over Jerusalem. Moving across the web of interconnected Matthean metaphors, we can see in Jesus the figure of Wisdom, in the search for a dwelling place, who has again enacted a symbolic journey in search of a home. The place of rest comes finally in Jerusalem, but in ignominy before the triumph; or does Wisdom leave the 'desolate' home and abandon the city?

But what does the invitation to the yoke mean, as portrayed by Matthew, for those who take it on and so become disciples? Alongside the curses and lamenting there is an ongoing refrain of benediction: 'blessed are your eyes...' (13.16); 'then the righteous will shine like the sun' (13.43, and not simply like 'stars', cf. Dan. 12.3); 'and they praised the God of Israel' (15.31). In the gospel, the 'crossroads' is a time of reclaiming the old, but also of recognizing the new (13.51-52). The parables of ch. 13 picture the uprooting of the weeds, but also selling all for the pearl of superlative value, and catching fish of every kind. We also hear in summary about what it means to be 'trained for the kingdom', and so are led to understand these parables as part of that training, part of the gentle 'learning' put forward as an invitation.

Our own declined parable pulls together several of these Matthean themes. It incorporates the critique of ch. 23 ('they do not lift a finger') with the invitation to easy labour; it contrasts unscrupulous stewards with the strange 'labourer'; it suggests that the yoke is a double one, pulled by disciple and teacher together. This latter picture, by the way, finds a probable intertextual precedent (or parallel; the dating is uncertain) in Wisd. 9.10, where we read: 'Send her forth from the holy heavens...that she may labor at my side, and that I may learn what is pleasing to you'. Certainly double, rather than single yokes were the common picture in the ancient world, as born out also by the related word groups of both Hebrew and Greek (*'ol* and *semed; zygos, zeugos, heterozygeo, suzeugnymi, syzygos,* etc.). The logion in the gospel is uttered in the context of Jesus' work alongside his disciples; our declension accentuates the theme of synergy latent in the logion. In contrast, the enemy is pictured as those who are, for now, within the household, but unwilling to labour in good faith, and using the yoke of Torah as a form of oppression rather than for good.

'I will give you rest'

From this perspective, the rest to be sought is not the rest of inheriting or regaining the land (as in Exodus), but the larger rest towards which the Sabbath pointed. One writer has pointed out how the discovery of wisdom themes in our logion has also meant that *anapausis* has received only slight attention.[18] Matthew's concentration upon the 'Son of Man as Lord of the Sabbath' suggests that he understood that Israel's real Sabbath had broken in with the deeds and words of Jesus. Thus, Jesus' Sabbath 'infractions' are presented as fulfilment of the Torah of mercy and not as the abolition of the old ways. To take on the yoke in this way is to acknowledge that the Sabbath of Sabbaths has at last arrived: 'He will not break a bruised reed or quench a smoldering wick until he brings justice to victory' (Mt. 12.20); '[M]any prophets and righteous people longed to see what you see, but did not see it, and to hear what you hear, but did not hear it'. (13.17). In the drama of the gospel, this labouring leads inexorably to the cross (for both Jesus and his followers); but the words left ringing in the readers' ears are 'Teach...them to obey everything that I have commanded, and remember, I am with you always'. The bearing of the yoke *together* is the last picture invoked by this command and promise. In the words of our last declension, 'so they carried together, and found rest from enemies in the land'.

A Return to the Root

Each of our declensions, in typical parabolic manner, works by comparison, seeking to open up various possibilities in the Matthean logion. In

18. Laansma, *I Will Give You Rest*, p. 9.

reading the logion through parabolic variations, we continually ask what is being 'thrown alongside' what? In these four declensions alone, we have seen Jesus compared to wisdom, the yoke paradoxically juxtaposed with rest, Torah compared with a new way (or scribal interpretation of Torah contrasted with the interpretation of Jesus), knowledge thrown alongside humility, teacher compared with teacher (or even teacher compared with disciple). Each of these comparisons, while made in a direct way through the parabolic form, does no violence to the more allusive logion, but explicates possible readings.

Similarly, each declined parable, because of its narratival character, traces a turning-point in the drama. In deference to the logion's mysterious aspect, the parables have been framed so as to still leave some space for interpretation: how exactly does transformation of the one who encounters the 'Inviter' take place? The parables vary concerning the centrality of this yoke-giver, who nevertheless continues to remain in view, at the very least becoming a catalyst for transformation. (The perceptive reader will have noted my relative lack of enthusiasm for Declension Two as an adequate reading for the Matthean logion; it is not, however, entirely without merit.) In Mt. 11.28-30, the self-effacing character of the caller and the focus upon the one who calls are held in tension, through the interplay between the first person address and an allusive word that obscures the face of the one who calls. In this way, the logion shows greater capacity for subtlety than any parabolic refraction, which must speak *about* the speaker in a third person narrative.[19] After all, these parables are 'declensions', in every sense of the word, offering themselves as useful modes for understanding or using the original word, but declining from its full potential. Parables, by their nature, play out a plot, add complication and come to resolution. However, in Mt. 11.28-30 the moment of transformation is put forward as a promise, and requires the listener's participation to be enacted.

This logion of invitation, yoke and rest differs in both form and function from the parables we have suggested, despite the illuminating capacity of

19. If the reconstructions of some are correct, we might wonder how it is that this logion was not framed in a more directive and less ambiguous manner, shaped inexorably by the mytho-logical compulsion or 'reflective mythology' of the early Church. See the discussion of J.E. McKinlay, *Gendering*, pp. 180-82 and the suggestions of E. Schüssler Fiorenza, 'Wisdom Mythology and the Christological Hymns of the New Testament', in *Aspects of Wisdom in Judaism and Early Christianity* (ed. R.L. Wilken; Notre Dame: Notre Dame University Press, 1975), pp. 17-43.

the composed variations. There is no actual transformation to be traced in the Matthean logion, nor is there an evident hook to swallow, such as is frequently the case in worldview-demolishing parables. Mt. 11.28-30 presents instead a tantalizing mystery and promise—a lure, so to speak, rather than a hook. What are the 'mysteries of the kingdom'? Who is the one who speaks? What and whose is the yoke promised? How is the carrying of burdens related to rest? Come and see. Here is a gentler enigma than the typical parable, but one whose devastation might be felt were the invitation to be seized.

WISDOM'S CHILDREN JUSTIFIED (MT. 11.16-19; LK. 7.31-35)

Barbara E. Reid

Women's Experience

The parable of Wisdom justified by her children (Mt. 11.16-19// Lk. 7.31-35) strikes a resonant chord with the experience of many women. It expresses the frustration of Jesus and John the Baptist, Wisdom's children, whose prophetic message is not accepted by the people of their generation. Neither John's asceticism with his severe message of repentance, nor Jesus' inclusive table practices and his proclamation of good news, finds a hearing. The final verse, however, promises ultimate vindication. Wisdom will win out: she is justified by all her children, and by implication, her children share in her justification.

In like manner, Wisdom's female children in the church today continue to experience the frustration of having been schooled in her Word and in her ways, yet find resistance, rejection, and even vilification when they attempt to proclaim the Word or preside at the Eucharistic table. This gospel parable can offer hope to women today with its assurance of vindication for all of Wisdom's children.

In the following analysis I will argue that there are both pitfalls and promise for women in the parable as it now stands in the Gospels of Luke and Matthew. I will use historical and literary critical methods to analyze the biblical text, working from a feminist liberationist perspective. I presume that the gospels have been written by men, from a patriarchal and kyriarchal[1] worldview, primarily serving patriarchal interests. I further presume that some parables, possibly this one included, have been preserved in circles of women disciples, and that these affirmed and legitimated the discipleship and ministry of women in the early Christian communities. I expect, then, that there will be tension in the form of the

---

1.   E. Schüssler Fiorenza (*But She Said: Feminist Practices of Biblical Interpretation* [Boston: Beacon, 1992], p. 8) coined this term to describe the interlocking structures of domination by elite males over women and disadvantaged men.

tradition as we now have it in the text. Parables that would be liberative for women have been tamed by the male evangelists in the process of transmission.[2] I recognize that my social location as a white, North American, middle-class, middle-aged, well-educated woman, living as a vowed religious, teaching in a graduate school of theology and ministry in the Roman Catholic tradition, shapes my own interpretive lenses.

> *Mt. 11.16-19*
> [16]'But to what will I compare this generation? It is like children sitting in the marketplaces and calling to one another, [17]'We played the flute for you, and you did not dance; we wailed, and you did not mourn'. [18]For John came neither eating nor drinking, and they say, 'He has a demon'; [19]the Son of Man came eating and drinking, and they say, 'Look, a glutton and a drunkard, a friend of tax collectors and sinners!' Yet wisdom is vindicated by her deeds'.

> *Lk. 7.31-35*
> [31]'To what then will I compare the people of this generation, and what are they like? [32]They are like children sitting in the marketplace and calling to one another, 'We played the flute for you, and you did not dance; we wailed, and you did not weep'. [33]For John the Baptist has come eating no bread and drinking no wine, and you say, 'He has a demon'; [34]the Son of Man has come eating and drinking, and you say, 'Look, a glutton and a drunkard, a friend of tax collectors and sinners!' [35]Nevertheless, wisdom is vindicated by all her children'.[3]

Literary Context and Function

The Matthean and Lucan versions of the parable, which come from the Q source, are very close in wording. Both evangelists have situated the parable in the context of Jesus' Galilean ministry. Each has portrayed Jesus as having incurred both success and opposition. With this mixed reception in view, the parable functions in both Matthew and Luke to sharpen the question of how the hearer of the gospel will respond to Jesus. Although the wording and context are quite similar in both versions, there

---

2.   On Luke's redactional tendencies to downplay the ministries of women see e.g., B.E. Reid, *Choosing the Better Part? Women in the Gospel of Luke* (Collegeville, MN: Liturgical Press, 1996), 'Luke's Mixed Message for Women', *Chicago Studies* 38 (1999), pp. 283-97; T.K. Seim, *The Double Message. Patterns of Gender in Luke–Acts* (Nashville: Abingdon, 1994).

3.   Biblical quotations are from the New Revised Standard Version unless otherwise indicated.

are slightly different emphases that emerge in each, due to the evangelist's redactional changes and to the way in which the parable relates to the differing theological themes in each gospel.

The Coming One (Mt. 11.2-6//Lk. 7.18-23)
In both gospels, the parable comes as the third in a series of units taken from Q.[4] In the first unit, John the Baptist sends some of his disciples to Jesus to ascertain if he is 'the one who is to come'[5] or whether they should look for another. The introductory verses vary. Luke connects the unit to the previous episodes with the line, 'The disciples of John reported all these things to him' (7.18). Matthew begins with a notation that John is in prison, a detail Luke places in 3.20. Matthew specifies that what John heard about was 'the deeds of the Christ'. The deeds (ἔργα) of the Christ (11.2) and the deeds (ἔργων) of Wisdom (11.19) frame the unit and serve to equate Christ with Wisdom.

Jesus replies to the query about his identity as the 'one who is to come' by instructing John's disciples to report to him what they have seen and heard: how those who were blind now see, those who had been lame walk, those with leprosy are cleansed, those who were deaf now hear, dead people have been raised, and those made poor have had the good news proclaimed to them (Mt. 11.5//Lk. 7.22). For the reader of Luke's Gospel this litany recalls Jesus' initial proclamation of his mission in Lk. 4.18 (modeled on Isa. 61.1-2). Both evangelists have depicted Jesus healing people who were blind (Mt. 9.27-31; Lk. 7.21), paralyzed (Mt. 8.5-13; 9.1-7//Lk. 5.17-26), leprous (Mt. 8.1-4//Lk. 12.5-16), and deaf and mute (Mt. 9.32-34//Lk.11.14-15). Both show Jesus raising dead people (Mt. 9.18-26//Lk. 8.40-56) and proclaiming good news (Mt. 4.17; 11.1; Lk. 4.43; 8.1).

Jesus' response to John's disciples underscores how their seeing should answer their question about the one for whom they are looking. Against the background of Isa. 35.5-6—

---

4.   In Matthew this section is part of a larger unit, 11.2-13.58 in which the questions of Jesus' identity and the significance of his deeds and teaching are central. See C. Deutsch, *Lady Wisdom, Jesus, and the Sages* (Valley Forge, PA: Trinity Press International, 1996), pp. 46-65.

5.   This expression does not appear in the Hebrew Scriptures as a messianic title. But see Ps. 118.26; Mal. 3.1; Isa. 59.20.

> Then the eyes of the blind shall be opened,
> and the ears of the deaf unstopped;
> then the lame shall leap like a deer,
> and the tongue of the speechless sing for joy.
> For waters shall break forth in the wilderness,
> and streams in the desert.

—it should be evident that Jesus is, indeed, the one issuing in the messianic era. Jesus' concluding word, 'Blessed is the one who takes no offense at me' (Mt. 11.6//Lk. 7.23) points ahead to the parable, which contrasts the desired response with the petulant refusal of the children in the marketplace. It furthers the recurring theme of the divided responses to Jesus' deeds.

Seeing and Believing

The theme of seeing and believing is particularly pronounced in the Gospel of Luke and is central to each of the four units in Lk. 7.18-50. While restoring physical sight is part of Jesus' mission (4.18), seeing is also a metaphor for perceiving the word of God.[6] Seeing Jesus' deeds of power is meant to lead one to glorify God (Lk. 5.26; 17.15-16; 18.35-43; 23.47)[7] and to follow Jesus (18.35-43). This theme is already sounded in the infancy narratives and is carried through all the way to the resurrection appearance stories. The shepherds, after seeing the newborn Jesus, 'returned, glorifying and praising God for all they had heard and seen' (Lk. 2.20). Simeon declares, 'my eyes have seen your salvation, which you have prepared in the presence of all peoples' (Lk. 2.30-31). The post-resurrection understanding of the disciples en route to Emmaus is described as 'their eyes were opened' (Lk. 24.31).

Seeing does not, however, always lead to believing. Both Matthew and Luke preserve sayings of Jesus in which he warns his disciples about the dangers of looking but not seeing, and hearing but not understanding (Mt. 13.13//Lk. 8.10). He later tells them, 'Blessed are the eyes that see what you see! For I tell you that many prophets and kings desired to see what you see, but did not see it, and to hear what you hear, but did not hear it'(Lk. 10.23-24//Mt. 13.16-17).

In unit one the reader is confronted with all the evidence to confirm the

---

6. See A. Culpepper, 'Seeing the Kingdom of God: The Metaphor of Sight in the Gospel of Luke', *CurTM* 21 (1994), pp. 434-43.

7. See D. Hamm, 'What the Samaritan Leper Sees: Narrative Christology of Luke 17.11-19', *CBQ* 56 (1994), pp. 273-87.

identification of Jesus as the one who is to come. In the next segment John's identity is clarified, which leads to the parable in the third unit which contrasts the styles of the two, while showing that they share the same rejection.

Looking for a Prophet (Mt. 11.7-19//Lk. 7.24-30)
Central to each of these three episodes is the identification of both John and Jesus as prophets. The first episode, with the allusion to Mal. 3.23, which speaks of the return of Elijah before the coming day of the Lord, establishes that Jesus is the coming one to whom the prophets pointed.[8] The second unit turns to the identification of John as a prophet 'and more than a prophet' (Mt. 11.9//Lk. 7.26).

Three times Jesus asks the crowd, 'What did you go out to see?' If they have objections to John's unbending asceticism, as opposed to a reed shaken by the wind, or are offended by his rugged dress (Mt. 3.4) in contrast to those decked out in gorgeous apparel, Jesus tells the crowds they are looking for the wrong thing in the wrong places. Those seeking a prophet will not only find one, but the very prophet of whom Malachi spoke, the messenger who prepares the way for the coming one. While there is differentiation in their roles,[9] both John and Jesus are presented here as powerful prophets of God. The third unit will underscore that the two prophets suffer the same divided response to their ministry as does every messenger of God.

Transition (Mt. 11.12-15; Lk. 7.29-30)
Matthew and Luke diverge in the transitional verses between these two Q units and the third one which contains the parable. Mt. 11.12 inserts a

---

8.   Very few prophets besides Jesus appear in the Third Gospel. Zechariah prophesies as he speaks his canticle (1.67). Gabriel announces that John the Baptist 'will be called prophet of the Most High' (1.76; see also 3.2; 20.6). Anna is the last prophet (2.36) mentioned before Jesus assumes this role. Luke casts Jesus as the promised 'prophet like Moses' of Deut. 18.15 (Lk. 9.28-36; Acts 3.22-23; 7.37). He also emulates the prophets Elijah and Elisha in his miracle working (Lk. 4.25-27; 7.11-17; 9.8, 10-17, 19, 30-33, 51). A particular Lucan theme is that of Jesus as rejected prophet (Lk. 4.24, 39; 13.33; 24.19-20; Acts 7.52). See further J.A. Fitzmyer, *The Gospel According to Luke I–IX* (AB, 28; Garden City, NY: Doubleday, 1981), pp. 213-15; R. O'Toole, 'The Parallels Between Jesus and Moses', *BTB* 20 (1990), pp. 22-29; R.E. Brown, 'Jesus and Elisha', *Perspective* 12 (1971), pp. 84-104.

9.   The subordination of John to Jesus, while stated in Mt. 11.11//Lk. 7.28, is not the main focus here. Both are prophets who have a similar reception and rejection.

sobering note about the violence suffered by the reign of heaven. Most likely this refers to Herod's actions against John and the violent opposition of other like-minded adversaries that attempt to block the coming of God's realm.[10] Matthew then asserts, 'For all the prophets and the law prophesied until John came; and if you are willing to accept it, he is Elijah who is to come' (11.13-14). There is an ambiguity as to whether Matthew is saying that John belongs to the new age with Jesus or whether he is the end figure of the age of the prophets and the Law. Matthew then explicitly identifies John with Elijah (v. 14). The quotation from Malachi in v. 10 has prepared for this. More than *a* prophet, John is *the* prophet who prepares God's people for the coming one who issues in the messianic age. Matthew concludes with an exhortation for anyone who has ears to hear (v. 15).[11]

Lk. 16.16 preserves a slightly different version of the sayings in Mt. 11.12-13 in a different context. Both Matthew and Luke consider John a prophet who bridges two stages of salvation history. But there is no exact Lucan parallel to Mt. 11.14. While Lk. 7.27 (// Mt. 11.10) casts John the Baptist as a new Elijah in his role as precursor of the coming one (so also Lk. 1.17, 76), the third evangelist suppresses the identification of John with Elijah in favour of portraying Jesus as the new Elijah in the role of eschatological prophet and miracle worker.[12]

Luke's transitional verses to the parable (7.29-30) set the scene differently from Matthew. In v. 29 Luke states that 'all the people who listened, including the tax collectors, and who were baptized with the baptism of John, acknowledged the justice of God [ἐδικαίωσαν τὸν θεόν]'. Balancing this statement is the conclusion of the parable about

10. Another alternative is that 'the kingdom of God is entering the world with explosive power and those who earnestly desire to enter it pay any price to become disciples' (J.P. Meier, *Matthew* [NTM, 3; Wilmington, DE: Glazier, 1980], p. 122).

11. A reprise of this exhortation appears in Mt. 13.43//Lk. 8.8.

12. Luke retains allusions to Elijah in reference to Jesus from his Marcan source in Lk. 3.16; 8.22-25; 9.8, 10-17, 19; 22.33, 39. Twice, Luke adds details to a Marcan story to highlight the parallel with Elijah: Lk. 4.2; 5.12. Many of the parallels between Jesus and Elijah are peculiarly Lucan: 4.16-30; 6.12; 7.11-17; 9.51, 54, 61-62; 12.49; 17.16; 19.1; 24.49; Acts 1.9. The Lucan Jesus rejects, however, the role of fiery reformer in 9.54, where James and John want him to call down fire from heaven as did Elijah. Another difference between Jesus and Elijah is found in Lk. 9.61-62, where potential followers of Jesus are not allowed to look back after putting the hand to the plow (cf. 1 Kgs 19.20). See further Fitzmyer, *Luke*, pp. 213-15; J.A.T. Roberts, 'Elijah, John and Jesus: An Essay in Detection', *NTS* 4 (1957-58), pp. 263-81; R. Swaeles, 'Jésus, nouvel Elie, dans saint Luc', *AsSeign* 69 (1964), pp. 41-66.

the children in the marketplace, 'Nevertheless, wisdom is vindicated [ἐδικαιώθη] by all her children' (7.35). The verb δικαιόω frames the Lucan version of the parable and sharpens its impact. In Lk. 7.29-30, the contrast is clearly set forth: there are those who are in right relation with God and those who are not. Those who have rightly perceived John the Baptist as God's prophet, and have accepted his baptism, are in right relation with God (7.29). The Pharisees and scholars of the law who have not so responded have rejected God's purposes (7.30). The parable then further elaborates on the rejection by 'this generation' of the offer made by God through John and Jesus (7.31-34). The concluding verse (7.35) affirms that despite this rejection, divine justification prevails.

The Parable of the Children in the Marketplace
(Mt. 11.16-19//Lk. 7.31-35)

There are few differences between the two versions of the parable. Minor variations in wording are not greatly significant until the concluding verse.[13] The structure is the same in both versions. The parable opens with a simile (Mt. 11.16//Lk. 7.31-32), followed by an explanation (Mt. 11.17-19a//Lk. 7.33-34, and a concluding saying (Mt. 11.19b//Lk. 7.35).[14]

Like many parables, the introductory verses set up a comparison, using the verb ὁμοιόω, 'to liken', and the adjective ὅμοιος.[15] The Aramaic *l^e* underlies these expressions and should be translated, 'It is the case with… as with…'[16] Thus, the comparison is not only between the characters 'this generation' and 'children', but involves the whole situation described. As will be clear below, there are two groups of children envisioned, one of which is the cipher for 'this generation'.

13. Matthew's elimination of ὁ βαπτιστής, ἄρτον and οἶνον in v. 18, for example, accords with his tendency to eliminate extraneous details. For detailed analysis of the differences in the two versions and a reconstruction of the text from Q, see W.J. Cotter, 'The Parable of the Children in the Market-Place, Q(Lk) 7.31-35: An Examination of the Parable's Image and Significance', *NovT* 29 (1987), pp. 289-304.

14. For analysis of the tradition history of the parable, see Fitzmyer, *Gospel According to Luke*, pp. 677-79; J.P. Meier, *A Marginal Jew. Rethinking the Historical Jesus* 2 (ABRL; Garden City, NY: Doubleday, 1994), pp. 144-54.

15. So also Mk 4.30; Lk. 6.47-49; 12.36; 13.18-21; Mt. 7.24, 26; 11.16; 13.24, 31, 33, 44, 45, 47, 52; 18.23; 20.1; 22.2; 25.1.

16. J. Jeremias, *The Parables of Jesus* (2nd rev. edn; New York: Charles Scribner's Sons, 1972), p. 101.

'The people of this generation' (γενεά)[17] are compared to children sitting in the marketplace calling to one another.[18] Both Matthew and Luke use the word γενεά, 'generation', in a pejorative sense. Disciples who are unable to cast out a demon are dubbed a 'faithless and perverse generation' (Mt. 17.17//Lk. 9.41). Jesus declares 'this generation' that seeks signs an 'evil generation' that will be condemned (Mt. 12.39-42; 16.4//Lk. 11.29-32).[19] Likewise, Jesus asserts, 'this generation' will be 'charged with the blood of all the prophets shed from the foundation of the world' (Lk. 11.50-51//Mt. 23.36). And he predicts to his disciples that he will suffer and be rejected by 'this generation' (Lk. 17.25).[20] While God offers mercy 'from generation to generation' (Lk. 1.50), the predominantly pejorative use of γενεά signals a likely negative response in this parable.

The parable likens 'this generation' to a group of children who stubbornly refuse to play with another group. No matter what the one group offers, whether pretending at wedding, or at funeral, the others refuse to participate.[21] The explanation in the next two verses relates this metaphor to the negative reception of the invitations issued by John and Jesus. 'This generation' responded to neither John's 'dirge' nor to Jesus' 'flute'.

The children seated in the marketplace introduces an image connected with court proceedings.[22] As the center of public life, the ἀγορά, market-

17. The difference between Luke's τοὺς ἀνθρώπους τῆς γενεᾶς ταύτης and Matthew's τὴν γενεὰν ταύτην is not significant.

18. Whereas Luke implies two groups calling out to one another, ἀλλήλοις, Matthew implies that there is only one group speaking τοῖς ἑτέροις, 'to others'. This difference in detail does not significantly change the meaning.

19. This passage makes a similar juxtaposition as Lk. 7.31-35 of a reference to Wisdom and a condemnation of 'this generation' for not responding positively to the prophets sent by God.

20. The pejorative use of γενεά continues in Acts. In his Pentecost speech Peter admonishes, 'Save yourselves from this corrupt generation' (2.40). In Acts 8.33; 14.16 γενεά is used of past generations whose purposes were opposite God's. There is a more positive nuance in two instances: God offers mercy from 'generation to generation' (Lk. 1.50), and 'all generations' recognize Mary's blessedness (Lk. 1.48). More neutral uses of γενεά occur in Lk. 16.8; 21.32 (// Mt. 21.32); Acts 13.36; 15.21.

21. Some see the figure in Luke's account as two groups of children, each wanting to play a different game. One group wants to pretend at wedding, the other at funeral, but they cannot agree. Matthew clearly has one group offering two different games to another unresponsive group. It is likely that Luke also is to be understood this way.

22. The insight that the image of the children sitting in the marketplace is one of judgment is Cotter's (see above, n. 14). She equates 'the children who call' with 'this generation', who falsely sit in judgment on John and Jesus. Because of the association

place, was the locale for commercial, social, religious, and civic inter-change. One might expect children in the ἀγορά to be running and chasing after one another in their play, not sitting while voicing their complaint about their unresponsive potential playmates. The verb κάθημαι, 'sit', is frequently associated with judgment, as in Mt. 27.19, for example, where Pilate sits on the βῆμα when Jesus is brought before him.[23] That the ἀγορά was used for court proceedings is evident from Acts 16.19, where Paul and Silas were dragged into the ἀγορά to be judged by the magistrates. In addition the verb προσφωνέω ('to call out to') connotes formal address, such as would take place in a court context (Lk. 23.20; Acts 21.40; 22.2).

The image, then, presented in the opening line of the parable introduces a note of judgment. It makes clear that John and Jesus' invitation is not merely a game in which children can participate or not as they will. Rather, it points toward the serious consequences that incur for those who refuse their call. The final verse, using another term from the legal world, δικαιόω, 'to justify', completes the court proceedings with the handing down of the verdict.

Calling and Banqueting

The auditory imagery of voices calling, flutes playing, dirges being sung (Mt. 11.17//Lk. 7.32) shifts to a culinary theme (Mt. 11.18-19a//Lk. 7.33-34). Both themes are associated with Wisdom's invitation to life and point forward to the final verse (Mt. 11.19b//Lk. 7. 35). Just as Wisdom sent out servant girls, calling from the highest places in the town (Prov. 9.3), so John called out his invitation in the desert (Mt. 3.3 //Lk. 3.4) and Jesus called out his message for anyone with ears to hear (Mt. 13.9//Lk. 8.8). Wisdom's invitation, like that of Yahweh (Isa. 25.6; 55.1; Ps. 23.5) is cast in terms of eating her bread and drinking her wine (Prov. 9.5). In like manner, banqueting with Jesus is associated with response to his invitation to discipleship.[24]

But just as Wisdom is rejected by the foolish (Sir. 15.7-8) so John is

of the verb προσφωνέω ('to call out to') with Jesus and the application of the parable to John and Jesus in Mt. 11.18-19//Lk. 7.33-34, I understand Jesus and John to be the ones calling and the agents of judgment.

23. For other examples of such usage see BAGD, s.v. κάθημαι, p. 491 and Cotter, 'Children in the Marketplace', pp. 299-301.

24. This theme is more prominent in Luke (5.30, 33; 7.36-50; 10.7; 11.37; 12.19, 22, 29, 45; 13.26; 14.7-24; 15.2; 17.8, 27, 28; 22.7-20, 30; 24.43), but is also present in Matthew (8.11; 9.11; 14.13-21; 15.27, 32-39; 22.1-14; 25.10; 26.17-29).

dismissed[25] as having a demon (as is Jesus in Mt. 12.24//Lk. 11.15), and Jesus is accused of being a glutton and a drunkard. This charge alludes to Deut. 21.20, where the phrase refers to a rebellious son. The final verse shows that this perception is false: Luke asserts that Jesus is a true son of Wisdom; Matthew makes him Wisdom incarnate. The additional slur that he is a friend of toll collectors and sinners surfaces a charge that reappears in both the Gospels of Matthew and Luke. Both evangelists interpret Jesus' table companionship with toll collectors and sinners as part of his missionary strategy to bring all into right relation. This is especially evident in the call of Matthew/Levi (Mt. 9.9-13; Lk. 5.27-32) and in Lk. 15.1-32, where the objection to Jesus' eating with tax collectors and sinners is voiced by his opponents.[26]

Wisdom's Children (Lk. 7.35)
It is in the final verse of the parable that there is the most significant divergence between Matthew and Luke. Most scholars hold that Luke has the more original wording: 'Yet Wisdom is justified by all her children'. The divine is portrayed as Lady Wisdom, whose justification is made evident by her children, preeminently, John and Jesus. Unlike the Gospel of Matthew, Luke does not identify Jesus with Wisdom. There are only a few explicit associations of Jesus with Wisdom in the Third Gospel. The infancy narratives assert that the child Jesus was filled with and grew in wisdom (Lk. 2.40, 52), and in Lk. 21.15 Jesus promises to give his disciples 'words and a wisdom' that none of their opponents will be able

25. Matthew uses ἐκόψασθε ('you did not mourn') in v. 17 where Luke has ἐκλαύσατε ('you did not weep', v. 32). In light of Matthew's use of the verb κόπτω in 24.30 (where Matthew has redacted Mark 13.26 in the 'Little Apocalypse') his redaction here may be intended to heighten the sense of eschatological urgency of John's mission. See Deutsch, *Lady Wisdom*, p. 50.

26. There are several other significant references to tax collectors in both Gospels. In the First Gospel, Matthew the tax collector is one of the Twelve (Mt. 10.3). In a saying unique to Matthew (21.31-32), Jesus asserts that tax collectors and prostitutes are entering the reign of God ahead of the chief priests and elders who oppose him. Significantly their response to John is mentioned here, akin to Lk. 3.12 where tax collectors are among those who ask to be baptized by John. Luke also has a parable in which a tax collector is justified rather than a Pharisee (18.10-14), and he tells of Zacchaeus, the chief tax collector, to whom salvation comes when he invites Jesus to eat in his home (19.1-10). One other reference to tax collectors occurs in Matthew's Sermon on the Mount. Jesus is exhorting his disciples to expand the bounds of their love, not to love only those who love them, since even tax collectors do this (Mt. 5.46). The parallel verse in Lk. 6.33 states that even sinners do this.

to withstand or contradict. In Lk. 11.49 it is unclear whether the reference to the 'Wisdom of God' speaking is to God or to Jesus.

The Lucan version of the parable advances the theme of justification, or right relation. While Paul and Matthew are more noted for this theme, it also plays an important role in the Third Gospel. In addition to Lk. 7.29, 35, the verb δικαιόω, 'to justify', occurs five more times in Luke and Acts. Twice in the Gospel it is used in a pejorative way to depict characters who try to justify themselves: the scholar of the law in 10.29 and the Pharisees in 16.15. In Lk. 18.14 the toll collector returns home from the Temple justified. In Acts 13.38-39, Paul speaks of all who were not able to be justified by the Law of Moses who are now justified by belief in Jesus.

The adjective δίκαιος, 'righteous', describes Zechariah and Elizabeth (1.6), Simeon (2.25), Joseph of Arimathea (23.50), Cornelius (Acts 10.22), and occurs in nine other sayings about the upright.[27] The adverb δικαίως, 'just', occurs once in Lk. 23.41 where it refers to the two criminals who have been justly condemned. The noun δικαιοσύνη, 'justification', occurs once in the Third Gospel, in Zechariah's prayer to serve God in holiness and righteousness (1.75).[28]

Most notable is that Luke changed the climactic declaration of the centurion at the death of Jesus from 'Truly this man was God's Son!' (Mk 15.39) to 'Certainly this man was innocent (δίκαιος)' (Lk. 23.47). In the Acts of the Apostles 'the Righteous One' (ὁ δίκαιος) becomes a title of Jesus in three key speeches (Acts 3.14; 7.52; 22.14).

The Lucan parable has a sorrowful edge to it, yet also a note of triumph. While there seems little hope in the Gospel that 'this generation' will respond positively to the invitation offered by God's prophets, John and Jesus, the invitation continues to be put forth. Right relation with God, personified as Wisdom, will ultimately prevail, as some will heed her call, and will banquet with her, as her true, upright children. Her child John embraced his mission 'to turn the hearts of parents to their children, and the disobedient to the wisdom of the righteous, to make ready a people prepared for the Lord' (Lk. 1.17). Her son Jesus went to his death trying to gather Jerusalem's children under his wings, despite their unwillingness (Lk. 13.34). To these exemplary children of Wisdom are added all those[29] who have embraced her invitation and who in turn speak it in their day.

27. Lk. 1.17; 5.32; 12.57; 14.14; 15.7; 18.9; 20.20; Acts 4.19; 24.15.
28. It occurs four other times in Acts 10.35; 13.10; 17.31; 24.25.
29. Luke's addition of 'all' in v. 35 reflects his tendency to universalize, as also in 4.15; 5.26; 7.16; 9.43; 18.43; 19.37.

The Parable Illustrated (Lk. 7.36-50)
The final episode of Lk. 7 brings to a climax the themes of seeing and
believing, justification, and proper recognition of Jesus as prophet, through
a colourful illustration of the on-going divided response to Jesus with two
contrasting characters. A woman who had been a sinner and who has
experienced forgiveness through Jesus acts with lavish gestures of love
toward him at the home of a Pharisee. By means of a parable (7.41-43),
Jesus confronts Simon with his incorrect perceptions. The woman is no
longer the sinner Simon sees her to be, and Jesus is the prophet Simon
does not suppose him to be (7.39). The two perceptions are intimately
linked. The key question, 'Do you see this woman?' (7.44a), and Jesus'
elaboration on what he sees (7.44b-47), confronts Simon with the necessity
to see the woman differently if he is to correctly perceive Jesus' identity.
Will he accept the invitation to become a child of Wisdom by accepting
her envoy who comes eating and drinking with sinners? Will Simon and
the others at table (7.49) remain solidified in their inability to see
themselves as the sinners Jesus has come to befriend in this banquet?[30]

Wisdom Personified (Mt. 11.19)
The redactional change of Matthew in his final verse makes Jesus himself
Wisdom personified, not simply a child of Wisdom. Just as Lady Wisdom
spoke in streets and marketplaces (Prov. 1.20-21) and found herself
rejected (Sir. 15.7-8; Wisd. 10.3; Bar. 3.12), so does Jesus who now
personifies her. The image of Jesus piping a tune evokes that of Lady
Wisdom the hymnist (1QPsa 18.12). The rejection of Jesus as prophet is
akin to that of Woman Wisdom, a prophet whose words of reproof are
ignored (Prov. 1.23-25). Jesus' eating and drinking recalls Wisdom, who
spreads her banquet and invites, 'Come, eat of my bread and drink of the
wine I have mixed' (Prov. 9.5). That Jesus' works (ἔργα, Mt. 11.2, 19)
identify his relation to God is akin to Wisdom Woman's participation in
God's works (ἔργα) at creation (Prov. 8.22-31). The language of
righteousness used of Jesus in Mt. 11.19 is evocative of Lady Wisdom,
who walks in the way of righteousness (δικαιοσύνη Prov. 8.20) and who
speaks with all righteous (δικαιοσύνη, Prov. 8.8).[31]

---

30. See further Reid, *Choosing the Better Part?*, pp. 107-23.

31. The theme of righteousness is a particularly Matthean theme. The noun
δικαιοσύνη appears in material peculiar to Matthew in 3.15; 5.10, 20; 6.1; 21.32.
Twice it occurs as a Matthean addition to Q sayings: Mt. 5.6 (// Lk. 6.21); Mt. 6.33 (//
Lk. 12.31). In addition to 11.19 the verb δικαιόω occurs in 12.37, a saying unique to

Matthew's portrayal of Jesus as Wisdom personified is most explicit in Mt. 11.19, but continues to surface throughout the Gospel.[32] It is a theme that first appears in Mt. 8.18-22 where the homelessness of the Human One recalls the rejection of Wisdom and her resultant homelessness on earth (Prov. 1.20; Sir. 24.7).[33] The whole of Mt. 11 shows the deeds of Christ (11.2) clearly identified with the deeds of Wisdom (11.19). With his redactional changes, Matthew has relativized the role of John and has sharpened the focus on the deeds of power of Jesus. The emphasis falls on the rejection of Jesus-Wisdom, not on the Elijah-like forerunner.

Concrete examples of towns that have rejected Jesus follow in Mt. 11.20-24.[34] The emphasis continues on the mighty deeds[35] of Jesus as the

Matthew. The adjective δίκαιος is found in peculiarly Matthean material in 1.19; 10.41; 13.43, 49; 20.4; 23.28; 25.37, 46; 27.4, 19, 24 and in Matthean redaction of Q material in Mt. 5.45 (// Lk. 6.28); 13.17 (// Lk. 10.24); Mt. 23.29 (// Lk. 11.47); Mt. 23.35 (// Lk. 11.50). Once it occurs in a saying from the triple tradition: Mt. 9.13//Mk 2.17//Lk. 5.32. It is important to note two instances in which δικαιοσύνη is associated with John the Baptist: Mt. 3.15 and 21.32.

32. J.M. Suggs (*Wisdom, Christology and Law in Matthew's Gospel* [Cambridge, MA: Harvard University Press, 1970]) was the first to delineate how Matthew transformed Q traditions, which depicted Jesus as one of Wisdom's rejected messengers, into a portrayal of Jesus as Wisdom personified. His work was furthered by F.W. Burnett (*The Testament of Jesus-Sophia: A Redaction-Critical Study of the Eschatological Discourse in Matthew* [Lanham, MD: University Press of America, 1981]) and C. Deutsch (*Hidden Wisdom and the Easy Yoke: Wisdom, Torah and Discipleship in Matthew 11.25-30* [JSOTSup 18; Sheffield, JSOT Press, 1987]; *Lady Wisdom, Jesus, and the Sages* [Valley Forge, PA: Trinity Press International, 1996]). D. Senior (*The Gospel of Matthew* [IBT; Nashville: Abingdon, 1997], p. 120) believes that 'Matthew intends to portray Jesus through the biblical metaphor of 'wisdom', the embodiment of God's presence in Israel'. Others, e.g., M. Johnson ('Reflections on a Wisdom Approach to Matthew's Christology', *CBQ* 36 [1974], pp. 44-64) are not convinced of the pervasiveness of the Wisdom christology in Matthew. D. Harrington (*The Gospel of Matthew* [SacPag 1; Collegeville: The Liturgical Press, 1991], p. 158) thinks the identification of Jesus with Sophia is clear enough in Mt. 11.25-30, but not as convincing for Mt. 11.19. F.T. Gench (*Wisdom in the Christology of Matthew* [Lanham, MD: University Press of America, 1997]) argues that wisdom motifs are present in Matthew, but not a Wisdom christology that identifies Jesus with Sophia. On Wisdom Christology in Q, see J.S. Kloppenborg, 'Wisdom Christology in Q', *Laval théologique et philosophie* 34 (1978), pp. 129-47; R.S. Sugirtharajah, 'Wisdom, Q, and a Proposal for a Christology', *ExpTim* 102 (1990), pp. 42-46; R.A. Piper, *Wisdom in the Q-Tradition* (SNTSMS 61; Cambridge: Cambridge University Press, 1989).

33. Deutsch, *Lady Wisdom*, pp. 43-45.

34. Luke places these reproaches in a different context: Lk. 10.12-15.

towns of Chorazin, Bethsaida, and Capernaum are excoriated for being like the petulant children in the marketplace, who have not responded to the mighty deeds of Jesus. The final section of ch. 11 (vv. 25-30) completes the identification of Jesus with Wisdom. In a thanksgiving prayer from Q[36] and the peculiarly Matthean invitation to rest (vv. 28-30) Jesus, like Wisdom, is shown to be the sage who teaches apocalyptic mysteries, interprets Torah, and calls disciples.[37] The invitation to come for instruction and to submit to Wisdom's yoke echoes Sir. 51.13-20. The linking of Wisdom's yoke and the promise of rest are similar to Sir. 6.18-37. In subsequent chapters Jesus is not only identified with Wisdom, but he is also teacher of Wisdom (12.1-8, 9-14; 13.1-53), interpreter of the Torah, revealer of eschatological mysteries, and possessor of Wisdom (12.41-42). The theme is rounded out in Mt. 13.54-58, where Wisdom and mighty deeds ($\delta\upsilon\nu\acute{\alpha}\mu\epsilon\iota\varsigma$) go hand in hand with one more query about Jesus' identity (13.54). Here the setting is his home town, where Jesus is not able to work many mighty deeds because of the townspeoples' lack of faith (13.58). The final portrayal of the Matthean Jesus as Wisdom is found in 23.34-36, 37-39, where Matthew places Wisdom's words on the lips of Jesus and shows them actualized in the present in him.[38]

The Function of the Parable
This parable serves as a vehicle for reflection on the mixed reception experienced by Jesus and his forerunner, John, and for subsequent followers who encounter the same. One of the functions of the parable is christological. It confirms that Jesus is the Coming One who ushers in the messianic age.[39] The complex of episodes to which the parable belongs

35. Although the term in Mt. 11.20, 23 is $\delta\upsilon\nu\acute{\alpha}\mu\epsilon\iota\varsigma$ rather than $\acute{\epsilon}\rho\gamma\alpha$, the emphasis is the same.

36. Luke's version is in a different context in 10.21-22.

37. Deutsch, *Lady Wisdom*, pp. 54-60.

38. The Lucan version of the saying (11.49), which probably preserves the original Q form, relays the saying in the third person, 'Therefore also the Wisdom of God said...' Matthew redacts the saying to the second person, changes the future tense of Q's $\acute{\alpha}\pi o\sigma\tau\epsilon\lambda\hat{\omega}$ to the present $\acute{\alpha}\pi o\sigma\tau\acute{\epsilon}\lambda\lambda\omega$ and adds an emphatic $\acute{\epsilon}\gamma\grave{\omega}$, thus solidifying the identification of Jesus as Wisdom, placing her words on his lips and showing their present actualization in him.

39. If there are circles of followers of John the Baptist in the purview of these Christian communities, the parable may also serve to establish that Jesus, not John, is the awaited one.

raises questions such as: What have you seen? What are you looking for? Where are you looking? How will you respond? These help explain that predetermined attitudes and expectations can keep some from perceiving correctly the One who is the envoy of Wisdom, or even Wisdom herself personified. The consequences of blindness or petulance are not neutral: judgment will ensue and these will not be counted among Wisdom's children.

In the Lucan community, where a prime tension point was inclusive table companionship, the parable most likely served to further that discussion of that issue by anchoring the community's inclusive practice in that of the just Jesus, Wisdom's child. In Matthew's community, where their self-definition in relation to those Jews who did not follow Jesus was a major concern, the parable most likely served to legitimate the teaching of Matthean leaders over that of their rivals. Opposition and rejection, then, are not signs of failure, but are seen as signs of legitimation for those who follow in the footsteps of the rejected Jesus and his predecessor.

Promise and Pitfall

From a feminist perspective this parable opens up both promise and pitfalls. First, the promise. The parable brings to the fore the image of Sophia as the female personification of the Divine.[40] The Wisdom traditions in the books of Job, Proverbs, Sirach, Wisdom of Solomon, and Baruch portray Sophia as the female personification of God's creative and saving action in the world:

> She fashions all that exists and pervades it with her pure and people-loving spirit. She is all-knowing, all-powerful, and present everywhere, renewing all things. Active in Creation, she also works in history to save her chosen people, guiding and protecting them through the vicissitudes of liberating struggle. Her powerful words have the mark of divine address, making the huge claim that listening to them will bring salvation while disobedience will bring destruction. She sends her servants to proclaim her invitation to communion. By her light kings govern justly and the unjust meet their punishment. She is involved in relationships of loving, seeking, and finding

40. In addition to providing a rich resource for female language for God, E. Schüssler Fiorenza has shown that the retrieval of Jewish and Christian discourses on Divine Wisdom also provides a framework for developing a feminist ecological theology of creation and a religious ethos that is inclusive of other religious visions. See 'The Sisters of Wisdom-Sophia: Justified by All Her Children', in *Sharing Her Word* (Boston: Beacon, 1998), pp. 160-83.

with human beings. Whoever loves her receives what in other scriptural texts is given by God alone.[41]

All these characteristics and activities ascribed to Sophia in the biblical Wisdom traditions are elsewhere attributed to Yahweh. To speak of the Divine in equivalent female terms is essential both for a fuller understanding of God and for an egalitarian theological anthropology. While no metaphor adequately encompasses the reality of God, to speak of the Divine without female metaphors overlooks whole strands of biblical tradition and results in a greatly impoverished theology. Moreover, without female images of God women are never seen as created in God's image. Violence against women and idolatrous male hegemony reigns unchecked.

Jewish Wisdom theology was not the creator of such female discourse about the Divine. Rather, it incorporated elements of the goddess cult, especially that of Isis, into its tradition.[42] By using current categories of goddess language, Wisdom writers spoke of the God of Israel in ways that had contemporary appeal. The remarkable thing was that it was able to do this without sacrificing its monotheism and without becoming assimilated to those cults.

Christian tradition takes another large step in the articulation of the Divine in female categories when Jesus is depicted with characteristics of Wisdom. Not only Matthew, but other early Christian writers say of Jesus what had also been said of Sophia, 'he is the image of the invisible God' (Col. 1.15), 'the one through whom all things were made' (1 Cor. 8.6), 'the power of God and the wisdom of God' (1 Cor. 1.22-24). The Fourth Gospel also portrays Jesus as personified Wisdom, though the terminology used is Logos instead of Sophia.[43] The promise inherent in such articulations is that when Wisdom categories are used of Jesus, then it is clear that the saving significance of Christ does not reside in his maleness. As Sophia incarnate, the Christ integrates divine femaleness with human maleness, overcoming gender dualism.[44] Wisdom christology enables both

41. E.A. Johnson, *She Who Is: The Mystery of God in Feminist Theological Discourse* (New York: Crossroad, 1992), p. 91. See also her article, 'Jesus, the Wisdom of God', *ETL* 61 (1985), pp. 261-94.

42. E. Schüssler Fiorenza, *In Memory of Her. A Feminist Theological Reconstruction of Christian Origins* (New York: Crossroad, 1984), pp. 130-40.

43. R.E. Brown, *The Gospel According to John* (AB 29A; Garden City, NY: Doubleday, 1966), pp. cxxv, 521-23.

44. E. Wainwright, *Shall We Look For Another? A Feminist Rereading of the*

women and men to see themselves as children of Wisdom, made in her image, redeemed in her love, and continuing her mission.

There are also dangers inherent in the effort to retrieve biblical Wisdom traditions. First, there can be a temptation to use Divine Wisdom to romanticize notions of femininity, which results in reinscribing gender dualism.[45] Extolling the feminine qualities of Divine Lady Wisdom can unwittingly make femininity transcendent and superior, thus divinizing patriarchal notions of cultural femininity. As a result, one does not come to grips with the sociopolitical implications of gender dualism that serves to keep kyriarchy intact. It is also important to realize that biblical Wisdom traditions are articulated within patriarchal bodies of literature that were shaped to serve kyriarchal interests.[46] In Jewish Wisdom literature, Sophia appears in discourse that is articulated in the form of instructions of a father to a son or as a fictive address to a young king. These articulations often combined a positive understanding of the divine female figure of Wisdom with a negative understanding of actual historical women.[47] Attempts at retrieving Wisdom traditions must be wary of unwittingly advancing kyriarchal agenda. In the case of Mt. 11.19, it is important to recognize that Matthew's identification of Jesus with Wisdom was most likely used to legitimate the authority of an all-male leadership while the female identity of the metaphor is absorbed into male figure of Jesus and disappears.[48]

In the New Testament, strands of Sophia christology have been relegated to the margins, and in some places, consciously submerged. In the Fourth Gospel, masculine language of *Logos* absorbs and replaces female depiction of the divine Sophia. Such a move dissolves the tension between the grammatical female gender of Sophia and the male gender of the earthly Jesus, thus silencing the traditions of God as Wisdom Woman incarnate.[49] A further complication is that in Western tradition many female expressions of the Divine have accrued to Mary. The marginal

Matthean Jesus (Maryknoll, NY: Orbis Books, 1998), p. 77; Schüssler Fiorenza, *Sharing Her Word*, p. 160.

45. Schüssler Fiorenza, *Sharing Her Word*, p. 177.

46. E. Schüssler Fiorenza, *Jesus: Miriam's Child, Sophia's Prophet* (New York: Continuum, 1994), p. 132.

47. Schüssler Fiorenza, *Miriam's Child*, p. 137.

48. Deutsch, *Lady Wisdom*, p. 147.

49. Schüssler Fiorenza, *Miriam's Child*, p. 153. See also J.E. McKinlay, *Gendering Wisdom the Host: Biblical Invitations to Eat and Drink* (JSOTSup 216; Sheffield: Sheffield Academic Press, 1996), pp. 179-207.

place of Wisdom christology in the New Testament and its misdirection into mariology can allow it to be seen only as an interesting added dimension to the predominant male paradigm. When Wisdom christology is simply regarded as a helpful way in which women can use a female metaphor to articulate and legitimate their experience, it ultimately does nothing to dislodge androcentricism.

Wisdom's Children Today

In the past, Divine Woman Wisdom sought a resting place among her people, but did not find one. Therefore, says *1 Enoch* 42.1-2, she has returned to heaven and has taken her seat among the angels. As feminists attempt to retrieve Sophia and her traditions from the shadows and restore her to her place among her earthly children, the parable of the children in the marketplace can help open a receptive space. When Luke portrays Jesus as another in the long line of Sophia's prophets who announce justice, right order and well-being for all God's creatures, especially those most marginalized, he gives hope to all those who today continue to proclaim and work for justice.[50] The divine presence and power to free is experienced in the midst of the struggles against oppression as Sophia accompanies disciples and leads them through the suffering to victory. When feminist preachers, teachers, and evangelists experience opposition and rejection, the parable can give courage and hope, recognizing that Sophia and all her prophets have always experienced such, but She has already conquered the forces of death itself. At the same time, it is important to recognize the limitations of Luke's version of the parable. In an androcentric world, it is easier to accept the image of Jesus as a child of Wisdom rather than see him as the incarnation of Sophia herself in the Matthean version.

50. L. Schottroff ('Wanderprophetinnen: Eine feministische Analyse der Logien-quelle', *EvT* 51 [1991], pp. 322-34) has raised theological and historical objections to feminist recovery of Wisdom traditions, arguing that these were used to serve the interests of elite males and that privileging such traditions eclipses the 'gospel of the poor' that is at the heart of Jesus' teaching. S. Schroer ('Jesus Sophia: Erträge der feministischen Forschung zu einer frühchristlichen Deutung der Praxis und des Schicksals Jesu von Nazaret', in D. Strahm and R. Strobel [eds.], *Vom Verlangen nach Heilwerden: Theologie in feministisch- theologischer Sicht* [Fribourg: Exodus, 1991], pp. 112-28), in contrast, argues that the Wisdom tradition appeals to the well-to-do not to exploit the poor. For further discussion see Schüssler Fiorenza, *Miriam's Child*, pp. 155-57; Wainwright, *Shall We Look For Another?*, pp. 77-78.

Matthew's rendition of the parable takes us one step farther in over-coming gender dualism. Followers of Jesus, whether female or male, can understand themselves to be children of Wisdom, made in the divine image, redeemed by the Christ who is her incarnate presence on earth, and whose deeds they continue to replicate. Despite this advance, there are still great difficulties to be overcome. In addition to those problems named above, the personification of the male Jesus as female Wisdom is further undermined if the phrase ὁ υἱὸς τοῦ ἀνθρώπου in Mt. 11.19 is translated 'Son of Man'. This emphatically male self-designation on the lips of a male Jesus in an androcentric narrative and a kyriarchal culture over-whelms any possibility for Sophia's voice to emerge. One step forward is to translate the phrase as 'the Human One', which not only replicates the more likely sense of Jesus' original self-designation, but also makes way for Wisdom's dwelling among her children.[51]

Finally, while we have sketched some liberative possibilities for interpreting the parable of the children in the marketplace, there is a far greater task of emancipatory theologizing that still awaits. As E. Schüssler Fiorenza has argued, recovery of ancient Wisdom traditions 'does not invite us to simply repeat the language of early Jewish and Christian reflective mythology about Divine Wisdom. Rather it compels us to con-tinue to struggle not only with conventional masculine language for G*d[52] but also with the exclusivist authoritarian functions and implications of such language. Theology must rearticulate the biblical symbols, images, and titles of Divine Wisdom–Chokmah–Sophia in a way that not only radically questions and undermines ossified masculine and absolutized language about G*d and Christ but also deconstructs the Western cultural sex/gender system'.[53] Biblical interpretation that so reconceptualizes the reigning mythology, and mobilizes cultural, sociopolitical, and religious imagination in the liberative struggle for meaning, offers new possibilities of emancipation and well-being for all Wisdom's children. At last, Wisdom would be justified.

51. Wainwright, *Shall We Look For Another?*, p. 75. For a philological analysis of the phrase see J.A. Fitzmyer, 'The New Testament Title "Son of Man" Philologically Considered', in *A Wandering Aramean* (SBLMS 25; Chico, CA: Scholars Press, 1979), pp. 143-60.

52. This is the spelling used by Schüssler Fiorenza 'to indicate the brokenness and inadequacy of human language to name the Divine' (*Sharing Her Word*, p. 187 n. 10).

53. Schüssler Fiorenza, *Sharing Her Word*, p. 179.

V
FINDING PARABLE

GATHERING: A MYTHIC PARABLE

Christin Lore Weber

There was a woman who went down each morning to the sea. There she gathered stones, feathers, driftwood and coloured bits of broken glass. She placed them in a basket woven of reeds that grew along a river flowing past her home. She rocked the basket like a child and sang a song composed of tears.

'Ah-eee', she sang, 'My babies are dying. Their hearts are crushed like an almond seed and the scent is bitter. Their eyes are streambeds run dry. Laughter that used to make my world a place of birds is silenced now and the land is seeded with bones'.

As she sang the tides thundered in and the waters broke against ancient rock, spraying her face, so that the salt of her tears combined with the salt of the sea. Finally the sea took back into itself all that the woman had not gathered that day, and when the waters swirled around her bare feet she turned and climbed the hill towards her house of river-rock and ferns.

On the north side of the house the woman placed each stone given her by the sea. Jasper and carnelian, obsidian and jade. She worked according to the only wisdom she possessed, but she could not make the stones fit.

Moving in a circle to the east she climbed her only tree, a dying willow, in the crook of which she added her feathers to a nest large enough for an eagle to have built. Feathers of gulls and of owls, of the red-tailed hawk, the great blue heron, the egret and the dove. She ran her fingers over soft down from the bluebird's breast and wisps of hummingbird's wings. But the nest remained empty.

In the south the woman made a mountain of glass, glass of every colour and shape, through which the sun passed like fire. But the fire burned the grass, leaving it parched and dry.

And in the west she wove the tangled arms of driftwood into the image of herself, facing the sea, reaching towards the emerald flash of each fading day for whatever could fulfill her heart's desire.

Tears and gathering were the woman's work and she was faithful.

In the tenth year of her work, as the woman returned from her morning gathering, she saw a girl-child coming toward her from the north and the child had no eyes. The woman left her basket by the place of stones and set off down the road to meet the child.

'What do you seek?' The woman asked the girl.

'I want to see', the girl replied.

'I have no power over sight', the woman told her softly, 'but if you will join me in my work with stones, some form of sight might well be granted you'.

So the girl stayed with the woman. Together the woman and the girl wove a basket made of river reeds and the woman gave the girl the task of gathering the stones. Each morning they went together to the sea; together they sang the woman's song; together they did the work of gathering. Then the tides rose, the waves thundered on the rocks, and their eyes filled with the water of the sea. The woman taught the girl the texture of jade and the way smoky quartz forms a wand.

Time passed. Some afternoons the girl without sight held the carnelian or the lapis against her throat or that place in her forehead the old woman called her third eye until she could feel the warmth of the sun as it passed through the rock and into her skin, her muscle, her nerve and finally into the bone that formed the stone-like structure of her own body. Each stone she held pulsed with light and colour as it brought its own part of her to life. Slowly she began to see herself from within, each part a brilliance, the whole of her a rainbow. Only then did the girl place the stones according to the vision in her heart, and every stone fit perfectly.

In the twentieth year of her work the woman who lived by the sea came up from her morning gathering accompanied by a woman with no eyes who was now a seer. Stones had become her eyes. Through them she saw past and future and every yearning in the world's heart.

'A child is coming down the road and her heart is crushed', she told the woman of the sea as they climbed the hill and reached the place where four roads crossed.

The woman looked to the east. She saw nothing, but on the air a scent of bitter almonds rose.

'I see no one', The woman told the seer.

'She will come'.

The child came. Her hair blew like feathers on the breeze. Her enormous eyes were haunted. Her body was like paper you could see through.

'What do you seek?' The woman asked the girl.

'I want to live', the girl replied.

'I have no power over life', the woman told her softly. 'But if you will join me in my work with feathers, then some form of life might well be granted you'.

So the girl stayed with the two women. Together they wove a basket of river reeds, one with a cover and hinges so that the feathers she would gather could not blow away. Each morning they went together to the sea. Together they sang the woman's song; together they did the work of gathering. The woman taught the girl with the crushed heart the art of weaving feathers into the large nest, now big enough to be a bed. Each night the child curled into the feather nest in the crook of the dying willow tree, and the spirits of the birds whose feathers had been lost sang to her in the darkness. In the mornings, by the sea, when the tides rose, when the salt spray mixed with her tears, and when the gulls cried out as they whirled above her, she began to feel in her chest a faint murmur like the beating of a heart.

In the thirtieth year of her work, the woman came from her gathering accompanied by the woman who was a seer and the woman whose heart had become a nest for giving birth. They saw a child coming up the road from the south. The woman whose heart was a nest ran to her, embraced her, took her hand and led her to the woman of the sea.

'What do you seek?' The woman asked the girl.

But the girl just looked at her with chipped eyes.

'She cannot speak', said the woman who was a seer.

'I cannot give anyone a voice', the woman told her softly. 'But if you will join me in my work with glass, then some form of speech might well be granted you'.

So the girl stayed with the three women. Together they wove a basket of river reeds and each morning they went together to the sea. Together they sang the woman's song; together they did the work of gathering. The woman taught the girl who had no voice how shards of coloured glass washed onto the beach. She told her these treasures were more difficult to find than any other of the gatherings. She explained the glass had splintered off the history of the world, of human striving. Each fragment told a story of loss, or anger, or revenge. But if they could be gathered and piled together in the sun, fire would pass through them and they would be cleansed. So the girl gathered glass. She spent her afternoons arranging and rearranging the fragments to catch the sun's fire. Years passed. One day the fire in the fragments of glass passed through her eyes and into her mind. The fire keened, it wept, it shrieked, it groaned and sobbed and whimpered. The fire cried with the voice of vengeance and betrayal, with the voice of love refused, with the voice hunger and of war. The woman listened. She wept. Her first sound was a moan. The fire had entered her heart. In the seventh year fire became her voice and it sang the song of humanity.

After forty years of gathering the old woman, accompanied by the woman who was a seer, the woman whose heart was a nest, and the woman who sang with the fire of sunlight through glass, went down in the morning to the sea. Together they sang the woman's song; together they did the work of gathering. When they were finished, the old woman sat with them on a large driftwood log and the tides came in and the waters swirled around their bare feet. Spray from the crashing waves salted their faces, filled their eyes, and wet their long hair.

'I am the woman who comes from the west', she told them. 'I am she who composed the song. I gathered the fragments from the sea. I am the tangled wood, turned to the setting sun. I gave you what I had and you completed it. But I still feel planted like a tree of bones on a hill at the world's end'.

'What do you seek?' the three younger women asked the woman of the sea.

'Rebirth', the old woman said.

The women took their baskets of stones, feathers, broken glass and driftwood and stood with them at the sea's edge. The wind rose and the tide swirled around their feet. The woman who could see far laid down her basket of stones. Jasper, agate, carnelian and jade tumbled into the rising tide. The woman whose heart was a nest lifted her basket of feathers to the wind that whirled them up and then settled them on the surface of the vast waters. The woman with the voice of fire tossed the glass shards from her basket into the sky where the sun's rays filled them with rainbows before they shimmered into the sea. And the old woman set her tangled wood afloat on the in the world's depth.

The four women joined hands and made a circle. They sang a new song.

'Lu-lay', they sang. 'We live and our children live. Our hearts blossom like almonds in the spring. Our eyes are promises of rain, sun and the changing moon. We rise from the gatherings we leave in the mothering sea'.

As the waters deepened, the women began to dance. They spiralled

312 The Lost Coin

round and round and the wind caught their long hair, winding it together. The currents pulled them down where the waters whirled. Faster and faster they spiralled with stones, feathers, glass and wood around them, until they were a blur of colour and form, inseparable.

In the morning there was a woman who came up from the sea. Her eyes shone with the wisdom of stones formed when earth was born, and she could see far. Her heart beat like the eagle's and was expansive as the sky. She was singing and the timbre of her voice resonated with the molten fire of volcanoes and the flicker of candles on Midsummer Night. Shells and seaflowers wound through her hair that shone with strands of gold, silver, mahogany and black. In her hands she carried a seedling tree.

The woman who came up from the sea stood at the top of the hill. She gazed to the north and a gathering of stones that fit together perfectly. She turned and gazed to the east where a nest of feathers invited eagles. She turned to the south where sun's fire passed through coloured glass like music. And then she stood beside a tangle of driftwood that resembled a gnarled old woman. She gazed over the sea toward the horizon as though she could see what lay beyond. And then she knelt on the receiving earth. On the edge where the world begins and ends, she planted the seedling tree.

BIBLIOGRAPHY

Abrams, M.H., *A Glossary of Terms* (New York: Holt, Rinehart and Winston, 3rd edn, 1971).
Adler, R., 'A Mother in Israel: Aspects of the Mother Role in Jewish Myth', in R. Gross (ed.), *Beyond Androcentrism: Essays on Women and Religion* (Missoula: Scholars, 1977), pp. 237-55.
Allan, R.J., *Rabbinic Passages to Help Interpret the Parables* (Storytellers Companion to the Bible, 9; Nashville: Abingdon, forthcoming).
Anderson, J.C., 'Matthew: Gender and Reading', *Semeia* 28 (1983), pp. 3-27.
Andrews, C., 'Modernizing God's Image', *National Post* (January 20, 1999).
Appelbaum, S., 'The Social and Economic Status of the Jews in the Diaspora', in S. Safrai and M. Stern (eds.), *The Jewish People in the First Century: Historical Geography, Political History, Social, Cultural and Religious Life and Institutions* (CRI, 2; Assen: Vangorcum, 1976), pp. 631-701.
Bailey, K.E., *Poet and Peasant and Through Peasant Eyes: A Literary-Cultural Approach to the Parables in Luke* (Grand Rapids: Eerdmans, 1983).
—*Poet and Peasant: A Literary Cultural Approach to the Parables in Luke* (Grand Rapids: Eerdmans, 1976).
—*Through Peasant Eyes: More Lucan Parables, Their Culture and Style* (Grand Rapids: Eerdmans, 1980).
Bal, M., *Lethal Love: Feminist Literary Readings of Biblical Love Stories* (Bloomington: Indiana University Press, 1987).
Balabanski, V., 'Matthew 25.1-13 as a Window on Eschatological Change', in *Eschatology in the Making: Mark, Matthew and the Didache* (Cambridge: Cambridge University Press, 1997), ch. 2.
Baldick, C., *The Concise Oxford Dictionary of Literary Terms* (Oxford: Oxford University Press, 1990).
Banks, Russell, *The Sweet Hereafter* (San Francisco: HarperCollins, 1991).
Barrett, C.K., *The Gospel According to St. John* (Philadelphia: Westminster Press, 2nd edn, 1978).
Beal, T., 'Opening: Cracking the Binding', in T.K. Beal and D.M. Gunn (eds.), *Reading Bibles, Writing Bodies: Identity and the Book* (London: Routledge, 1997), pp. 1-11.
Beauvoir, S. de, *The Second Sex* (New York: Vintage, 1974).
Beavis, M.A., *Mark's Audience: The Literary and Social Setting of Mark 4. 11-12* (JSNTSup, 33; Sheffield: Sheffield Academic Press, 1989).
—'Parable and Fable', *CBQ* 52 (1990), pp. 473-98.
—'Ancient Slavery as an Interpretive Context for the New Testament Servant Parables, With Special Reference to the Unjust Steward (Lk. 6. 1-8)', *JBL* 111 (1992), pp. 37-54.
—'The Foolish Landowner (Luke 12. 16b-20)', in V.G. Shillington (ed.), *Jesus and His Parables: Interpreting the Parables of Jesus Today* (Edinburgh: T. & T. Clark, 1997), pp. 55-68.

Bechtel, L.M., 'Rethinking the Interpretation of Genesis 2. 4b-3. 24', in A. Brenner (ed.), *A Feminist Companion to Genesis* (FCB, 2; Sheffield: Sheffield Academic Press, 1993), pp. 77-117.

Bernard, J.H., *A Critical and Exegetical Commentary on the Gospel According to St. John* (2 vols.; Edinburgh: T. & T. Clark, 1928).

Betz, H.D., 'The Logion of the Easy Yoke and of Rest (Matt. 11: 28-30)', *JBL* 86 (1967), pp. 10-24.

Blatz, B., 'The Coptic Gospel of Thomas', in W. Schneemelcher (ed.), *New Testament Apocrypha 1: Gospels and Related Writings* (Louisville, KY: Westminster/John Knox Press, 1991), pp. 110-33.

Blessing, K., 'Desolate Jerusalem and Barren Matriarch: Two Distinct Figures in the Pseudepigrapha', *Journal for the Study of the Pseudepigrapha* 18 (1998), pp. 47-69.

—'Luke's Unjust Steward Viewed from the Window of Psychiatrist Milton Erickson', Annual Meeting of the Society for Biblical Literature, Psychology and Biblical Studies Group, Washington, DC, 23 November 1993.

Blume, E.S., *Secret Survivors: Uncovering Incest and Its After-Effects in Women* (New York: Ballantine, 1990).

Bohn, C.R., 'Dominion to Rule', in J.C. Brown and C.R. Bohn (eds.), *Christianity, Patriarchy, and Abuse: A Feminist Critique* (New York: Pilgrim Press, 1989), pp. 105-16.

Bormann, L., and E. Schüssler Fiorenza (eds.), *Religious Propaganda and Missionary Competition in the New Testament World* (Leiden: E.J. Brill, 1994).

Bornkamm, G., 'Dei Verzogerung der Parusie. Exegetische Bemerkungen zu zwei synoptischen Texten', in W. Schemauch (ed.), *In Memoriam E. Lohmeyer* (Stuttgart: Verlag Katholisches Bibelwerk, 1951), pp. 116-48.

Borsch, F.H., *Many Things in Parables: Extravagant Stories of New Community* (Philadelphia: Fortress Press, 1988).

Boucher, M., *The Parables* (Wilmington: Michael Glazier, 1981).

Brawley, R.L., *Text to Text Pours Forth Speech: Voices of Scripture in Luke–Acts* (Bloomington: Indiana University Press, 1995).

Brock, R.N. and S.B. Thistlethwaite, *Casting Stones: Prostitution and Liberation in Asia and the United States* (Minneapolis: Fortress Press, 1996).

Broner, E.M., *Her Mothers* (Bloomington: Indiana University Press, 1985).

Brown, P., *The Body and Society: Men, Women, and Sexual Renunciation in Early Christianity* (New York: Columbia University Press, 1998).

Brown, R.E., 'Jesus and Elisha', *Perspective* 12 (1971), pp. 84-104.

—*The Gospel According to John I-XII* (AB 29; Garden City, NY: Doubleday, 1966).

Buckley, J.J., *Female Fault and Fulfillment in Gnosticism* (Chapel Hill: University of North Carolina Press, 1986).

Bultmann, R., *Geschichte der Synoptischen Tradition* (Göttingen: Vandenhoeck & Ruprecht, 2nd rev. edn, 1931).

—*History of the Synoptic Tradition* (Oxford: Basil Blackwell, 1963).

Burguière, P., and O. Temkin (eds.), *Soranos D'Ephèse. Maladies des Femmes* (2 vols.; Paris: Les Belles Lettres, 1990).

Burnett, F.W., *The Testament of Jesus-Sophia: A Redaction-Critical Study of the Eschatological Discourse in Matthew* (Lanham, MD: University Press of America, 1981).

Butler, S., *Conspiracy of Silence: The Trauma of Incest* (San Francisco: Volcano Press, 1978, 1996).

Bynum, C.W., *Holy Feast and Holy Fast : The Religious Significance of Food to Medieval Women* (Berkeley: University of California Press, 1987).

Callaway, M., *Sing, O Barren One: A Study in Comparative Midrash* (SBLDS, 91; Atlanta: Scholars, 1986).

Camp, C., '1 and 2 Kings', in C.A. Newsom and S.H. Ringe (eds.), *The Women's Bible Commentary* (London: Westminster/John Knox Press, 1992), pp. 96-109.

Carles, E., *A Life of Her Own* (Harmondsworth: Penguin Books, 1992).

Carlston, C.E., *The Parables of the Triple Tradition* (Philadelphia: Fortress Press, 1975).

Carter, P., *Feminism, Breasts and Breast-Feeding* (New York: St. Martin's Press, 1995).

Cartlidge, D.R., 'Combien d'unités avez-vous de trois à quatre?; What Do We Mean By Intertextuality in Early Church Studies?', in D.J. Lull (ed.), *Society of Biblical Literature Seminar Papers* (Atlanta: Scholars Press, 1990), pp. 400-11.

Cassem, N.H., 'A Grammatical and Contextual Inventory of the Use of κόσμος (in the Johannine Cosmic Theology', *NTS* 19 (1972-73), pp. 81-91.

Cassuto, U., *A Commentary of the Book of Genesis* (vol. 1; trans. I. Abrahams; Jerusalem: Mages/Hebrew University, 1961).

Castelli, E., '"I Will Make Mary Male"; Pieties of the Body and Gender Transformation of Christian Women in Late Antiquity', in J. Epstein and K. Straub (eds.), *Body Guards: The Cultural Politics of Gender Ambiguity* (New York: Routledge, 1991), pp. 29-49.

Clifford, R.J., *Proverbs* (Louisville: Westminster/John Knox Press, 1999).

Cloke, G., *This Female Man of God: Women and Spiritual Power in the Patristic Age, AD 350-450* (London: Routledge, 1995).

Corley, K.E., *Private Women, Public Meals: Social Conflict in the Synoptic Tradition* (Peabody, MA: Hendrickson, 1993).

Cotter, W.J., 'The Parable of the Children in the Marketplace, Q (Lk.) 7:31-35: An Examination of the Parable's Image and Significance', *NovT* 29 (1987), pp. 289-304.

Crossan, J.D, 'Kingdom and Children: A Study in the Aphoristic Tradition', *Semeia* 29 (1983), pp. 75-95.

—'Parables', *Harper's Bible Dictionary* (P.J. Achtemeyer, gen. ed.; San Francisco: HarperSanFrancisco, 1985), pp. 747-49.

—*Sayings Parallels: A Workbook for the Jesus Tradition* (Philadelphia: Fortress, 1986).

—*The Historical Jesus: The Life of a Mediterranean Jewish Peasant* (San Francisco: HarperCollins, 1992).

—*The Essential Jesus: Original Sayings and Earliest Images* (San Francisco: HarperSanFrancisco, 1994).

Culler, J., *On Deconstruction: Theory and Criticism after Structuralism* (Ithaca: Cornell University Press, 1982).

Culpepper, A., 'Seeing the Kingdom of God: The Metaphor of Sight in the Gospel of Luke', *CurTM* 21 (1994), pp. 434-43.

Dalman, G., *Arbeit und Sitte in Palästina, Vol. 4: Brot, Öl und Wein* (Hildesheim: Greog Olms, 1964).

Daly, B.O., and M.T. Reddy, *Narrating Mothers: Theorizing Maternal Subjectivities* (Knoxville: University of Tennessee Press, 1991).

Davidson, J., *Courtesans and Fish Cakes; The Consuming Passions of Classical Athens* (New York: St. Martins Press, 1998).

Davies, W.D., and D.C. Allison, *A Critical and Exegetical Commentary on the Gospel According To St. Matthew* (2 vols.; Edinburgh: T. & T. Clark, 1988–1991).

Derrett, J.D.M., 'Law in the New Testament: The Parable of the Prodigal Son', *NTS* 14 (1967), pp. 56-74.

Deutsch, C., *Hidden Wisdom and the Easy Yoke: Wisdom, Torah and Discipleship in Matthew 11: 25-30* (JSNTSup, 18; Sheffield: JSOT Press, 1987).

—*Lady Wisdom, Jesus, and the Sages* (Valley Forge, PA: Trinity Press International, 1996).

De Virgilio, G. 'La valenza teologica dell'espressione: "πραΰς εἰμι καὶ ταπεινὸς τῇ καρδίᾳ" (Matthew 11, 29)', *RevistB* 45 (1997) pp. 409-28.

Dewey, J., 'From Storytelling to Written Text: The Loss of Early Christian Women's Voices', *Biblical Theology Bulletin* 26 (1996), pp. 71-78.

Dewey, K., '*Paroimiai* in the Gospel of John', *Semeia* 17 (1980), pp. 81-90.

DiQuinzio, P., *The Impossibility of Mothering: Feminism, Individualism, and the Problem of Mothering* ((New York: Routledge, 1999).

Dixon, S., *The Roman Mother* (London: Croom Helm, 1988).

Doanne, J., and D. Hodges, *From Klein to Kristeva: Psychoanalytic Feminism and the Search for the 'Good Enough' Mother* (Ann Arbor, MI: University of Michigan Press, 1992).

Dodd, C.H., *Historical Tradition in the Fourth Gospel* (Cambridge: Cambridge University Press, 1965).

—*Parables of the Kingdom* (New York: Charles Scribner's Sons, 1961).

Donahue, J.R., *The Gospel in Parable: Metaphor, Narrative, and Theology in the Synoptic Gospels* (Philadelphia: Fortress Press, 1998).

Downing, F.G., 'Cynics and Christians, Oedipus and Thyestes', *Journal of Ecclesiastical History* 44 (1993), pp. 1-10.

du Plessis, I.J., 'Reading Luke 12: 35-48 as Part of the Travel Narrative', *Neot* 22 (1988), pp. 217-34.

—'Why did Peter ask His Question and How did Jesus Answer Him? Or: Implicature in Luke 12: 35-48', *Neot* 22 (1988), pp. 311-24.

Dupont, J., 'Vin vieux, vin nouveau (Luc. 5, 35)', *CBQ* 25 (1963), pp. 284-304.

Epstein, J., and K. Straub (eds.), *Body Guards: The Cultural Politics of Gender Ambiguity* (New York: Routledge, 1991).

Epstein, L.M., *Sexual Laws and Customs in Judaism* (New York: Nyau, 1967).

Erikson, M., 'The Confusion Technique in Hypnosis', in E.L. Rossi (ed.), *The Collected Works of Milton H. Erikson on Hypnosis I* (New York: Irvington Publishers, Inc., 1989), pp. 258-91.

Evans, C.A., *Luke* (NIBC; Peabody, Mass.: Hendrickson, 1990).

—*Saint Luke* (Trinity Press International Commentaries; Philadelphia: Trinity Press International, 1990).

Evans, C.A. and J.A. Sanders, *Luke and Scripture: The Function of Sacred Tradition in Luke–Acts* (Minneapolis: Fortress Press, 1993).

Exum, J.C., 'The (M)other Place', in Exum, *Fragmented Women. Feminist (Sub)Versions of Biblical Narratives* (JSOTS 163; Sheffield: Sheffield Academic Press, 1993), pp. 94-147.

Eynikel, E., and K. Hauspie, *A Greek-English Lexicon of the Septuagint* (2 vols.; Stuttgart: Deutsche Bibelgesellschaft, 1992, 1996).

Fehribach, A., *The Women in the Life of the Bridegroom: A Feminist Historical-Literary Analysis of the Female Characters in the Fourth Gospel* (Collegeville, MN: Liturgical Press, 1989).

Fetterley, J., *The Resisting Reader: A Feminist Approach to American Fiction* (Boston: Beacon, 1978).

Fewell, D.N., 'Joshua', in C.A. Newsom and S.H. Ringe (eds.), *The Women's Bible Commentary* (London: Westminster/John Knox Press, 1992), pp. 67-77.

Fiensy, D.A., *The Social History of Palestine in the Herodian Period* (Lewiston, NY: Edwin Mellen, 1991).

Firmage, E., 'Zoology (Fauna)', in D.N. Freedman (ed.), *Anchor Bible Dictionary* (New York: Doubleday, 1992), pp. 1109-67.

Fitzmyer, J.A., *The Gospel According To Luke I-IX* (AB 28; Garden City, NY: Doubleday, 1981).

—*The Gospel According to Luke X-XXIV* (New York: Doubleday, 1985).

—'The New Testament Title 'Son of Man' Philologically Considered', in *A Wandering Aramean* (SBLMS, 25; Chico, CA: Scholars Press, 1979), pp. 143-60.

Ford, R.Q., *The Parables of Jesus: Recovering the Art of Listening* (Minneapolis: Fortress Press, 1992).

Forestell, J.T., *The Word of the Cross: Salvation as Revelation in the Fourth Gospel* (AnBib 57; Rome: Biblical Institute Press, 1974).

Frantham, E. et al., *Women in the Classical World: Image and Text* (New York and Oxford: Oxford University Press, 1994).

Fraser, S., *My Father's House: A Memoir of Incest and Healing* (Toronto: Doubleday Canada, 1987).

Freedman, D.N. (ed.), *Anchor Bible Dictionary* (New York: Doubleday, 1992).

—*Eerdmans Dictionary of the Bible* (Grand Rapids, MI: Eerdmans, 2000).

French, V., 'Midwives and Maternity Care in the Roman World', in M. Skinner (ed.), *Rescuing Creusa: New Methodological Approaches to Women in Antiquity* (*Helios* 13.2, spec. edn, 1987).

Fricke, W., *The Court-Martial of Jesus: A Christian Defends the Jews Against the Charge of Deicide* (trans. S. Attanasio; New York: Grove Weidenfeld, 1990).

Friedl, E., 'Moonrose Watched Through a Sunny Day', *Natural History* 8 (1992), pp. 34-44.

Friedman, S.S., 'Creativity and the Childbirth Metaphor: Gender Differences and Literal Discourse', *Feminist Studies* 13 (1987), pp. 49-82.

Fuchs, E., 'The Literary Characterization of Mothers and Sexual Politics in the Hebrew Bible', in A.Y. Collins (ed.), *Feminist Perspectives on Biblical Scholarship* (Atlanta: Scholars, 1985), pp. 117-36.

Fulmer, C., *Cry of Ramah. Songs by Colleen Fulmer: Dances by Martha Ann Kirk* (Albany, CA: Loretto Spirituality Network).

Funk, R.W., R.W. Hoover and the Jesus Seminar, *The Five Gospels: The Search for the Authentic Words of Jesus* (New York: Polebridge, 1993).

Garland, D., *Reading Matthew: A Literary and Theological Commentary on the First Gospel* (New York: Crossroad, 1993).

Gärtner, B., *The Theology of the Gospel of Thomas* (London: Collins, 1961).

Gateley, E., *A Warm, Moist Salty God: Women Journeying Towards Wisdom* (Trabuco Canyon, CA: Source Books, 1993).

Gench, F.T., *Wisdom in the Christology of Matthew* (Lanham, MD: University Press of America, 1997).

Genovese, E.F., 'For Feminist Interpretation', *Union Seminary Quarterly Review* 35,1/2 (1979-1980), pp. 5-14.

Glasson, T.F., 'Carding and Spinning in Oxy. Pap 655', *JTS* 13 (1962), pp. 313-32.

Goldberg, A.M., 'Torah aus der Unterwelt? Eine Bemerkung zu Rom. 10, 6-7', *BZ* 14,1 (1970), pp. 127-31.

Good, R.S., 'Jesus, Protagonist of the Old in Luke 5: 33-39', *NovT* 25 (1983), pp. 19-36.
Goodwin, A., 'Right to Remain Silent', *Pastoral Psychology* 41 (1993), pp. 359-76.
Goulder, M.D., *Midrash and Lection in Matthew* (London: SPCK, 1974).
Gower, R., *The New Manners and Customs of Bible Times* (Chicago: Moody Press, 1987).
Green, J.B., *The Gospel of Luke* (Grand Rapids: Eerdmans, 1997).
Griffith, S., 'Asceticism in the Church of Syria: The Hermeneutics of Early Syrian Monasticism', in V.L. Wimbush and R. Valantasis (eds.), *Asceticism* (New York: Oxford University Press, 1995), pp. 220-45.
Grosz, P.R., *Sexual Subversions: Three French Feminists* (Sidney: Allen and Unwin, 1981).
Guelich, R.A., *Mark 1-8. 26* (Word Biblical Commentary 34A; Dallas: Word, 1989).
Guijarro, S., 'The Family in First Century Galilee', in H. Moxnes (ed.), *Constructing Early Christian Families* (New York: Routledge, 1997), pp. 42-65.
Haberman, B.D., 'Praxis-Exegesis: A Jewish Feminist Hermeneutic', in K. Pui-Lan and E. Schüssler Fiorenza (eds.), *Women's Sacred Scriptures* (London: SCM Press, 1998), pp. 91-101.
Hagner, D.A., *Matthew 1–13* (World Biblical Commentary 33A; Dallas: Word, 1998).
Hall, D.J., *The Steward: A Biblical Image Come of Age* (Grand Rapids: Eerdmans, rev. edn; 1990).
Halperin, D.M., J. Winkler, and F.I. Zeitlin (eds.), *Before Sexuality: The Construction of Erotic Experience in the Ancient Greek World* (Princeton, NJ: Princeton University Press, 1990).
Hamm, D., 'What the Samaritan Leper Sees: Narrative Christology of Luke 17.11-19', *CBQ* 56 (1994), pp. 273-87.
Hare, T., *Remembering Osiris: Number, Gender, and the Word in Ancient Egyptian Representational Systems* (Stanford: Stanford University Press, 1999).
Harley, J.E., *The Book of Job* (NICOT; Grand Rapids: Eerdmans, 1988).
Harrington, D., *The Gospel of Matthew* (SacPag; Collegeville: The Liturgical Press, 1991).
Hartin, P.J., 'Angst in the Household: A Deconstructive Reading of the Parable of the Supervising Servant (Lk. 12: 41-48)', *Neot* 22 (1988), pp. 373-90.
Hays, R., *Echoes of Scripture in the Letters of Paul* (New Haven: Yale, 1989).
Hedrick, C.W., 'Parables and the Kingdom: The Vision of Jesus in Fiction and Faith', *Society of Biblical Literature Seminar Papers* 26 (1987), pp. 368-94.
—*Parables as Poetic Fictions: The Creative Voice of Jesus* (Peabody, MA.: Hendrickson Publishers, 1994).
Heil, C., 'Zeugnisse eines Schriftlichen griechischen vorkanonischen Textes Mt. 6, 28b Sinaiticus*, p. Oxy, 655 I 1-17 (EvTh36) und Q 12, 27', *ZNW* 89 (1998), pp. 30-44.
Herman, Judith, *Father–Daughter Incest* (Cambridge, MA: Harvard University Press, 1987).
Herzog II, William R., *Parables as Subversive Speech: Jesus as Pedagogue of the Oppressed* (Westminster: John Knox, 1994).
Hiebert, P., 'Widows', in B.M. Metzger and M.D. Coogan (eds.), *The Oxford Companion to the Bible* (Oxford: Oxford University Press, 1993), pp. 795-98.
Horsley, R.A., and J. Draper, *Whoever Hears You Hears Me* (Harrisburg, PA: Trinity, 1999).
Howard-Brook, W., *Becoming Children of God: John's Gospel and Radical Discipleship* (Bible and Liberation Series; New York: Orbis, 1994).
Howell, D.B., *Matthew's Inclusive Story. A Study in the Rhetoric of the First Gospel* (JSNTSup, 42; Sheffield: Sheffield Academic Press, 1990).
Humphrey, J.W., J.P. Oleson and A.N. Sherwood, *Greek and Roman Technology: A Sourcebook* (London and New York: Routledge, 1998).

Huntington, P., *Ecstatic Subjects, Utopia, and Recognition: Kristeva, Heidegger, Irigaray* (Albany, NY: State University of New York Press, 1998).

Ian, M., *Remembering the Phallic Mother: Psychoanalysis, Modernism, and the Fetish* (Ithaca, NY: Cornell University Press, 1993).

Ilan, Tal, *Jewish Women in Greco-Roman Palestine: An Inquiry into Image and Status* (TSAJ, 44; Tubingen: J.C.B. Mohr/Paul Siebeck, 1995).

Imbens, A., and I. Jonker, *Christianity and Incest* (Minneapolis: Fortress Press, 1992).

Iser, W., *The Act of Reading* (Baltimore: John Hopkins University Press, 1978).

—*The Implied Reader* (Baltimore: Johns Hopkins University Press, 1974).

Isherwood, L., and D. McEwan, *Introducing Feminist Theology* (Sheffield: Sheffield Academic Press, 1993).

Jeremias, J., 'ΛΑΜΠΑΔΕΣ Mt. 25.1. 3f.7f'., *ZNW 56* (1965), pp. 196-201.

—*The Parables of Jesus* (New York: Charles Scribner's Sons, 1972).

Jobling, David, 'The Bible and Critical Theory Seminar' (University of Queensland; Brisbane, 21 September, 1999).

John, V.J., 'Nature in the Parables of Mark: An Inquiry into the Use of Nature Images in Mark Chapter 4 with Special Reference to Their Significance for Ecological Concerns', Ph.D. Diss. at South Asia Theological Research Institute of Serampore College, Bangalore, India.

Johnson, E.A., 'Jesus, the Wisdom of God', *ETL* 61 (1985), pp. 261-94.

—*She Who Is. The Mystery of God in Feminist Theological Discourse* (New York: Crossroad, 1992).

Johnson, L.T., *The Gospel of Luke* (Collegeville, MN: Liturgical Press, 1991).

—'Something Fundamental is Afoot', *Commonweal* 120 (29 January 1993), pp. 17-22.

Johnson, M., 'Reflections on a Wisdom Approach to Matthew's Christology', *CBQ* 36 (1974), pp. 44-64.

Joines, K.R., *Serpent Symbolism in the Old Testament: A Linguistic, Archaeological and Literary Study* (Haddonfield: Haddonfield Press, 1974).

Jülicher, A., *Die Gleichnisreden Jesu* (vol. 2; Tübingen: J.C.B. Mohr, 1910).

Kee, H.C., ' "Becoming a Child" in the Gospel of Thomas', *JBL* 82 (1963), pp. 307-14.

King, K.L., 'The Gospel of Mary Magdalene', in E. Schüssler Fiorenza, *Searching the Scriptures: Volume 2: A Feminist Commentary* (New York: Crossroad, 1994), pp. 601-34.

—'Kingdom in the Gospel of Thomas', *Forum* 3 (1987), pp. 48-97.

Kingsbury, J.D., *Matthew as Story* (Philadelphia: Fortress Press, 1986).

Kirshenblatt-Gimblett, B., 'The Concept and Varieties of Narrative Performance in East European Jewish Culture', in R. Bauman and J. Scherzer (eds.), *Explorations in the Ethnography of Speaking* (Cambridge: Cambridge University Press, 2nd edn, 1989), pp. 283-308.

—'A Parable in Context: A Social Interactional Analysis of Storytelling Performance', in Dan Ben-Amos and Kenneth S. Goldstein (eds.), *Folklore: Performance and Communication* (The Hague/Paris: Mouton, 1975), pp. 105-30.

Kingsbury, J.D., *Matthew as Story* (Philadelphia: Fortress Press, 1986).

Klauck, H.J., *Allegorie and Allegorese in synoptischen Gleichnistexten* (2nd edn; Münster: Aschendorffsche Verlagsbuchandlung, 1978).

Klijn, A.F.J., 'The "Single One" in the Gospel of Thomas', *JBL* 81 (1962), pp. 271-78.

Kloppenborg, J.S., 'Wisdom Christology in Q', *Laval théologique philosophie* 34 (1978), pp. 129-47.

—*The Formation of Q: Trajectories in Ancient Wisdom Collections* (Philadelphia: Fortress Press, 1987).

Koester, C.R., *Symbolism in the Fourth Gospel: Meaning, Mystery, Community* (Minneapolis: Fortress Press, 1995).

Korsak, M.P., 'Genesis: A New Look', in A. Brenner (ed.), *A Feminist Companion to Genesis* (FCB, 2; Sheffield: Sheffield Academic Press, 1993), pp. 39-52.

Kraemer, R.S., *Her Share of the Blessings: Women's Religions among Pagans, Jews, and Christians in the Greco-Roman World* (New York: Oxford University Press, 1992).

Kraemer, R.S., and M.R. D'Angelo, *Women and Christian Origins* (Oxford: Oxford University Press, 1999).

Kramer, S.N., 'BM 98396: A Sumerian Prototype of the Mater Dolorosa', *Eretz Israel* 16 (1982), pp. 141-46.

Kristeva, J., *New Maladies of the Soul* (trans. R. Guberman; New York: Columbia University Press, 1995).

—*Revolution in Poetic Language* (trans. M. Waller; New York: Columbia University Press, 1984).

Kysar, R., 'The Making of Metaphor: Another Reading of John 3: 1-5', in F.F. Segovia (ed.), *What Is John?: Readers and Readings of the Fourth Gospel* (SBLSS, 3; Atlanta: Scholars, 1996), pp. 21- 41.

Laansma, J., *I Will Give You Rest* (Mohr Seibeck, 1997).

Lacks, R., *Women and Judaism: Myth, History and Struggle* (Garden City: Doubleday, 1980).

Lambdin, T.O., *The Nag Hammadi Library* (ed. J.M. Robinson; Harper: San Francisco, rev. edn, 1990).

Lambrecht, J., *Once More Astonished: The Parables of Jesus* (New York: Crossroad, 1981).

Laqueur, T., *Making Sex: Body and Gender from the Greeks to Freud* (Cambridge: Harvard University Press, 1992).

Lee, D.A., 'Women as "Sinners": Three Narratives of Salvation in Luke and John', *Australian Biblical Review* 44 (1996), pp. 1-5.

Lefkovitz, C.H., 'Sacred Screaming: Childbirth in Jerusalem', in D. Orenstein (ed.), *Life Cycle: Jewish Women on Life Passages and Personal Milestones* (vol. 1; Woodstock: Jewish Lights Publishing, 1994).

Lefkowitz, M.R., *Heroines and Hysterics* (London: Duckworth, 1981).

Lefkowitz, M.R. and M.B. Fant (eds.), *Women's Life in Greece and Rome: A Source Book in Translation* (Baltimore: The John Hopkins University Press, 2nd edn, 1992).

LeGuin, U.K., 'The Hand That Rocks the Cradle Writes the Book', *New York Times Book Review* (January 22, 1989), pp. 1, 35-37.

Lenski, G.E., *Power and Privilege: A Theory of Social Stratification* (Chapel Hill: University of North Carolina Press, 1984).

Levine, A.-J., 'Matthew', in C.A. Newsom and S.H. Ringe (eds.), *The Women's Bible Commentary* (London: Westminster/John Knox Press, 1992), pp. 252-62.

—*The Social and Ethnic Dimensions of Matthean Salvation History* (SBEC, vol. 14; Lampeter: Edwin Mellen Press, 1988).

Lew, M., *Victims No Longer: Men Recovering from Incest and Any Other Sexual Child Abuse* (New York: Nevraumont Publishing Co., 1988).

Lewis, N., *Life in Egypt Under Roman Control* (Oxford: Clarendon Press, 1983).

Lieberman, S., *Tosefta* (New York: Jewish Theological Seminary of America, 1995).

Lieu, J., 'The Mother of the Son', *JBL* 117 (1998), pp. 61-77.

—'Scripture and the Feminine in John', in A. Brenner (ed.), *A Feminist Companion to the*

Hebrew Bible in the New Testament (FCB, 10; Sheffield: Sheffield Academic Press, 1996), pp. 225-40.

Lincoln, B., 'Thomas-Gospel and Thomas-Community: A New Approach to a Familiar Text', *NovT* (1997), pp. 65-76.

Lindars, B., The Gospel of John (Grand Rapids, MI: Eerdmans, 1972).

— 'Two Parables in John', *NTS* 16 (1970), pp. 318-29.

Luz, U., *Das Evangelium nach Matthäus (Mt. 18-25)* (EKKNT, 476; Zurich: Benziger Verlag, 1990).

—*Matthew 1-7: A Commentary* (trans. W.C. Linss; Minneapolis: Augsburg Fortress, 1989).

MacDonald, D.R., *The Legend and the Apostle: The Battle for Paul in Story and Canon* (Philadelphia: Westminster, 1983).

—*There is No Male and Female: the Fate of a Dominical Saying in Paul and Gnosticism* (HDR, 20; Philadelphia: Fortress Press, 1987).

MacGregor, G.H.C., *The Gospel of John* (London: Hodder and Stoughton, 1928).

Mack, B., *A Myth of Innocence: Mark and Christian Origins* (Philadelphia: Fortress Press, 1988).

—'Q and a Cynic-like Jesus?', in W.E. Arnal and M. Desjardins (eds.), *Whose Historical Jesus? Studies in Christianity and Judaism* (vol. 7; Waterloo, ON: Wilfrid Laurier University Press, 1997), pp. 25-36.

Maher, V. (ed.), *The Anthropology of Breast-Feeding: Natural Law or Social Construct* (Providence, RI: Burg Publishers, 1992).

Malina, B., *The New Testament World* (Atlanta: John Knox Press, 1981).

Malina, B. and R. Rohrbaugh, *Social-Science Commentary on the Synoptic Gospels* (Minneapolis: Fortress, 1992).

Manlowe, J.L., *Faith Born of Seduction: Sexual Trauma, Body Image, and Religion* (New York/London: New York University Press, 1995).

Marks, E. and I de Courtivron (eds.), *New French Feminisms: An Anthology* (New York: Schocken Books by arrangement with University of Massachussetts Press, 1980).

Massingbaerde Ford, J., 'The Parable of the Foolish Scholars (Matt. XXV 1-13)', *NovT* 9 (1967), pp. 107-123.

—*Redeemer, Friend, and Mother: Salvation in Antiquity and in the Gospel of John* (Minneapolis: Fortress Press, 1997).

Matthews, C., *Sophia: Goddess of Wisdom: The Divine Feminine From Black Goddess to World Soul* (Bath: Bath Press, 1991).

McBride, M., 'Power', in L. Isherwood and D. McEwan (eds.), *An A to Z of Feminist Theology* (Sheffield: Sheffield Academic Press, 1996), pp. 183.

McCloskey III, C.J., 'Go Sin No More', *Columbia* 79, 4 (April, 1999), pp. 18-20.

McFague, S., *Metaphorical Theology: Models of God in Religious Language* (Philadelphia: Fortress Press, 1982).

McGuire, A., 'Women, Gender and Gnosis in Gnostic Texts and Traditions', in R.S. Kraemer and M.R. D'Angelo, *Women and Christian Origins* (New York: Oxford: Oxford University Press, 1999), pp. 257-99.

McKenna, M., *Parables: The Arrows of God* (Maryknoll, NY: Orbis Books, 1994).

McKinlay, J.E., *Gendering Wisdom the Host: Biblical Invitations to Eat and Drink* (Gender, Culture, Theory, 4; JSOT, 216; Sheffield Academic Press, 1996).

McNamara, M., *The New Testament and the Palestinian Targum to the Pentateuch* (AnBib, 29; Rome: Pontifical Biblical Institute, 1978), pp. 70-81.

Meeks, W., 'The Image of the Androgyne: Some Uses of a Symbol in Earliest Christianity',
	HR 13 (1974), pp. 165-208.

Meier, J.P., *Matthew* (NTM, 3; Wilmington, DE: Glazier, 1980).

—*A Marginal Jew. Rethinking the Historical Jesus* (Anchor Bible Reference Library; Garden
	City, NY: Doubleday, 1994).

Meyers, C., *Discovering Eve: Ancient Israelite Women in Context* (New York: Oxford
	University Press, 1991).

—'Gender Roles and Genesis 3.16 Revisited' in A. Brenner (ed.) *A Feminist Companion to
	Genesis* (FCB, 2; Sheffield: Sheffield Academic Press, 1993), pp. 129.

Miller, A., *Thou Shalt Not Be Aware: Society's Betrayal of the Child* (London: Pluto Press,
	new edn, 1998).

Miller, B.F., 'Study of the Theme of "Kingdom": The Gospel According to Thomas: Logion
	18', *NovT* 9 (1967), pp. 52-60.

Miller, R.J. (ed.), 'The Gospel of Mary', *The Complete Gospels* (San Francisco:
	HarperSanFrancisco, 1994), pp. 357-66.

Minear, P.S., *Matthew: The Teacher's Gospel* (New York: Pilgrim Press, 1982).

Montefiore, H., and H. Turner, *Thomas and the Evangelist* (SBT, 35; Naperville: Alec R.
	Allenson, 1962).

Morrison, T., *Beloved* (Harmondsworth: Penguin Books, 1987).

Moxnes, H., *The Economy of the Kingdom: Social Conflict and Economic Relationships in
	Luke's Gospel* (Philadelphia: Fortress Press, 1988).

—*Constructing Early Christian Families: Family as Social Reality and Metaphor* (London:
	Routledge, 1997).

Murphy, R.E., *Proverbs* (Word Biblical Commentary, 22; Nashville: Thomas Nelson, 1998).

Musil, A., *Arabia Petraea III* (Vienna, 1907, re-printed Hildesheim 1989), pp. 194-95.

Neill, S., and N.T. Wright, *The Interpretation of the New Testament 1861-1986* (Oxford:
	Oxford University Press, 2nd edn, 1988).

Neirynck, F., *Q-Synopsis: The Double Tradition Passages in Greek* (Leuven: University Press,
	1988).

Neusner, J., *A Rabbi Talks with Jesus: An Intermillennial, Interfaith Exchange* (New York:
	Doubleday, 1993).

Newman, B.M., *A Concise Greek-English Dictionary of the New Testament* (Stuttgart: Biblica-
	Druck, United Bible Societies, 1971).

Newsom, C.A. and S.H. Ringe (eds.), *The Women's Bible Commentary* (Louisville: West-
	minster/John Knox Press, 2nd edn, 1998).

Niditch, S., 'Genesis', in C.A. Newsom and S.H. Ringe (eds.), *The Women's Bible Com-
	mentary (*London: Westminster/John Knox Press, 1992*)*, pp. 10-25.

Nolland, J., *Luke 1-9.20* (World Biblical Commentary, 35A; Dallas: Word, 1989).

O'Day, G.R., 'Johannine Theologians as Sectarians', in F.F. Segovia (ed.), *What is John?
	Readers and Readings of the Fourth Gospel* (SBLSS, 53; Atlanta: Scholars, 1996), pp.
	199-203.

O'Toole, R., 'The Parallels Between Jesus and Moses', *BTB* 20 (1990), pp. 22-29.

Oakman, D.E., 'The Countryside in Luke Acts', in J.H. Neyrey (ed.), *The Social World of
	Luke–Acts: Models for Interpretation* (Peabody, MA: Hendrickson, 1991), pp. 151-80.

—*Jesus and the Economic Questions of His Day* (Lewiston/Queenstown: Edward Mellen,
	1986).

Ottosson, M., ' הרר', *TDOT* 3, pp. 458-61.

Pable, M., 'Returning to the Father's House in Time for the Jubilee of the Year 2000', *Columbia* 79, 4 (April 1999), pp. 10-12.

Patterson, S.J., *The Gospel of Thomas and Jesus* (Sonoma, CA: Polebridge Press, 1993).

Perkins, P., *Hearing the Parables of Jesus* (New York/Ramsay, NJ: Paulist, 1981).

Peskowitz, M., 'Roundtable Discussion: What's in a Name? Exploring the Dimensions of What 'Feminist Studies in Religion' Means', *JFSR* 11 (1995), pp. 111-15.

—*Spinning Fantasies: Rabbis, Gender and History* (Berkeley: University of California Press, 1997).

Piper, R.A., *Wisdom in the Q Tradition* (SNTSMS, 61; Cambridge: Cambridge University Press, 1989).

Plath, M., 'Der Neutestamentliche Weheruf über Jerusalem', *TSK* 78 (1905), pp. 455-60.

Pomeroy, S.B., *Goddesses, Whores, Wives, and Slaves: Women in Classical Antiquity* (London: Random House, 1975).

—*Women in Hellenistic Egypt* (New York: Schocken, 1984).

—*Women's History and Ancient History* (Chapel Hill: University of North Carolina Press, 1991).

Potterie, I. de la, ' "To Be Born Again of Water and the Spirit'—The Baptismal Text of John 3, 5', in I. de la Potterie and S. Lyonnet (eds.), *The Christian Lives by the Spirit* (trans. D.V. Flynn; New York: Alba House, 1971).

Praeder, S.M., *The Word in Women's Worlds* (Wilmington: Michael Glazier, 1988).

Pregent, R., 'Wisdom Passages in Matthew's Story', *Society of Biblical Literature 1990 Seminar Papers* (Atlanta: Scholars Press, 1990), pp. 469-93.

Pui-Lan, K., and E. Schüssler Fiorenza (eds.), *Women's Sacred Scriptures* (Concilium 1998/3; London: SCM Press/Maryknoll, NY: Orbis Books, 1998).

Redmond, S.A., 'Christian "Virtues" and Recovery from Child Sexual Abuse', in J.C. Brown and C.R. Bohn (eds.), *Christianity, Patriarchy and Abuse: A Feminist Critique* (New York: Pilgrim Press, 1989).

Reid, B.E., *Choosing the Better Part: Women in the Gospel of Luke* (Collegeville, MN: Liturgical Press, 1996).

—'Luke's Mixed Messages for Women', *Chicago Studies* 38 (1999), pp. 283-97.

Reinhartz, A., 'From Narrative to History: Resurrection of Mary and Martha', in *'Women Like This': New Perspectives on Jewish Women in the Greco-Roman World* (Atlanta: Scholars Press, 1991).

—'To Love the Lord: An Intertextual Reading of John 20', in F. Flack, R. Boer, C. Kelm, and E. Runions (eds.), *The Labor of Reading: Essays in Honour of Robert C. Culley* (Semeia Studies; Atlanta: Scholars Press, 1999), pp. 46-69.

Rich, A., *Of Woman Born: Motherhood as Experience and Institution* (New York: Bantam Books, 1981).

Ricoeur, P., 'Biblical Hermeneutics', *Semeia* 4 (1975), pp. 29-148.

—'Stellung und Funktion der Metapher in der biblischen Sprache', in P. Ricoeur and E. Jungel, *EvT, Special no.: Metapher: zur Hermeneutik religiöser Sprache*, pp. 45-70.

Ridderbos, H.N., *The Gospel According to St. John: A Theological Commentary* (Grand Rapids, MI: Eerdmans, 1979).

Riley, G.J., 'The Influence of Thomas Christianity on Luke 12.14 and 5.39', *Harvard Theological Review* 88 (1995), pp. 229-35.

Ringe, S., *Luke* (Louisville: Westminster/John Knox, 1995).

Riniker, C., 'Die Gerichtsverkundigung Jesu', Ph.D. Diss., Berne, 1991.

Ritchie, N., 'Women and Christology', in E. Tamez (ed.), *Through Her Eyes: Women's Theology From Latin America* (Maryknoll, NY: Orbis, 1989), pp. 81-95.

Roberts, A. and J. Donaldson (eds.), *The Ante-Nicene Fathers, Vol. 4: Fathers of the Third Century: Tertullian, Part Fourth; Minucius Felix; Commodian; Origen, Parts First and Second* (Grand Rapids, MI: Eerdmans, repr., 1997).

Roberts, E., and E. Amidon, (eds.), *Earth Prayers From Around the World: 365 Prayers, Poems, and Invocations for Honoring the Earth* (San Francisco: HarperCollins, 1991).

Roberts, J.A.T., 'Elijah, John and Jesus: An Essay in Detection', *NTS* 4 (1957-58), pp. 263-81.

Rodorf, W. and A. Tuilier, *La Doctrine des douze apôtres (Didache)* (SC, 248; Paris, 1978).

Rohrbaugh, R.L., 'A Dysfunctional Family and Its Neighbors', in V.G. Shillington (ed.), *Jesus and His Parables: Interpreting the Parables of Jesus Today* (Edinburgh: T. & T. Clark, 1997), pp. 141-64.

Rolland, P., 'Les Prédecesseurs des Mc. II, 18-22 et parallèles', *RB* 89 (1982), pp. 370-405.

Rousselle, A., *Porneia: On Desire and the Body in Antiquity* (trans. F. Pheasant; Oxford: Basil Blackwell, 1988).

Rowlandson, J. (ed.), *Women and Society in Greek and Roman Egypt: A Source Book* (Cambridge: Cambridge University Press, 1998).

Ruddick, S., *Maternal Thinking: Towards a Politics of Peace* (London: Women's Press, 1990).

Ruether, R.R., *God and the Rhetoric of Sexuality* (Philadelphia: Fortress Press, 1978).

—*Sexism and God Talk: Toward a Feminist Theology* (Boston: Beacon Press, 1983).

—*Women and Redemption: A Theological History* (Minneapolis: Fortress Press, 1998).

—'The Western Religious Tradition and Violence Against Women in the Home', in J.C. Brown and C.R. Bohn (eds.), *Christianity, Patriarchy and Abuse: A Feminist Critique* (New York: Pilgrim Press, 1989).

Rushton, K., 'The Parable of Jn. 16. 21: A Feminist Socio-Rhetorical Reading of a (Pro)Creative Metaphor for the Death-Glory of Jesus' (Brisbane Australia: School of Theology, Griffith University, 2000).

Safrai, S., 'Home and Family', in S. Safrai and M. Stern (eds.), *The Jewish People in the First Century: Historical Geography, Political History, Social, Cultural and Religious Life and Institutions* (CRI, 2; Assen: Vangorcum, 1976), pp. 728-92.

Saiving, V., 'The Human Situation: A Feminine View', *Journal for Religion* (April, 1960).

Sawicki, M., *Seeing the Lord: Resurrection and Early Christian Practices* (Minneapolis: Fortress Press, 1994).

Sawyer, J.F.A., 'Daughter of Zion and Servant of the Lord Isaiah: A Comparison', *JOST* 44 (1989), pp. 89-107.

Schaberg, J., 'Fast Forward to the Magdalene', *Semeia* 14 (1996), pp. 33-45.

—*The Illegitimacy of Jesus: A Feminist Theological Interpretation of the Infancy Narratives* (San Francisco: Harper and Row, 1987).

—'Luke', in C.A. Newsom and S.H. Ringe (eds.), *The Women's Bible Commentary* (Louisville, KY: Westminster/John Knox Press, 1992), pp. 275-92.

Scheildel, W., 'The Most Silent Women of Greece and Rome: Rural Labor and Women's Life in the Ancient World', *Greece and Rome* 42 (1995), pp. 210-13.

Schmidt, K.L., 'Kollaō perikollaō', TDNT, III.

Schnackenburg, R., *The Gospel According to St. John* (New York: Crossroad, vol. 1, 1982).

Schneiders, S.M., '"Because of the Women's Testimony": Re-examining the Issue of Authorship in the Fourth Gospel', *NTS* 44 (1998), pp. 517-35.

—'Born Anew', *TToday* 44 (1987–88), pp. 189-96.

—*The Revelatory Text: Interpreting the New Testament as Sacred Scripture* (San Francisco: Harper & Row, 1991).

—'John 20: 11-18: The Encounter of the Easter Jesus With Mary Magdalene—A Transformative Feminist Reading', in F.F. Segovia (ed.), *What Is John? Readers and Readings of the Fourth Gospel* (Atlanta: Scholars Press, 1996), pp. 155-68.

Schottroff, L., *Lydia's Impatient Sisters: A Feminist Social History of Early Christianity* (Louisville, KY: Westminster John Knox Press, 1995).

Schroer, S., 'Jesus Sophia: Der trägeder feministischen Forschung zu einer frühchristlichen Deutung der praxis und des Schicksals Jesu von Nazaret', in D. Strahm and R. Strobel (eds.), *Vom Verlangen nach Heilwerden: Theologie in Feministisch-Theologischer Sicht* (Fribourg: Exodus, 1991), pp. 112-28.

Schüssler Fiorenza, E., 'Wisdom Mythology and the Christological Hymns of the New Testament', in R.L. Wilken (ed.), *Aspects of Wisdom in Judaism and Early Christianity* (Notre Dame University Press, 1975), pp. 17-43.

—*In Memory of Her: A Feminist Theological Reconstruction of Christian Origins* (New York: Crossroad, 1983).

—*Bread not Stone: The Challenge of Feminist Biblical Interpretation* (Boston: Beacon, 1984).

—*But She Said: Feminist Practices of Biblical Interpretation* (Boston: Beacon Press, 1992).

—*Discipleship of Equals: A Critical Feminist Ekklesia-logy of Liberation* (London: SCM Press, 1993).

—'Transforming the Legacy of the Women's Bible', *Searching the Scriptures: A Feminist Introduction* (New York: Crossroad, 1993), pp. 1-24.

—*Jesus: Miriam's Child, Sophia's Prophet: Critical Issues in Feminist Christology* (London: SCM Press, 1994).

—*Searching the Scriptures: A Feminist Commentary* (New York: Crossroad, 1994).

—*Sharing Her Word: Feminist Biblical Interpretation in Context* (Boston: Beacon, 1998).

—*Rhetoric and Ethic: The Politics of Biblical Studies* (Minneapolis: Fortress Press, 1999).

Schweickart, P., 'Reading Ourselves: Towards a Feminist Theory of Reading', in E. Showalter (ed.), *The New Feminist Criticism: Essay on Women, Literature and Theory* (New York: Pantheon Books, 1985), pp. 17-44.

Scott, B.B., 'The Empty Jar', *Forum* 3 (June 1987), pp. 77-80.

—*Hear Then the Parable: A Commentary on the Parables of Jesus* (Minneapolis: Fortress Press, 1989).

Seim, T.K., 'The Gospel of Luke', in E. Schüssler Fiorenza (ed.), *Searching the Scriptures: A Feminist Commentary* (New York: Crossroad, 1994), pp. 728-62.

—*The Double Message: Patterns of Gender in Luke–Acts* (Nashville: Abingdon Press, 1994).

Senior, D., *The Gospel of Matthew* (Nashville: Abingdon, 1997).

Shillington, V.G. (ed.), *Jesus and his Parables: Interpreting the Parables of Jesus Today* (Edinburgh: T. & T. Clark, 1997).

Skeat, T.C., 'The Lilies in the Field', *ZNW 37* (1938), pp. 211-14.

Sloyan, G.S., 'The Gnostics' Adoption of John's Gospel and Its Canonization by the Catholic Church', *BTB* 26 (1996), pp. 125-32.

—*John* (Interpretation; Atlanta: John Knox, 1988).

Smith, P.R., *Is It Okay To Call God 'Mother'? Considering the Feminine Face of God* (Peabody, MA: Hendrickson Publishers, 1993).

Soskice, J.M., *Metaphor and Religious Language* (Oxford: Clarendon Press, 1992).

Stanton, E.C., *The Woman's Bible* (Boston, MA: Northeastern University Press, 1993).

Steck, C., *Israel und das gewaltsame Geschick der Propheten* (WMANT, 23; Neukirchen: Neukirchen Verlag, 1967).

Stein, R.H., 'Parables', in B.M. Metzger and M.D. Coogan (eds.), *Oxford Companion to the Bible* (Oxford: Oxford University Press, 1993), pp. 567-70.

Steinberg, N., Review of *Discovering Eve: Ancient Israelite Women in Context*, by C. Meyers, *Critical Review of Books in Religion* (1990), pp. 162-66.

Street, G.C., 'Women as Sources of Redemption and Knowledge in Early Christian Traditions', in R.S. Kramer and M.R. D'Angelo, *Women and Christian Origins* (New York: Oxford University Press, 1999), pp. 330-54.

Strobel, F.A., 'Zum Verstandnis von Mt. XXV 1-13', *NovT* (1958), pp. 199-227.

Stroker, W.D., 'Extracanonical Parables and the Historic Jesus', in C.W. Hedrick (ed.), *Semeia 44: The Historical Jesus and the Rejected Gospels* (1988), pp. 95-120.

Suggs, J.M., *Wisdom, Christology and Law in Matthew's Gospel* (Cambridge, MA: Harvard University Press, 1970).

Sugirtharajah, R.S., 'Wisdom, Q, and a Proposal for a Christology', *ExpTim* 102 (1990), pp. 42-46.

Swaeles, R., 'Jesus nouvel Elie, dans Saint Luc', *AsSeign* 69 (1964), pp. 41-66.

Tamez, E. (ed.), *Through Her Eyes: Women's Theology from Latin America* (Maryknoll, NY: Orbis Books, 1989).

Tarrech, A. Puig i, *La Parabole des dix vierges (Mt. 25, 1-13)* (AnBib, 102; Rome: Biblical Institute Press, 1983).

Temkin, O. (trans.), *Soranus' Gynecology*, II, 67-70b (Baltimore: Johns Hopkins University Press, 1991).

Tenney, M.C., 'The Gospel of John', in F.E. Gaebelein (ed.), *John-Acts* (EBC, 9; Grand Rapids: Zondervan, 1973), pp. 3-203.

Theissen, G., 'Itinerant Radicalism: The Tradition of Jesus Sayings from the Perspective of the Sociology of Literature', in N.K. Gottwald and A.C. Wire (eds.), *The Bible and Liberation: Political and Social Hermeneutics* (Berkeley: Radical Religion Reader, 1976), pp. 84-93.

Thomson, M.B., 'The Holy Internet: Communication Between Churches in the First Christian Generation', in R. Bauckham (ed.), *The Gospel for All Christians: Rethinking the Gospel Audiences* (Grand Rapids: Eerdmans, 1998), pp. 49-70.

Thurer, S.L., *The Myths of Motherhood: How Culture Reinvents the Good Mother* (Boston: Houghton Mifflin, 1994).

Tojesen, K.J., *When Women Were Priests* (San Francisco: Harper & Row, 1993).

Tompkins, J.P. (ed.), *Reader Response Criticism* (Baltimore: Johns Hopkins University Press, 1980).

Traina, C.L.H., 'Maternal Experience and the Boundaries of Christian Sexual Ethics', *Signs* 28 (2000) pp. 369-405.

Trible, P., 'Eve and Miriam: From the Margins to the Center', in H. Shanks (ed.), *Feminist Approaches to the Bible* (Washington: Biblical Archeological Society, 1995), pp. 5-24.

—*God and the Rhetoric of Sexuality* (London: SCM Press, 1992).

Trocmé, E., 'Jean 3, 29 et le thème de l'epoux dans la tradition pré-évangelique', *Revue des Sciences Religieuses* 69 (1995), pp. 13-18.

Vaage, L., *Galilean Upstarts: Jesus' First Followers According to Q* (Valley Forge: Trinity Press International, 1994).

Valantasis, R., *The Gospel of Thomas* (London: Routledge, 1999).

Van den Heever, G.A., 'Theological Metaphorics and Metaphors of John's Gospel', *Neot* 26 (1992), pp. 89-100.

Van Wolde, E., *A Semiotic Analysis of Genesis 2-3: A Semiotic Theory and Method of Analysis Applied to the Garden of Eden* (Assen: Van Gorcum, 1989).

Vermes, G., *The Religion of Jesus the Jew* (Minneapolis: Fortress Press, 1993).

Via, D.O., *The Parables: Their Literacy and Existential Dimension* (Philadelphia: Fortress Press, 1967).

Wahlberg, R.C., 'The Assertive Widow', *Jesus and the Freed Woman* (New York and Mahwah, NJ: Paulist Press, 1978), pp. 104-27.

Wainwright, E., *Towards a Feminist Critical Reading of the Gospel According to Matthew* (Berlin, NY: Walter de Gruyer, 1991).

—'Matthew', in E. Schüssler Fiorenza (ed.), *Searching the Scriptures; A Feminist Commentary* (New York: Crossroad, 1994), pp. 635-77.

—*Shall We Look for Another? A Feminist Reading of the Matthean Jesus* (Maryknoll, NY: Orbis Books, 1998).

Weber, C.L., *A Cry in the Desert: The Awakening of Byron Katie* (Manhattan Beach, CA: Work Foundation Inc., 1996).

—*Circle of Mysteries: The Women's Rosary Book* (St. Paul, MN: Yes International, 1997).

—*Altar Music: A Novel* (New York: Scribner, 2000).

Wegner, J.R., *Chattel or Person? The Status of Women in the Mishnah* (Oxford: University Press, 1988).

Westbrook, R., 'Punishments and Crimes', in D.N. Freedman (ed.), *Anchor Bible Dictionary* (New York: Doubleday, 1992), pp. 546-56.

Wicker, K.O., 'Teaching Feminist Biblical Studies in a Postcolonial Context', in E. Schüssler Fiorenza (ed.), *Searching the Scriptures: A Feminist Introduction* (New York: Crossroad, 1993), pp. 367-80.

Williams, A.M., *Rethinking 'Gnosticism': An Argument for Dismantling a Dubious Category* (Princeton, NJ: Princeton University Press, 1997, 1999).

Wimbush, V. L., and R. Valantasis (eds.), *Asceticism* (New York: Oxford University Press, 1995).

Winter, M.T., *The Gospel According to Mary: A New Testament for Women* (New York: Crossroad, 1994).

Wire, A.C., 'The God of Jesus in the Gospel Sayings Source', in F.F. Segovia and M.A. Tolbert (ed.), *Reading From This Place: 1. Social Location and Biblical Interpretation in the United States* (Minneapolis: Fortress Press, 1995), pp. 277-303.

Witherington, B., III, *Jesus the Sage: The Pilgrimage of Wisdom* (Minneapolis: Augsburg Fortress, 1994).

Wordelman, A.L., 'Everyday Life: Women in the Period of the New Testament', in C.A. Newsom and S.H. Ringe (eds.), *The Women's Bible Commentary* (Louisville: Westminster/John Knox Press, 2nd edn, 1998), pp. 482-88.

Wyatt, N., ' "Supposing Him to be the Gardener" (John 20, 15). 'A Study of the Paradise Motif in John', *ZNW* 81 (1990), pp. 21-38.

Yalom, Marilyn, *A History of the Breast* (New York: Ballantine Books, 1997).

Zöckler, T., *Jesu Lehren im Thomas Evangelium* (Leiden/Boston/Köln: E.J. Brill, 1999).

Zornberg, A.G., *The Beginning of Desire: Reflections on Genesis* (New York: Doubleday, 1995).

INDEXES

INDEX OF REFERENCES

BIBLE

INDEX OF AUTHORS

The Lost Coin